The Time
of Their
Lives

Joyous harlequin from my friend, Warren Chappell, an illustrator for Knopf and other houses, Warren always accompanied his many letters with an original drawing. This one represents my pleasure in writing this book.

—AL SILVERMAN

The Time
of Their
Lives

The Golden Age of
Great American Book Publishers,
Their Editors and Authors

Al Silverman

T·T

Truman Talley Books
St. Martin's Press ❦ New York

www.stmartins.com

The author is grateful for permission to reprint these copyrighted materials:

"And Yet the Books" by Czeslaw Milosz, used as an epigraph, from *The Collected Poems of Czeslaw Milosz, 1931–1987.* Copyright © 1988 by Czeslaw Milosz Royalties, Inc. Reprinted by permission of HarperCollins Publishers.

"For Roger W. Straus on His 78th Birthday" by Joseph Brodsky from *Roger W. Straus: A Celebration.* Copyright © 2005 by Farrar, Straus and Giroux. Reprinted by permission of Farrar, Straus and Giroux, LLC.

Excerpt from *Never Let Me Go* by Kazuo Ishiguro, used as an epigraph, reprinted by permission of Random House, Inc.

"Hail to Our Chief" by Dr. Seuss, reprinted by permission of Audrey Geisel.

Library of Congress Cataloging-in-Publication Data

Silverman, Al.
    The time of their lives : the golden age of great American book publishers, their editors and authors / Al Silverman. —1st ed.
        p.   cm.
    ISBN-13: 978-0-312-35003-1
    ISBN-10: 0-312-35003-1
    1. Publishers and publishing—United States—History—20th century. 2. Authors and publishers—United States—History—20th century. 3. Publishers and publishing—United States—Biography. 4. Book editors—United States—Biography. I. Title.
    Z473.S575 2008
    070.50973'0904—dc22   2008006233

First Edition: September 2008

10 9 8 7 6 5 4 3 2 1

For Rosa,
with love

CONTENTS

CONTENTS

ACKNOWLEDGMENTS

This book could never have been written without the astonishing contributions of 120 eyewitnesses to my golden age. Almost everyone I talked with had vibrant memories of the period. I am particularly grateful to Oscar Dystel, the mighty head of Bantam Books in its best days, who was the first one to tell me how much he liked my idea, and who urged me to plow ahead. He and other heads of houses—George Braziller, Arthur Thornhill, Jr., of Little, Brown, Tom Guinzburg of Viking, Larry Hughes of William Morrow, and Roger Straus of Farrar, Straus and Giroux—gave me unstinting encouragement throughout the writing of this book. I am also indebted to Anne McCormick for allowing me to borrow her husband, Ken McCormick's, oral history.

I would like to thank my editor, Truman "Mac" Talley, for championing the book among his St. Martin's colleagues. It is an honor for me to be among those distinguished as "A Truman Talley Book." St. Martin's president, Sally Richardson, provided her unstinting support throughout the time it has taken me to complete my task—almost five years now. Also at St. Martin's I received instant help from Terra Gerstner, whose skills in the production process saw me through its rough passages. I also had a sensitive and scrupulous copy editor, Mark LaFlaur, who made

ACKNOWLEDGMENTS

corrections and suggestions that improved almost every page of the manuscript. And Robert Cloud, the production editor, kept at me until I answered all his intelligent queries.

My agent, Robin Straus, was on top of things right from the start when I first floated the idea past her. Robin served double duty, allowing me to interview her and her husband, Joe Kanon, who was a leading publisher before becoming a bestselling thriller author.

I would have been in deep soup often if I hadn't had Bruce Stark, my computer tutor, instantly answering my cries for help. And David A. Smith, involved in "Writer Services" at the New York Public Library, guided me in my research efforts to learn more about the early heads of American publishing companies.

My biggest stroke of luck came when I hired Dana Benningfield, a wonderful actress (I've watched her perform her magic on the stage), to transcribe my interview tapes. Soon she was asking editorial questions about my material. I found her queries both practical and wise, and I sent one of my earliest chapters to Dana, asking her to edit it. Immediately, I discovered that she was not an amateur editor at all, but a skilled editor. I am deeply grateful for all her efforts in making this a better book. My transcriptions were then handed over to another smart actress, Stephanie Dorian, who worked faultlessly at that task. Thank you, Steph.

I can't say that any one of our grandchildren, ages three to twenty, actually did any work on the manuscript, but Ella, Zoe, Jonathan, Erin, Emma, Louis, and Russell, each in their own way, took me out of myself into the land of laughter. Cheers to all of them for constantly giving me perspective.

None of this, of course, would have happened without the steadfast support of my wife. Rosa stood by me, as she always has, when I was high and when I was low, always making life more livable. Thank you, darling, for being you.

AND YET THE BOOKS
by Czeslaw Milosz

And yet the books will be there on the shelves, separate beings,
That appeared once, still wet
As shining chestnuts under a tree in autumn,
And, touched, coddled, began to live
In spite of fires on the horizon, castles blown up,
Tribes on the march, planets in motion.
"We are," they said, even as their pages
Were being torn out, or a buzzing flame
Licked away their letters. So much more durable
Than we are, whose frail warmth
Cools down with memory, disperses, perishes.
I imagine the earth when I am no more:
Nothing happens, no loss, it's still a strange pageant,
Women's dresses, dewy lilacs, a song in the valley.
Yet the books will be there on the shelves, well born,
Derived from people, but also from radiance, heights.

Translated from the Polish by Czeslaw Milosz and Robert Hass

The Time
of Their
Lives

INTRODUCTION

In May 2003 my wife, Rosa, and I were packing our belongings, preparing to move from our house in the country, where we had spent thirty-eight happy years, to an apartment in New York City. The new owner, we insisted, would have to give us six months to properly deal with, well, a lifetime of memories.

So there we were, up in our lavishly disordered attic, where we once saw a raccoon walking away from us with a snarl on his face, as if we were intruding in *his* house. Old scraps of paper kept falling out of mildewed paper bags that had been in our attic for years and years. One fragment that I had long forgotten about fluttered to my feet. It was a *Kirkus* review of an anthology I had assembled from pieces plucked out of the Book-of-the-Month Club *News* over the years. The book was published by Little, Brown in 1986 at the time of the Club's sixtieth anniversary. Reading that review—it was a favorable one—I thought, Gee, am I having an epiphany?

Several friends over these late years of my life, wanting to see me toiling again, had suggested that I write a memoir. Well, I never wanted to write a memoir. Too many people are writing memoirs, especially now that they can get their book—even if they only want a single copy—printed in three minutes on Jason

Epstein's Espresso Book Machine. (There's more about Jason and his Espresso in chapter 10, on Random House.).

As we went on stripping our attic, I attacked a group of magazines that I would definitely take with me to New York. Over the years I'd collected first issues of magazines; final ones, too, when ill fate struck. I found myself holding an oversize first edition as gently as I could, because it was crumbling a bit in my hands— the first issue of a magazine calling itself *The New York Review of Books*. In 1963 a strike had shut down all the daily newspapers in New York City, so a small group of high-minded women and men—including Robert Silvers and Barbara Epstein and her husband, Jason Epstein—created a magazine meant to be a stopgap for booklovers during the strike. Up in the attic I stopped to read a "To the Readers" column, explaining the magazine's purpose in life. "The hope of the editors," it began, "is to suggest, however imperfectly, some of the qualities which a responsible literary journal should have and to discover whether there is, in America, not only the need for such a review, but the demand for one." Forty-five years later, need, if not demand, has prevailed.

And it began to come to me that from the success of a magazine born almost exactly at a time when books were most beloved by a reading public, plus the accumulated joy of my sixteen years at the Book-of-the-Month Club and nine years as an editor with Viking/Penguin, I had unearthed the existence of a bygone golden age in American book publishing.

Thinking further, my conceit expanding by the second, I determined that the golden age had to be the years from 1946, as the harrowing savagery of World War II was washing away, to the late 1970s and early 1980s, before the era of publishing ossification had fully set in. Ossification had begun in the 1960s when the great old-line book people began to be replaced by bottom-line businessmen.

At first I felt that my period of awe might be resisted by certain

INTRODUCTION

high-minded American publishers, especially those who strad-
dled the decades before and after World War II. I could hear them
letting out a clamorous cry on behalf of the great works of the
1920s and 1930s, when the novels of Ernest Hemingway and
Scott Fitzgerald and Thomas Wolfe were being nurtured by the
master editor of the period, Maxwell Perkins. In reality, only one
or two of my eyewitnesses to history made the claim that it was
the earlier period that shone brighter than the postwar years covered here.

I see now that there were other memories pushing at me. In
the fall of 1989, I was invited to teach at Yale in its Residential
College Seminar programs. Within Yale University are twelve
colleges, each of which can offer up to two new courses not in
Yale's curriculum. All I needed was an idea for such a course. So I
went to where I often go when in a muddle: to the book. I proposed
a course called, "Defining Contemporary America Through the
Novel: 1970 to 1990." Two of the Yale colleges decided this was
what they wanted. And so I was accepted to become one of those
outsiders teaching at Yale.

I picked twelve novels of that period for my class to read.
They were not necessarily among the finest novels of those two
decades, but they were significant in that each novel would focus
on an unsettling element in contemporary life. For instance, for
"the age of extreme anxiety," I gave them Don DeLillo's trea-
sured *White Noise*. For "the reality of the minority experience,"
there was Toni Morrison's breakout novel: *Song of Solomon*. For
"the hopes and fears and tensions of middle class American families," I chose *Dinner at the Homesick Restaurant* by Anne Tyler.
(How about this opening sentence from her novel: "While Pearl
Tull was dying, a funny thought occurred to her.")

My other novels with defining themes for those two decades
were *The Women's Room* by Marilyn French; *Rabbit Is Rich* by
John Updike; *Final Payments* by Mary Gordon; *A Flag for Sunrise*

3

by Robert Stone; *The Bonfire of the Vanities* by Tom Wolfe; *In the Days of Simon Stern* by Arthur A. Cohen; *The Chaneysville Incident* by David Bradley; *In Country* by Bobbie Ann Mason; and *A Thief of Time* by Tony Hillerman.

Teaching at Yale, I guess, had me sneaking up closer to what I really wanted to do. In the end, though, I think it was two nonfiction masterpieces—published within my golden age—that gave me the impetus to proceed: *The Children of Sanchez* by Oscar Lewis and *The Glory of Their Times* by Lawrence S. Ritter. Both books treaded the same path. Oscar Lewis told the story of a poor family in Mexico City through what he called "a new technique whereby each member of the family tells his own life story in his own words." Larry Ritter, a remarkable human being and a warm friend (he died in 2004), lugged a tape recorder to the homes of some great old-time baseball players, inviting them to tell their stories about baseball and life in the early twentieth century. The renowned baseball announcer, Red Barber, called *The Glory of Their Times* "the single best baseball book of all time."

Both of those books were strictly oral histories. *The Time of Their Lives,* I decided, would become a hybrid of sorts—part oral history, part narrative history, part I'm not sure what. My job would be to go out, as Lewis and Ritter had done, and let my editors, publishers, heads of houses, and other involved witnesses tell me about the glories of their time. I never expected that so many of them would end up saying to me, "Those were the happiest years of my life."

And so I set out on what became for me a voyage of discovery.

SEVERAL YEARS AGO, in a front-page review for *The New York Times Book Review,* Paul Theroux, who was reviewing the third volume of *The Life of Graham Greene* by Norman Sherry, wrote: "It is impossible now for any American under the age of sixty or so to comprehend the literary world that existed in the two decades after World War II, and especially the magic that fiction writers exerted upon the public."

More recently, Louis Menand in *The New Yorker,* writing about Edmund Wilson, called Wilson's time "a world where print was still king, and literature was at the center of a nation's culture."

There was truly a blast of fresh air sweeping through America, giving books room to emerge with cultural primacy in the country. Television was still very new. Electronic technology was stirring, but half asleep. Bookstores were almost all independent. And the U.S. government was making it easy for veterans to go to college almost for free under the G.I. Bill. It was an exhilarating time for those of the middle class to position themselves, if they wanted to, among this new educated public.

Who broke through first in the golden age? Why, the World War II veterans who yearned to write about their wartime experiences. The early war novels by Norman Mailer, Irwin Shaw, James Jones, Gore Vidal, and others thrust them into the center of the cleansing new culture.

IT STARTED ON the dot in 1946 when Farrar, Straus opened for business. You will see in the first chapter that Roger Straus set the tone for the grand era by going on a Nobel Prize binge. He and his great editor, Robert Giroux, ended up with seventeen Nobels.

Those Nobels came from writers all over the globe. At the end of a destructive war, Europe's sense of idealism and romanticism had come crashing down, leaving promising young authors adrift, alone. So American book publishers began to launch their own Marshall Plans. It wasn't just the old-timers—the Knopfs and Random Houses and Vikings and Harpers and Doubledays—who were in on the gold rush. The new publishers, from Farrar, Straus to Grove Press's Barney Rosset to Atheneum, were also scooping up the best of the literature from France, Germany, Italy, Latin America, and the rest of the world.

For example, in 1950, Richard Seaver, a young American living in Paris, fell in love with two novels by an unknown Irish novelist also living in Paris, Samuel Beckett. Three years later, Seaver tipped off Barney Rosset about Beckett. As a consequence, Rosset went to France and brought back *Waiting for Godot* for his Grove Press. That was the beginning of an astonishing publishing career.

Another discovery came early on at Atheneum. Mike Bessie, one of the most celebrated editors of the period, acquired André Schwarz-Bart's *The Last of the Just*, a work of art that Book-of-the-Month Club judge Gilbert Highet called "the saddest novel I have ever read, almost as sad as history."

SO, SUDDENLY, the authors of old found themselves buttressed by the new authors, who were everywhere. I loved working with authors during my years as an editor at Viking, but for this book, I interviewed only Toni Morrison and E. L. Doctorow. That was because they were editors first, novelists second (at least chronologically). I think of this book as a sort of love song to the editors of the era. I believe that there were more magnificent editors working during my period than in any other time in the history of our sometimes odd and lonely profession.

Keith Jennison, who had a strong career in book publishing in almost every capacity, said this about the editing experience in his book, *The Best of Times:* "The great New York editors worked from the premise that the editor and author worked together to ask more of the book than would ever again be asked by any reader or critic." I don't think that editors, at any time—save maybe for Maxwell Perkins—have ever gotten their full due. For years, many heads of houses barely tolerated their editors. George H. Doran, whose publishing company merged with Doubleday in 1927, had this to say about editors: "Every publishing house of consequence has its competent editor in chief. Frequently he is a partner in the business, but rarely is he the dominant figure, for modern publishing demands the merchant of quality as director-in-chief."

Alfred A. Knopf went even further. In an interview he gave *The Saturday Review* in 1972 (one of the magazines of which I have, unhappily, a final issue), Knopf said, "The most fundamental change in book publishing was the increased importance of the editor. In the early days, things were quite simple. The book came in. We published them as written." Perhaps that was what was truly meant by the much overused term for book publishing, "a cottage industry."

I can name at least fifty men and women of the era who would qualify for the Editors' Hall of Fame, if we had one. (Perhaps this book will be a start.) You will meet many of them at their jobs and learn how a great editor can make a writer write well. Four editors need to be mentioned here.

Let's start with Robert Giroux, whom his publishing partner, Roger Straus, called "the best living editor of the time." Bob, now 94, has long since retired, but when I last talked with him, he remembered how he refereed a match in his office between two heavyweights—T. S. Eliot and Carl Sandburg. You will see how Giroux handled them and other such literary brawlers.

Robert Gottlieb spends his time these days editing Bill Clinton's books and writing marvelous essays for various magazines. When, in the golden age, he was the editor of editors at Simon & Schuster, and then at Knopf, he claimed some of the most wondrous fiction and nonfiction authors of the period—everyone from Chaim Potok, Joseph Heller, and John le Carré to Miss Piggy. In this book he speaks, with wisdom as well as wit, about the editing profession.

Early in 2007, Robert Loomis was feted for his fifty years on the job at Random House. The authors he brought to his house include William Styron, Maya Angelou, Daniel Boorstin, Neil Sheehan, Jonathan Harr, John Toland. The list goes on and on.

Corlies "Cork" Smith, right off, became the legend of legends among all who worked with him and knew him. The first thing he did as an editor was fasten on to the secretive Thomas Pynchon, who is one of the strangest of characters in the golden age, and also maybe one of the bravest of writers. It was a working relationship, but a friendship, too, the editor doing what he could to help make Pynchon a twentieth-century master of literature.

Cork took to literature, but he enjoyed doing other things, too. His first book for his new publishing house, Viking Press (the house he loved the most), was Jimmy Breslin's *Can't Anyone Here Play This Game?* (Who else but the original New York Mets team?) Throughout his career Cork moved in all directions, seeking anybody who was a stylist, or had a story to tell, or both.

What about the women? They came late to power and glory because the heads of houses at the time didn't understand that women could play this game at least as well as men. The barriers began to break in the 1960s when recognition came to tremendous commercial and literary editors of fiction and nonfiction such as Carole Baron, Lisa Drew, Ann Harris, Judith Jones, Charlotte Mayerson, Fran McCullough, Leona Nevler, Betty Prashker, Elizabeth Scharlatt, Elisabeth Sifton, Nan Talese, Drenka Willen, Marian Wood, and Genevieve "Gene" Young.

Two of these women, Carole Baron and Leona Nevler, made their marks by using their quicksilver minds to add zest to the paperback revolution. It was the time when paperbacks were blowing the roof off the industry and leaving fresh money on the table of just about every house in town. You will hear about those ferocious years from some of the founding fathers and mothers: Ian and Betty Ballantine, Oscar Dystel, Jason Epstein, Larry Hughes,

Helen Meyer, Victor Weybright, and many other clean-up hitters, almost all of them swinging for the fence.

Vladimir Nabokov had just the word for what was happening in book publishing: *Shamantzvo*—"the enchanter-quality, the ability to keep people wanting more"—a word that applied to both general trade hardcovers as well as paperbacks.

ON NOVEMBER 19, 2003, riding up the escalator in Broadway's massive Marriott Marquis hotel, I met a woman a step in front of me whom I'd had the privilege of knowing in my working days. I hadn't seen her for a few years; I asked her what she was doing. She told me she had just left the publishing company, where she had held a senior position, after it was sold to a foreign conglomerate. "I'm an agent," she said in a determined voice, but her eyes looked lifeless.

Oddly, riding the same escalator was a friend who had just been retired from his longtime executive publishing job. He told me he might do some agenting, too, or maybe write a book. He was seeking to find his way in what he called "the new climate of the industry." This was a dispiriting opening to an event I had been looking forward to—the fifty-fourth National Book Awards dinner. I asked myself, *Why am I here?* I was here because I was starting work on this book, and I thought it would be smart to compare the kids of today in book publishing to the graybeards I would be seeing. But I hadn't expected to hear right off such sad stories from good people who'd lost their jobs and were showing up to be seen, not forgotten.

I sipped some wine as the room began to fill up with beautifully dressed women, so many of them so young, wearing the colors of the rainbow, next to whom most of the men were looking drab in their monkey suits. I chatted with a couple of agents with their spouses, and some guys who, I remember, were still residing in executive suites. Then Kris Puopolo, a lovely bright young woman, came up to me, looking radiant. Kris had begun her book publishing career at Viking in my time there, working as an assistant to a couple of editors. I knew that she was now a senior editor at Doubleday's Broadway Books label, looking mostly for nonfiction, she said. I told her what I was up to, then said, "It's different now, isn't it?"

"Yes," she said, "but if you love books it almost doesn't matter how you're treated. You're working with your author."

Indeed. The main reason Kris was here was because she had a National Book Award nonfiction finalist, Anne Applebaum, for her book *Gulag,* a narrative history of the Soviet concentration camps. Alas, Applebaum did not win the NBA award, but later on she did win a Pulitzer Prize.

I had a couple of nominees to root for, too. One was Tom Boyle for his novel, *Drop City.* I had worked with Tom on several of his books at Viking, and we had become good friends.

The other was George Howe Colt for his nominated nonfiction work, *The Big House: A Century in the Life of an American Summer Home.* George's work was a love letter to the past. Built in the early 1900s, the house on Cape Cod belonged to everyone in his family, but it had to be put on the market in the 1990s because they couldn't afford it anymore. Shortly before I left Viking I had tried to buy *The Big House,* but I was beaten out by Scribner.

Sadly, neither Boyle nor Colt won an award. But I did have one sure-thing awardee: Stephen King, this year's winner for his "Distinguished Contribution to American Letters." I felt happy that he was finally receiving his due, although I know he would have preferred to have been at least once in his life an NBA fiction nominee. No chance. Some stern guardians of literature kept referring to him as "a rich hack."

Speaking of that, in his acceptance speech, King noted drily,

"There are some people who have spoken out passionately about giving me this medal. There are some people who think it's an extraordinarily bad idea."

Why? I'll tell you why. It began back in 1952 when Arnold Hano, the editor in chief of a small paperback house called Lion Books, tried to nominate his best author, Jim Thompson, for his novel, *The Killer Inside Me.* Arnold never heard from the NBA. In Robert Polito's *Savage Art,* a hard-hitting but sympathetic biography of Thompson, Polito wrote: "Prior to meeting Hano, Thompson published only three novels. . . . Working alongside Hano during 1952–54, he swiftly realized fourteen books—more than half of his life's achievement. . . . Hano trusted Thompson like no publisher did before or after him." Arnold Hano, an almost lifelong friend of mine, went on to his own happier career as an author.

Thompson became one of the greatest and most neglected bad boys of contemporary American fiction. He earned an underground reputation that carried him even beyond Raymond Chandler and Dashiell Hammett. One book reviewer wrote of Thompson, "The great merit of the novels of Jim Thompson is that they are completely without good taste." If the National Book Award people back then had chosen *The Killer Inside* in 1952, how different the war between high culture and popular culture might have been.

But there was Harold Bloom, responding to King's "distinguished contribution to American literature," by saying of the author, "He is a man who writes what used to be called penny dreadfuls."

Later that evening, Shirley Hazzard won the fiction prize for her novel, *The Great Fire.* Shirley Hazzard is an admirable author. I regard *The Transit of Venus* as one of the finest novels published in the golden age. She is also a gatekeeper to literature, but a less fevered guardian, perhaps, than Harold Bloom. In her acceptance speech she said thank you, and then she shot this rebuke at King for mentioning a number of genre authors, such as Elmore Leonard and Peter Straub, who maybe deserved to be honored by the award givers. "We have this huge language so diverse around the earth," Hazzard said, "that I don't think giving us a reading list of those who are most read at this moment is much of a satisfaction."

Many American intellectuals, the elite palace guard, read mysteries and such for enjoyment, but generally draw an impenetrable line before the words "popular culture." To me, this attitude stifles the joyous totality of the reading experience. There is always going to be a gulf between high art and popular entertainment, but there is also a bridge between them for people to walk back and forth as they choose. And they do.

The battle over reading values struck particularly hard in the paperbound industry. Oscar Dystel, who ran Bantam Books for years like a wizard, always loved reading good commercial fiction. He was nervous about literary fiction. "The problem," he told me, "was, can we afford the book because it's a great book, or can we take the book that can't miss?" His answer was that "the heart of our business was a good book that people enjoyed reading."

Of all the heads of houses of paperback firms, the one who had the widest breadth of understanding about the reading experience was Victor Weybright. He knew what he wanted to acquire in the commercial field, but he never underestimated the power of the literary novel. Weybright bought for New American Library marvelous works of fiction such as *The Naked and the Dead, Doctor Zhivago,* and Ralph Ellison's *Invisible Man.* He was also the one, you will see, who broke open the industry to the novels of African-Americans.

Marc Jaffe, who worked for both Victor Weybright and Oscar Dystel, had the most fun with Dystel. But he felt that Weybright, of all the paperback publishers, was the No. 1 discoverer of authors. When Marc was at NAL, he once asked Weybright what made him decide to publish a trifecta of Erskine Caldwell, William Faulkner, and James T. Farrell. "Well, Marc," Weybright said, "what I did was lay down on the floor all of the competitive, or selection of competitive books, and I saw a big gap there. And here were these important contemporary authors of quality, who had some sense—in terms of content—of what the popular world was all about. And we went after them." One of them, Erskine Caldwell, broke the bank for Victor. By 1961, Caldwell had sold more than sixty-four million books around the world.

I give the last word on the literary civil war to John Farrar, a distinguished publisher in his time, who wrote the following in 1950 for *The American Scholar:* "It would be a bore for me to publish only for the 'highbrow.' I like the 'middlebrow.' I like the 'lowbrow.' I have always despised the literary snob. I like a good story, and I am bored by a pretentious, dull book, no matter what scholarly cloak it wears."

ONE THING I almost forgot about the rise and fall of the golden age described here. It began to falter not when the book publishers who loved books gave way to those who preferred profits to reading. It happened when publishers and editors began cutting back on their drinking. If there is one national flower in book publishing, it is the martini. You will have to read this book to find out how the flower lost its bloom in . . . how do I put it? . . . the sadder years.

But here's to you, anyway.

October 2007

Part I

THE NEWCOMERS

1

YOU ARE WHAT YOU PUBLISH

Farrar, Straus and Giroux

The first list of a new publishing house is always an adventure.
A new imprint on a book gathers character through the years,
and it is our hope that readers will come to know ours and,
perhaps, to feel a certain friendship for it.

—JOHN FARRAR AND ROGER W. STRAUS, JR., 1946

O n the Monday morning of December 8, 2003, after New York City had been hit by its biggest December snowstorm ever, I headed downtown to see Roger Straus. I wanted him to recall for me a life well spent as the founder of postwar America's most distinguished new American publishing house—seventeen Nobel Prizes in literature, twelve of them since 1970. Alfred A. Knopf's venerable house, considered the most literary of them all, had twelve Nobels between 1916 and 1964. But Farrar, Straus and Giroux set the postwar standard for literary excellence in the glory years of book publishing.

I wondered if Roger would show up for our meeting. He was nearly eighty-seven years old, with serious health problems, and he had just come out of the hospital after two weeks of fighting pneumonia. When I called his office I was happy to hear that he was back and would see me.

Roger and I had done good deeds together during my years at the Book-of-the-Month Club; so many of the books he published had become our books. We also bumped into each other now and then after a late afternoon weekend movie at our Westchester County cinema paradiso. On those impromptu occasions Roger was entirely without portfolio; he wore scruffy suburban work clothes, and talked with unbecoming shyness in the presence of our wives.

I was coming to Farrar, Straus and Giroux to converse with Roger, as I had explained to him earlier over the phone, about the book I was writing, on what I perceived to be the golden age of publishing. "It began," I said, "in 1946, when you gave birth." I told him that Farrar, Straus would probably be my first chapter. I think he liked the idea of marching ahead in the field, and so here he was, greeting me at the door of his corner office overlooking a rare setting outside—a marshmallow blanket of snow blinking in the sun atop all of Union Square.

I was not surprised to see a thinner, worn-looking Roger. His face carried a post-hospital pallor and his eyes were puffy. But he was still his dapper self, wearing a camel's hair jacket over his chocolate brown shirt, khaki pants, a flamboyant ascot shielding his neck. His silken white hair seemed pulled back tighter than ever, giving him the look of a matador who had outlived his bulls. His voice, though muted some from his illness, registered strongly, especially when he plunged into his biblical arsenal of obscenities. He moved out from behind his desk, put a chair opposite mine, and issued his first indelicacy. He was talking with a certain delight about Sheila Cudahy, who had come to Farrar, Straus in 1953 as editor in chief after Roger bought her late husband's Chicago book publishing company, Pellegrini & Cudahy.

"She was a goddamn good editor," Roger told me. "Started

our children's division, weighed about eighty pounds soaking wet. I'll tell you what she brought in that made her reputation. She brought in Nelson Algren. She spent some time in Chicago working with him on *A Walk on the Wild Side,* telling him to take 'fuck' out and put 'shit' in. He listened to her and did what she wanted." She must have done good. *A Walk on the Wild Side* is still in print.

ROGER DIED ON May 24, 2004, five months after our conversation. I was lucky to have been with him when he was looking back with some pleasure, I think, at what he had been able to accomplish. It was light-years away from the wealth piled up by past generations of Strauses. His father had been president of the American Mining and Smelting Company; his mother was a Guggenheim whose father owned a copper mine. What Roger sang out at our meeting were some of his personal delights: the discoveries of his life: Carlo Levi's *Christ Stopped at Eboli*; poet Joseph Brodsky, the author he regarded with the most warmth; Susan Sontag, "my closest friend"; Philip Roth, his best living American "dialogue" writer; Edmund Wilson and Isaac Bashevis Singer, both spirited away from other houses; Gayelord Hauser, the bestselling author who saved Roger's company in those early years.

Hauser's *Look Younger, Live Longer* was published in 1950 just as the buzzards had begun to circle overhead, ready to pick at the undeveloped bones of Farrar, Straus. Hauser was the Dr. Atkins of his time, a handsome gentleman about town with such dear friends as Greta Garbo, specializing not in low-carb, high-protein diets, but in the blessings offered by yogurt and blackstrap molasses. That mix oozed *Look Younger, Live Longer* toward a sale of 500,000 copies. "It carried us along for a while," Roger said with a touch of unsettling humility. Most of all, the book helped him take up more ambitious searches, for books that mattered.

Early in his reign, Roger had invited to lunch two successful and hard-drinking partners in a literary agency, Diarmuid Russell and Henry Volkening. ("Drink," a British publisher once observed, "has always been crucial in the book trade," and so will be covered in this book in a measured way.) "We went to their favorite French restaurant," Roger told me, "where a number of martinis were consumed. I finally said, 'I don't want to be too boorish about this, but the reason I'm buying lunch for you guys is that I want to publish the kind of authors that you represent— Welty-like, Malamud-like, blah, blah, blah.' And one of them, probably Henry, said to me, 'Why should we give you an author like you've described until after we've had a chance to show Harcourt, Brace, Scribners, blah, blah, blah?' Jesus Christ, they were right. I wouldn't either if I was in their position."

In those early years it was more or less hit-or-miss publishing. Roger and his wife, Dorothea, went prospecting in Italy, the country they loved. With the help of a well-connected Italian scout, the two brought back *Christ Stopped at Eboli* and rising young novelists Alberto Moravia, Giovanni Guareschi, and Cesare Pavese.

Since it was in his nature, Roger also aggressively pursued authors from other houses who were known to be aggrieved by their present publishers. One day in the late forties he got a call from an old friend at Random House.

"How would you like to publish Edmund Wilson?" Roger was asked. Wilson had done *The Shock of Recognition* for Random House's Modern Library, two volumes on the development of literature in the United States.

"Of course I would like to publish Edmund Wilson," Roger said. "Why the fuck aren't you publishing Wilson?"

"Wilson can't stand Bennett and the rest of the boys over there, and I can't hold him." Ah, Roger thought, a chance to upend Bennett Cerf, who not only governed Random House and was one of the most feverish quipsters of his time, but who also delighted in stealing authors from other houses.

Roger called Wilson, and they had lunch. "So I said all the things I'd say when one is in hot pursuit. I asked him what he was working on. He said he was collecting all his essays. 'I'll buy them,' I said right off." Roger didn't remember whether the advance to Wilson was $2,000 or $2,500, "but that's how we began. And," he said with some pride, "he never left me for a moment after that. I published all his books." Edmund Wilson did get on well with Roger Straus, who, he once wrote, "made me laugh and cheered me up."

If Roger had one distinct feeling about his profession, it was an everlasting belief in his writers. "He was there in my thirties, forties, fifties and sixties," John McPhee said, speaking at the memorial service held for Roger in New York, "and was still leading me up the street on a leash when I entered my seventies."

Straus's relationship with his editors, however, was different. He was tough on them, held many in slight regard—perhaps because they were contending with him for authors—and treated them with disdain. One of his strongest editors in chief, Aaron Asher, who brought with him Philip Roth, Brian Moore, and Arthur Miller, among others, spent five years at the house and couldn't stand his boss. Another superb editor, Henry Robbins, who discovered Joan Didion and Tom Wolfe, also ended up fleeing Roger. Partly it had to do with the firing of a woman at Farrar, Straus who meant very much to Robbins, but there were editorial spats as well.

Roger even had difficulties with his son, Roger Straus III. I always found young Roger to be a sweet-natured individual who seemed to fill his difficult role with much grace. But I didn't sense that he had the driving ambition of his father. The breakup came in 1993 when the son left the company over "philosophical differences" with his father. Some people who were there felt that the father had become annoyed with his son for wanting to steer the house in a more commercial direction. Whatever the reason, young Roger worked at Times Books, then settled in as a serious photographer, a profession he still follows.

In the beginning, however, Roger did at least find a partner whom he respected and who brought resolute credentials to the new publishing house.

JOHN FARRAR once confessed: "I have no sense of humor and a vile temper." A veteran of two world wars, Farrar had made his reputation right after World War I as editor of the prestigious literary magazine *The Bookman*. The magazine was then owned by Doubleday, Doran, a powerhouse publisher of the time, where Farrar was also a prominent editor.

In 1929, five months before the Wall Street crash, Farrar left Doubleday, Doran to form a new publishing house with Stanley Rinehart, his business manager on *The Bookman,* and Stanley's brother, Frederick. The Rinehart boys were sons of Mary Roberts Rinehart, probably the richest bestselling author of her time. She was so rich that she never bothered to look at her royalty notices but, instead, complained to Stanley that she never seemed to receive money from the company. So one Christmas her son bought a huge strongbox and filled it with thousands of one-dollar bills and sent it to his mother for the holiday. "Stanley, dear," she called on Christmas morning, "can you guess what I just received from Farrar & Rinehart? It's unbelievable—a real treasure chest brimming over with crisp new dollar bills. Now I'm worried that your new firm will go bankrupt."

No need to worry about that. One thing John Farrar took with him from Doran was the unsold stock of an unsuccessful Edgar Allan Poe biography that he had previously acquired, written by an unknown professor named Hervey Allen. He had also bought the right to look at a future work by Allen—"a long novel as yet untitled." In 1933, in the teeth of the Great Depression, Farrar, Rinehart offered, for $3 retail, a 1,224-page historical novel by Hervey Allen. The first printing of *Anthony Adverse* was 17,000. Its second printing was 200,000. In the two years that *Anthony Adverse* topped the bestseller list, it sold 500,000 copies, and it kept on going and became a competitor to *Gone With the Wind* over the next twenty years.

Roger Straus was happy to have Farrar with him. "He knew everybody and everybody knew him," Roger said. "They knew he was honest. They knew he was a good editor. He had this respect from among his peers."

Hugh Van Dusen, who became an editor at Harper's in 1956 and stayed on full-time until 2006 (but is still in the office three days a week), had a different take on John Farrar. Hugh met him when he was job hunting. "Farrar knew my parents slightly," Hugh said, "and so my father asked if he would see me." (Hugh's father, Henry P. Van Dusen, was president of Union Theological Seminary in New York.) Farrar invited Hugh to have lunch with him.

"I found Mr. Farrar to be one of the most inarticulate great men I ever met," Hugh said. "He was sort of fumbling around during lunch, trying to find something of importance to say about publishing to this young guy who was just graduating from Harvard." Farrar may have sounded inarticulate, but he was not without a kernel of gold to bequeath the youngster. "As we were about to leave," Hugh recalled, "he stopped and turned to me and, I think, even grabbed my arm for emphasis, and he said, 'You know, publishing is all about memory.'" Perhaps the old Farrar was telling the young Van Dusen that *institutional memory* has always been vital in book publishing, not just for connecting the past to the present, but also for finding truths from the past that could light up the present and even the future. Farrar provided many such insights to Roger Straus until illness came along and robbed him of his own memory.

IN 1955, his company nine years old, and not yet sure of its footing, Roger hired the person he needed most. And he did it even though he understood from the beginning that Robert Giroux's heart would never belong to Daddy. Three years older than Roger, Giroux had been a wunderkind at Columbia University in the mid-1930s, an abiding influence on a group of book-loving students with literary aspirations. Among his classmates were Herman Wouk, John Berryman, Robert Gerdy, who became an editor at *The New Yorker,* and Thomas Merton. Merton introduced himself to Giroux, then the editor of the literary magazine *Columbia Review,* in 1935 when he came to show Giroux some of his writings. Merton himself was editor of the college humor magazine, *Jester.* Thirteen years later, in 1948, it was Giroux who told Merton that his book, *The Seven Storey Mountain,* would be published by Harcourt, Brace. Giroux had gone to work for Harcourt in 1940 as a junior editor, Merton had entered a Trappist monastery in Kentucky in 1941, and by the time Merton's classic was published, Giroux was a commanding editor of the house.

Roger claimed that he had first gone after Bob Giroux in 1946 when he was putting his company together. At lunch the publisher offered Giroux the job as editor in chief.

"Oh, my God, Roger," Bob said, "I can't afford to."

"What do you mean you can't afford to? We haven't talked about money."

"No, no. What I mean is I have this sinecure with Harcourt, Brace and, you know, you may make it or maybe you won't." Roger thought that was a fair assessment at the time. Bob was also having a good time in his early years at Harcourt. For one, he had inherited Carl Sandburg. "I used to go out with him because he was a troubadour," Bob told me. "He was one of the earliest folk singers, and he published a book at Harcourt called *The American Songbook*. My favorite song of his was 'My Name Is Sam Hall and I Hate You One and All.' Well, he had a noose around his neck; he was going to be hanged."

Bob talked about a convergence of greatness at the Harcourt offices—the meeting of Carl Sandburg and T. S. Eliot. "I know Eliot didn't think much of Sandburg's poems, and Sandburg was very critical of Eliot because, he said, he had no sense of humor. I thought, they must never meet each other because they're on opposite ends of the spectrum politically. Well, one day Eliot visited the offices. And I had him with me, and suddenly one of the secretaries called me and said, 'Mr. Sandburg has just arrived.' And I said, 'Put him in Mr. Harcourt's office,' which was way down at the end. 'I don't want them to meet.' I had to leave Eliot to go to the john or something, and I was probably gone five minutes. When I came back, Carl was sitting in my office, right next to Eliot, and Eliot had a big grin on his face. Carl said, 'Bob, look at that man's face. Look at the suffering in that face.' And Eliot shot back, 'You can't blame him for the people who ride on his coattails.' "

Six years later, when Roger heard that there was trouble at Harcourt, he took Giroux to lunch again and said flat out, "You know, my offer is still open. Do you want to come?"

"Yes, I would," Bob said. He left Harcourt still in a state of rage because management had refused to let him buy a book that was rightfully his—a first novel that the then-unknown author, J. D. Salinger, wanted him to have.

ROBERT GIROUX

Jerry Salinger was publishing these stories, mostly in *The New Yorker,* and they were, one after another, fantastic. So I wrote him a very short note from Harcourt, care of Bill

Shawn, the editor of *The New Yorker,* a reclusive figure whom I had gotten to know. In the note I said, "I know that every editor in town is asking to see your first novel, but I have a proposal to make. Let me publish all your stories right now." Never heard from him.

About a year later I was eating a sandwich at my desk when our receptionist called. "Mr. Salinger is here," she said, "and he wants to meet you." I said, "Mr. Salinger? What's his first name?" And she said, "Jerome, his name is Jerome." I said, "Send him in."

In he came. He was very tall, dark-haired, had a horse face. He was melancholy looking. It's the truth—the first person I thought of when I saw him was Hamlet.

"Giroux," he said. I said something like, "Right. It's nice to meet you, Mr. Salinger."

"Giroux," he said again. "Mr. Shawn has recommended you to me. But I want to tell you that to start me out it would be much better to publish my first novel instead of my stories." I laughed, thinking, you want to be the publisher, you can have my seat. But I said, "I'm sure you're right about that." And I said, "I will publish your novel. Tell me about it." He said, "Well, I can't show it to you yet. It's about half finished." I said, "Well, let me be the publisher." And he said yes, and we shook hands.

When Jerry Salinger left, I was thrilled. He'd come in to see me, which is the last thing in the world I expected, and which probably happened because of Shawn. Anyway, I thought it was something the firm should be proud to publish.

A year later a messenger came to the office with a package from Dorothy Olding, Salinger's agent at the Harold Ober literary agency. I opened it, pulled out the manuscript. There on the top page I read the title: *The Catcher in the Rye.*

YOU ARE WHAT YOU PUBLISH

I read it that night and was thrilled and delighted that we would be able to publish a first novel of such originality. It never occurred to me that my new boss, Eugene Reynal, would not back me up.

Reynal had recently sold his publishing house, Reynal & Hitchcock, to Harcourt, and he had become head of Harcourt's trade division. He had a mixed reputation. He'd come from old money; gone to Harvard, Oxford—he even smoked initialed cigarettes. But I had to get on with him. I gave him the book to read. He didn't like it, didn't understand it. He asked me, "Is this kid in the book supposed to be crazy?" And I said, "No, he's not. He's disturbed in many ways, but he's not crazy. He's very lucid about what he thinks, and very imaginative. Gene," I said, "I've shaken hands with this author. I agreed to publish this book."

"Yes," he said, "but, Bob, you've got to remember, we have a textbook department." And I said, "What's that got to do with it?" He said, "This is a book about a kid going to prep school." So he sent it to the textbook people, who read it and said, "It's not for us."

The next thing I knew Reynal had rejected the book without telling me. I remember apologizing to Salinger. He said, "Ah, it's okay. I expect things like that. It happens." Well, I never thought it would happen to me.

Giroux came to Farrar, Straus without Salinger, but he did bring along seventeen other authors who constituted seemingly half the total literary talent in America at the time, including Thomas Merton, John Berryman, Robert Lowell, Flannery O'Connor, Jack Kerouac, Peter Taylor, Randall Jarrell, and Bernard Malamud. They don't make lists like that anymore. In 1996 Alan

Williams, a masterful editor and a much loved colleague, put together a fiftieth anniversary volume of excerpted pieces from books published by the house over the half century. In his introduction Williams called Giroux's Pied Piper sweep "almost certainly the greatest number of authors to follow, on their own initiative, a single editor from house to house in the history of modern publishing."

There was one other author besides Salinger who Giroux wasn't sure would follow him: T. S. Eliot, who had won the Nobel Prize during Giroux's reign at Harcourt, Brace and who described the ideal of writing this way: *"The common word exact without vulgarity, the formal word precise but not pedantic, the complete consort dancing together."* There then came the day when Bob rushed into Roger's office, waving a telegram in his hand. He read it to Roger: " 'I congratulate you in your new association. Of course, my next book will be with you on your new imprint. T. S. Eliot.' "

One of the last questions I asked the ailing head of his house that December morning in his office as we gazed out his windows, watching the shovels falling on the snow, dealt with the relationship between these two strong-willed individuals. "Roger," I said, "do you think that Bob is the greatest living book editor?"

He was silent for a moment, working out his thoughts. Then he said: "It couldn't be anyone else." But quickly he offered this P.S.: "You know, he did have a temper."

In 1964 Roger made Robert Giroux chairman of the board and changed the name of his company to Farrar, Straus and Giroux.

WHEN I MET with Bob Giroux in early May 2004, he was ninety years old, living in Tinton Falls, New Jersey, hard by Asbury Park, in a tree-shaded retirement home. He was waiting for me down in the lobby with Charlie Reilly, who has been with Bob since they first met in grammar school in Union City, New Jersey, home of the Giroux family. Both gentlemen on this hot day were dressed semiformally—summer sports jackets, open-necked sports shirts, slacks. To me, Giroux looked at least twenty years younger than his age. His wavy white hair was fresh and fluffy, his eyes were clear and alert, and there was an air of authority to him that friends said he'd always had. Herman Gollob, a renowned editor of this golden age (see chapter 4 on Atheneum) told me, "I thought Robert Giroux would be a tall, slender, aristocratic guy—you know—with a cocktail in his hand. Here's this guy looking like a ward heeler." Jack Kerouac's mother had a different take on Giroux when she met him. "You don't look like a publisher," said Gabrielle Kerouac, "you look like a banker." Even now, on a cane Bob Giroux moved with the authority of a banker, bent but unbowed.

My wife, Rosa, was with me. She had grown up in nearby Long Branch, and she wanted to go see the house where she was born, which we did after spending most of the day with Bob and Charlie. They paid Rosa courtly attention. Their apartment was cozy, with a terrace off the living room that was, of course, overflowing with books. As we talked Bob's voice was earthy and commanding, and his memory, except for names, was still razor sharp.

He held court by himself, telling story after story. One of the most unusual tales was about an odd publishing discovery. It came on a day in 1960 when a woman living in Bob's apartment building approached him. "I have a brother," she said, "who's a priest. He's stationed in Rome and wants to write about the Vatican Council. His name is Father Francis X. Murphy, and he's coming to New York. Will you see him?" Bob said he would.

The great Second Vatican Council was scheduled to commence in the fall of 1962 (the first one had begun in 1870). Two thousand five hundred bishops of the Roman Catholic Church would crowd into St. Peter's Basilica for four years to work out extensive changes in the Church's doctrine and practice. Father Murphy told Bob that he was a Redemptorist priest and would be an observer in the Council. "I would like to write about the Vatican Council for *The New Yorker*," he declared right off.

This stumped Giroux. "*The New Yorker* doesn't do much with religion," he told the priest.

"I'm not going to write about religion," Father Murphy said. "I'm going to write about politics. The Vatican Council is a political meeting. I read *The New Yorker*. I know what they publish and I admire their style, and I think I can write in their vein."

Sure, Bob thought. But since he had nothing to lose he said, "Write me a few pages about what you have in mind, and I'll try to get the editor, William Shawn, to look at them." When the material came in, Bob couldn't help but be impressed. "Very good phrasing," he told Shawn, "and in the *New Yorker* style." Shawn agreed and asked to meet the source, but Bob said that would be impossible. This priest would require complete anonymity. Shawn went along and Father Murphy, under the pen name Father Xavier Rynne, would write "Letters from the Vatican" each year that the Vatican Council was in session. *The New Yorker* would print excerpts, and Farrar, Straus and Giroux would publish the volumes. "A whole Catholic generation of writers was formed by reading these accounts of how things were done," a young FSG editor, Paul Elie, who still works there, told me. In 2004, Farrar, Straus and Giroux republished the Rynne diaries in a one-volume edition. Francis X. Murphy died in 2002, deep into his nineties, and even those who disagreed with his liberal approach to the Council regarded him as "one of the great clerical raconteurs."

Bob received an extraordinary bonus for his recruitment of Xavier Rynne. Bob's friend, Robert Fitzgerald, the brilliant translator of classical languages, who was intimately involved with Vatican II and was living in Italy with his family, found tickets for Bob and Charlie to attend the last day of the conference when the Pope and all the cardinals would walk down the aisle and out the door. It promised to be a historic moment. There was a catch, however. The tickets were for general admission. Fitzgerald told his guests, "You must gather in the open square in front of St. Peter's, and go to your particular section." Then he gave them a coach's advice. "You'll find it crowded with Italian nuns. They all tend to be short. The thing you must remember about them is that they can run very fast. They'll lift up their skirts and tear like hell for the side door. You have longer legs than they have. Get up near the wooden horses, and take off!"

"We did," Bob crowed like a teenager. "You know where the main altar was with the Bernini columns. We ended up looking down on it, and we were in the first row. These nuns were furious because they thought they deserved the first row. But nobody had told them how fast *we* could run."

When it was over, the doors that had been closed all the years the Vatican Council was in session were finally opened. Bob fondly remembered the moment: "And we walked out onto the Vatican Square into a heavenly sunlight."

As he went on that lazy afternoon in May 2004, a sweet smell of honeysuckle wafted into the room, just in time, it seemed, as he began to speak of Bernard Malamud.

It was Alfred Kazin, a scout for Harcourt, Brace, who, in 1950, introduced Bob to Malamud. The two found they had much in common, not the least being that both had been born in the same year, 1914, in the same month, April, and that nothing was more important to both of them than the book. They became Bob and "Bern" to each other.

At that time Malamud was working on a first novel, about baseball, seeking to find his voice. Bob liked *The Natural,* but the reason he gave Bern a two-book contract at Harcourt was because of a short story he had read in the *Partisan Review*, "The Magic Barrel." Bob felt it was a masterpiece, and figured that Malamud's second book, all things being equal, would be a volume of short stories that would feature "The Magic Barrel."

Harcourt published *The Natural* in 1952 to very good reviews; later it became a celebrated movie starring Robert Redford. When Bob left for Farrar, Straus, Bern did not accompany him; the second book still belonged to Harcourt. But one day he received a call from Malamud.

"Bob," Bern said, "they've turned down the book."

"I can't believe they'd turn down your stories," Bob said.

"Oh, it's not my stories," Bern said. "I've written a novel called *The Assistant*. Would you like to see it?" Bob said of course he would. He read the novel immediately. He was stunned by *The Assistant,* which was based on Malamud's mother and father's life running a small neighborhood grocery in Brooklyn, and Bob thought that Malamud had found his voice. In 1957, Farrar, Straus published *The Assistant* to critical acclaim. (Not long ago John Updike said, "I think in *The Assistant,* Malamud wrote a wonderful book—better to my mind than *The Great Gatsby.*")

In 1959, Malamud's short story collection was published under the title of the story Bob loved the most, *The Magic Barrel.* Soon after, Malamud received a call from Roger Straus. "Are you sitting down?" Roger said. Malamud said he was. "You've just won the National Book Award for *The Magic Barrel.*" Malamud was filled with pride. So was Straus, for it was the first major American literary award for his house. Malamud came through again in 1967, winning both the National Book Award and the Pulitzer for his novel *The Fixer.*

In March 1986 the Malamuds and Bob Giroux were dinner guests at Roger and Dorothea Straus's home. Bern was happy. He said he was four chapters from the end of his new novel. The next day, working at his desk, he died of a heart attack. On Bob Giroux's ninetieth birthday, Bernard Malamud's widow, Ann, called to wish him all the happiness in the world.

I keep thinking about that phone call and remembered something Malamud had told his class one day at Bennington College. He was trying to describe the writing ordeal, something he was going through at that time in his life: *"Before the first word strikes the page, or the first decent idea occurs, there is the complicated matter of breaking the silence."* How well he came to break the silence.

THE HIRING OF Robert Giroux by Roger Straus, despite the uneasiness each felt for the other, was, as the present leader, Jonathan Galassi, told me, "the beginning of the real FSG."

And it was. Roger remained as always the house's central nervous system. Galassi said that Roger read every book FSG published. He was the boss who, almost every day of his life, came into his office and clucked over his troops. "I don't think Roger was in essence a *literary* person," Galassi explained. "He created himself into a publisher, and he created FSG. And he kept it going. What really mattered to him was the organism of the company. I always felt he had an affinity with the authors because they were creative, too. He sort of saw them as his peers."

It was more difficult for Roger, however, to classify his editors as "peers," for he felt he was above them all—even the one, you could say, who made the house. At one point in a conversation I had with Bob Giroux after Roger's death, I did ask him how the two of them had gotten along through those years. There was in his voice a certain restraint. "He was very smart," Bob said, "a very good backer of books. But there were times when he thought I was trying to steal his thunder in one way or another."

There were two particular moments in the history of the company in which each baldly antagonized the other. In 1971 Bob proposed that FSG do a twenty-fifth-year anthology showcasing the house's most prideful works. Roger was enthused, and they moved ahead on it. Henry Robbins did much of the pickings for the book, and Bob wrote the introduction. On one page he depicted the publisher with his legs up on his desk, talking with Jimmy Van Alen, who was one of the company's original moneymen (and who also, it should be revealed here, invented the tiebreaker in tennis). Roger took the introduction home to read. The next day he told Bob, "My wife thinks you're making fun of me."

"I'm not making fun of you."

"I want to take it out."

"I won't take it out."

"Then we won't publish the book."

And they didn't, even though it was in the catalog and on press.

Many years later, in 2002, *The New Yorker* published a profile of Roger Straus titled "Showboat." In it, Straus was quoted as saying to Giroux, "The trouble with you is that you've been in publishing a hundred and seven years, and you still don't know the difference between an editor and a publisher."

When we met two years later, Bob was still livid about the description. "I never wanted to be a publisher," he said. "He hired me as his editor. I was his editor," he said, his voice rising. "And I was a damn good editor. There's nothing great about the word *publisher* per se, except that one publisher—I think it was the second Nelson Doubleday—said, 'I publish books. I don't read them.' No editor would ever say that," Bob said, calming down, thinking about his years in the company. "I loved being there, and the firm really rose."

The problem was that they were a team of mismatched personalities: Straus glib, flamboyant, power-driven, with a hunger for books that would go places, yet stingy with his forces; Giroux austere (he was Jesuit-trained, after all), conservative in dress, with an elegant mind that translated into a purity about his calling. Yet the center somehow held. Straus and Giroux needed each other because they shared the same fervent desire to find enduring works of literature. And both understood that it could only happen in the sanctity of an editorially driven publishing house.

Paul Elie joined the company in 1993. At that time he was working on a book of his own, about the interconnected lives of four Catholic "literary saints": Dorothy Day, Thomas Merton, Flannery O'Connor, and Walker Percy. Except for Dorothy Day they were all Giroux authors, and Bob helped make Elie's conception work. *An American Pilgrimage* was published in 2002 to much deserved praise. "Robert Giroux was more of a teacher, with his knowledge of taste," Elie told me, trying to gauge his superiors. "It was important to me to hear Mr. Giroux talking, him and his peers trying to figure out what was true or what was phony. One of the things I've understood in my work here—and this is true of Jonathan and Roger as well, considering that they're all brilliant men—their power is not intellectual. They go by instinct, gut reaction. They marry people to ideas in a way that's so nimble, you hardly know they're doing it."

Roger was nimble in other ways, too, as, for instance, how he netted Isaac Bashevis Singer, a novelist who would take Farrar, Straus and Giroux all the way to Stockholm. For years FSG's rival, Knopf, had published the works of Isaac Bashevis Singer's older brother, Israel Joseph Singer. Funny, I remember a bestselling I. J. Singer novel, *The Brothers Ashkenazi,* coming into our house when I was a kid. This novel could have been about my parents' life in what they called "the old country." They had no money to buy books, but my Aunt Rose, a schoolteacher and a lover of books who was living with us, brought it home. I read *The Brothers Ashkenazi* when I was a little older and loved it almost as much as *Anthony Adverse.*

"You like my work?" I. J. Singer would push Alfred Knopf, "my brother is even as good, if not better than I am." Finally, as Roger Straus heard it, "Alfred told Harold Strauss, his editor in chief at the time, to go see this guy who was writing for *The*

Jewish Daily Forward, writing in Yiddish on a typewriter whose carriage moved from right to left." Harold Strauss bought the novel, *The Family Moskat,* for $500. "That was a fair price in those days," Roger said, "and Knopf published it. But unbeknown to Isaac, Knopf cut the book by about twenty-five percent without his permission. So," as Roger explained it, "Isaac said, 'Fuck off, boy, I'm leaving him.' I heard about it, and in 1958 we published *Satan in Goray.*"

There followed, with Giroux as his editor, a grand parade of Singer novels and stories—and in 1978 Isaac Bashevis Singer won the Nobel Prize. Roger said that Singer had published ten novels without an agent. "I handled all of his work by myself. Finally, I thought, this is very incestuous what I'm doing. I can't be your publisher and your agent and fuck you one way or another. He wasn't very pushy, but I knew I had to get him an agent."

That isn't quite the way Bob Lescher remembers it. Bob was a major editor for nine years at Henry Holt and at Harcourt, then changed course to become a highly regarded literary agent (Dr. Benjamin Spock was one of his first clients). Bob was tipped off that Singer was looking for an agent, so he took the author to lunch. It was a cordial affair, and then Lescher got down to business. "Tell me, Mr. Singer, why do you want an agent? You've dealt with Mr. Straus and Mr. Giroux directly all these years. They appear to have published you superbly. Do you have trouble, for example, reaching Mr. Straus?"

"You know," Singer said, "in the old days when I wanted to reach Roger Straus I'd call him and he took my call. Now I call and the secretary says, 'He's on the phone with Mr. Solzhenitsyn." Singer waved his hand in the air. "I don't mean to take anything away from Mr. Solzhenitsyn," he said, "he's a perfectly good novelist . . ." With that, Lescher signed on as Singer's literary agent and today is the executor of the Singer estate.

In 1982, FSG published Singer's *Collected Stories*—forty-seven of them, headed by his incomparable "Gimpel the Fool." In his author's note to the collection, Singer wrote with intensity about the essence of what he called *genuine* literature: *"Genuine literature informs while it entertains. It manages to be both clear and profound. It has the magical power of merging causality with purpose, doubt with faith, the passions of the flesh with the yearnings of the soul. It is unique and general, national and universal, real and mystical."*

Singer died in 1991 at the age of eighty-seven. His widow, Alma, called Bob Giroux to attend his interment at a New Jersey cemetery. Immediately, Bob noticed the headstone, with a misspelled word—"the *Noble* Prize." The mistake was fixed later, but Bob seized on it when he spoke and praised "the extraordinary, even *noble* literary career of Isaac Bashevis Singer."

ON THE ONE WINTRY DAY we spent together—the last time I would see Roger—he reminisced about the Nobel Prizes. He spoke with pride about his two major commercial authors, Scott Turow and Tom Wolfe, but the Nobel Prize was Roger's Congressional Medal of Honor. In 1970 the winner was the one who had gotten into Mr. Singer's bald head a bit—Aleksandr Solzhenitsyn. It came out all right when, eight years later, Singer joined Solzhenitsyn in the Nobel pantheon. Straus's other Nobelists were Pablo Neruda, Czeslaw Milosz, Elias Canetti, William Golding, Wole Soyinka, Joseph Brodsky, Camilo José Cela, Nadine Gordimer, Derek Walcott, Seamus Heaney—the last three coming within five years of each other! "The best part of that," Roger said, "is that it will never happen again."

Of all those literary heroes, the one Roger loved the most was Joseph Brodsky. Roger carefully took from the top of his desk a heavy piece of glass—a replica of the Brodsky Medallion struck by the Nobel foundation. "Joseph wasn't married then," Roger explained, "and he put me down as next of kin. That did two things for me. It got me this medal, and it also got me a private interview with the king and queen. Only next of kin got in to meet the king and queen."

"Joseph was like a son to Roger," said Jonathan Galassi. "I think he was totally loyal and appreciated Roger in a certain way. They didn't sit around talking about people. They had this very connected relationship."

For Roger's seventy-eighth birthday, Brodsky wrote a poem to him that includes these three stanzas:

He is tall,
He is wise.
He sports loud
coats and ties.

He's a Mensch!
He's a Gent!
His fast talk
is intelligent.

If I were
Some young dame,
'round him
I'd lose my shame.
Since I am
an old fart,
I just lose
my mind or heart.

Roger was not in the office for Brodsky on January 28, 1996, when he made his last visit. But Paul Elie was there. "He asked me to get him a pack of cigarettes," Paul said. "I, for once, just couldn't do it. And he came back and he said, 'Ah, you did not get cigarettes, did you?' And I said, 'Joseph, I couldn't.'"

"'Ah—see, you are growing. Last year you would not have been able to resist me.'"

Joseph Brodsky died that night. He was fifty-five years old.

THE POETS DIE young. The heads of publishing houses—those who are what they publish—tend to live longer lives. Upon the death of Roger Straus in May 2004 there swelled forth a string of memorial services, running from New York to London and, later in the year, to the Frankfurt Book Fair. The tributes were deferential to a degree, but Roger's contentiousness created certain oratorical opportunities for those who mourned him.

Christopher MacLehose, a brilliant British literary publisher in the Straus tradition, may have best expressed the shadings of Roger's psyche in his remarks:

"Not content with rivals, Roger created for himself among his peers, sometimes with breathtaking provocations, bitter enemies, and these he kept in good repair. He had the soul of a buccaneer and, not seldom, the turn of phrase of an ordinary seaman." But MacLehose also proclaimed, "No American publisher I know did more for his writers."

Of all the houses I cover in this book, FSG is the only one—up to now, at least—that has not materially changed after being bought by another company. In 1997, Roger actually offered his house to the Georg von Holtzbrinck Publishing Group, Stuttgart, because he knew and respected the Holtzbrinck family and their dedication to publishing serious works of literature.

The legacy that was laid down for the house in the time of Roger Straus and Robert Giroux, and that is now being attended to with excellence by president and publisher Jonathan Galassi, may have been best expressed after Roger's death by Verlyn

Klinkenborg of *The New York Times:* "His firm was often discussed as if it were an antique, an inefficient old relic in a world of streamlined publishing machines. But, as Mr. Straus knew and demonstrated, the only meaningful efficiency in publishing is excellent taste."

2

WISHING FOR A FAIR WIND

Grove Press

I had a very good publishing career, but not money-wise.
We got rid of the money.

—BARNEY ROSSET

W hen Barney Rosset was in high school at the ultra-progressive Francis W. Parker School in Chicago, he was captain and star tailback on the football team, and he picked up an obsession for Henry Miller. When he was full-grown, he was active at tennis, softball, and Ping-Pong, and he was determined to publish *Tropic of Cancer*.

Before Barney was finished with his book publishing career, Henry Miller had fallen to him as one of his vanguard of golden age authors—Samuel Beckett, Jorge Luis Borges, Jean Genet, Eugène Ionesco, Marguerite Duras, William S. Burroughs, Frantz Fanon, and Octavio Paz were happy to join Grove Press. "Try to imagine a non–Grove Press America," said publisher John G. H. Oakes, in a 1999 speech honoring Barney Rosset, "that is, an America where Barney Rosset never made his indelible mark—and you'll see why it's easy to call him the greatest influence on American culture in the postwar era."

Publishing Henry Miller's *Tropic of Cancer* had not come easy. The book had been banned in the United States (and a host of other countries) since its publication in 1934. When Rosset founded Grove Press in 1951, his strategy for sliding by the censors and book-banners was to use the unabridged *Lady Chatterley's Lover* as a blocking back for *Tropic of Cancer*. He knew he would be challenged for publishing *Chatterley*—a novel, incidentally, that he never personally loved. But he understood that D. H. Lawrence passed literary standards; scholars and lawyers could make a case for him on that basis. Henry Miller was not so highly regarded. So Rosset would go first with *Chatterley*, and if the American court system ruled favorably, it would clear an opening for the book he did love and run it in for a touchdown. It took a bit of doing.

Rosset had entered the publishing business almost on a whim. (One of his editors, Kent Carroll, was once heard to say: "Rosset has a whim of steel.") In 1951, at twenty-nine years old, he was feeling depressed rather than steely. One of the causes of his dejection was his failure as a filmmaker. This had been his occupation of choice after coming out of the army, partly because his best friend in high school, Haskell Wexler, was flourishing in Hollywood; indeed, Wexler would become one of the film industry's most revered cinematographers. (It was such a close friendship it survived Wexler's first marriage, to Barney's high school sweetheart.) Three years earlier, Rosset had produced a documentary called *Strange Victory* (an allusion perhaps to Billie Holiday's famous song about lynching, "Strange Fruit") about how the United States may have won a world war but was failing domestically in the war against racism. The film didn't work, and even he came to dislike it.

Barney was then living in Paris with Joan Mitchell, the daughter of a Chicago doctor and of a mother who was the editor of *Poetry* magazine. Mitchell was beginning her career as a painter;

she was, in every way, as tough and independent as Rosset. They married in France, then came back to America and settled in Greenwich Village among the young American artists who were opening new pathways in art, as Rosset would do in avant-garde literature. Soon after, Joan Mitchell left Barney to pursue her own career as a painter. She would, in fact, become an acclaimed abstract expressionist.

This was a most uncomfortable period in Barney's life. The loss of Joan Mitchell hurt a lot (although he survived to marry three more times). He took courses at the New School for Social Research and went to work for a magazine called *Monthly Review Press.* "I was trying to do something over there," he told me, "but they decided that I might seem to be too liberal and left wing. But, chrissakes, I had a convertible car, and I got a parking ticket delivering the magazine. I was fired. I mean, like I was an unpaid intern. So I lost that. And then came the books. I liked them."

One day a friend of Joan Mitchell's from Chicago blew into town with two suitcases filled with books. She told Barney that these two guys she knew had started a book publishing house called Grove Press. The books in the suitcases were their inventory. They had only published three books in three years and wanted out. Barney bought the company for three thousand dollars, half contributed by his banker father. Soon, the new owner of the orphaned Grove Press, now filled with a purpose in life, was kicking open the doors and releasing a mighty draft of cool, fresh, unabridged air over the American book publishing industry.

The early nineteen-fifties was the opportune time for Barney Rosset to do what he was determined to do. There were unprecedented opportunities abroad. At the end of a destructive world war that had destroyed much of Europe, crippling the continent's sense of promise and possibilities, talented young authors were thrashing around, unread and unpublished. So American publishers began looking outside the United States for "orphans" who could really write. It wasn't just the Knopfs and Random Houses and Vikings and Harpers and Doubledays and the other good old boys who were in on the cultural gold rush. The new publishers, beginning with Farrar, Straus and George Braziller, were scooping up their share of the literary lode from France, Germany, Italy, Latin America, and the rest of the world. In 1953, Barney Rosset, having become a political radical when he was ten years old, began going after books no one else would publish.

Richard Gallen, once a Grove Press lawyer, told me, "Barney's business was always on a precipice. There was no one editorially doing what he was doing at that skill. In terms of drama, European literature, avant-garde literature, sexually provocative literature—there was no one doing it in America. No one. But somehow when I came, they were short of money; and when I left, they were short of money."

I CAUGHT UP with Barney Rosset at his East Village loft on an early January evening in 2004. The first thing he insisted on telling me was that "the most important part of my life wasn't publishing. It was high school. By far. Then I would say the army, then publishing." Surprised by his unexpected confession, I watched Barney and his longtime companion, Astrid Myers. Astrid was patiently trying to put into order the files scattered all over the house. She was looking for material to clarify Barney's life, to the extent that that was possible. He thought he knew where to find what he wanted, but Astrid was stumped.

The turmoil in his apartment that evening had to do with Barney trying to write his autobiography, and he was running on overtime. He sat at a working table that looked out over a long stretch of apartment. In the middle of the room was a covered Ping-Pong table where Barney had played with the elite of book publishing. "The last time I ever played Ping-Pong," he said, "was right here with George Plimpton." Plimpton was then helping Barney put the finishing touches to his *Paris Review* interview, published in the winter 1997–1998 issue. Barney, at five-feet-five, seemed a lot younger than his eighty-two years. His face was unlined and bore a little-boy pout that bordered on obstinacy. But Barney understood himself. When things began to go bad, it was his doing. Late in life he was disposed to say, "I made most of the major decisions in a second, and spent many years regretting them."

As we conversed, Barney spoke about his longing for his high school years, and of the person who meant the most to him in his early life. It wasn't his wealthy Jewish father, or his Irish Catholic mother. It was a distinguished public servant named Robert Morss Lovett. I vaguely remembered Lovett from the many jobs he had held in President Roosevelt's administration, and the troubles he got into during the war when the House Un-American Activities Committee (HUAC) began chasing after alleged communists in government.

Lovett had been a professor of English at the University of Chicago for forty-five years, and taught such students as Nelson Algren, Vincent Sheehan, and James T. Farrell. It was Lovett who helped Farrell find a publisher for his heralded *Studs Lonigan* trilogy, which, in its use of scatological language, was well ahead of its time.

"He was many, many, many things," Barney said of Lovett. Almost as an afterthought, he added modestly, "And he was the grandfather of my high school girlfriend."

Oh, I thought, so this is what it's all about. "Would you like to have married her?" I asked Barney.

"Hmm," he murmured. "Yes, I would." Barney's life has always been balanced by the twin pursuits of justice and pleasure.

When it was time for Barney to pick a college, he decided on Swarthmore College. "I chose it mostly," he said, "because the guy who came around sort of looking for students was an ambulance driver from the Spanish Civil War and a Quaker." Barney also thought Swarthmore (in Pennsylvania) was closer to Vassar, where his sweetheart was matriculating.

In that year spent at Swarthmore, Barney became, he insisted, "absolutely involved" with Henry Miller. In the literary underground he found a copy of the unexpurgated *Tropic of Cancer*. "I liked it enormously," he said, "so I wrote my freshman English paper on the book." He received a B-minus from his professor who, noting Miller's and Rosset's unfettered anti-Americanism, commented drily, "Perhaps the jaundice is in the eye of the beholders."

Barney, who never did believe in pursuing a higher education (he had also learned that Vassar was located in Poughkeepsie, New York, nowhere near Swarthmore), quit Swarthmore after his first year. In 1942 he enlisted in the army. He was put into the Army Signal Corps' photographic division and ultimately was sent to a lonely outpost in Kunming, China. At this point, confused about his life, he characterized himself this way: "a raw, semi-trained second lieutenant in the Signal Corps, twenty-two years old, and without a clue as to what was going on."

He thought he had come to the China of his dreams, filtered into his mind from the pages of Edgar Snow's *Red Star over China*. He had read that book when he was in the ninth grade and never forgot about its favorable recital of Mao Tse-tung and his Red Army. But instead of Mao, he found himself alongside the ragged remnants of Chiang Kai-shek's army. Barney felt that if these poor peasant children posing as soldiers represented Chiang Kai-shek's Kuomintang government, the only hope for the China of the future would come from Mao. In a letter to his parents at that time he wrote: "The Central government in China includes the biggest bunch of grafters and crooks I have ever seen."

In 2002, Barney put together a collection of his "War Photographs" for a New York gallery—graphic photos of Chiang's soldiers either wounded or dead, accompanied by an even more graphic account of Barney's military and sexual adventures in that desolate, dangerous edge of the world. His wartime experience left other deep impressions, and when he started Grove Press, he was receptive to suggestions about literary developments in the Far East.

In 1955, Barney was spiritually led to Japan by John Nathan, a Japanese translator he knew. As a consequence, Grove Press published Donald Keene's two monumental works on Japanese literature. Nathan also told Barney about a young Japanese novelist he had translated: Kenzaburo Oe. Barney published Oe's first two novels in America, *A Personal Matter* (1964) and *Teach Us to Outgrow Our Madness* (1969). He and Oe became close friends and each traded visits to the other's country. When, in 1994, Oe was awarded the Nobel Prize in literature, Barney and Astrid were invited to Stockholm for the ceremonies.

It was good having John Nathan's help, but from the beginning of his days at Grove Press, Barney Rosset relied heavily on his own literary instincts. These *whims* of his would fling him around like a high-flying kite.

SOME TIME DURING his first active year as a publisher, Rosset was glancing through the second issue of an English language literary magazine called *Merlin,* published in Paris by a group of young expatriate writers and translators. It was there that he read a story about a writer Rosset had never heard of: Samuel Beckett. The article was written by an American named Richard Seaver. Rosset wrote Seaver at the offices of *Merlin:* "I've just started this small publishing house, and I'm very interested in your magazine and especially in a couple of the writers." Rosset told Seaver he was coming to Paris and would like to meet with him, with hope that he could perhaps direct him to Beckett.

Dick Seaver, like Barney Rosset, was an athlete. (In later years the two of them formed a fearsome tennis doubles team.) At the University of North Carolina, Seaver was captain of the wrestling team. He also became a Francophile. In his senior year he signed up for French I and French II, although his teachers said to him, "You can't take I and II at the same time. That's not done." Seaver not only did it, but in the last semester of his senior year, he conquered French III and IV. And off to Paris he went.

Early in 1952, looking in the display window of a Paris publishing house, Les Éditions de Minuit, Seaver noticed the covers of two books—*Malone* and *Molloy*—by Samuel Beckett. He bought *Malloy* and was overwhelmed. It was for Seaver a shock of discovery. He went on to read everything he could find by Beckett.

RICHARD SEAVER

In Paris I became involved with a disparate but fascinating literary group—English, Scottish, American, South African—who had just founded an English-language literary magazine, *Merlin,* edited by a man named Alex Trocchi, who was also a budding novelist. The first issue had just come out, and one of its contributors and a friend of mine, Pat Bowles, introduced me to Trocchi. We hit it off immediately, and knowing I'd been in Paris for several years, Alex asked me if there were any Paris-based writers *Merlin* should publish. I thought immediately of Beckett, whom I had just discovered, and who, as I said to Trocchi, "had knocked my socks off."

As I talked to Alex about Beckett, he became increasingly enthusiastic. "Jesus," he said, "he sounds just right for our magazine. Why don't you write a piece about him for the next issue?" So I did. It was the first one written in English on Beckett. When the issue appeared, I wrote Beckett a note that said: "If you have anything, we'd love to publish you in the magazine." I didn't know where to send it, so I brought my letter and the magazine containing my piece—"Samuel Beckett: An Introduction"—to Jerome Lindon, the publisher of Les Éditions de Minuit, one of the great publishers of the twentieth century, who was doing everything that Beckett wrote. I didn't hear from Beckett for weeks and weeks. Everyone who knew Beckett had told me that he was the most meticulous, polite, and courteous of men. Why hadn't he written back? Well, I finally did hear from him; it was late summer, and he had been away, he explained. "I have three stories written in French," he said. "If you'd like to see any of them, I'll send them to you."

The first story he sent us was called "La Fin (The End)," which I thought was extraordinary. I wrote him and told him how wonderful it was and asked, "Would you kindly translate it?" He said he couldn't, he was in the midst of other kinds of work (which I found out later included the original staging of *Waiting for Godot*). The next time I saw Lindon, he told me, "You know, he has a novel in English—the last novel he wrote in English in 1945, just at the end of the war. He tried to publish it in England and got turned down by everybody. You might ask him about it." So I did.

At that time I lived behind the Boulevard St. Germain on the Rue du Sabot, in a ground-floor ex-warehouse that before the war had been used as a banana-drying emporium! By now, *Merlin* had its offices there, too. One night, I think in November of 1952, there was a knock on my door. It was pouring rain and here was this tall gaunt figure standing there. He said, "Here. Here's *Watt*." And I said, "What?" He said, "Yes, *Watt*." It was Abbott and Costello all over again, and

I knew this had to be Mr. Beckett. "Oh, my god," I said, "you're soaked. Please come in for a cup of tea. A drink?" "No, no, no, I couldn't. Thank you very much. I'm on my way somewhere." So off he went, leaving his novel, *Watt,* behind.

The manuscript was encased in a black imitation leather binding; he had wrapped the thing in paper and had it under his coat. It must have been eight o'clock at night, and I started to read *Watt* out loud to the *Merlin* gang. It was so funny and so wonderful that I kept reading it till my voice gave out. Then Trocchi picked it up. Then Patrick. Then the poet Christopher Logue. We read the whole damn manuscript until about four in the morning—by the way, getting drunker and drunker. But it got funnier and funnier as we got drunker.

I wrote Beckett the next day and said we'd love to extract something from it. And he said, "Okay, but do you mind if I pick the extract?" Uh-oh. Would he pick the most complicated, esoteric extract? He did, which we published without question.

Years later, when I really got to know him, I asked one day, "Were you testing our literary purity when you chose that section from *Watt* for the magazine?" All he did was grin.

In *The Grove Press Reader,* published in 2001 on the fiftieth anniversary of the publishing house, there is a fascinating series of letters between Barney Rosset and Samuel Beckett. In the first letter, written on June 18, 1953, as Grove Press was readying publication of *Waiting for Godot,* Rosset explained how he had come to Beckett. "Sylvia Beach is certainly the one you must blame for your future appearance on the Grove Press list," Rosset wrote. (Beach, who ran the famous Shakespeare & Company bookstore in Paris, was the one who first brought James Joyce to the attention of the world by publishing *Ulysses* in 1922. Beckett worked for a while as Joyce's secretary.) "After she talked of you," Rosset went on, "I decided that what Grove Press needed most in the world was Samuel Beckett." Odd that in this letter Barney never mentions Richard Seaver. An oversight? I don't think so. Barney liked to keep the spotlight on himself.

Beckett wrote back quickly and delivered a homily about his convictions: "With regard to my work in general, I hope you realize what you are letting yourself in for. I do not mean the heart of the matter, which is unlikely to disturb anybody, but certain obscenities of form which may not have struck you in French as they will in English, and which frankly (it is better that you should know this before we get going) I am not at all disposed to mitigate." *Mitigate?* Barney Rosset never bothered to find out what the word meant; it certainly wasn't in his vocabulary. Beckett's last words in the letter were: "Thanking you for taking this chance with my work and *wishing us a fair wind* . . ."

Later in the summer the two met for the first time in the bar of the Pont Royal hotel, a hangout for Sartre and Camus. Rosset was with his second wife, Loly, an attractive German woman, and Beckett was due at 6 P.M. "This very handsome gentleman," Rosset recalled in his *Paris Review* interview, "walked in wearing a raincoat and said, 'Hi, nice to meet you. I've only got forty minutes.' He was all set to get rid of us! At four that morning he was buying us champagne."

After that, the salutations became: "Dear Samuel," then "My Dear Barney," each wishing the other further hope for a fair wind. And Barney named one of his sons Beckett.

Waiting for Godot was published by Grove Press in the fall of 1954. Rosset printed a thousand copies, and in the first two years only sold about four hundred. Was he wrong about Beckett's appeal?

Some years ago, French sociologist Pierre Bourdieu developed a typology of publishing houses based on whether publishing

decisions were oriented toward a short or long life span. Bourdieu divided book publishing into two parts—houses that "are
geared to the rapid turnover and quick obsolescence of their
products" and "houses geared to a long-term perspective . . . in
the hope that once a book is part of the backlist, it will continue to
find new buyers." These patient houses, Bourdieu felt, tended to
accumulate what he called "symbolic capital." The example he
used to solidify his theory was Les Éditions de Minuit's experience with *Waiting for Godot*. The French edition was published
in 1952 and in the first five years sold 10,000 copies. The cumu-
lative sale by 1968 was 65,000 copies.

The year that *Waiting for Godot* opened on Broadway, starring
Bert Lahr as Estragon, the book began to move for Grove Press.
And even though the Broadway production lasted only six weeks,
the play caught on elsewhere in the United States. Barney Rosset
claims that Grove ended up selling over two million copies. How
about that for symbolic capital?

Barney Rosset and Dick Seaver did meet in Paris in that *Godot*
period, and they had dinner together along with Barney's new
wife, Loly, and Dick's wife, Jeannette, who was not only comely,
but a violin prodigy in France.

At dinner, Seaver asked Rosset, "How big is Grove now?"

"You're looking at half of it," Barney said. "Loly is my sales
manager." Ten years later Grove Press had 350 employees.

Dick spent the next two years in the navy, and after that he
worked a year in Venezuela. When the Seavers returned to New
York in 1957, they were ready to settle down. One of the first
people he went to see was Barney Rosset. "Maybe there's something we can do together," Barney told Dick.

"I'd love to," said Dick. He saw what Barney was doing, publishing the new guys from France—Beckett and Jean Genet and
Eugène Ionesco—and spreading out to other countries, too. He
was ready to be a part of Grove Press's global quest for literary

excellence. But Barney never called him back. So Dick went to work for another new postwar publisher, George Braziller (see next chapter).

Two years later, in 1959, Seaver finally heard from Barney Rosset. "Listen, I really need you," Barney said. "We're about to get much bigger, and we're going to get in much more trouble than we have in the past because we're going to publish *Lady Chatterley's Lover* in about three months, and there's going to be a lot of action, and it's going to be a lot of fun. Come on."

"Sure," Dick Seaver said. He left Braziller and stayed with Grove for twelve years.

BRINGING SEAVER TO Grove Press was a rare act of reason—or maybe I should say of premeditated calculation—by the normally impulsive Barney Rosset, who, as Dick Gallen pointed out to me, "took life by the neck and shook it up." He certainly was in the habit of exploding first and thinking about the consequences when the smoke settled. Much of the time Rosset's hiring policy was based on impulse—the sound of a person's voice, or the look in his eyes, or on just pure swagger. One morning a man with a long beard showed up in the Grove offices. When asked what he was doing there, he said, "I'm your new salesman."

"You are? When did Barney hire you?"

"Last night, in this bar where I work."

Finally, someone asked him about his qualifications. "I once sold Christian memorabilia and Bibles in the Bible Belt," he said. The bearded ex-bartender lasted six months at Grove.

The hiring in 1956 of Fred Jordan, who of all Barney's editors was the longest-serving, and always the most loyal, wasn't quite that off the wall, but still odd. "When I got to meet Barney, I started to give him my résumé," Fred told me the day I went to see him at his home in Croton-on-Hudson. "He waved it off. So right away I was on the defensive. 'Look,' I said, 'whatever risks you're taking, I'm taking greater risks. I will do the job, and you can fire me anytime you want if you don't like me.'

" 'OK,' Barney said in his offhand way. 'I'm going to Europe.' He never told me—'you're hired.' He said, 'We'll see what happens.' And that's the way it was for the next thirty-five years or so."

Fred Jordan felt he always understood Rosset. "What you see is what you get," he said. "How many people are there like that? It's quite extraordinary. After you've been with him for a while, it's very hard to work with anybody else because he's such an authentic person."

Rosset grew to respect Fred, too. He told an interviewer from the literary quarterly *Tin House*, "I found out after a few years [with Fred] that he had a strong sense of what he was saying and feeling, and his instincts were good. Not necessarily that I always agreed with him, but a certain sensibility echoed strongly."

In his first couple of years with Grove Press, Fred looked after marketing and sales, and read the books that came in in German—he had been born in Vienna. One of his early discoveries for the company was a German playwright, Rolf Hochhuth. Fred recommended to Rosset that Grove publish his play *The Deputy,* which was creating a stir because it was about Pope Pius XII's reluctance during World War II to speak out against the Holocaust. Barney said okay. Because of the controversy over the play, a Broadway version of *The Deputy* became a big hit. It was also the first play to make the bestseller list.

When Dick Seaver came in to be managing editor, and also to edit Barney's two-year-old literary magazine, the *Evergreen Review,* Jordan became an editor. But he always deferred to Barney's whims. "I would never, never buy anything without him," Fred told me. "He had a very firm judgment. He could look at something and say yes or no. You would tell him what you thought, and as he got more and more confidence in you, he would rely on you."

"Did he disappoint you," I asked Fred, "by saying no to things you wanted?"

"Very often," Fred said. "Barney was a personal publisher. He published what he liked and nothing else. So I never pitted my ego against his. I couldn't have lasted."

Dick Seaver's approach to Barney was the opposite of Fred's. He said, "A lot of people just kowtowed to him because he was a tyrant. Barney knew that whatever I told him was what I thought, not what he wanted to hear. And I think he respected me for that. In fact, he once said to me, 'You're the brother I wish I had.'"

IN 1959, WITH his list growing, and his reputation rising in the world of book publishing, Barney Rosset felt it was time to take on the book-banners.

The battle for *Lady Chatterley's Lover* began with a skirmish. Barney dispatched Mark Schorer, a professor of literature at the University of California, Berkeley, to Taos, New Mexico, to try to convince Lawrence's widow, Frieda Lawrence-Ravagli, that Grove Press should be the American house to publish the unexpurgated novel. Frieda knew Schorer and admired him, especially for the high literary esteem in which he held her husband. Schorer's essay "On *Lady Chatterley's Lover*" had appeared in the first issue of the *Evergreen Review* in 1957. (From 1957 to 1973, each issue of the *Evergreen Review* was a rich treasury of new and provocative literary voices from around the world, featuring the Beats and Black Mountain poets as well as Jean-Paul Sartre, Susan Sontag, Kenzaburo Oe, Octavio Paz, and Carlos Fuentes, among many others.) One of the lesser reasons for Barney's starting *Evergreen* was that he could use it as a bully pulpit for books he wanted to publish that he knew would probably run into trouble. "Barney treated the Schorer piece deliberately," Fred Jordan said, "as a kind of preparation for the publication of *Lady Chatterley's Lover,* so we would have some critical apparatus."

Alas, Frieda Lawrence died before she could give Rosset her legal blessing for the book. And Lawrence's British literary agents said no. In the end, Barney decided: "We'll publish it ourselves."

The unexpurgated *Lady Chatterley's Lover* became an immediate bestseller. Elated, Barney now sought to get arrested—the right way. The right way, he knew, would be to send the book through the mails so that it would be seized by the post office. Then his offense would be a federal one. That was exactly what happened.

There was only one person, Barney felt, good enough to be his general in the campaign: Charles "Cy" Rembar. Rembar's tryout for the job was his facility as an infielder in the Long Island Hamptons' softball league; Barney played third base on the same team. As we have learned, this was his way of hiring people. He knew that Rembar—lean, studious, and articulate—would be a standout lawyer in the case. Rembar himself loved the challenge of trying to pull down the obscenity laws that had kept authors of the widest reputation—James Joyce was a prime example—out of the hands of American readers. "The law in the time of *Chatterley*," Rembar wrote in his brilliant book, *The End of Obscenity,* "recognized two kinds of books: literature, which produces cortical responses, or in any case emotional responses from somewhere above the belt, and pornography, which gets you in the groin." The Rembar brief to the postmaster general concluded that "appeal to sexual interest does not create obscenity."

The trial took place on May 14, 1959, and lasted one day.

After the opening statements, Cy Rembar put the sire of Grove Press on the stand. He asked Rosset about his motive for publishing the book:

"I consider *Lady Chatterley's Lover* to be a great book [why shouldn't he, under the circumstances, be permitted an exaggeration or two?] and a significant part of the heritage of the English-speaking people. As a publisher in a free marketplace, I am also looking for stimulating, challenging, possibly profitable opportunities to publish good books."

This was the true vision Barney Rosset had brought to book publishing and that he maintained all his life.

"It occurred to me," Barney went on to say, "that it would be incomprehensible, if this book were published today, that the public would be shocked, offended or would raise any outcry against—but rather they would welcome it as the republishing, the bringing back to life, of one of our great masterpieces, and therefore I went ahead and published it. Thus far all of my anticipated feelings have been rewarded . . . with the exception," he concluded slyly, "of this hearing."

Rembar's star witness from the outside was Malcolm Cowley, who modestly defined his occupation as being "a literary critic and historian." That is exactly what he had been in his forty years at his trade, from literary critic of *The New Republic* to editor of *The Portable Faulkner* and an almost lifelong literary consultant for the Viking Press. When Rembar asked Cowley to give his estimate of the position Lawrence held in English literature, the opposing counsel immediately objected. He was overruled.

"Very briefly," Cowley said, "he is considered to be the most significant English novelist after Joseph Conrad." Then he explained why the heart of *Lady Chatterley's Lover* was the description of sexual encounters: "because Lawrence is trying to advocate in the book sexual fulfillment in marriage. That is the purpose of the sexual acts throughout."

On cross-examination, Cowley was asked, "Is it your feeling, Mr. Cowley, that it is vital and indispensable to use these so-called four-letter words as they are used in this book?"

He was ready for that. "It was vital to Lawrence to use them. It wouldn't have been vital to another writer; but to his purpose of trying to remove sentimentality from the sexual act and at the same time reveal passion and tenderness. The original title of the book, you know," Cowley said mischievously, "was *Tenderness.*"

Despite Cowley's heroics the postmaster general ordered that the book could not travel through the mails.

Rembar immediately sued and asked a federal court to take the case. There were appeals back and forth, with Grove Press winning one, losing the next. But on March 6, 1960, the case came to an end. The Court of Appeals cleared *Lady Chatterley's Lover.*

NOW IT WAS Henry Miller's turn.

Miller was living in the Big Sur region of California when Barney Rosset went to see him early in 1959. The meeting did not go well. Perhaps it was because Barney was feeling queasy staring down from the cliffs at the thrashing waves of the Pacific. He was invited to sit on a sofa that hung over the down slopes, but pleaded vertigo. Barney liked Miller all right, thought that Miller was a mild-mannered guy, but with a mind of his own. But Henry Miller wasn't overly interested in having Grove Press take on his most infamous book. For starters, New Directions was his publisher in America. He would give *Tropic of Cancer* to the owner, James Laughlin, if he wanted it. But Laughlin shied away from court fights. Miller also had another rather weird objection. "If you make my book a success," he told Barney, "the next thing I know it will be used in college texts."

"He didn't want to be mainstream," Barney told me. "He liked being an outlaw. We were taking away that right."

Barney bombarded Miller with letters and also sent him a copy of the newly published *Lady Chatterley's Lover,* so different from Knopf's abridged edition. Miller wrote back on July 9, 1959. "Looks good," Miller said about the Lawrence, "and it is of course a big step forward—but how slowly everything proceeds. The 'Cancer' will be twenty-five years old this September. Soon I'll be dead. . . . One has to die first, if you notice, before the ball gets rolling. . . . My own view is that it may take another fifty or a hundred years before these banned books of mine can circulate freely in this country. But I may be wrong."

Rosset was sure he was wrong. He pled his case with two friends of Henry Miller's. One was Maurice Girodias, who had published the unabridged *Tropic of Cancer* in his Olympia Press in Paris. The other was Ledig Rowohlt, whose house, Rowohlt, had also published the naughty version in Germany. He and Barney had become best friends. "I loved him," Barney said. "He was my favorite publisher in the whole world." One day Barney received a telegram from Girodias and Rowohlt, who were in Hamburg, Germany. Henry Miller was with them. "Come right over," the telegram said. "Miller will give you the book." Barney took the next flight out to Hamburg and sealed the deal when he got there by playing Ping-Pong with Miller.

But of course it wasn't going to be that easy to publish the book. "*Chatterley* was basically one lawsuit," Fred Jordan told me, "and that was against the post office. We won a federal victory. *Tropic of Cancer* was fifty cases, in almost every state in the country. We had guaranteed booksellers all around the country that we would defend them. And that's what we did." Red ink began to bleed all over Barney Rosset's business.

Barney's attorney, Charles Rembar, decided that the Illinois Supreme Court, flush in Barney's home state, would be a good target for the publisher. But they declared unanimously against Grove Press.

Rembar then sent an urgent appeal to the court of last resort, the United States Supreme Court.

There were no briefs, no arguments, no trial. The court decided only on the papers filed and, by a 5–4 majority, ruled that *Tropic of Cancer* was not obscene.

Barney Rosset had opened the doors not only for *Tropic of Cancer* but for other works of fiction that would never have made it into public print if he hadn't done what he had always set out to do: use the books he was publishing, as he once wrote, "as battering rams to storm the ramparts of literary censorship."

ONE DAY IN December 1959, Barney attended a Dell sales conference in Connecticut. Dell at that time was distributing Grove Press books in paperback. Their biggest Grove book was *Lady Chatterley's Lover,* although, it should be noted, the Dell edition did not have the publisher's name on the book; they were still fearful of losing their license.

That first evening of the sales conference the clatter of a poker game could be heard in the Dell hospitality suite, four tables of Dell salesmen poking cards back and forth. Barney was enjoying himself, playing at one of them. Much later in the evening only one table was operating. Barney was one of the occupants. The game was five-card draw, and the person on his left, whose name Barney had not caught, pushed almost all the chips he had to the center of the table. Barney, who had drawn three cards, saw him. The youngster, with confident ease, displayed his cards—a three-aces' full house! You can't do much better than that in five-card draw. But, wait. Barney began turning over his cards, one by one, announcing with an exaggerated hush to his voice, "See, I have two pairs—all kings." Well, four of a kind always beats a full house. The young Dell salesman, whose name was Nat Sobel, turned gray all over and felt, he told me, "like I was struck dead." Barney said good-bye to him. Sobel passed out in the hospitality suite on what he called, "drink and disappointment."

Next morning the sales conference was to begin at 8 A.M. Helen Meyer, the boss at Dell, was a stickler about the time. Sobel didn't wake up until after 9 A.M., with a terrible hangover. He staggered to his room, showered, downed some coffee, and reported for work at 9:45. He was hoping to slip in discreetly at the back of the conference hall. Unfortunately for him, Dell had printed up memo pads for every one of the reps, and he had to go right up front—his name was at the dead center of the dais. He remembers sitting down and hearing Helen Meyer whisper, "Who is he?"

Barney Rosset was also there that morning, noticing his poker opponent's extreme discomfort. He became interested in the kid. He did some checking on him and found out that although he had been in book publishing for only about a year, Sobel was one of the best salesmen on the Dell paperback sales force; he had done particularly well with Grove's list.

Three months after the Dell melodrama at the sales conference, Barney called Sobel, who, even after the sales conference, was still employed.

"Are you the guy who appeared two hours late for the Dell sales conference?" asked Barney.

Sobel, thinking it was a joke, said, "Yes, I'm the guy."

"I'm Barney Rosset. Kid, I like your style. I'd like to hire you as assistant sales manager at Grove Press, with one proviso: If you ever run sales conferences at Grove, they never begin before 10 A.M."

On those terms, with a dollop of money also offered, Nat took the job, but not before telling Barney to his face that in that poker game, "I think you were one lucky sonofabitch." Barney took it in good grace. Sobel turned out to be the lucky one. Six months after his arrival, the sales manager at Grove quit. Barney, convinced he had a good, tough one in Sobel, promoted him to sales manager, giving Nat enough room to flourish. And, for the next decade, flourish he did, as did Barney Rosset.

THROUGHOUT THE 1960S, Rosset and his crusaders created a golden age for their house. They continuously secured for the beleaguered company books that *worked*—first, the books that no other American publishers would touch: William S. Burroughs's *Naked Lunch* ("a work of genius," Barney called it); Frank Harris's *My Life and Loves;* John Rechy's *City of Night;* Jean Genet's *Our Lady of the Flowers* and *The Thief's Journal,* both banned in the United States until Rosset came along; Pauline Réage's *Story of O,* and Hubert Selby, Jr.'s *Last Exit to Brooklyn.* Many of these works first appeared in part in the *Evergreen Review,* and most are still being read today.

Not all of Grove Press titles, however, had to bear the Rosset erotic signature. Dick Seaver, who over the years translated forty to fifty authors from the French (among them Françoise Sagan, Eugène Ionesco, Marguerite Duras, and the Marquis de Sade), found and translated Frantz Fanon's *The Wretched of the Earth* (Grove, 1963). The book had been published in French (*Les Damnés de la terre*) in 1961, the year that Fanon died at age thirty-six. A powerful work, it helped establish the black liberation movement, especially in the desperately poor colonized countries.

In 1965, Barney took over another transcending work from Doubleday, *The Autobiography of Malcolm X.* When Malcolm X was assassinated early that year, Doubleday had had the book in galleys. Nelson Doubleday then gave it up, saying, "I don't want my secretaries to be killed because of this book." Barney Rosset was willing to take a chance, and he paid Alex Haley, who had put the book together, $20,000 to complete it.

A highlight of the decade for Grove Press was Fred Jordan's discovery of the book that would become the house's biggest seller in the period: *Games People Play: The Psychology of Human Relationships* by Eric Berne, M.D. It was also a good example of in-house teamwork (which was never Rosset's bent) at its best.

Games People Play came to Fred Jordan because he had published Berne's previous book, *Transactional Analysis in Psychotherapy,* which sold only a few hundred copies. But Jordan was convinced that this new one could break out. Barney wasn't convinced. So *Games People Play* was published in 1964 with a modest first printing of three thousand copies. Now, this was the period when Grove was still suffering lingering aftershocks from the legal battles over *Tropic of Cancer*. Nat Sobel says he will always remember the humiliation and irony of having to go every Friday to the offices of Bookazine and Dynastine, two major book jobbers, to collect a check from them on the basis of the sales of *Cancer,* "just so we could meet the payroll."

At the time that *Games* was published, Sobel was on a three-week trip to the West Coast, visiting all the major bookstores. As soon as he returned, he rushed to see the boss.

"Look, Barney, I have a hunch."

"What hunch?"

"I'd like us to take out a big ad to promote *Games People Play.*"

"Whoa," Barney said, "we've gone back for two thousand more copies. What's your hunch?"

"Barney, on this trip, I saw three people—one in L.A., one on the plane to San Francisco, and one in San Francisco—reading *Games People Play.*"

"So?"

"God is telling me something—that we need to spend some money and really go with this book."

"Okay. I'll buy that."

It was the daddy of the book, Fred Jordan, who came up with the idea of how to spend the money: run a co-op ad with the Doubleday bookstore in New York, and then feature the ad prominently in *The New York Times*. The ad would be timed for the American Psychiatric Association's convention in New York. Sobel saw to it that copies of the book would be on sale there, promoted at a professional discount.

Jordan wrote a very selling ad in the form of an open letter to young psychiatrists. "After that ad came out," Sobel said, "hordes of shrinks at the convention were buying *Games.*" That was not the end of it. Jordan's "letter" drew such interest from *Life* magazine that they hired Kurt Vonnegut, Jr., to review the book. It was a powerful selling review. Grove went on to sell 600,000 copies in hardcover.

"Lots of money was made in 1967, '68, '69, and the beginning of '70," said Dick Gallen.

And then Barney Rosset was back on the precipice.

IN MY CONVERSATIONS with Dick Gallen, he said it was a Grove editor named Harry Braverman who edited the Malcolm X autobiography. "He was a very bright, scholarly, socially concerned human being," Gallen said. Harry Braverman was more than that.

"On those occasions when Barney would be somewhat mercurial," Nat Sobel said, "Harry was a very good, calming influence. Gradually, over the years that I was there, he had a number of different jobs with more and more responsibility to the point that when we were all vice presidents, he was a senior vice president, and clearly the number-two person. And then he left to run the *Monthly Review Press*," a socialist magazine of some repute. The reason Braverman left was that Barney had refused to publish a book by Bertrand Russell on America's war crimes in Vietnam. "Harry's leaving was really a critical thing," Sobel said. "Barney no longer had a counterbalance, somebody who could say to him, 'Don't do that. You're putting too much on the line for the whole company to do that.'"

Had Harry Braverman stayed at Grove, he might have talked his boss out of indulging his old obsession: film. Barney had gone ahead and bought a sixteen-millimeter avant-garde film library called "Cinema Sixteen." Soon after, he was on his way to Sweden to pay $100,000 for the American film rights to an erotic film called *I Am Curious (Yellow)*. Everyone I talked to about this reckless move of Barney's said pretty much the same thing—that *I Am Curious (Yellow)* marked the beginning of the end of the Rosset reign at Grove Press.

"You bring a film through Customs," Dick Gallen told me, "they have a right to seize it if they deem it obscene. So the film came into the country, was shown to Customs and seized by Customs." Gallen was one of the Grove lawyers suing the United States government to get the film released from Customs.

The trial, Grove Press vs. the U.S. government, was held on February 4, 1968. "I was nervous," Gallen remembered, "focusing really on what I had to do and not so much on what was going on around me. The government presented the case by showing the film, and rested its case. No witnesses. We produced about ten witnesses: intellectuals, literary people (Norman Mailer was one of them), sociologists. The jury took about two hours and declared—'Guilty!'"

The Grove lawyers appealed to the United States Second Circuit Court in New York and won. "We thought the government would then appeal to the Supreme Court," Gallen said, "because this was an important obscenity case. And they didn't. So in New York State, *I Am Curious (Yellow)* was deemed not obscene and could play in theaters. The movie opened to lines around the block." But lots of the moviegoers were disappointed. One reviewer put it this way about the Swedish film: "Is it art or Europorn? By the end of this mess, you don't really care."

Still, Barney Rosset insisted on showing the film wherever it could be shown. Dick said, "I advised Barney not to open the movie in many states, just to go very slowly to make sure that we were on solid ground. Barney wouldn't listen. I don't know what his rationale was, I mean, he just didn't want to wait. He'd been waiting so long. And it got seized; theater owners were arrested in Baltimore and several other places. There must have been twenty lawsuits. Had he waited, it might have been possible to get through this without any lawsuits."

In Baltimore the movie was deemed obscene. Appeals were turned down and it finally went to the Supreme Court. Barney had a killing setback there. Justice William O. Douglas, open-minded about all literature, had written an article for the *Evergreen Review*, and received a small fee; he thus disqualified himself from the Supreme Court decision. Without Douglas, the court deadlocked, 4–4, and so upheld the obscenity ruling of the U.S. Circuit Court in Baltimore. In the end, *I Am Curious (Yellow)* did little for Grove Press financially.

Barney compounded his problems by putting his editors to work to find films rather than books. "There was a point," Dick Seaver said, "where the book business was having to support the film business. Grove Press had more unreleased films in its coffers than MGM, and no public."

In his *Paris Review* interview, Barney was hard on himself, especially regarding his judgment. "Because we made a lot of money on *I Am Curious (Yellow),*" he said, "I went and bought a lot of foreign films—which were no longer commercially viable because all the art theaters had closed down, overnight, in 1970. . . . There had been a big market for foreign films in this country, and suddenly it was gone. After *I Am Curious* played, that was the end. We killed our own market."

ROSSET HAD BEEN an intemperate owner over the years, completely sure of himself when it came to buying books, and completely unwilling to engage in the business aspects of book publishing. He was smart enough and tough enough to deal with profits and losses, but he never wanted to. It wasn't his way of living—wasn't "that strong romantic streak in his life," is the way Fred Jordan put it. The romance for him came in breaking all the taboos the industry had tolerated over the years, not worrying about how much money his company had to bring in to survive.

He sold his company in 1985 to Ann Getty, of Getty Oil, and Sir George Weidenfeld (later Lord Weidenfeld), a British publisher (formerly of Weidenfeld & Nicolson). A year later, the Getty management dumped Barney Rosset, the man who had done more than any other American publisher to liberate literature—who, indeed, had spent his life serving the book.

As the years went by, Barney found some comfort in being lionized by the publishing industry. He won lifetime achievement awards from the PEN American Center, *The Paris Review*, the Small Press Center, the National Book Critics Circle, and, from the government of France, the medallion of the Commandeur de l'Ordre des Arts et des Lettres. In 2002 the Association of American Publishers presented him with the Curtis Benjamin Award for Creative Achievement. It had only taken the AAP twenty-odd years to acknowledge Rosset's achievements. The medals piled up for Barney Rosset. However, as this tough-minded American romantic said to me when I visited him in 2004, the money had gone away. "People have the idea that I have a lot of money, but I don't. Honestly, I can tell you I haven't got any. Zero."

Had he taken too many chances? Well, in 1962, Barney decided to publish a bilingual edition of a South American poet in Spanish and English. Barney's sales director, Nat Sobel, had immediately objected. "You know," Nat told Barney, "I don't think I can sell this book. Nobody's ever heard of the guy."

"I didn't think you could sell the book," Barney said.

"Well, then," Nat asked, "why are we publishing it?"

"You know," Barney said, "every once in a while we need to put something back into the body of publishing that is worthwhile, and this is worthwhile."

"The book, titled *The Labyrinth of Solitude,*" Nat told me, "turned out to be the first publication in the English language for Octavio Paz." The work, nine deeply felt essays celebrating Mexican culture and character, is still in print. In 1990, Paz won the Nobel Prize for literature.

"It turned out to be a good gamble," Nat Sobel said, almost sheepishly. "But that's not why he did it."

"This is worthwhile." Put that on Barney's gravestone.

3

A QUEST TO KNOW MORE
ABOUT THE WORLD

George Braziller

I was doubly fortunate in the early years to have no
preconception about my role as publisher. I simply
felt that I was on a quest to know more about the
world and how others interpreted it, and every
new discovery opened doors to others.

—GEORGE BRAZILLER

We have seen that for Barney Rosset our period was the
best of times and the worst of times. For George
Braziller, it was neither. What he sought was simply
the opportunity to seek the best. And he had his victories.

They knew each other, of course. Barney and George were the
best of friends, but they were competitors, too—essentially because they were feeding from the same vast trough. Seeking his
fortune in book publishing, Barney Rosset went out of the country. So did George Braziller. They were both rebels, but each in
his own way. Barney Rosset was a rebel who would muck up the
face of book publishing. George Braziller challenged tradition,
but left it standing. The other distinction was that Barney Rosset

came from money, whereas George Braziller did not. He always counted his change.

There was a certain hauteur on Rosset's part about Braziller. Soon after Seaver went to work for Braziller, Barney did offer Seaver a job. Seaver said to him, "I've just taken a job."

Barney was outraged. "Where?"

"George Braziller."

"Oh," Barney said, "you're not going to like it there." And Barney was right, Seaver didn't always like it there. Still, he stayed with Braziller for two years, where he learned a lot about book publishing, especially how book clubs worked.

In the mid-1950s, Braziller was making it with the two book clubs he had founded when he was barely out of knickers—first the Book Find Club and then the Seven Arts Club. He was doing so well, in fact, that he was now thinking about publishing books of his own. It wasn't an easy decision to make because his clubs had enabled him to move his wife and two children into a home in fashionable Westchester County. It was while he was in London on book club business that he decided to seek a second opinion. And he would go right to the top. He called Sir Allen Lane for an appointment.

In 1935, Allen Lane had founded Penguin Books, a line of inexpensive but good-quality fiction and nonfiction paperbacks. Penguin transformed the landscape of publishing in England, as book publishing in America would later be transformed by what came to be called the paperback revolution. In a 2005 biography on Allen Lane published in England, author Jeremy Lewis called Lane "the greatest publisher of the twentieth century."

Braziller didn't know about that, but he did know, as he told me, that "Sir Allen had been knighted for his advanced instincts in creating Penguin." And though Sir Allen had never met George, he certainly knew about his Book Find Club, which was modeled to some degree on the successful Left Book Club in Britain. So Lane invited Braziller to his office on Music Street.

"The floors were creaking as I came into his office," George remembered. Not knowing quite what to say, he got right down to the point of his visit. "Sir Allen," he asked the century's "greatest" publisher (he was, after all, knighted in 1952), "what advice would you give to a young American who wants to start his own publishing house?"

Lane answered immediately: "Take lots and lots of gambles, but small ones."

George Braziller never took lots and lots of gambles (he left those to Barney Rosset), but when he felt he had to gamble—such as in starting his own book publishing company—he gambled big. George Braziller, Inc., celebrated its fiftieth anniversary in 2005.

Braziller, everyone kept telling me, is a hard person to measure, but I never found him to be that way. He had come up a different road from the large Ivy League contingent of book publishers, but that may have been good for him in the profession. He was pure, you see—he never went to college, but sort of snuck into the book business by the back door. He was more a lone eagle than a member of the old boys' network. Being a loner, though, may have been one of his weaknesses in his relations with the people who worked for him. "He was a pain in the ass," is the way Dick Seaver put it, "but I loved him, and still do."

So do many elder statesmen in publishing who knew him well. George was a complicated person who found within himself multiple gifts, including the gift for sniffing out literature and bringing meaningful art books to the attention of an art-loving audience. It is the way he has spent his life.

GEORGE BRAZILLER

I was young, but already married, and the first job I had was as a shipping clerk at $15 a week for my brother-in-law. He had started a small remainder operation, you know, buying books cut-rate from publishers who had overprinted them. After about a year I asked him, "How about a raise?" He said, "How much do you want?" I said, "A dollar." He said, "Braz"—that was my nickname—"we can't afford it." I said, "Then I'm quitting."

I go home and say hi to my wife, Marsha. I said, "Well, I quit." "Yeah," she said, "that's nice. What are you going to do now?" I said, "I'm going to start a book club."

"It wasn't actually a book club then. It was remainders I got from my brother-in-law. That's how I started. I still remember the title of the first book: *The Liberators,* by John Hyde Preston. I bought ten copies for a quarter each, and I sold them for fifty cents. In one pocket was the debit. In the other pocket was the credit. My sister, my brother—my other relatives—they said, okay, every month we'll buy a book from you. And from ten, twenty friends, you know the story: I built it up to a hundred or so.

Of course, I knew all about the American book clubs—the Book-of-the-Month Club, the Literary Guild. I also knew that in England there was a book club called the Left Book Club. It was started by a great English publisher, Victor Gollancz. I said to myself, Gee, why don't we do something like that here?

The way I did it was to go and speak before union groups. I would go to a union hall, make a little speech, and sign up people.

Then came the war. I said to my wife, "You're going to have to take over." She stepped in and took over.

Late in 2003 I went up to George Braziller's cramped little office on Madison Avenue and Thirty-third Street. There was a woman sitting at the desk. "Your name?" she asked briskly. "Al Silverman," I said. "You're here to see George," she said, pronouncing his name with affection. "George!" she hollered, "you have a visitor." Behind a room divider, surrounded by books and papers, George flashed a smile.

He and I had known each other from back in the early seventies when the Book-of-the-Month Club began picking off Braziller titles at a faster clip, it seemed, than we did from many long-established houses. It was almost as though he was publishing books especially for us: those exquisite illuminated manuscripts he had found right out of New York's Morgan Library or Istanbul's grand museum, the medieval masterpieces lying in locked, temperature-controlled rooms of museums all over the world. It seemed that only George Braziller could bring them back to life. They were perfect book club choices for our crowd, as he well knew, having learned such things from his own book clubs.

Here he was, in his late eighties, as trim as a quartermaster, standing straight and steady in his trademark Harris tweed suit. His face was barely lined, and his green eyes, slitted like a Sherpa's, still delivered light. He swims, he told me, almost every day, and spends a lot of time walking in Central Park, near where he lives. In fact, he suggested that we walk to the park and converse there, but I told him the birds and the squirrels would be making too much noise. So he took me to a quiet Korean restaurant near his office. We sat upstairs, where we were alone, and he ordered good healthy veggie food for both of us.

This oddball intellectual spoke in a voice similar to that of a rabbi's, deep and sonorous, with sudden homey lapses into Brooklynese when he was excited: *"It was a great, great manuscript in the Italian school that was almost psychedelic—purples and greens and oranges. It was a sight to hold this here manu-script in my hands. Oh, what a feeling!"* The most vivid memory I have of George—I told him this at our lunch—was when the two of us, on a cold gray morning in Frankfurt, Germany, were walking to the Frankfurt Book Fair. He said then that in 1945, right after V-E Day and the end of the war in Europe, he and his gun company, which had fought its way through France and Germany, had been sent to Frankfurt. As we came toward the train station, he stopped, looked around and spread out his arms.

"Frankfurt," he pointed toward the station, "was where the exodus was. If you were going to get discharged, or if you were going to be sent back to the States, that was the place you were sent to. But what I remember was standing where that station is today. The station was bombed out—not totally, but it was a wreck. I remember stopping there, looking around. The city of Frankfurt was as flat as a tabletop. You could look north, south, east, and west for miles—nothing, nothing. They flattened Frankfurt."

I asked him, over soup, what he had been doing in Frankfurt at that time. "Every soldier wanted to go home," he said. "But the war was still on with Japan. We were just hanging around, sort of wasting our time, cleaning guns and all that. I figured out something to keep myself interested. I got an idea to do a book about my outfit. I remember going to the captain. 'Braziller,' he said before I could open my mouth, 'come on, what are you up to? Are you up to something?' I said, 'We were a fighting outfit, sir. Why don't we do a history?' He said, 'I'll let you know.' Sure enough, the next day I get a call that the colonel wants to see me. So I go in, give him the old salute. 'I hear you want to do a book,' he said. I was nervous as hell, but I sold it to him. I actually stayed in Germany and did the book on the history of my company and got it printed in Frankfurt. And then I was able to go home."

George Braziller was discharged in 1946. For a while he liked parading around town in uniform. Edwin Seaver (no relation to

Richard Seaver) at that time was working for the Book-of-the-Month Club as publicity manager. He remembered George coming to the office one day. In his book, *So Far, So Good,* Seaver describes George wearing a "well-fitted Eisenhower jacket and highly polished paratrooper boots, with the bottoms of his immaculately pressed pants tucked into them."

George's uniform made barely an impression on his wife, Marsha. She was just happy he was home. Hugging her husband, she said, "Okay, you're here. Take over." She brought him up to date on the goings-on with their little company. Marsha did have a decision for George to make. "We've been thinking about taking this book," she said. She handed him a first novel called *Focus* by an author named Arthur Miller. *Focus* became Braziller's first postwar Book Find Club selection. And it also brought about a lifelong friendship between him and Arthur Miller.

His book club, like the Left Book Club in England, did veer left, but George also chose literary works that never became bestsellers, yet fed intellectual appetites. He knew what was going on in the literary world. One of his good friends was Arthur Rosenthal, who owned the Basic Book Club (Basic Books under Rosenthal later became a prominent imprint). He and Braziller sometimes played golf together. At one of those outings Rosenthal, seeking advice, asked George how he could do better with his own club. "It's very simple," George answered, "just copy my ads." Rosenthal was not impressed.

But at a later date Rosenthal told Braziller that he was looking to do a book on Freud, and he named the analyst he thought would be right for it. "Terrible idea," George said. "Why don't you go see Ernest Jones in London? He's writing a biography of Freud." Rosenthal did just that and wound up with the pearl of Basic Books: Ernest Jones's incomparable three-volume biography of Freud. He also got to date one of Jones's daughters.

Braziller liked to present books to his members that the more conservative big book clubs refused to take. The most notable Book Find Club selection of 1948, full of four-letter words never before seen in an American novel, was Norman Mailer's *The Naked and the Dead.* John P. Marquand, a novelist of note and also a judge at the Book-of-the-Month Club, reviewed the book in the club's magazine, and was of two minds about it. "Aside from many moments of startling horror," Marquand wrote, "*The Naked and the Dead* has a larger vocabulary of plain and fancy four-letter words than I have ever seen in print and is conclusive proof that literature is at last released from prudery and, some might add, from many limits of common decency." Marquand did go on to praise the novel for its "fine authenticity." It rolled up big numbers for the Book Find Club.

GEORGE BRAZILLER was doing well with the book clubs, but he had a growing urge to double up and become a book publisher. And in 1955 he founded George Braziller, Inc.

"I didn't know a damn thing about publishing and quickly lost a little bit of money," he said in a 2005 interview with *The Brooklyn Rail* magazine, celebrating his firm's fiftieth anniversary. "But in those days, there was a response to book publishing. You could count on the bookstore—people were interested in literature."

But he didn't yet have the money to do what he wanted to do. Also, his wife had become seriously ill and medical bills began to pile up. She died in 1971, and her death had a major effect on George and his three children. So he decided to sell his book clubs. He found a buyer right off—Time-Life, as the Henry Luce empire was then called. They paid him a million dollars for the two clubs and made him a consultant.

"I have to tell you the role of a consultant," George said, with a shade of a smile on his face. "They told me they wanted me to be an adviser and offered me $25,000 a year, which was a helluva lot of money in those days. 'We'd like to give you a three-year contract,' they said, so I stupidly said, 'Why don't we make it a year? Then, if we like each other, I'll stay on.'"

Two weeks after signing his contract, the Time-Life suits held the first meeting with their consultant. They told Braziller that they would like to move his office from where it was on lower Park Avenue to Rockefeller Center. They asked him what he thought about that.

"Well," the adviser said, "we're paying four dollars a square foot. I don't know what it will cost up there, but don't you think we ought to stay with the four dollars?" As George describes it, "They all looked around, wagged their heads, and said they'd prefer to move."

Shortly afterward, there was a second meeting. This time the consultant was told, "George, we're thinking of going on to a computer." "If you're asking for my advice," George said, "you guys just decided to move. Why don't you absorb the move first?" Again, they wagged their heads. The consultant was never invited to another meeting. He was paid his $25,000 for attending two meetings, and his consulting responsibilities were fulfilled. He could now give all of his attention to the George Braziller publishing house.

George admits that the realization of his dream came slowly. He knew it would be difficult to get big books from agents because he couldn't pay them enough. It would be easier, he felt, in Europe. So, in 1958, he went to Paris.

He found the city in chaos. General Charles de Gaulle's Fifth Republic had just come to power, but the city was locked in a general strike; the uprising in Algeria was at its height and *plastiques* were being thrown on the streets. The war in Algeria alerted Braziller to literary possibilities. He heard about a book just about to be published by Les Éditions de Minuit, the same house that Dick Seaver admired for publishing Samuel Beckett. *La Question* by Henri Alleg was an autobiography that centered on the practices of terror and torture by the French army stationed in Algeria. Alleg wrote from firsthand experience, being one of those who had suffered in their hands. Shortly after publication, the book was banned in France. George took a copy back with him to New York and handed it off to Dick Seaver to read in French and give him his opinion.

"This is a wonderful book, a very important book," Seaver reported to Braziller, "but I can't imagine people in America will be interested in it."

"Well," the boss replied with anger, "write me a report." Seaver did, but reiterated his fears about selling it. "You forget about what the market will be," George growled. "Let me figure that out." He did figure it out. He had it translated, and in a Braziller coup he persuaded Jean-Paul Sartre to write an introduction to *The Question,* published in 1958. "The book became a bestseller," Seaver said, not at all displeased that he had been wrong.

With ample sales from *The Question*—it became a backlist staple—Braziller was able to keep his business a step or more ahead of the creditors. But he always did need financial help, and kept close watch on his overhead.

In Paris, George looked for someone to work with him who knew the French market. He was fortunate to find a woman with a brilliant literary background: Maria Jolas. She had been born Maria McDonald in Louisville, Kentucky, went to Europe at a young age, and married Eugene Jolas, also an expatriate American, who had become a close friend of James Joyce. In 1927, Eugene, Maria, and Elliot Paul started *transition,* an avant-garde literary magazine. The magazine lasted until 1930 and after an interruption was published again from 1932 to 1939. Braziller was introduced to her in the fifties when she was widowed, and they became friends and colleagues.

The first book Maria Jolas pointed George toward was a novel by Nathalie Sarraute called *Portrait of a Man Unknown*. It had been published in France in 1947 but had never found a buyer in the United States. It was a difficult novel, about the relationship of a miserly father and his daughter; Sartre called it an "anti-novel." It was actually the start of a modernist movement called *le nouveau roman* ("the new novel")—writers who were willing to challenge the traditional structures of narrative fiction. Maria Jolas translated *Portrait* into English, and George published it in 1958. Nathalie Sarraute and George became the best of friends, and she continued to be published by Braziller until her death in 1999 at the age of ninety-nine.

Publishing Sarraute led George to find other significant *nouveau roman* writers who were looking to be published in America—Claude Simon and Sartre, who were both awarded Nobel Prizes (although Sartre refused to accept his); Marguerite Duras, Claude Mauriac, Alain Robbe-Grillet, and Yves Berger. In his 2005 catalog, writing with pride about the house's fiftieth anniversary, George Braziller said, "I was doubly fortunate in the early years to have no preconception about my role as publisher. I simply felt that I was on a quest to know more about the world and how others interpreted it, and every new discovery opened doors to others."

So he began to cover the world. He published Nigeria's Buchi Emecheta, as well as Neil Jordan of Ireland, David Malouf of Australia, and Orhan Pamuk of Turkey. The author he loved the most, and who stayed with him until her death in 2004, was Janet Frame of New Zealand, best known for her moving autobiography, *An Angel at My Table*.

As time went on, George began to find exciting new novelists. In 1964 he published a first novel about the Korean War that had been turned down everywhere—R. E. Kim's *The Martyred*. It became a bestseller.

Later, when the Vietnam War was at its height, George got a

call from Dore Ashton, an art critic who would help him move into a new phase of his publishing life. But her call was not about an artwork. She had just heard from Ronald Glasser, a doctor who had been in Vietnam and who had written a novel about his experiences. A publisher had held his manuscript for six months, then turned it down. Would George be willing to read it? The manuscript was given to him that day, and George read it through the night. The next morning he called Glasser and told him he would publish *365 Days*. It was one of the first novels published about the Vietnam experience and was a winner from the beginning. Thirty-four years after its 1971 publication and its successful life as a Braziller paperback, George republished *365 Days* in a new hardcover edition to help mark his company's fiftieth anniversary.

"I have to tell you," and George did tell me, "in the sixties *The New York Times* was reviewing every one of our books." That was George Braziller's time. In my introduction, I mention Louis Menand's recollection of that time when "literature was at the center of a nation's culture." It was true, and here were the *new* American publishers taking advantage of the situation—Kurt and Helen Wolff, who had their own imprint at Harcourt Brace Jovanovich; Barney Rosset, and George Braziller—literary radicals who were accumulating their fair share of the spoils.

At the 1963 Frankfurt Book Fair, Kurt Wolff was killed instantly when a trolley ran over him. When we talked about Frankfurt, George was still mourning Wolff's passing. He fondly recalled chatting with Wolff shortly before his death. "We stopped and shook hands, and we exchanged some gossip. And I remember saying to him, 'Kurt, you know, you're my competition.' And he said, 'Oh, no, you're *my* competition.' And then came the tragedy, the tragedy."

As soon as he had established his literary credentials, George Braziller made another of his rare gambles. He moved sideways from literature, though keeping it in his ken, to the illustrated book. "It was kind of easy," George told me, "because the art world then . . . no one was doing any art books. The only publisher here was Harry Abrams. So I figured, why not take a chance on it?"

IN THE 1930S and 1940s, Harry N. Abrams, a small man with a powerful physique and a way with words, was working at the Book-of-the-Month Club as advertising manager and production manager. It was an odd combination for him to take on, but he was good at both tasks. After the war he wanted to go out on his own. In 1950 he resigned to form the first American book publishing house devoted solely to art books.

From the beginning, Abrams had the touch for putting together handsome, oversized books of art. And he was a genius at promotion. In 1957 he published H. W. Janson's *Picture History of Painting*, which he had written with his wife, Dora Jane Janson. It was a huge, erudite volume, full of striking full-color photographs from the masters of art throughout history. Harry managed to sell it to Time-Life Books, the Book-of-the-Month Club, and many foreign language publishers. He sold 375,000 copies. Later, he published Janson's *History of Art*. It went out with a first printing of 130,000 copies. The Book-of-the-Month Club became one of his most dependable customers.

When I came to the Club, I got to know Harry pretty well. The first time my wife and I were invited to his and his charming wife, Nina's, New York apartment we were struck dumb by the paintings with blue-ribbon names attached to them hanging frame-to-frame on the Abramses' walls. It was as if we had just entered the Louvre. They even had one room that was dedicated solely to pop art—Warhol and the other celebrated artists of the genre.

Harry and I would have lunch a couple of times a year at his favorite restaurant, Laurent, then one of the grandest rooms in the city. There, Harry was treated like a caliph. After the gossip was exchanged (he was a first-rate gossiper), the talk would turn to what he was getting ready to show to the Club. Almost always it was some larger-than-life art book that no other house could afford to do, but that would, he told me, be terrific for the Book-of-the-Month Club audience.

In 1966, finding himself low in capital, Harry Abrams decided to sell his company. He was grabbed up by the Los Angeles Times–Mirror Corporation. A few months after the sale, Nina Abrams was having lunch in a Caribbean winter getaway with Ed Fitzgerald, who was then running the Literary Guild. (You will hear more about Ed Fitzgerald, whom I consider my life mentor, in chapter 7 on Doubleday.) In his book, *A Nickel an Inch,* Ed describes listening to Nina tell him, "Fitz, the Times-Mirror is just providing the capital to expand it. Harry will still be in complete control of it." Fitz said, "Nina, don't kid yourself. When you sell it, you sell it."

Nina turned out to be right, at least in the beginning. The Times-Mirror did leave Abrams pretty much alone for a few years before the inevitable squeeze began.

All the while George Braziller was never particularly fearful of the high-octane Abrams competition. "What we tried to do," he said, "were things that Abrams wasn't doing. That's when I started the American Artist series and the Architecture series, and then I went on to do the Medieval Art series." And on and on until, gradually, it was the art books that were carrying the house.

George found his mother lode when, one day in 1964, he was reading *The New York Times* and saw art critic John Canady's review of a Catherine of Cleves exhibit at the Morgan Library. "I didn't know a damn thing about medieval art, but the Morgan was right around the corner from my office. I went over there to see what he's making a fuss about.

"I walked in and I see this here art book, a hundred and fifty-seven illustrations from this *Hours of Catherine of Cleves*—you could see it illuminated—and I just went berserk." George felt that the book contained a series of some of the most beautiful illustrations of the Bible ever made. "Right then and there, I asked to speak to the director. 'Who are you?' they said. I said, 'Tell the director I want to do a book on this.'

"Sure enough, he came out and saw me. His name was Fred Adams. So I said, 'Yeah, I'd like to do the book.' I didn't know what I was doing, but we did it."

George found someone who did know what he was doing. John Plummer, a former curator and fellow emeritus of the Morgan Library, wrote the introduction and commentaries for the book. Braziller then sent the finished manuscript to the Netherlands, where they knew how to print such a complex book. "John Canady reviewed it in *The Times*," George recalled, "and that Christmas we sold about twenty thousand copies of *Catherine of Cleves*. Oh, God, I remember that so well." The Book-of-the-Month did well with it, too, and George suddenly found himself in the illuminated manuscript business. He found an art-loving public for the richness of these fifteenth-century miniatures, each illuminated page accompanied by biblical commentary. Almost every Christmas for fifteen years he published some such manuscript for his public.

And then he fell in love with the art book of his life.

IT HAPPENED in Paris one year as he was going around, thinking how he could build his list. He noticed that publishers were suddenly doing books about the contemporary artists of the time. He heard about one Greek publisher in particular, Efstratios Teriade, who had become famous for commissioning the artists themselves to create works of art that he could publish in a book. "They were actually in a desperate situation," George told me, referring to the

World War II period. "This was just before the war, during the war, and right after the war. Literally, these artists were broke. If you bought an artist a meal he would hand you a painting."

Sensing the plight of the French contemporary masters' lives, Teriade, who lived in Paris, created a series of magazines called *Verve*—each issue featuring the work of Chagall, Léger, Picasso, Matisse, and many other major artists. Braziller was astounded by what he saw. He was particularly taken by a *Verve* edition of a Matisse that nobody had ever seen before.

In 1941 Matisse had had a serious operation, and he thought he would never be able to paint again. So, while he was bedridden, he began cutting out various images, "a form filtered to the essentials," is the way Matisse spoke of it. And Teriade put the Matisse cutouts into a book. The book was titled *Jazz*. George said, "I remember asking Teriade if he would give me permission to do a popular edition of *Jazz* in the United States." Then he paused for about twenty seconds, shaking his head, his eyes welling up: "And he almost said yes—he *almost* said yes." In the end, Teriade said no.

But George Braziller, who found it difficult to take no for an answer, would not give up. "Every time I went to Paris I would call on him. And he always said no." And so one year George turned to Pierre Matisse, the son of Henri Matisse and proprietor of an art gallery in New York. "Mr. Matisse," George said as if he were speaking to Allen Lane, "I've been wanting to do this here book for a long time. Can I have your permission?"

"You need Teriade's permission," the young Matisse said.

"Teriade won't give me permission."

"Well," said Matisse, "I'm not going to give you permission."

Another year went by, and George Braziller called once more on Pierre Matisse, with the same request. This time Matisse surprised him: "Well, why don't you do it, and don't tell me?" It would, of course, have been a pirated edition.

Glumly, George said, "I don't want to do that."

One more year went by, and this time Matisse, presumably worn down, said to Braziller, "Okay, you can do it." George still has the sheet upon which Matisse wrote: "Permission granted." And Teriade never contested its publication.

Riva Castleman explains, in her introduction to *Jazz,* how Henri Matisse managed to put together his fabulous cutouts. She quotes from a letter the master wrote to Teriade in 1944: "Send me a white cane." What he meant, Castleman said, was that he needed glasses, "tinted to seventy percent because the dazzling colors of the cut shapes were practically driving him blind."

Castleman ends her introduction with these words: "The dark rhythms, roiling counterpoint, happy staccatos, and jolting dissonance of this *Jazz* will sound forever. Matisse has taught the eye to hear."

Jazz was published here in 1983 and was a smashing success. It secured George Braziller's reputation as a master of art books.

GEORGE AND I finished our lunch at the Korean restaurant, and we walked out into the street on a day that was filled with Matisse light. Here he was, walking just a bit slower than he once did (this was three years before George was feted everywhere when he turned ninety), but his mind still full of ideas. "After here, we're [meaning himself] going up to the Met," he said, "and we're maybe going to do a wonderful book, a form of Japanese tapestry. There are a number of things on tapestry in the West. Japanese—it's neglected." He gave me a tender smile. We shook hands, and I walked off in a different direction, but not before I stopped to watch him moving on toward the Met to continue his life's work.

4

AN UNCERTAIN PARTNERSHIP
OF EQUALS
Atheneum

No one can be seriously in publishing for any length of time and
not want the full challenge, in partnership with others, of
directing his own publishing house.

—SIMON MICHAEL BESSIE

O n the Sunday morning of March 15, 1959, *The New
York Times* carried a rare book publishing story on its
front page. The scoop was that three men, all familiarly
known in the trade, were about to start a new publishing house.
They were Simon Michael Bessie, senior editor at Harper &
Brothers; Hiram Haydn, editor in chief of Random House; and
Alfred A. Knopf, Jr., always known as "Pat," a vice president in
his father's distinguished company. "It is," said an anonymous
publisher on the newspaper's front page, "as if the presidents of
General Motors, Chrysler and Ford left their jobs to start a new
automobile company."

It had all started a year earlier, on the day that Mike Bessie sat
down to lunch with Pat Knopf. Bessie had become an editor at

Harper's in 1946, and through those years a friendship had grown between the two of them. Pat felt that Mike was one of the smartest editors in the business; he had, for instance, nailed John Cheever's first novel, *The Wapshot Chronicle,* which won the National Book Award for fiction in 1958. "I don't suppose anything would persuade you to leave Harper's," was the way Knopf started the conversation.

Bessie, a born orator, looked straight into Pat Knopf's eyes and declaimed: "Yes, there is one thing that will persuade me to leave, and that is if I could join you in your firm, which I presume you will be taking over when your parents retire. If I could join you as an editor and partner, I'd be willing, though my means are not great, to buy some stock."

"Are you serious?" Pat responded with delight. "Well, I'll talk to my parents."

The skinny on Pat's father and mother, the formidable Alfred A. Knopf and the even more formidable Blanche Knopf, was that "Blanche in the office would only be mean to women, and Alfred would only be mean to men." It was more than that. When ruffled, which was often, they were both mean of spirit. Their personal reputations wavered back and forth, but not their professionalism. Together, Alfred and Blanche succeeded in making their house, before World War II and after, the most renowned of any in American book publishing. Perhaps their noblest distinction was the reshaping and redesign of the American book: A Knopf book almost always looked beautiful (and still does). It was said that if you owned ten Knopf titles (you would recognize them by Knopf's colophon, the borzoi, or Russian wolfhound, prancing on the title pages) you could make yourself a suit of clothes with the cloth. So why wouldn't Mike Bessie want to join hands with Pat Knopf, especially if an inheritance could be secured for him?

Bessie's keen sense of opportunity was almost as impeccable

as his editorial instincts. And clearly, so was his timing. Almost out of the blue one day, Pat Knopf's mother and father informed their son that they were thinking they might retire before long and would perhaps turn the business over to him. But since Pat was less experienced with the editorial side of their house—he was heavily involved with sales and marketing—his parents suggested that he would be wise to seek out an editor of some stature who would be willing to buy into the business and become his partner.

A short while after their lunch together, Pat Knopf called Mike Bessie and said, "They're interested."

"We went through a little dance," Mike recalled, "trying to work out details about my coming over to Knopf." But the two soon found themselves caught in a spiderweb. It turned out that while Pat had talked to his father about bringing Bessie on board, he had not spoken to his mother; she was away, as was her custom, searching the literary publishing houses in Paris for the book that would knock everyone's socks off back home. When she returned, the Knopfs' random idea of their son eventually taking over the company was forgotten. Blanche had a snap conversation with Pat rejecting the idea of Bessie, after which Pat immediately contacted Mike.

"This is the most difficult call I've ever had to make," Pat said. "It won't work."

"She won't have it," Mike told me. "She didn't want me there." Mike had his idea as to why. "She and I had become absolute rivals—I mean direct rivals. See, I'd lived in France before the war, and I was getting quite a few good French books because I knew people there—books that she wanted."

The outcome of it all must have been a huge disappointment to the only child. Pat Knopf had come out of the Army Air Force in World War II a hero, flying B-24 bombers over Germany. "As soon as he decided to fly, he thought he'd get killed," said Herman Gollob, perhaps Pat's best-loved editor. "But he never turned back on a mission." Pat asserted himself, became a squadron commander and did have some close calls. "I guess the bottom line of the story," Pat said, reflecting on his career in the one conversation I had with him, "was when I called my mother and my father and said I was coming home. My father said, 'What are you going to do?' It came out of my mouth—'I guess I'm coming to work for you.'"

And that's what he did. Pat believed then that he would someday succeed his parents, for wasn't it a normal custom of book publishing (as with other family businesses) that if a son worked for his father's company, the crown would, in the course of time, be his? As the years wore on, in the Knopf organizational chart, Pat was listed as "secretary and trade books manager." But everyone who worked with him at Knopf knew that such titles didn't encompass all he did there. In the executive committee meetings, he also acted as a buffer when one parent or the other became testy, which was often. Pat himself was sometimes maligned, too, by the father or mother, and never seemed to receive approbation from either parent. "His mother thought he was a *galumphing* salesman," was how Bessie put it.

When Blanche Knopf said no to her son about Mike Bessie, Pat must have begun to feel it was time to move on. And the fact that Bessie had mentioned a willingness to put money into Knopf reinforced Pat's desire to step out and risk forming a new company.

Pat and Mike had another lunch together, this time with Richard Ernst, a cousin of Mike Bessie's wife at the time, Connie Ernst Bessie. Ernst had also been a classmate of Mike's at Harvard. Ernst began the business part of the luncheon by saying to his cousin: "Pat tells me that you and he had—lightly at least—discussed the possibility of starting a firm of your own. I think it's a great idea, and I'm prepared to put some money in."

And so Pat Knopf had himself a publishing company.

THE TWO FOUNDERS, Knopf and Bessie, now bound tightly to each other, both felt they would need a third "founding partner," someone with an impeccable publishing pedigree. They wanted to show the world the seriousness of the new house's intent, and they pointed to the same person, Hiram Haydn, who was friends with them both.

Haydn, tall, handsome, and well-respected, had begun his publishing career in 1945 with the Crown publishing company and then moved to Bobbs-Merrill in Indianapolis. There, he had published his biggest book, Ayn Rand's *The Fountainhead.* In 1955, Bennett Cerf lured Haydn to Random House to become his editor in chief. Haydn was also the editor of the prestigious Phi Beta Kappa magazine *The American Scholar.* He would serve there with distinction for thirty years.

One of the reasons for Bennett Cerf's hunger to hire Haydn was that Hiram had made it his business to seek out young writers. Cerf, worrying that his great authors at Random House—William Faulkner, John O'Hara, and Robert Penn Warren—were wearing down, loved the idea of an editor who spent so much of his time seeking out new talent. For twelve years Haydn had taught a novel workshop at the New School for Social Research, where he was constantly encountering writers who he felt had a future. Among his student discoveries were William Styron and Mario Puzo. "We'll need the best of them," Cerf had told Haydn. "All you have to do is see to it that two out of twenty develop that way." Haydn had published Styron's first novel, *Lie Down in Darkness,* at Bobbs-Merrill, and he expected to bring Styron to Random House. He did bring along Ayn Rand's next novel, *Atlas Shrugged.* So he was already on his way to meeting Cerf's oddly generous quota.

Yet here he was, only four years later, flirting with Pat Knopf and Mike Bessie. Knopf and Haydn had become friends when they began commuting together from Connecticut to Grand Central Station; Pat and his wife, Alice, socialized often with Hiram and his wife, Mary. At the same time, Mike Bessie was calling Hiram his "best friend." Whenever Haydn needed a place to stay in the city, he often wound up with the Bessies in their Greenwich Village digs. So it seemed to be good fellowship all around.

Still, Haydn was torn about what to do. He was enjoying his job at Random House, especially commingling with Bennett Cerf's partners, Donald Klopfer and Robert Haas. Unlike the mercurial Cerf, Klopfer and Haas were reserved gentlemen, and Haydn didn't mind answering to them. Several times, when Cerf felt that Haydn was buying a book that wouldn't work, Klopfer would suggest he trust his editor in chief's judgment. But there did come a time when Haydn wanted to buy a book no one else wanted.

At *The American Scholar* Haydn had published several essays on aspects of nature by an anthropologist named Loren Eiseley. Hiram met with Eiseley and suggested he combine his essays into a book with transitional lines in between. With Haydn's help, Eiseley turned in an impressive manuscript, and Haydn, much excited by it, gave *The Immense Journey* to his colleagues to read. At the sales conference, they all ganged up on him. "I could not persuade the powers at Random House," Haydn wrote in his candid and controversial memoir, *Words & Faces,* "that this beautifully written book would find any sizable audience." Lew Miller, the Random House sales director, told Haydn that he agreed with him about the writing, and then barked, "That's why it won't sell." In a burst of passion Haydn said, "This is a book that will last forever." With much reluctance, Cerf agreed to publish *The Immense Journey,* but he put no immediate resources behind it. It slowly caught on, and it has, so far, lasted "forever."

What ultimately made Hiram Haydn decide to leave Random House and join the Knopf-Bessie team, he said in his book, was "the possibility of being on my own, to collaborate on running our own business." How many frustrated editors in the fragile trade had, over the years, imagined themselves being allowed to buy any book they wanted? Haydn felt that, at the least, he would have that opportunity with Pat Knopf and Mike Bessie.

The team was in place, and the only thing they hadn't yet figured out was a name for their company. At an early board meeting Haydn received a phone call from Loren Eiseley, who was in Philadelphia. In a burst of excitement he told Haydn that he had just won the Athenaeum Institute's Award for "the promotion of literary and scientific learning." Haydn hung up the phone with an inspiration. "Why not," he said to his mates, "call ourselves *Atheneum* [dropping the second 'a']?" Indeed, why not?

IN THE BEGINNING the Atheneum trio worked well together. There had been initial disappointment because each had assumed he would bring a key author from his former house to Atheneum: Mike Bessie was counting on John Cheever; Hiram Haydn on William Styron; Pat Knopf on John Hersey. Alas, Cheever, Styron, and Hersey decided to stay loyal to their current publishers. Fortunately, the founders all had close relationships with other talented writers.

The strongest Atheneum book for its first list (Summer-Fall 1960) was a Mike Bessie coup, *The Last of the Just* by André Schwarz-Bart, the story of the persecution of the Jews from the 1100s to the Holocaust. It became a surprise bestseller.

Bessie took secret delight in beating out his primary competitor for the book, Blanche Knopf. "She staged a terrible scene with the French publisher," Mike said. " 'I don't care what Bessie paid for it,' she said (I had paid $2,500). 'I'll give you twice the money.' " By that time, Schwarz-Bart had won the Prix Goncourt, a prize similar in prestige to our National Book Award, and Blanche knew what an award-winning author was worth. "But," Mike said with some relish, "it was ours."

Bessie scored again in 1961.

"I can't tell you what I owe to Teddy White," Mike said. "Teddy and I were in the same class at Harvard, but a year apart. And we became friends. One day in 1959 we had lunch together. Teddy told me, 'I'm writing a textbook about American politics.'

"Oh," I said, "what is your publisher doing?"

" 'Well, that's what's bothering me. They're trying to get me not to do it.' "

Mike went on to tell me that Theodore H. White's plan was to do two to four books about each presidential election, beginning in 1960. "I thought it was a brilliant idea. And I knew one thing about Theodore, if I knew nothing else. And that was, he couldn't write a textbook if he tried—his writing was too popular. He'd made his mark as a first-class journalist with *Life* magazine. I told him I thought it was a brilliant idea, and that it should be a trade book. He looked at me and said, 'You mean you would like to take this on in your new house? Have you got the money?'

" 'Yes,' I said, 'we've got plenty of money. Our money's fresh, clean.' [Mike never lacked for presumption.] 'By the way, you want an advance, I presume.' "

" 'Oh, yes,' he said, 'I want a good advance.' I asked him how much he wanted. 'I want $20,000.' " That was a good price for the times, but the partners all agreed to it. It was a wise decision. *The Making of the President, 1960* won the Pulitzer Prize for general nonfiction and became a huge bestseller. The others in the series that followed over the years didn't do as well.

Hiram Haydn's early contributions were a bit more modest. He did have one bestseller in 1962, *The Rothschilds* by Frederic Morton. And, like Bessie, he was also winning prizes for his books: Randall Jarrell's *The Woman at the Washington Zoo: Poems and*

Translations won the National Book Award for poetry; Joan Williams's *The Morning and the Evening* won the John P. Marquand Award for the best first novel of the year. Haydn also contributed to the financial health of the company by bringing in two close friends to invest in Atheneum and sit on its board. One was William M. Roth, a millionaire and a brilliant economist. The other was Marc Friedlaender, an editor who ended up running Atheneum's paperback program, which Pat Knopf had started.

Pat was moving smartly in other directions, too. He saw to it that Atheneum would be well represented in poetry when he hired Harry Ford away from his father's house. At Knopf, Ford had been in charge of both production and editing poetry. Over the Atheneum years, Ford brought in Pulitzer Prize poetry winners Anthony Hecht, Richard Howard, W. S. Merwin, and James Merrill. Merrill also won a National Book Award for Atheneum, as did Howard Moss and Conrad Aiken. Pat also saw to it that Atheneum's children's publishing program would grow to be one of the most notable in the business. Jean Karl, its first editor, won many prestigious children's books awards for the house. Later, one of book publishing's greatest children's publishers, Margaret McElderry, brought her genius to Atheneum.

So it seemed that Knopf, Bessie, and Haydn were working peacefully together. Still, as early as 1963, ruptures had begun to form between them. "During the first couple of years," Haydn wrote in *Words & Faces,* "we were very indulgent towards each other about the acceptance of manuscripts. I don't know how many times Pat said to me, 'If it's good enough for you, it's good enough for me.' And Mike and I seldom read the same scripts—rather, we congratulated each other on whichever new acquisition."

The immediate situation with Haydn was that he wasn't bringing in books that became bestsellers. Haydn did publish a first novel from one of his students at The New School—Mario Puzo's *The Fortunate Pilgrim.* It didn't sell many copies, either.

Then Puzo gave Haydn the outline of a book he wanted to do about the Mafia. Here was one time at least when all three of the founding partners were on the same page. "Hiram was very dubious about it," Mike remembered, "and so was Pat." So, too, was Bessie when he got back from a trip to Europe. "I have to sit here and say . . . ," he said to me, pausing for a second, as if he were about to confess to a crime. "I don't know what I exactly said to Pat and Hiram, but it was something like 'Everybody's discovered the Mafia; the Mafia is coming out of our ears.' And that's how Puzo's *The Godfather* got away—because we turned it down." That may have been the last time the partners acted in unison.

It was individual egos and the pressures of the business that eventually began to affect their trust of one another. Haydn was irritated because Mike Bessie was making all the trips to Europe; he felt he should have a turn overseas. But Pat Knopf objected. He told Hiram that Mike was the man for Europe and that Hiram should be seeking out new young American writers. Haydn continued to make a fuss, and with utmost reluctance Pat let him go to Europe. That's when the relationship between Knopf and Haydn evaporated.

"Basically," Mike said coldly, "Pat and I—we divorced Hiram. We had an impossible situation."

The nub of it was that, beyond Pat Knopf's dissatisfaction with Haydn, Atheneum was in severe financial trouble. "Pat's fear," Haydn wrote in his memoir, "was of failure. He had made that heroic break. It was his assertion of manhood, of freedom from the tyrannical father. It became his life."

In the end, the divorce from Haydn came about by a memorandum from Haydn's friend, William Roth, now a leading stockholder of the company. The memo, written in 1963, addressed to Haydn, Bessie, Knopf, and Marc Friedlaender, spelled out with absolute clarity the essence of a book publishing company—as wise a definition as I have read about the nature of our profession, then and now: *"Publishing is a marginal business, and it is particularly difficult to build up an entity that has any real dollar value and therefore an assurance of future existence."*

Roth then got more specific: "I have been concerned ever since Atheneum began, that rather than living from bestseller to bestseller, it would be necessary somehow to build up a continuum of income that would give the company value and stability as a 'going concern.'" That was what hit home with Pat Knopf since he himself desperately sought that continuum of income. But there was another thing he always sought—complete control of his company. It was a preoccupation that stunted his usefulness as a publisher.

On November 3, 1963—Hiram Haydn's birthday, as it happened—the three founding partners met. Pat Knopf's opening words stung Haydn just as Pat had so often been stung by his father: "I've lost faith in your judgment." Mike Bessie stood silently by Pat's side.

In 1964, Haydn left Atheneum and went to work for Harcourt Brace Jovanovich, taking at least one author with him. Two years earlier, Haydn had discovered and bought a first novel by a young North Carolina writer named Reynolds Price. *A Long and Happy Life* didn't make any money for Atheneum, but received glowing critical reviews, and it was the beginning of a long and rich literary career for Price. It was also the beginning of a close friendship between Haydn and his author. "I left Atheneum," Price said, "because he and I loved each other."

Hiram Haydn died in 1973, and his memoir, *Words & Faces*, was published the following year. His unfavorable depiction of the breakup with Knopf and Bessie, in a memoir that was surely meant to settle scores with his old partners, left bruises on Pat Knopf and Mike Bessie that can still be felt. It harshly documented that time in their lives when it was supposed to be one for all, and all for one, but never was.

Robert Loomis, Random House's peerless editor, told me how

devastated Haydn had been when Styron refused to move to Atheneum. And then he recounted a weird story about Hiram that might have been apocryphal. "He had his first heart attack," Bob Loomis said, "and in the hospital he saw the sepulchral figure of a monk wearing a cassock, at the foot of his bed, laughing in a crazed way, saying, 'We know what it's all about.' He told his wife, Mary, 'the monk was here.' A year later when Hiram had had another heart attack, he was home, in his bed. His wife heard him call out: 'Mary! The monk is here!' She ran upstairs, and Hiram was dead."

Haydn's death did not strengthen the camaraderie between the original founding partners. Mike Bessie stayed on at Atheneum until 1975, but the company now was really Pat's. It was up to him, and nobody else, to find new people who might bring his company hope, if not deliverance.

IN THE YEAR that Hiram Haydn departed, and before the coolness deepened between Pat and Mike, the two had invited a gifted young fellow, Herman Gollob, to be editor in chief. With Gollob on board, the house began to swing.

Gollob is a purebred Texan. A graduate of Texas A&M, he never lost his Texas voice: *"See, here again, man. This is all this kind of shit: luck and timing."* What he was telling me one lovely day toward the end of 2004 was how he moved from Little, Brown in Boston to Atheneum in New York: "all this kind of shit"—which included astrology, as it connected to Gollob's future in book publishing.

When Herman came over to our apartment to talk about his life in publishing, he looked almost exactly as I remembered him from years ago: small, a little bent, but still a gamecock. His flashing brown eyes seemed to slip out of the sockets when on fire, and his mouth was set in a way that would enable him to chew glass. He dove into his recollections with passion.

"I had not heard from Mike and Pat at Atheneum for, like, six weeks," he snapped at me as if this insult had happened just yesterday, "and I'm not going to get that job." He was feeling particularly frustrated one morning in his Boston office, so he picked up a newspaper and began to check the astrology section. His secretary saw what he was doing. "Well, look," she advised him, "I know this astrologer and she's terrific. She's an old lady, and for five dollars she'll read your chart."

Hmmm, Herman thought, why the hell not? So he called, and the woman immediately asked, "When were you born?" He told her. Did he know the time of his birth? He told her. "Well, come up in about five days," she said, "and I'll have your chart ready."

"On the fifth day," he said, "I walk up these three flights of stairs. There are like twenty cats in this apartment. I see a tiny, silver-haired lady, silver-rimmed glasses, with pink cheeks, twinkling; she really looked like a woman who was out of a fairy tale. And she had charts all over the goddamn wall.

" 'Here's the first thing I can tell you,' she said. 'You're up for a new job, and you're going to get it. It'll take you away from town, and you're not going to find out about it soon, but you won't be leaving until September.' " Gollob beamed with the memory. "I felt this burden lifting from my soul."

Finally, one day in July, Herman got the call from Mike Bessie: "We very much want you to join us at Atheneum." Gollob was anxious to start his new job, but Bessie told him not to come until after Labor Day. Gollob was annoyed about the delay, but he wasn't about to buck his astrologer.

Luck and timing seemed to flow right along in the Texan's path from the beginning of his career. He had started out in Hollywood as a messenger for Paramount Pictures, thinking he would go on to become a movie producer, or run MGM. He then switched to the training program at the leading theatrical agency,

MCA. He enjoyed being a servant to the stars, such as Alan Ladd and Gregory Peck and Dinah Shore, but it was stifling, too. Someone whose advice he valued told Herman he should go to New York and become a book editor. So he moved to New York, but he did not become a book editor immediately.

Here, again, came luck and timing, along with that Hollywood component—connections. He had brought with him to New York a letter of introduction to a woman named Helen Strauss. Back then, she was the doyenne of literary agents, running the William Morris Agency in New York with an iron hand. So Herman called her up.

"Gollob," she said, "I've been waiting for your call. A young man who was working for me has just been drafted. And I need somebody."

Naturally, Gollob got the job.

It was 1958, and he felt like he was in heaven. "Helen Strauss was as tough as can be—fearless and absolutely brilliant," he said. "She took James Michener out of textbook editing and made him a writer. She put together *Tales of the South Pacific* and made the deal for the all-time great musical, *South Pacific.*"

Gollob fondly remembered the moment he met the legendary literary agent. "She was sitting in the office, and she was on the phone. Had one of her billion Harlot cigarettes in her mouth; she chain-smoked that foreign cigarette; I used to steal them from her. I heard her say, 'Don't be a horse's ass, damn it!' Then she hung up. And I thought, anybody who can tell somebody 'Don't be a horse's ass' and hang up in his face is somebody I want to work for."

They got along famously—except for the day when he boasted to her that he had just taken Mike Bessie to lunch. Helen Strauss was furious. "I didn't hire you to take Mike Bessie and Hiram Haydn and Bennett Cerf out to lunch," she said. "I handle the big guys. You take out these young editors who've got a future ahead of them." She named one of them: Alan Williams.

Alan Williams was then Lippincott's New York editor, and he and Gollob immediately began what would become a lifelong friendship. If a genie could have granted me one wish for this book, it would have been for Alan to return so I could talk with this most enlightened and beloved editor of the period. The way Gollob described Williams was the way I think of him, too: "He had that boyish, sly wit, was as amiable and generous as he could be. He knew everything, and never showed it off. It was just there. He was funny and just a lovable human being."

One day, when their friendship had deepened, Williams called and told Herman Gollob, "I've got some news. I've just been hired by Little, Brown to be their New York editor. Let's have lunch." It turned into a long wet lunch. About 3 or 4 o'clock Herman said, "You know, I'm thinking of quitting this goddam job. I want to be an editor, just like you, Uncle Alan."

Alan looked at Herman and smiled. "Well, we have an opening in Boston."

When Herman returned from lunch, his eyes rolling in his head, he walked into Helen Strauss's office and said, "I'm quitting." She asked why. "Because," he said, "I'm going to be interviewed for a job at Little, Brown."

"Oh, you're going to be *interviewed* for it. I can smell your breath from over here, by the way. Why don't you go home and collect your senses, and then come in here on Monday and talk to me."

So he came in on Monday, cold sober, and said, "I'm still going to leave."

"All right," she said. Helen Strauss picked up the phone instantly and called Arthur Thornhill, Sr., in Boston. Thornhill, the head of Little, Brown, was widely admired as a publisher and a gentleman. "Arthur," she said, "there's a young man here who is stupid enough to want to leave me and go off to work at Little,

Brown. Now he's going to be interviewing people. I just want you to know that I think very highly of him."

Herman got the job.

ONE OF THE first things I asked Gollob that day we spent together was which uniform would he wear when he was named to the Book Publishing Hall of Fame. In his weighty career, Herman had played on a lot of teams—Harper's Magazine Press, Doubleday, Simon & Schuster, the Literary Guild, as well as Little, Brown and Atheneum. "I'd have to say the place closest to my heart," Herman told me, "was Atheneum. For one thing, Pat Knopf is a guy I just loved. As far as I'm concerned he was a finer publisher than his old man was. He certainly was a more decent human being. And tough! He could be ruthless, too. He let nothing stand in his way to make that company float."

When Gollob was leaving Boston to work for Pat Knopf in 1964, Little, Brown's editor in chief, Ned Bradford, said to him, "You can have Clavell and Barthelme. They're your guys." Gollob had published *Come Back, Dr. Caligari,* Donald Barthelme's collection of short stories at Little, Brown. The editor and author had been close friends back in Houston; Gollob was the first to head east, then Barthelme followed before *Caligari* was published. But James Clavell—he was Gollob's true discovery.

HERMAN GOLLOB

I owe Clavell to Alan Williams. Barbara and I were on our honeymoon. We had married in April '61. We stopped in New York City. I wanted her to meet my good friend Alan Williams, who was then Little, Brown's New York editor. We're sitting in his office having coffee, and I see this huge pile of yellow manuscript pages. It must have been over a foot tall. I said, "What's that goddamn thing?" Alan said, "That's *King Rat*. You know, this guy's sent it here two or three times, and we keep turning it down. Everybody in New York has turned it down, at least once."

I said, "*King Rat*? I love that title. What is it?" He says, "Well, it's about a Japanese prisoner-of-war camp." And I said, "Hell, I'm gung ho on prisoner of war camp novels." "Well, you want to read it?" I said, "Okay."

A couple of weeks later the manuscript arrived from New York. So I start to read it and it's horrible. It was written in a language that only vaguely approximated English. I discovered though that I was compelled to read it no matter how bad it was. I was wanting to know what happens next. So there was something there. Edmund Wilson said about Fitzgerald's *This Side of Paradise:* "Every fault a novel can have but one. It cannot fail to live." That's how I felt about the *King*.

So I went to work on it. I swear to God, I agonized over it, worked every day, seven days a week, about twelve hours a day for six weeks. It was about 1,200 pages. I cut it almost in half.

Clavell was a screenwriter-director in Hollywood (mostly low-budget adventures at Twentieth Century Fox), and I sent him the manuscript. He wrote me a letter back saying, "I wanted to beat my wife up when I saw this letter, because I wanted to take my razor on somebody. But I'll do what you say—most of it, anyway."

King Rat became a successful book, and then was made into a powerful movie, with George Segal playing the lead. Too bad—McQueen would have been ideal for the role.

Clavell didn't know what he was going to do for his next book. And I said, "You know, Michener had a big score with

Hawaii. Why don't you write a novel about Hong Kong—from the beginning up to the present. He said, "Yeah, I think I'll do that." So he moved there. Just like that. Meantime, Pat Knopf and Mike Bessie hired me as a senior editor at Atheneum [1964]. A dream opportunity. And one of the first deals I made was for Clavell's epic-in-progress. The advance was $7,500. Little, Brown had paid $5,000 for *King Rat;* Clavell didn't really need the money because he had his Hollywood money.

Months pass. Finally, he called me up. "Laddie," he said, "I think I might have a little problem here." I said, "What's that?" He said, "I've written about 800 pages of this novel, and I'm only on the second week of the founding of the colony."

Well, yeah, that is something of a problem; it'll end up 900 million pages long. I said to him, "Is there enough drama in the founding?" He said, "Well, the founding is very interesting and exciting." "Okay," I said, "the founding it is."

The manuscript came in, and it was, in a way, worse than *King Rat,* because Clavell had never written an historical saga before. There was some feeling in the house that maybe we should abandon the novel, but not from Pat Knopf. He said, "We brought you in here to do Clavell, and you're going to do this goddam book." I said, "Okay." End of argument.

When we finished the book, we still didn't have a title. Clavell sent me thirty titles, and the title he wanted—I swear to God—was *Whither Goest Thou Wind.* I said to him, "You mean like *Gone With the Wind*?" That was that.

All through the novel the head man was a *taipan*—one word, lower case. It meant that he was chief, a man of power and authority. So I said to Clavell, "What if you dashed *taipan*? And then you capitalize it every time you use it, so it might give it some mythological force." He said, "Well, you can do anything you want." "Let's go with *Tai-Pan.*"

So I go to Mike Bessie and he said, "Nah, we can't call it that. Nobody will understand what it's all about. They'd think it was Taiwan." And Pat Knopf said, "I don't give a goddamn what he says. You want to call it *Tai-Pan,* you call it *Tai-Pan.*" And that was it.

Gollob actually served two terms at Atheneum, first as senior editor, 1964–1967; then as vice president and editor in chief, 1971–1975. In the interim he became executive story editor at Palomar Pictures, an ABC subsidiary in New York, a position he left in 1969 to start a new publishing house with a University of Texas graduate, Willie Morris.

Morris was then the youngest editor in chief of the oldest magazine in American history: *Harper's* magazine, founded in 1850. His magazine was receiving all kinds of awards, and now he wanted to tack on a book publishing company. So he and Gollob founded Harper's Magazine Press. But in a dispute with the owners of the magazine, Morris left *Harper's*, and Herman left, too. He didn't want to stay there without his buddy.

Almost immediately, Pat Knopf called Gollob and asked him to come back to Atheneum, and Herman did, as vice president and editor in chief. His relationship with Knopf was tumultuous and, as much as he admired Pat, he also pounced into fights with him. "I used to quit all the time," Herman told me. "Pat could be very tough, impulsive." As was Gollob. "I'd quit, take the stuff off my wall, bring it home. He'd call me and make up. I'd come back." Herman came back all right, but he never unpacked. The pile was in a corner of his office: Pat Knopf couldn't miss seeing it.

During his second term at Atheneum, Herman edited Clavell's

most successful novel, *Shogun*. And he came across a first novel about pro football which knocked him over, *Semi-Tough* by Dan Jenkins, a Texan who at the time was a near-legendary senior writer at *Sports Illustrated*. Gollob went on to edit, at Atheneum, Jenkins's classic golf novel, *Dead Solid Perfect*, and two sequels to *Semi-Tough*, one when he was working at Simon & Schuster, the other at Doubleday. The agent, Sterling Lord, had sent the manuscript first to Random House, but they turned it down. Sterling knew that Gollob was a graduate of Texas A&M, and Dan Jenkins went to TCU. The agent figured, "This is a shoo-in," and he sent the manuscript to Gollob.

Pat Knopf also read the original manuscript and, as Herman remembered, "didn't dig it that much. There was a lot of Texan stuff in there, and there was a lot of profanity—the *fuck* word was used a lot." Skeptical, Pat asked Herman, "Are you sure you want to do it?" Herman knew it needed an enormous amount of work, but he was crazed to do it, and told Pat as much. So, for an advance of $6,000, a deal was struck.

Jenkins came in and talked for a long time with Gollob about revisions; the editor told his author what he had to do. Four months later, Jenkins's new version appeared in the mail. "It made me so goddamn happy, just elated," Herman said. *Semi-Tough* was published in 1972 and became an instant bestseller, second on the *New York Times* bestseller list in its first week of publication. And after an all-out paperback auction directed by Pat Knopf, New American Library won it for $250,000.

Herman Gollob's final gift to Pat Knopf and Atheneum was a huge historical novel, *Aztec,* by Gary Jennings, about the ancient Mexican empire. *Aztec* was published in 1980 and sold to paperback for $800,000. By then, Herman had left the company.

His wooer this time was Doubleday's Literary Guild. "I figured," he told me with a straight face, "that if Al Silverman could make it in the book club business, anyone could." He was right about that. Pat Knopf was hurt when Gollob left in 1979, but it was only one blow to the house of Atheneum that brutal year.

The nation was in an economic slowdown. Interest rates were over twenty percent, which meant it was extremely difficult for the smaller financially troubled publishing houses to borrow from the banks. Atheneum wasn't the only one feeling the heat—the historic house of Charles Scribner's Sons (established in 1846) was being burned, too. In an attempt to strengthen both companies, Charles Scribner, Jr., proposed a merger with Atheneum.

"We at Scribner's always got along well with Pat Knopf," Charlie Scribner wrote in his lovely and painfully honest memoir, *In the Company of Writers,* "and it occurred to us that we might increase our business by adding to ours that of another established company."

In July 1978, Pat Knopf and Charles Scribner, Jr., shook hands on a friendly takeover, which made Scribner chairman and Knopf vice chairman. Effective in the fall of 1978 the two-pronged house would now be called "the Scribner Book Companies," enabling Atheneum to carry on independently. It helped, too, that Pat Knopf soon found a fitting successor to Herman Gollob in Tom Stewart.

TOM STEWART was no idler, neither in publishing nor in love. A slim, handsome young man with laughing eyes, Tom was at Harvard in the late 1960s, while his future wife, Amanda Vaill, a slender, beautiful young woman with an easy laugh, was attending Radcliffe. The two met in Cambridge, and everyone began to call them "Scott and Zelda." Amanda executed the best revenge by writing a charming book, her first, *Everybody Was So Young,* about Sara and Gerald Murphy, who were expatriate friends of Zelda and Scott (though far richer) and very much of the spirit of Fitzgerald's lost generation.

Tom Stewart and Amanda Vaill became engaged when they were juniors. Tom hoped to stay in New York that summer and maybe find something in book publishing. His soon-to-be mother-in-law, Pat Vaill, ran an upper-crust Park Avenue jewelry company called Seaman Schepps (which Amanda coauthored a book about). One of Pat Vaill's customers was the president of Viking, Tom "Tommy" Guinzburg, as she called him (son of Viking's founder, Harold K. Guinzburg). And Tommy Guinzburg gave Tom Stewart a summer job.

"In that wonderfully diffident way of his," Tom said about Guinzburg, "he told me that publicity would be a good place to begin because it's a nerve center, and you can see where a lot of things go."

Tom did indeed get to see where a lot of things went at Viking that summer. But the moment he remembers most came in the bathroom, standing alongside Malcolm Cowley. "I'm majoring in English at Harvard," Tom told me with gusto, "and I'm thinking, *My God, you're standing here peeing next to one of the great men of American letters.*" It was enough to turn a young man toward the literary profession. In 1970, after earning a bachelor's degree in English literature, summa cum laude, he began his eighteen-year career in book publishing.

Tom landed his first full-time job as a junior editor for Richard Grossman, who had his own imprint under the Viking umbrella. In 1965, Grossman had published Ralph Nader's best muckraking book, *Unsafe at Any Speed.* Tom marched vigorously up the publishing ladder. He served three three-year terms—the first with Richard Grossman at Viking; the second with Farrar, Straus and Giroux; and the third with Harcourt Brace Jovanovich. And then it was on to his longest and most complex tenure, with Atheneum.

Several of Tom's friends had suggested he explore the Atheneum position that Gollob had just abandoned for the Literary Guild at Doubleday. It just so happened that, at that time, Pat Knopf was about to embark on his annual five-week business and pleasure trip to Europe. Pat did spend a couple of weeks working in London, carrying manuscripts into his plush hotel, the Connaught. "I think he must have brought fifteen or twenty books in the time he was there," said Betty Prashker, a leading editor back then for Doubleday, who was also seeking British titles. "And I said to Pat, 'How do you possibly have the time to read these manuscripts?' He said, 'Well, I don't read them. I listen to the pitch, and if it sounds good, I buy it.' "

Pat, not always pitch-perfect in his choices, needed someone who had the instinctive feel for books. From London, he called his treasurer, Marvin Brown, a man he loved (as did I when I worked with Marvin at Viking in the 1990s), and told Marvin to see Stewart, but "go ahead and hire somebody." Marvin Brown liked everything he'd heard about Tom Stewart, and he felt even better after talking with him. So, with Pat's backing, he hired Tom.

"After I had been there about three weeks," Tom said, "Pat, just back from England, came into my office. His first words were: 'Stewart, you've been here just long enough to start screwing up!' It was something that I'd done that I should have asked him about," Tom said. "Because, you know, one of the things about Pat is that he has hot buttons you're not aware of." Tom figured he'd better prove himself quickly, and the first thing he set out to do was to improve his manners.

One of the company's sales reps had told him about a woman named Judith Martin, who was writing a column on etiquette for *The Washington Post* under the byline of "Miss Manners." "Somebody's got to get her to do a book," the rep told Tom. He looked into the Miss Manners material, was thoroughly impressed, and wrote Judith Martin a note saying, "You're wonderful." Tom thinks that he may have been the fifty-third person in book publishing to have complimented Martin, and he never expected to hear from her.

Miss Manners, the very embodiment of proper etiquette, wrote and declined his offer, saying, "Thank you very much. Other people have talked to me, and I've got a novel, and I have decided that I'm not going to do anything with the Miss Manners book until I place the novel."

"Well, send it to me," Tom said. And she did. When he received her novel, *Gilbert Came a Dealing,* Tom found it to be a bit of a mess. Still, he could see how it might work. He told Martin that she needed to change the book from it being a narrative filled with transitions to being a series of scenes—make it more like *Auntie Mame,* Tom suggested. He then worked out a two-book deal with Judith Martin. "We'll edit the novel now," he told her, "but let's do the etiquette book first. See, it will make the novel more successful." And that's exactly what happened. But it took a bit of doing to make *Miss Manners' Guide to Excruciatingly Correct Behavior* one of the books of the year, and an enormous bestseller for Atheneum. (In 2005 this first Miss Manners volume was "freshly updated.") Tom had to fight it out with Pat Knopf.

"We had a first printing, then a second printing," Tom said, "and Pat was willing to have Atheneum, a cash-poor company, *run an ad.* That was a big deal. We were going to run a fairly modest ad in the daily *New York Times.* I looked at the layout for this ad we were going to run. It was flat and boring. I walked into Pat's office first thing in the morning, and threw it down on his desk and said, 'This ad sucks! It doesn't say—second printing before publication. It doesn't say, a Book-of-the-Month Club selection. It doesn't have any of the three great quotes we got for the book. It's just a tombstone. It's not selling the book.' I said all this to Pat—stood up to him for the first time, told him I was right. And from that day on Pat and I were friends."

They became more than friends. Some people referred to Tom as Pat Knopf's surrogate son.

At the same time that Tom was scoring with Miss Manners, another editor, Neil Nyren, was bringing in strong commercial books, too. Nyren bought Andy Rooney's sharp personal and political commentaries; he acquired Garrison Keillor's first book, a short story collection; and he began the career of a new mystery writer, Jonathan Kellerman. "All in all," Tom said, thinking of those days, "we had a pretty good run."

Then in May 1984 came the Macmillan Corporation's acquisition of the Scribner Book Companies. "It was paradise for about a year and a half," Tom said, "because that was when Daddy Warbucks buys you, but he's not controlling you yet. When Macmillan began its reorganization of Scribner's and Atheneum was when it all started to go to hell."

In 1989, Tom Stewart, then the president of Atheneum, left the company to join *Fortune* magazine, where he went on to become one of the best business journalists in the country. He also wrote a well-received book, *Intellectual Capital: The New Wealth of Organizations,* that was not published by Atheneum, possibly because it was not exactly a part of the new wealth of organizations.

Lee Goerner, an editor of high repute while working at Knopf, became Atheneum's publisher in 1989. (I first met Lee at the Book-of-the-Month Club after we had chosen as a Main Selection a book he had discovered, edited, and translated, Isabel Allende's first novel, *The House of the Spirits.*) He published some wonderful books over the next five years.

Goerner died in 1995. His widow, Katherine McNamara, who published a valuable online literary journal, *Archipelago,* recalled a lunch her husband once had with Thomas Pynchon. "I think it was during the unsettling year before Atheneum was shut down," she wrote in *Archipelago.* "He and Pynchon were saying good-bye when Pynchon took him lightly, affectionately, by the lapels and half-growled, 'Only publish good books.'"

Goerner didn't forget. Among the last books Atheneum published were Dr. Jonathan Shay's *Achilles in Vietnam: Combat Trauma and the Undoing of Character*, of which Lee sent copies to fellow publishers with the inscription, "Lest we forget," and an elegant edition of Sir John Hale's *The Civilization of Europe in the Renaissance*. Following Macmillan's acquisition by Simon & Schuster, Atheneum trade was effectively shut down on the last day of June 1994, except for its children's imprint, which is very successful to this day.

IN HIS CAREER at this house that became his own, Alfred A. Knopf, Jr., always tried to publish good books, and he did publish many—Robert Ardrey's *African Genesis;* Edward Albee's *Who's Afraid of Virginia Woolf?;* Luigi Barzini's *The Italians*—all alive and well today, among many others. Someone once characterized those who had started their own publishing houses as being "idiosyncratic, driven." Pat Knopf may have been more idiosyncratic and driven than most. It was in his blood. Having lived through a stunted childhood, as an only child of parents who had no time to love him (if, indeed, that was ever their inclination), he successfully freed himself from his parents' strictures by making his own way in book publishing. He surrounded himself with experts, some of the best in the field, who helped him run the company. It was not General Motors, or Ford, or Chrysler. But Atheneum was his company, and it completely possessed him. Considering the circumstances, the publishing house he ran deserved a longer life.

5

A MOST UNUSUAL COG IN THE PROFESSION

St. Martin's Press

I've been so lucky in my life and in my job, because the start of
Tom McCormack's trade publishing coincided with the whole
glory days of book club auctions and the rise of paperbacks.
And for St. Martin's, the books were just getting
better and better, so the growth kept coming.

—SALLY RICHARDSON

T he first person I talked with for this chapter was Thomas
McCormack, who retired from St. Martin's Press in
1997. Today St. Martin's is running at full steam, as it
has ever since Sally Richardson became McCormack's successor. In my time at Book-of-the-Month Club, Sally was the
rights director, and a dream to work with. But it was Tom Mc-
Cormack who was there at the beginning, because he was the
company's George Washington.

I remember him as one who scarcely raised his voice. I did not,
however, let that mislead me. Tom McCormack's reputation was

that of a tough guy—editor; egoist; pedant; playwright; raconteur; skeptic; publisher—who, having been an orphan himself, spent twenty-eight years seeing to it that St. Martin's Press, also born as an orphan in 1952, was properly raised.

We met on an early morning in October 2004 in his large, sunny apartment overlooking Central Park. McCormack, as slim as a ballet master, was drinking coffee out of a Brown University cup and wearing a baseball cap lettered *Red Sox*. Well, why not? It was the October that would turn out to be one of the happiest of this blue-collar Bostonian's life. His team would finally exorcise the ghost of Babe Ruth to win its first baseball championship in eighty-six years.

Here is how McCormack began his monologue when I asked him (innocently, I thought) if he had been a snotty kid.

"Yeah," he answered, "I was a snotty little kid, always first in his class, and I used to bust IQ tests to the point that they asked me to test tests."

If this sounds close to self-satisfaction, listen to McCormack build on the story. When he was in a philosophy class at Brown University, still a teenager, he made friends with a twenty-four-year-old undergrad who had recently come back from World War II. After the professor returned their first exam, an essay on philosophy, Tom pulled an A, his friend a C–.

Walking out of the class, the vet asked to see Tom's paper. He read it and said to Tom, "Yeah, I can see you do have a flair for bullshit."

If so, this talent of Tom's, I figured, might also help him in detecting the BS in others. Including me. So I immediately told him what my book would be all about: a golden age of book publishing, beginning in 1946, and burning bright into the early 1980s, when the flame began to flutter.

Immediately Tom McCormack began reminiscing about the time of his life in book publishing. For him, it began with his first position at Doubleday, then Harper's, and New American Library, and it flourished in the seventies when he made St. Martin's Press a viable, profitable, and most unusual cog in the trade publishing world. At his retirement, Thomas McCormack was the second-longest-tenured CEO in postwar book publishing, though a distant second to Roger Straus, who had been the owner of his own toy store for over fifty years. As Tom talked about his years, always in that voice of his, subdued but full of confidence, I felt dreamy, as though I were watching spring flowers coming to bloom before my eyes.

ST. MARTIN'S PRESS was born a bastard, conceived not by American parents, but by the sire of an aristocratic British family called the Macmillans.

It was in 1843 that the brothers Daniel and Alexander Macmillan established their publishing house, Macmillan Publishers Limited, in Cambridge, England. Daniel died in 1857, but in 1869, with the firm having become highly successful, Alexander Macmillan came to the United States. Now that the Civil War was over, Macmillan felt that the company was ready to set up shop in the United States. And so Alexander arranged with an experienced American bookseller, George Edward Brett, to run a Macmillan sales agency in New York.

This first Brett, "a man of strong character, quick decision and earnest convictions," according to *Publishers Weekly,* did such a good job selling the English-based Macmillan books throughout the U.S.A. that he decided to try publishing and selling American books, too. Toward the end of the century one of George Edward Brett's sons, George Platt Brett, came to work for the house. Upon the death of his father, Brett was told that his company would become independent, though still under the command of Macmillan and Company Ltd. of London. In the

Macmillan hierarchy, George P. Brett was deemed the United States' "resident publisher."

Brett's fundamental principles of successful publishing—"offering good manuscripts, selling books effectively, and attention to office work promptly"—worked so well that by 1931 Macmillan had become the largest publishing house in the United States. When Brett died in 1936, his son, also George P. Brett, took over the company.

This Brett had come into his inheritance at a propitious time. A year earlier Harold H. Latham, who had been editor in chief since 1920, went on a scouting expedition for new writers. His first stop came in Atlanta, where he learned from Lois Cole, who had worked in Macmillan's office there, that a friend of hers, an *Atlanta Journal* reporter named Peggy Mitchell, was working on a novel. Brett went to see Mrs. Mitchell, whose formal first name was Margaret. She told him that she was only writing for her own amusement. But the night before Latham was to leave Atlanta, Mitchell showed up with a huge manuscript in hand. "Take the thing before I change my mind," she said. He did, and *Gone With the Wind* was published in 1936. By the end of its first year, it had sold 1,375,000 copies.

In June 1936, Margaret Mitchell wrote a letter to Harry Scherman, the founder of Book-of-the-Month Club, in which she tried to explain what her book becoming a Main Selection meant to her.

"When I heard that you all had selected it, it was too much to be borne and I went to bed and was ill, with an ice pack and large quantities of aspirin."

She also confessed to Harry Scherman that she could never read authors "like Tolstoi and Dostoevsky, and probably Thackeray and Jane Austen, too." But now she would try to. "When people are kind enough to mention them in the same breath with my book, I ought to be able to do more than duck my head and suck my thumb and make unintelligible sounds."

There you have Margaret Mitchell, crossing the Rubicon.

BY THE END of World War II, the reigning Brett, who lacked his father's energy and instincts, saw Macmillan's No. 1 ranking among American publishers fade quickly: Doubleday, McGraw-Hill, and Prentice-Hall had all pulled ahead of Macmillan. In 1951, Brett made a difficult decision. He prevailed on the English Macmillans to sell their stock to the American company. He took 61.3 percent from the London shareholders. This windfall helped Brett for a while, but Macmillan U.S.A., now on its own and short of capital, was open to invasion from other companies. As for the London Macmillans, they were relieved of the burden of trying to bolster a company that had, over the years, become financially weak. But now they found themselves without a voice in the country that was apparently going to dominate the remainder of the twentieth century.

"Within two years of the sale," Tom McCormack told me, "they realized, 'Oh, shit, we've lost the arm that used to distribute our books. Let's start another company to do that.' " And so they did in 1952, unveiling St. Martin's Press, named after historic St. Martin's Lane, where Macmillan had sat in London for generations.

Thinking small, Sir Harold Macmillan, the future prime minister who now ran the family enterprise, made St. Martin's Press a company that was, in effect, only a jobber for the books that came off Macmillan London's press. "That original 1952 St. Martin's Press," McCormack said drily, "was not originating any books." In 1956, St. Martin's Press was allowed to buy books and became a wholly original American publisher.

HIS NAME AT BIRTH, in 1932, was not Tom McCormack. It was Michael Gerard Griffin. For the first nine months of his life he was in the Brighton, Massachusetts, Foundling Hospital, and then was shunted to various foster homes. When he was four years old, thanks to the Catholic Welfare Bureau, Tom was adopted by a man named Thomas McCormack. This father had fought in the First World War. After the war he worked nights as a printing pressman. When young Thomas was eleven years old he saw a movie called *The Adventures of Mark Twain*, starring Fredric March. "Here's this magical moment," Tom recalled, "when we see Samuel Langhorne Clemens, back from the West, 'going to write that up.' And he starts to write his real name and he scratches it out and writes, 'Mark Twain.' I was thrilled like crazy. The next morning I ran all the way to the library and took out *Tom Sawyer*." That was the first of his many visits to the library. "I got so lucky," he said. "I just didn't know anyone that has had more luck, sheer luck, than I've had in my day."

Neither his father nor his mother, Lida McCormack, had any schooling of their own, so it was strange for them to see their boy, some years later, going off to college to study philosophy. "Don't worry," Tom told his parents. "When I get my degree I'm going to go down to New York and get a job at one of those big publishing firms."

And that's just what he did, but not right away. He graduated from Brown in 1954, then went into the army, spending two wonderful years assigned to the American embassy in Rome. After that, there was a scholarship to study philosophy at Harvard. But he quit to write a novel and made another kind of discovery: "It was not given to me to write novels."

In 1959, Tom heard from an old friend from Brown who was then working at Doubleday that they had a trainee program, and he suggested that Tom go over and see them. He did. He was interviewed and was hired by Doubleday's editor in chief, whose name was Ken McCormick. (You will read much more about this legendary book person in the Doubleday chapter.)

Tom's first assignment was to work on Anchor Books, a quality trade paperback imprint devoted to literature that had been founded in 1953 by Jason Epstein. By the time McCormack came to Doubleday, Epstein had gone to Random House. But he was remembered. "There was an editor at Anchor who liked to tell funny stories about Epstein," Tom said, "who, I guess, evidently could have a rather high-flown vision of himself. So she used to poke fun at him, and everyone would laugh except me. And she said, 'I notice Tom isn't laughing.' And I said, 'Look, all I know is that he could not have been the dunce that he's depicted as here. Because look what he's created.'"

Then, as the sixties began, Tom moved into hardcover trade, working mostly for the executive editor, LeBaron R. "Lee" Barker, Jr. Lee Barker and Ken McCormick were the two great Doubleday editors of the time. Between the two, they'd had eight wives, but the marital turnover never impaired their editing skills. Barker particularly liked to bring young editors around, and he became kind of a mentor to Tom.

Lee Barker, who was Herman Wouk's editor, gave Tom the editorial letters he sent to Wouk when they were working on *The Caine Mutiny;* the letters show how Wouk accepted Barker's editorial recommendations. "You remember the strawberry incident in the novel?" Tom said. "Wouk had a duplicate called 'the coffee incident.' And Lee said to him, 'Herman, you've already done it.' So they cut it.

"Then he gave me his letters to Wouk on *Youngblood Hawke.* He had a lot of suggestions, but by this time Herman was so grand he wasn't taking suggestions from anyone. The result was that that book had the largest number of returns of any book ever published by Doubleday until that time."

Tom learned a lot from Lee Barker about the art of editing, and, later in life, became a stickler about editing, almost to the point of pedantry. His greatest learning experience, however, about all the major elements in book publishing, came from a man named Leonard Shatzkin—lessons that would continue to influence Tom's decision-making throughout his career. Doubleday was about to start a new "quality" paperback imprint called Dolphin Books. It seemed that everyone in publishing was getting into this new American dream machine—republishing classics in mass market and trade paperback editions. It was Len Shatzkin who convinced Doubleday's president, Doug Black, and John Sargent, who ran the trade division, that with Doubleday's distribution system, they would be able to flood paperbacks into places that they'd never been before. And Doubleday could fill the slot with its own backlist classics titles—without paying royalties, since almost all the titles were in the public domain (because the copyrights had expired). Once he received the go-ahead, Shatzkin went to Tom and said, "I want you to put together the first Dolphin list."

"I suppose what you mean," McCormack said, "is that you want me to go through all the classics and see the really important ones that have never had an edition—"

"No!" Shatzkin interrupted him. "Just the other way around. We're going to do the ones everybody's done, because those are the ones that sell. And we're the ones with the strong sales force. So we're going to pick everything."

Shatzkin's assignment for young McCormack was specific: Find a hundred books that had had more editions in print than any other, for Dolphin to publish on January 15, 1961. One day in November Tom crawled into Shatzkin's office. "I didn't make it," he admitted, breathing heavily. "I got only ninety-six." "Ha!" Shatzkin shouted. "I thought you'd get about seventy."

Shatzkin had also told Tom that the No. 1 book for Dolphin of the ninety-six should be the one that had the most editions in print. Tom found that *The Scarlet Letter* had eighteen available editions. He also remembered that when they had four hundred

Dolphin books in print, the title that sold the most was *The Scarlet Letter.*

I would love to have met with Leonard Shatzkin for this book, but he died in 2002 at the age of eighty-three. Fortunately, I was able to spend time with his widow, Elke, and her likable son, Mike. For twenty-five years Michael Shatzkin has been doing what his father had done in his lifetime—seeing to "the physiology of book publishing," as Tom McCormack calls it. Mike prefers to describe himself as merely "a provocative observer of the industry." Mike and I talked, of course, about his dad's influence on McCormack. "Tom's a very smart guy," Mike told me. "He did learn a lot from my dad, but he learned a lot about interpreting it his way, too."

In 1964, Tom McCormack moved from Doubleday to Harper & Row. Bob Barnes, the Doubleday sales manager who had been most involved with Dolphin, asked Tom to follow him to Harper's, where they would work on an exciting new project: the distribution of Penguin Books. Cass Canfield, the head of Harper & Row, had made an agreement with Allen Lane, Penguin's canny founder, to distribute Penguin Books in the U.S. But the day before the deal was to be finalized, Lane called up and said, "I've changed my mind." Canfield was a gentleman. He told Barnes and McCormack, "Don't worry, I hired you away. I'm going to take care of you. We'll start our own paperback line." It would be called Perennial Books. And Tom McCormack would be its editor in chief.

Tom spent three good years at Harper's, putting together a powerful paperback line of classics for Perennial. Then he moved over to Harper's hardcover books. He was assigned to a division handling specialty books—"nonfiction assemblage," Tom called it—which was not exactly up his alley. "I was to go to the magazines, for instance, and get the *House & Garden* book of flower arranging and the *Cosmopolitan* book on cosmetics. And I was just wrong for that job. I hated myself because I wasn't earning my keep."

So he left Harper's and took a job at New American Library that was more to his liking: to run Mentor Books and the Signet classics. The highlight of his eighteen-month stay at NAL was buying a mass market paperback titled *The Double Helix*. "That was fun," he said, "because I had no idea what I was given in page proofs; I'd never heard of Watson or Crick. I read it on the weekend. And I remember coming in Monday raving about it. I told them, 'This is a great book, we have to have this goddam book." They listened to Tom and bought paperback rights for *The Double Helix* from Atheneum for $80,000. It turned out to be a solid investment.

Feeling refreshed, Tom McCormack was ready to move on, and in 1969 the Macmillan guys in London asked to see him about a job with their new American company.

ST. MARTIN'S PRESS was hurting again, and not for the first time. For too many losing years through the mid-fifties, the Macmillans shook up the American company. Ian McKenzie, a Scotsman, took over the direction of St. Martin's from Daniel Macmillan. Sherman Baker was his able editor in chief.

One day, Baker found himself facing a thousand-page manuscript. Hardly anyone sent St. Martin's manuscripts for consideration unless they were desperate, so Baker figured (rightly) that this monster had been turned down everywhere. But he started to read it. Most of the manuscript consisted of short stories about trout fishing in the upper Michigan peninsula. But in the middle of it was a story involving a tense courtroom drama. The author of the manuscript was John D. Voelker, a supreme court judge in Michigan, who wrote under the pseudonym of Robert Traver. Sherman Baker loved this one short story enough to buy the entire book that was called *Trout Madness*. In 1958, *Anatomy of a*

Murder became St. Martin's first No. 1 bestseller. Later, the novel became a high-grossing film starring Jimmy Stewart and Lee Remick. Baker got full value from Traver's large manuscript; he published the short stories about trout fishing, and *Trout Madness* stayed in print for many years at St. Martin's.

Bolstered by that unexpected success, Ian McKenzie went on a buying frenzy. "He was so lofty," McCormack said to me, "that he would say to people in London, 'Last year, we lost a hundred thousand dollars; this year, we'll lose *a hundred and fifty* thousand dollars.'" So Morris Macmillan, Harold's son, was sent over to fire McKenzie. They did that, then they sent down the number two man from Canada, Frank Upjohn, to run St. Martin's. It was Upjohn who interviewed McCormack to be the head of the trade department.

"I got to his office at 4 o'clock in the afternoon," Tom said, "and I knew I was in trouble when we both became aware of the New York Life Insurance Company's big clock banging at 8:00 at night."

This was a time when Tom McCormack was less interested in book publishing than he was in writing plays. He'd just written a one-act play that was taken by a playwright's unit headed by Edward Albee. It would play a week off-Broadway. So Tom told Frank Upjohn, "I'm scribbling, and that's what I want to do."

Upjohn understood, but the Macmillan family didn't. They wanted Tom to head up the trade division, so they sent other bigwigs to see him. Finally, courted from all sides, Tom figured that he'd just put the playwright pencil down for a little bit while he got settled in at St. Martin's—then, maybe, get back to the theater.

It wasn't that easy. The new head of the trade division was on the job forty-eight hours when Frank Upjohn, the new head of the American company, was carried out on a stretcher with an ulcer. Upjohn recovered enough to come back to St. Martin's for the rest of 1969. Then, according to McCormack, Upjohn said, "Look, all I want to do is go up and sit on my ass in the Canadian woods." And that's what he did. Immediately, Tom got the call from London—"You're the man"—inviting him to head the company.

First, Tom asked to see the ledgers. The treasurer brought them in. "He explained to me that the left side is called the *assets*," Tom said, "and the right side is called the *liabilities*. I knew nothing, but I could see this company was dying. They had lost $150,000 and it was a tiny little company, with thirty-three employees. You couldn't lose that kind of money back in 1969."

The job, as the Macmillans explained it, would be mainly for McCormack to handle the academic books that Macmillan of London was shipping to New York for St. Martin's small college and school divisions. Tom told them he was only interested if he could be allowed to develop the trade division. They said okay, as long as he didn't neglect the other things.

Tom began to make his moves quickly. There was a children's department. He found that it wasn't working so he folded it. He examined the school division, another loser. He folded it. Then he began applying the principles he had learned from Leonard Shatzkin. "If it wasn't for him," Tom said, "there's no doubt in my mind, I would not have been able to see what the hell needed doing down at St. Martin's Press when I got there."

The following year, in 1970, St. Martin's made a profit of $8,000. It was a start. And it emboldened him to make two key additions to his company.

IT WAS TIME. In Tom's first six months on the job, he had studied St. Martin's past and present, made easy cuts and laid out the house's future in his head. Now he needed to get help.

The first thing he did was to call Anne McCormick. He had gotten to know her at Doubleday where she was working in subsidiary rights. But she had recently moved to Knopf. The reason was that she had married Ken McCormick at Doubleday, and the company's elders frowned on husbands and wives working together. Tom told Anne, "I'm looking for a *you* to run rights here."

She said immediately, "I think you ought to talk with Sally Gately over at Doubleday." Sally Gately was facing a similar problem. She was about to marry Sandy Richardson, one of Doubleday's major senior editors. So she, too, had to find another place to go. Tom invited her to his office in the storied Flatiron Building.

A word should be said about this unusual home of St. Martin's Press, which seemed to have been made for the likes of Tom McCormack. Constructed in 1902, it is the oldest skyscraper in New York, sliced like a wedge of pie where Fifth Avenue and Broadway converge at Twenty-third Street. If you view it head on, it is like the prow of a huge ship churning right toward you. And that was about the way McCormack came at Sally Gately when he took her to lunch at the Gramercy Hotel and told her of his dreams for the company:

"I decided to spend six months looking around to see what I need, and that's why I'm talking to you. I don't know what you're going to do because right away there's not going to be a job. But you're looking for a job, and I'm looking to change it all. So why don't you come on board?" He made her an offer before they'd finished lunch, and she accepted. Not long after that she became known as Sally Richardson.

Sally and I met in April 2005 in the large comfortable office she has occupied as president of the trade division since 1995. She had come a long way from the boisterous seventies, when she was still under thirty and handling subsidiary rights for Tom McCormack. We had gotten to know each other around that time when she was hand-delivering manuscripts to the Book-of-the-Month Club that she thought were important for St. Martin's and, she hoped, were also right for us. As I have said, Sally was grand to work with—honest, unassuming, tart-tongued, with a totally warm personality—and very attractive, too. I hadn't seen her close up for a long time, but she looked much the same as she had back then, with her ash blond hair setting off a pale complexion, and startling blue eyes that somehow seemed more vulnerable than I had remembered. But she had been going through hard times, losing her husband, Sandy, in 2004 after a long and difficult illness.

I asked Sally what it was like for her at the beginning to be working in the hot center of a new and much smaller house than Doubleday, with a vastly different book publishing culture. "I've been so lucky in my life," she said, "and in my job, because the start of Tom's trade publishing coincided with the whole glory days of book club auctions and the rise of paperbacks. And for St. Martin's, the books were just getting better and better, so the growth kept coming."

How did Tom do it? I asked her. "Tom was like a contrarian," she said. "You know, at this time every house was saying to their people—cut back and focus and concentrate. And he said, 'No, no—just the opposite.' He said that if we weren't paying too much for the actual physical books we were importing from London, and if we didn't spend a lot of money on cover art or anything, we could sell to the libraries.

"And that's what Tom did. He had everything calibrated. He brought in the British books that he didn't pay too much for, and they sold from 3,000 to 12,000 copies, mostly to the libraries, which gave us a firm base on library dollars. The library was like our allowance, like an annuity. And so you could experiment more on other parts of the list with more exciting books."

The trouble was that in those introductory years nobody—in the United States or England—seemed willing to offer St. Martin's the exciting books they needed to accelerate growth. "Tom would go to them," Sally said, "full of vim and vigor, and they would say, 'It's lovely to meet you and I'll probably have something for you some day, but meantime I do a lot with Random House and Doubleday . . .' He was frustrated, so his London bosses said to him, 'Come to London. We'll set up a lot of appointments with British agents.'

"Tom went to London," Sally went on, "and he didn't know anybody and nobody knew him, and they gave him the usual treatment: 'No, I don't have anything, and my big authors are spoken for, and I don't have any new ones, but I'll keep you in mind.'

"Tom began to get mad. 'Look,' he said, 'I'm right here now. I want to buy fifty books in the three weeks I'm here.' It was so frustrating for him," said Sally.

TOM McCORMACK

It was 1971 and I was on one of my first editorial trips to London. My job was to carry my beggar's basket to publishers and agents, hoping that they'd lend me manuscripts of books for which American publishing rights were available. Trouble was, the people I visited had hardly heard of St. Martin's Press and they'd never heard of me at all—so they were reluctant to show me anything they considered had much American potential.

On the last day of my visit, I went to the David Higham Literary Agency. I was sent into the smallest office to see the low man on the Higham totem pole, a man named David Bolt. David was not about to risk a fresh new manuscript on me, but he wanted to show me some courtesy. I saw him roll his eyes desperately along a shelf of bound books—works already published in London—which meant they had long ago been read and rejected by editors from New York.

Finally, he tugged down a slender book with a jacket depicting a sixteen-year-old boy pulling on a horse. I later learned it had by that time sold a total of 1,200 copies in Great Britain. *If Only They Could Talk* looked like a young-reader's book to me, and St. Martin's didn't do young-reader books. But I figured beggars can't be choosers, and, besides, I could tell a courtesy gesture when I saw it, and I wanted to show courtesy back. I did tell David it was my last day, so I couldn't read it while I was there. "Don't worry," he said breezily.

Back in New York, I put the book on the pile filling the reader table my wife, Sandra, and I had next to our bed. Eventually, Sandra got it. When she finished, she looked at me meaningfully and said, "I think you'd better read this one." No exaggeration. I read the first chapter, and I knew this writer was a kind of a storytelling genius. It was an eight-page episode about a sick horse, a surly farmer, and a dedicated, good-humored veterinarian. The author's name was James Herriot. He was the veterinarian, and he lived in a remote town in Yorkshire, England.

I went to Higham's agent-counterpart here, Claire Smith at the Harold Ober agency, and I put to her a theory.

"Claire," I said, "there are two kinds of books—caper books and milieu books. A caper book you begin tonight and you want to finish tonight—like say a good murder mystery. A milieu book is a book that draws you into its world, and you love it, and you don't want to finish it tonight, you want to look forward to getting back into that world and being with its people tomorrow night, and even for the weekend. Herriot's book is a milieu book, but it's only caper-length—192 pages. This book should be twice that length. I need more words from Herriot, Claire."

"How lovely that you should say so," Claire replied, and she plucked down from her shelf another bound, jacketed volume by Herriot. It also had an unworthy title, *It Shouldn't Happen to a Vet*. The cover illustration was a cartoon, and it too was 192 pages. I read it immediately, called Claire, and asked, "Do you think I might talk to the author?" She gave me his number.

I planned to tell him I wanted to combine the two books. But in truth neither book had an ending—it just provided a year's worth of the veterinarian's memoirs and stopped. At the end of the second book, he'd obviously met the girl who would be the love of his life. As I stared at the phone, I figured I'd also ask him for three more chapters and have our James marry his Helen and thus give us an ending. I could see him picturing a fast-talking, cigar-smoking Madison Avenue type he's never met, yammering, "He should marry the goil!" What would this country animal doctor in northern England make of it?

What he'd make of it would be magic. He understood what I was after even better than I did. I was ready just to add the second book onto the first and the three chapters onto that. Instead, James melded the two books—putting all the winter chapters together, all the spring chapters, et cetera—creating a memoir of one year in the life of our hero. And our hero marries the girl. James gave us an ending that to this day chimes like the sound of music.

All we needed now was a title. I turned to my colleagues for suggestions. The leading choice from the Americans was *Cow in the Waiting Room*. "No, no," I cried. "I want something that connotes the ages of nature, the great roll of the planets through the seasons, something yummy like that." We had a British guy in our marketing department, Michael Brooks, and he said, "There's a doxology that is regularly sung over there, 'All things bright and beautiful, all creatures great and small, all things wise and wonderful, the Lord God made them all.' "

That's how we came to call our new 442-page milieu book *All Creatures Great and Small*. It was the first of a long series of number-one bestsellers that, before he died, made James Herriot the most widely read memoirist of the generation in the entire world.

Tom's most important hire, next to Sally Richardson, was Thomas L. Dunne; he joined the company in 1971. And—wouldn't you know it—he, too, was a graduate of Brown University. I met with Tom Dunne in his office, where he had eleven people working in his imprint. Thomas Dunne Books, founded in 1986, publishes some 175 titles a year—hardcover, trade paperback, and mass market paperbacks. (St. Martin's Press publishes about seven hundred more titles a year, not counting Dunne's. Len Shatzkin would have loved to hear that.)

Dunne, an extremely busy fellow, was most patient with me as we talked. In a way, he seemed to have absorbed the nature of the person who had hired him—McCormack's intensity, self-confidence, and cynicism, but with a harder edge. They also fought a lot with each other. Tom Dunne gave me an example of such an occasion.

"I wasn't being paid that much to begin with, so it was small money. He had the time to fight me over five hundred dollars. He would argue, 'Look at it this way, look at it that way.' He went back and forth and back and forth. I don't even remember how it was solved; we probably split the difference. But years later somebody, maybe it was the finance guy, told me that Tom McCormack had to make some amount of profit, or they would shut down the company. If that was the case he could have saved himself a lot of time by just telling me what was going on." Well, Dunne hadn't been around for very long, and Tom McCormack wasn't ready to share confidences with a rookie he was not yet sure of. But the younger Tom was learning from his elder.

"Tom had his own insights," Dunne said. "He had to be taught finance, but he was never—what am I trying to say?—taken with bullshit; by that, I mean the finance jargon. To Tom, it was simply dollars in and dollars out, and what was left over was profit. Watch the cost, and focus on profit, profit, profit. Tom just wanted to know how much money was in the bank at the end of the day."

Dunne went on to explain how his boss insisted that each book make a profit. "It could be a small profit. If a small profit is multiplied a hundred times, then it's a big profit."

As an example, Tom pointed to a bookshelf full of Thomas Dunne books. He mentioned one in the stacks, *Digital Fortress* by Dan Brown. "That was Brown's first book," he said (before *The Da Vinci Code*). "I paid four thousand for it, and we kept it in print. In the last two years we sold almost four million copies." Some example! But it sure did help me understand Tom McCormack's approach to book publishing.

The thing that none of my interviewees seemed to mention about McCormack was that he was an ace at what Len Shatzkin's son Mike referred to in a juicy way as "the Black Art"—selecting books. "If you pick the right books," Mike explained, "then a lot of the sins of bad business are forgiven. And if you don't pick the right books, all the efficiency in the world can't save you." But when Tom McCormack threw his arms around *All Creatures Great and Small,* it caused some consternation among his colleagues in the Flatiron Building.

Sally Richardson remembers that when McCormack came back from London, "flushed with triumph with this new buy, we were all making fun of him. We kept saying, 'Tom, you're crazy. That's not what's selling. Sex is selling and big novels are selling, but not a story about a vet in 1937 in Yorkshire. That's never going to work.' " Tom Dunne seconded the notion.

When the book—with a ten-thousand-copy print run—landed in the stores, it looked like the doubters might have been right. Reviews came in slowly. McCormack was trying everything, even offering to veterinarian magazines the first serial rights for next to nothing. Still, attention was not being paid. All of a sudden, *The Chicago Tribune* ran a front-page review in its Sunday *Book World* section, which began: "If there is any justice, *All Creatures Great and Small* will become a classic of its kind."

Tom Dunne said it was then that Tom McCormack exhibited his genius. The head of the house had two decisions to make: whether or not to reprint, and how to maximize such a glowing review. Demand for the book was growing in the Chicago area, but nowhere else. Tom McCormack focused on returns so much— another Len Shatzkin carryover—that the company's returns, which averaged around fifteen percent, were way below the industry standard of forty percent. Of course, much of that gap was due to the basic elements of McCormack's approach to the game, namely: "make sure you use your fixed overhead up to capacity and publish as many books as you can as long as each one has more revenues than disbursements." He was doing just that with the British titles he bought, all packaged for publication, with hardly a drop of fixed overhead; the libraries would take whatever was left.

Second, he had to figure out how to use the fabulous *Chicago Tribune* review.

Tom decided to hit on two flanks. He ordered a massive 50,000-copy reprint for his tiny company, which would never be so tiny again. And he bought a full-page ad in *The New York Times Book Review* (which had not yet reviewed the book) and pasted the *Chicago Tribune*'s stunner to that expensive page. That did it. "So it looked as though we would survive," Tom said. In 1971 the company's profits had gone to $55,000, "and the year after that, when we introduced *All Creatures Great and Small,* to six-figure profits"—only five years after the company had been losing $150,000. St. Martin's was no longer a small company. And then came James Herriot's next winner—*All Things Bright and Beautiful.*

Oscar Dystel, the proprietor of Bantam Books, had bought the paperback rights to the Herriot works, but became nervous when McCormack sent him the jacket of *Bright and Beautiful.* What disturbed him was the cover blurb: "The warm and joyful sequel to *All Creatures Great and Small.*"

"You know, Tom," Oscar said, "sequels don't work. Don't call it a sequel."

"Oscar," Tom replied, "I am convinced that if there's anybody they want more of the same from, it's James Herriot, and that's what I'm going to do." Tom said that the second Herriot far outsold the first one "because, by then, *All Creatures Great and Small* was out in mass market and had built up a following."

After the first two Herriots came *All Things Wise and Wonderful* in 1977 and *The Lord God Made Them All* in 1981. You could say that the Lord Herriot made St. Martin's Press.

All of a sudden, St. Martin's became the secret Cinderella of book publishing. That's because Tom figured it would be easier to buy books at the right price if he kept his beggar's cup in play. (Not any more. The most recent paperback version of *All Creatures Great and Small* carried this line on its cover—"Multi-Million Bestseller.") It wasn't just that the book was selling so well north, east, west, and south of Chicago. St. Martin's had acquired it on the cheap: a $2,000 advance for the first volume, and not much more for the others. Added to that was the fact that St. Martin's was paying only a 12.5 percent royalty per book; not the usual 15 percent. Tom did volunteer to raise the royalty rate, but Herriot graciously declined Tom's offer. "This man really made me," the author told his agent.

Let's say they made each other. James Herriot was the one who opened up the world for St. Martin's Press, especially in London. No longer would McCormack have to flail his arms at all those live books in the agents' quarters, ready for the plucking for everybody, it seemed, except Tom McCormack. A few years later, when he and Sandra went to London, they actually received a call from Bruce Hunter at the lordly Higham agency.

"Listen, it just occurred to me that you're in town," Hunter said, as if St. Martin's were still an afterthought. "We're actually holding an auction in New York for this manuscript, but it's going to be a lot of money." McCormack told Hunter to send the manuscript to his hotel.

The manuscript was 1,529 pages long, an historical novel set in late nineteenth-century India at the height of the British Raj. It was written by M. M. Kaye, a seventy-year-old British woman who had been raised in India. She called her book *The Far Pavilions*. Both Sandra and Tom read chunks of it, and both were hooked. It was a milieu book for them, one they wanted never to end. Sandra was now an editor at her husband's company, well regarded for her skill in finding books. "This is a book we must have," Sandra told her husband. He smiled: "Ain't no one gonna win this book except us."

The bidding might have been closer, but the book's champion at Simon & Schuster, Michael Korda, was on vacation. S & S backed out, and McCormack got *The Far Pavilions* for $120,000. He then saw to it that the ending was modified for an American audience that tended to find unhappy endings disagreeable; the lovers were allowed to survive their disagreeable final crisis. That did it for Bantam, which bought paperback rights from Sally Richardson for $500,000.

By that time, in the late seventies, St. Martin's was hitting its stride. McCormack's strategy was to stay clear of "big book" auctions; he didn't much like dealing with agents, anyway; he thought they were muddying relationships between authors and editors. His gang kept buying loads of books in the Shatzkin manner, for small prices and small profits.

One such writer who had come to St. Martin's for a modest price was Rosamunde Pilcher. Both Tom Dunne and Sally Richardson loved her. Dunne had edited all her books, became her friend, visited with her regularly at her home in Scotland, and now publishes her son, Robin's, novels. The first ten Pilchers, romance novels, Tom said, "did okay, but nothing special." One day Sally Richardson told Pilcher, "Your books are wonderful; you should be writing bigger books."

"Oh, I can't," Pilcher said, "because my publisher in London wants them to only be a certain length."

And Sally said, "Don't worry. Write bigger, and if they turn you down, we'll give you the money they would've given you, plus some."

So Rosamunde Pilcher wrote bigger, and her eleventh novel, *The Shell Seekers,* was her breakthrough book, becoming a No. 1 bestseller.

IN THE MID-1980s, a young editor at St. Martin's, Michael Denneny, bought what Tom McCormack calls "the biggest single book of the gay world to this day," *And the Band Played On* by Randy Shilts, with the subtitle: "Politics, People, and the AIDS Epidemic." When Sally sent manuscripts to the Book-of-the-Month Club, there were lively go-rounds between our reader-editors. Some were excited by the book—nobody had yet written the definitive story about the growing AIDS tragedy—but some of us worried that it might be too raw for our members. Fortunately, one of our great reader-editors at the club, Joe Savago, took us naysayers on. When Joe read a book he loved, he was able to express such passion in his written reports and such emotion during discussions that he often made us see things his way. This time he urged us with a grave heart to take a book he felt would be around forever. We did take it, and he was there to savor the success of *And the Band Played On.*

One day shortly thereafter, he came into my office and said to me, "Al, I'm dying." In one of our lowest moments at BOMC, we lost Joe Savago to AIDS.

At St. Martin's, however, the book was creating a controversy between Tom McCormack and his sales and marketing people. Tom wanted to put out a tremendous number of copies on the book, but it looked as though there would be an initial lay-down of only 15,000 copies. At the same time, he wanted to put a price of $25 on the book. "You're talking about how you want us to get out 30,000," said his sales manager. "You're going to have to price it at $19.95."

"Twenty-five dollars," said the boss. "That's the price of the book." *And the Band Played On* sold over 100,000 copies in hardcover. For Tom McCormack, it was a matter of intuition, his confident sense of the Black Art, and the gut feeling that the people who would want this book would want it very much, and they would pay whatever they had to for it.

THE MOST EXPENSIVE book Tom McCormack ever bought was *The Silence of the Lambs.* But he wasn't the one who discovered it.

One day in the late seventies, McCormack took Richard Marek, a terrific editor of the golden age, to lunch. Marek had worked at a number of houses—Dial Press, Macmillan, World, Crown, Putnam's—and in his time he found and/or developed such writers as Robert Ludlum, Peter Straub, James Baldwin, Richard Condon, and John Irving. At that lunch Tom invited Marek to join St. Martin's with his own imprint. Dick warned Tom, "I will single-handedly up your returns rate." Tom, less cranky than he used to be, said, "Yeah, I know, but maybe we'll publish some good books." Marek joined St. Martin's in 1978.

"I thought Tom was the most brilliant person I had known in publishing," Dick Marek told me. "St. Martin's was making money hand over fist at a time in American publishing when everybody was struggling, and when the corporations were starting to buy the book companies, then wondering what the hell would they do with these tiny little places they had bought."

Richard Marek wanted to go after one book, if it ever got written. He had read a second novel from Thomas Harris. It was titled *Red Dragon.* "I thought it was the best real horror thriller that I had read by an American author," Dick said. "Everyone knew that Harris was working on a sequel that would follow the career of Hannibal Lecter—but nobody knew when it would be finished and who would publish it. Putnam had published Harris's first novel, *Black Sunday,* and six years later, *Red Dragon.* But the new one would be up for grabs.

Dick asked his longtime colleague, Joyce Engelson, who had come with him to St. Martin's, to try to find out what was going on with the new novel. Joyce told Harris's agent, Gloria Safire, "If Tom's next book ever goes free, Dick Marek would like to talk with you about buying it."

Along the way Marek and Tom Harris became pals. "We used to meet in dark bars in New York," Dick said. But there was still no book forthcoming.

And then, one day, Gloria Safire called Marek. "I've got wonderful news," she said. "Tom's study burned down, and he's going to need money to fix it."

Tom McCormack gave Harris $750,000 to fix it. It was the first book he bought for both hardcover and paperback rights. And he still says, "It was the best buy I ever made."

Alas, before Tom Harris finished the book, Dick Marek had left

St. Martin's to become publisher and president of E. P. Dutton. "When I got to read Tom's book," Dick said, "I told him it was perfect." But when it came in to St. Martin's, Tom McCormack didn't think it was perfect. He sent a long editorial letter to Harris with seven or eight key editorial suggestions. Harris came back and told McCormack he would not change a thing, and that if Tom insisted, he would leave St. Martin's and take his book with him. This really irked Harris's new high-powered agent, Mort Janklow. He and McCormack had never gotten along, and after Marek left St. Martin's, Janklow told Sally Richardson, "There's no way in hell I'm going to let that book be published by St. Martin's." Tom got his dander up and said, "Well, we have the contract and it's *here*."

St. Martin's published *The Silence of the Lambs* in 1988, but as Tom Harris wished it published. And a year later Sally Richardson took on the responsibilities of dealing with Harris on the paperback edition.

Sally had advanced steadily over the years, and in the early 1980s Tom McCormack decided to put her in charge of the company's new mass market line. At first Sally objected. "God, I don't know how to handle paperbacks," she told Tom. "I don't know anything about them."

"Well, neither do I," Tom said, "but it's not a brain science, and we'll learn." And they did.

Later Sally directed the trade paperbacks, too. When the trade paperback imprint was given a new name in 1995, it was Griffin, McCormack's birth name, but as Tom pointed out, "It made a great colophon. A griffin is half lion, half eagle." A few years later Tom promoted Sally to publisher of the hardcover business.

Now, here she was, asking Tom Harris to meet her in St. Martin's offices to discuss the paperback jacket. "I was terrified," she told me. "I had done a bunch of jackets and I had them on two windowsills. So Harris came in and he was very leery about being here, and I was nervous as hell, because I knew how important it was. And he saw all the covers, and I think he just realized in an instant how much we cared. So then we had a good meeting, and now he's a friend. I love Tom Harris."

BEFORE I ALLOWED Tom Dunne to go back to work that morning when I visited him, we started to reminisce. "We were poor," Tom said with a bit of a chuckle, "but drunk and happy. You know, we'd go out to those long lunches, and we'd all have a grand old time. And at every sales conference there was dancing. I'm not kidding. Three times a year we'd all go to some big, cheap Italian-type meal with red wine and sometimes marijuana in the bathroom, and then everyone would go dancing till four o'clock in the morning. I mean, it doesn't happen now. But it was like we were all young and stupid."

"Yeah," I said, thinking back to so many of my conversations with the linchpins of the golden age, who liked to drink and had struggled so much trying to fight off the consequences. "The drinkers have disappeared, that's for sure," I said lamely, not realizing that Tom Dunne had been one so affected.

"Well," he said, "they either died or, like myself, ended up in recovery, but happily."

It took a while for Tom to get happy, and he suffered through days when he didn't know how or if he could go on. He told me about one of those moments when a bitter fight broke out between him and Tom McCormack.

"He called me into his office one day when I was really feeling sorry for myself. I was very overstressed. It was like all hell was breaking loose, and I couldn't keep everything together. I knew I was really shorthanded and that I needed to add to my staff, and I was at my wits' end."

The first thing McCormack said to Dunne, was, "Now I don't want you to get upset."

Already seething, Dunne said sardonically, "Of course not."

McCormack told Dunne that somebody had called him, complaining that Dunne hadn't been calling back fast enough.

"You son of a bitch, I thought, *you wouldn't have called that person back either.* It was complete bullshit and he should have known that, and I went completely nuts. I just started screaming at him. He started screaming at me. Spit was flying and we were ready to come to blows, at which point for no good reason the personnel director opened Tom's door and said, 'Hi, I'm ready for the meeting.' So the air went out of the balloon."

Perhaps Tom McCormack didn't sleep well that night, because the next day he came to Dunne, hat in hand, and said, "Look, I know you're overtaxed, and you're obviously doing too much, and you need some help. So hire anybody you want in the price range we agreed on."

The person Tom Dunne wanted was Ruth Cavin, who had been buying mysteries for Walker and Company. Cavin had done a bang-up job at Walker, a house that was even more frugal than St. Martin's. She could never buy a mystery for more than two thousand dollars, yet she always seemed to find some promising new writer. She would bring these good ones along and eventually lose them to a house that had more money to spend. She was more than happy to have Tom Dunne liberate her.

When Tom McCormack heard whom Dunne had chosen, he wasn't so happy. "I guess you don't know how old she is," he said. Tom Dunne knew that Cavin was older than he, but he had never asked her age. "She's seventy-one," McCormack informed him. "But I said you could hire whomever you want. Uh, she won't be around here much longer."

As I write this, Ruth Cavin, now just shy of ninety years old, is still with Tom Dunne, editing some fifty books a year. The happiest part of my visit came when Ruth popped into his office, still a stately, vigorous woman, even with a bad back. She looked at me and said hello, but didn't immediately recognize me until Dunne mentioned my name. "Oh, my," she said, "I know you, yes." We hugged and kissed. I had known her and her husband both personally because we lived in White Plains, and we used to see each other from time to time at publishing parties or when we lunched together. I had followed her career and greatly admired her for her grace and strength and amazing energy. I told Tom Dunne that he was lucky to have her.

WHEN I WAS walking back home from the Flatiron Building, I thought about St. Martin's and the odd array of people who had worked there over the years—odd, but nonetheless dedicated to Tom McCormack's vision of what a book publishing house should be. I thought back to some of the other new houses that I was also writing about—Farrar, Straus and Giroux, Grove Press, George Braziller, Atheneum—all of which had literary aspirations, with editors who kept looking for the next Joyce, Hemingway, Proust, or the next Faulkner, even though they never found them. FSG had all those Nobel Prizes; Grove Press had Samuel Beckett and the legacy of freeing D. H. Lawrence and Henry Miller from the censors; George Braziller could take pride in bringing to America marvelous foreign authors and *Jazz,* the last fantastic work made into a book by Matisse; and Atheneum had André Schwarz-Bart's *The Last of the Just,* among other achievements.

By contrast, at St. Martin's you hardly ever heard the L-word mentioned. Literary fiction and literary nonfiction were not among McCormack's publishing ambitions. This was a house that truly cared for popular entertainment and filled its needs with category fiction (mysteries, science fiction, gothics, romances, and the like), but also commercial works of high quality, such as Rosamunde Pilcher's *The Shell Seekers.* Tom McCormack claims that by the early eighties "we had published more fiction than anyone else in the English-speaking world." Well, he certainly found a way to make that formula work when he was there, as Sally Richardson does today with a much changed and expanded publishing house.

In 1995, the once great Macmillan colossus was sold to the Georg von Holtzbrinck Publishing Group of Stuttgart. And the Holtzbrinck family took over St. Martin's Press as they would Farrar, Straus and Giroux, Henry Holt, Times Books, and other imprints. That introduced such changes as direct reporting, five-year plans, and close coordination with the other American properties. It was not a world Tom McCormack was likely to enjoy, even though he had made those drastic changes needed to save the company when he took over. He would leave peaceably.

He chose to retire on his sixty-fifth birthday, January 5, 1997. And the first thing he did was to take that pencil down from the shelf, after years of neglect, and begin scribbling at his plays again.

Meanwhile, his troupe plays on at St. Martin's.

INTERLUDE: THE PRETTIEST
BACKLIST IN THE BUSINESS

Even though Donald S. Lamm's father had been an editor at Macmillan (before the Depression left him without a job), book publishing was not an immediate thought for Don Lamm. After serving in the U.S. Army Counter Intelligence Corps, Don studied seventeenth-century English literature at Oxford University before looking for a job. In 1956, after an interview with George Brockway, the executive editor at W. W. Norton & Company, Don became a college traveler and, after three years on the road, an editor in the college department. In 1976 he succeeded Brockway as the president of the oldest and largest publishing house owned entirely by its employees. Although the college department has been a profit engine for Norton since the 1950s, over the same years trade editors have delivered a solid range of bestsellers to the house, among them William J. Lederer and Eugene Burdick's *The Ugly American,* Betty Friedan's *The Feminine Mystique,* Douglass Wallop's *The Year the Yankees Lost the Pennant* (remembered best as *Damn Yankees*), Joseph P. Lash's *Eleanor and Franklin* (a National Book Award winner), Vincent Bugliosi's *Helter Skelter,* Patrick O'Brian's novels about the British Navy, Michael Lewis's *Liar's Poker,* and Jared Diamond's *Guns, Germs, and Steel,* as well as volumes by such award-winning poets as Adrienne Rich,

A. R. Ammons, and Rita Dove. Don once explained the job he inherited and handled with verve: "Judgment in publishing ought to reflect three factors: taste, experience and—intuition." Emphasizing this last word, he raised a moistened finger to the wind.

DONALD LAMM

I won't say that our firm was casually run, but we never really put the kind of emphasis on endless accounting drills. There was the assumption that the president and the treasurer would work hand in glove on financial matters. I don't think it was until 1978 or so that we began to do forecasts and budgets. We just had this notion that we would prosper if we kept doing what we did—the college department producing at least one new successful textbook a year, the trade department periodically turning out bestsellers while maintaining what Bennett Cerf once dubbed "the prettiest backlist in the business."

During a lunch close to the time George Brockway decided to retire—he had been chairman of the board—I asked George, "If there is one thing you could advise me about running the shop, what would that be?"

And he replied, "Never get involved in auctions."

Of course, he was right. You get intoxicated by the chase, and before long you're paying far more advances than most books warrant. But times changed, and the firm could no longer stand aloof from auctions after the early eighties.

Even before then there was one auction that gave us a particular delight. It happened in the mid-sixties. We were one of three firms that were approached by the agent Dorothy Olding, to consider making an offer on the memoirs of Dean Acheson. The other firms involved were Harper's and Random House. George immediately gathered the board together and said, "Look, we have a choice. We can make a substantial offer for Acheson's memoirs, or we can move uptown to larger quarters." We were now sort of captive tenants in a building acquired by Yeshiva University down in lower Fifth Avenue. The board was unanimous: "Let's go for Acheson."

So we made an offer of $180,000, which was huge for Norton, the highest we'd ever gone. In an effort to give further evidence of our zeal to secure the memoir, George and I had also collaborated on a letter to Acheson. We knew that he was not only one of the greatest secretaries of state in our history, but an elegant writer, too. We suggested to Acheson that, in addition to a large trade sale, there were some changes in organization that would enable us to pull out individual paperbacks for college use. Dorothy Olding said that appealed greatly to Acheson. And so did the fact that we opted for what turned out to be Acheson's favorite title for the book.

Within thirty-six hours, we heard that Harper's had made a smaller offer. As for Random House—at that time a creature of RCA—Bennett Cerf called Dorothy, naming an offer that was higher than ours and saying that he was waiting to have it cleared by General Sarnoff, RCA's one-star CEO. When she told that to Acheson, his response was caustic and decisive: "Dorothy, I have spent too much of my life waiting for things to be cleared by generals. Let's go with Norton."

Present at the Creation: My Years in the State Department was published in 1969 and won the Pulitzer Prize for history. Five years later we were able to move uptown.

Part II

THE SURVIVORS

The earlier years—the ones I've been telling you about—
tend to blur into each other as a kind of golden time, and
when I think about them at all, even the not-so-great things,
I can't help feeling a sort of glow.

—KAZUO ISHIGURO, *NEVER LET ME GO*

6

INDEPENDENT PUBLISHING
AT ITS HEIGHT

The Viking Press

Only a writer can understand how a great editor is a father,
mother, teacher, personal devil and personal god.

—JOHN STEINBECK

Before I make the outrageous suggestion that the hallmark
of Viking's success as an independent publishing house
has been the continuous excellence of its editorial staff, I
should disclose that I spent nine years in the 1990s working for
Viking in an avuncular editorial role.

That is, because of my advanced age, they gave me authors of
advanced stature, whose editors had left town: Saul Bellow,
Robertson Davies, William Kennedy, and T. C. Boyle. I did have
a grand time fussing over their latest works. By fussing, I mean
since these authors were all painstaking craftsmen and perfec-
tionists, as well as visionary, I learned to stay out of their way,
becoming . . . well . . . sort of a stowaway on each author's ship.
I was still allowed to bring in new authors on my own. Much in
the way Viking editors acted both before, during, and after my

golden age, my acquisitions were a mixture of fiction and nonfiction, both literary and popular. It felt so good being in the company of dedicated kids like Dan Frank (though at least a generation younger, he was my mentor, for I had never before been a book editor), Carolyn Carlson, Kathryn Court, Pam Dorman, Nan Graham, Courtney Hodell, Kris Puopolo, David Stanford, Dawn Seferian, Amanda Vaill, Mindy Werner, and Wendy Wolf. Over half of the crowd is still at their life's work.

I was also given the opportunity there to explore the past on my own, reading archival correspondence between authors and their editors down in the basement. One day I was amazed to stumble over a 1931 contract for James Joyce's next novel, untitled. In it was an insertion that Joyce insisted had to be part of the contract: If the author's editor, B. W. Huebsch, should leave the Viking Press to go to another firm, Joyce and his book would be allowed to follow him. In those days, such an "editor's clause" must have been exceedingly rare. That Joyce novel turned out to be *Finnegans Wake*. It was published in 1939, and Ben Huebsch was indeed its American editor.

FIVE MONTHS AFTER opening the store for business in August 1925, twenty-five-year-old Harold K. Guinzburg made the move of his life. He and his partner, George S. Oppenheimer, bought the distinguished B. W. Huebsch and Company, which, after publishing many illustrious authors, had fallen on hard times. The other significant move they had made earlier was to name their company. (It became exclusively Guinzburg's company in 1933, when Oppenheimer left to write screenplays in Hollywood, some with Dorothy Parker.) Rockwell Kent designed the colophon, a Viking ship (Kent also designed the Random House colophon). The partners took resonance from the image of the ship, calling their vessel, though not yet seaworthy, "a symbol of enterprise, adventure and exploration in the publishing field—to acclaim treasure when we find it, but avoid calling brass, gold." Fair enough. Their first treasure was Ben Huebsch.

Huebsch had started his own firm in 1901; it was noted by several literary historians that he had thus become the first Jew to enter general publishing in the United States in the twentieth century. His greater claim to fame, however, was discovering the Irishman James Joyce. (I hope that Mr. Huebsch will forgive me, for I have just violated a prime Huebsch dictum. The patron saint of Viking could not stand editors who claimed to have discovered an author. "The author is not a discovery," Huebsch always insisted. "The author is the discoverer." Maybe so, but I still maintain that it is the editor who has to dig out the pearl in the sand pile and clean it up.)

Alfred A. Knopf, who had first met Huebsch in 1912 and later became a friend, spoke of Huebsch this way: "He helped people who really knew how to write, was able to discuss their work with them in terms of equality, and believed that writers should write, and publishers should publish."

In addition to Joyce, Huebsch brought with him to Viking such authors as D. H. Lawrence, Sherwood Anderson (he published Anderson's masterwork, *Winesburg, Ohio*), Van Wyck Brooks, Thorstein Veblen, plus a young editor, Marshall Best, who would one day succeed Huebsch as editor in chief. In fact, the three iconic editorial guideposts for Viking, almost from its birth into the 1960s, were Ben Huebsch, Marshall Best, and a Romanian giant of letters, Pascal Covici.

In a long and dazzling career, Huebsch became an august figure in book publishing all over the world. In 1921 an international writers' organization called PEN was founded by John Galsworthy. The next year, Huebsch helped establish the PEN American Center. The only mistake he may have made as an editor (which he laughed off) was turning down a big trashy novel that he couldn't stand. So *The Egyptian* by Mika Waltari went elsewhere, selling millions of copies all over the world.

In 1956, Huebsch retired from full-time work and became a roving editor for Viking, scouting for books all over the world. "At noon, when he was on the premises," Harold Guinzburg's son, Tom, recalled with a smile, "Ben would emerge from his office with a cane, tap his way down editorial row, and turn to one of our young assistants, asking, 'Would a lovely youngee like yourself keep an elderly gentleman company for lunch?' And they'd go out and come back an hour and a half later, both of them in love with each other. He was so courtly."

On October 18, 1964, Huebsch was in London working with the Joyce estate, and he sent Tom Guinzburg a note: "Nothing much new," he wrote, "I had the usual kind of three hours with the estate people. I'll be taking a nap in a minute and going on to Sweden tomorrow." Huebsch died that night in his sleep. He was in his eighty-ninth year.

PASCAL COVICI had spent a frustrating ten-year period trying to make a financial success of Covici-Friede, the publishing house he shared with Donald Friede. In 1938, when the company was about to fold, Harold Guinzburg sent Covici a telegram: "Don't you want to get off the ship?" Covici did, bringing his first mate, John Steinbeck, right along with him.

Covici was a big, strong, larger-than-life figure with a shock of white hair. Malcolm Cowley, Viking's priceless editorial consultant over the years, described Covici's physical presence this way: "The big shoulders, the clear blue eyes under white hair, the hand on one's arm, the piratical slouch of his brown hat, the bold features breaking into a smile, the slow chuckle that became a booming laugh, the drawer on his desk that opened as he reached for a cigar." Other major literary critics described him as being the equal of Maxwell Perkins. "Every author Pat worked with," Tom Guinzburg said, "had to have the best treatment. Whether it was Bellow or Arthur Miller or Steinbeck, or even some first novelist,

Pat would be in the office, banging on my desk—'Come on, Tom, this one is the most important book we've ever published! Come on, Tom, we have to have some advertising, we must do this for this one young man!'

"I can remember when Artie Miller was married to Marilyn Monroe," Tom went on. "There she was, sitting in the Covici kitchen by herself, while Miller was out rehearsing the play he was working on. Monroe spent a lot of those evenings with the Covicis, even trying to learn something about Jewish food. She was just so far out of her depth, but was so nice about it. She'd say, 'Yeah, well, *latke*, I mean, what is it?' Later in the evening Miller would come to collect her."

Covici seemed to understand what each of his authors, especially his key ones—Miller, Bellow, and Steinbeck—needed from him. My wife, Rosa, and I once visited Saul Bellow at his Vermont home, and one of the first things Saul asked me was whether I had known Covici. Sadly, I hadn't. Saul spent the rest of the afternoon describing a character that belonged in a Bellow novel. He dedicated *Herzog* "To Pat Covici, a great editor and better yet, a generous friend."

In 1935, still at Covici-Friede, Pat Covici was reading John Steinbeck's novel, *In Dubious Battle*. "I had a letter from Covici which sounded far from over-enthusiastic," Steinbeck wrote. "It gave me some confidence in the man. I like restraint." He then went on to quote what Covici said: " 'I am interested in your work and would like to arrive at an arrangement with Miss McIntosh [Steinbeck's agent].' My estimation of him went up immediately." Covici became Steinbeck's editor and stayed with him ever after. In 1952, when he had finished *East of Eden,* Steinbeck wrote to Covici: "The dedication is to you with all the admiration and affection that has been distilled from our singularly blessed association of many, many years."

Covici died in 1964, two months before Huebsch. "Like an old prospector," Bellow said at the memorial service, "Covici rose every morning to look for treasure, never doubting he would strike it rich." Steinbeck voiced his love for Covici by saying, "For thirty years Pat was my collaborator and my conscience. He demanded of me more than I had, and thereby caused me to be more than I should have been without him."

How could the young ones coming into the house in those post-war years—Helen Taylor, Denver Lindley (on the day President Kennedy died, Taylor and Lindley ran off and got married; no one seems to have known about their romance), Catherine Carver, Aaron Asher, Alan Williams, Elisabeth Sifton, Cork Smith—how could these talented editors not have felt the touch of angels on their shoulders?

Jonathan Galassi, Farrar, Straus and Giroux's brilliant head of house, never worked for Viking, but he remembers, when he was a student in England, being invited to breakfast by Alan Williams. "I was very starry-eyed," Jonathan said, "totally gaga, wanted to work there. It was a fabulous editorial department. This was independent publishing at its absolute height."

IT WAS CLOSE to that, all right, but the president of Viking Press, Thomas H. Guinzburg, surely had something to do with it. In a large part it was because he grew up inspired by the Viking heritage—its editors—and by the abiding influence of his father over the years. When Tom was nine years old, Harold Guinzburg brought him a children's book in manuscript form. Young Tom looked at the pictures and then read the opening sentence: "Once upon a time in Spain there was a little bull and his name was Ferdinand." He found the story so easy and nice to read that he told his father, "I want to read it again."

"Four million copies later," Tom told me with a shy smile, recalling the pleasure of reading *Ferdinand the Bull,* "the experience made me feel like I might someday be suited for my father's profession." He loved his father, and he tried hard to emulate him. When Harold Guinzburg went off to war—he was one of the founders of the Office of War Information (OWI)—the son, at age eighteen, joined the Marines.

It was a bewildering experience. For one thing, Tom immediately discovered that his parents had never really prepared him for the slings and arrows of anti-Semitism. At 6 A.M. on a Sunday on his third day in the Marines, his platoon leader summoned the group to church. "All right, you fuckheads, get out of here and get in line! Everybody who's a Protestant, you get in that line. You Catholics get in the other line. Anybody else—make your own line."

Guinzburg just stood there, not knowing what to do. "You fuckhead!" the corporal screamed. "What line are you on?"

"Well, sir," said the recruit, "I'm not religious."

"Oh, yeah?" He grabbed Tom's dog tags hanging around his neck. "Jesus," he said, "what a name. What's that H stand for?"

"He— . . . Hebrew?" Tom intoned as a question, because he had never set foot in a synagogue or a temple. He was told, "Go make your own fucking line."

In February 1945, Private Guinzburg struggled onto Iwo Jima with eighty others from his battalion. Tom said, "Only eight or nine made it." One historian described the attack against the Japanese defense as "throwing human flesh against reinforced concrete." Later, Tom suffered a concussion and was burned in the leg by a mortar shell filled with napalm. He came back from war, as many of us did, reborn. And, at Yale, his father's college, he began to solidify his ambitions.

One of his favorite teachers at Yale was Norman Holmes Pearson, who, Tom said, "was probably the most popular English professor on the Yale campus." During the war Pearson had worked for Harold Guinzburg in the OWI, so he kept an eye on the son. In his senior year, Tom was managing editor of the *Yale Daily*

News. One day he got a message to report to Norman Pearson's office. When he walked in, Pearson said to him, "What are you going to do next in your life?"

"Well," Tom said, "I'm drawn toward publishing."

"Let me give you some advice," said his professor. "Go sow some more wild oats. Your father's one of the great men that I've ever known. But if you work for him now he's going to treat you harshly, because he probably thinks you need it."

Tom did as he was told. For two years in Paris he hung out on the Left Bank with a gang of literary expatriates, most of whom had been his childhood friends—George Plimpton, Peter Matthiessen, William Pène du Bois, Harold Humes, John Train, William Styron, and Donald Hall (a recent poet laureate of the United States). They got into serious stuff, too, including the founding of *The Paris Review* in 1953. Tom came back to New York to work for Viking in 1953, heeding his father's advice to "go do some manual stuff—be a salesman, work in the publicity department. You're not going to be an editor right away. How could you be? Just because you're smart doesn't mean you know anything about publishing." So he started in publicity.

Tom had the good luck to be befriended by one of the sterling Viking elders, Malcolm Cowley. While becoming the literary historian of the American Century—among his best-known works are *A Second Flowering: Works and Days of the Lost Generation* and *And I Worked at the Writer's Trade*—Cowley served the company for over fifty-six years. Tom actually met him for the first time before going to work for his father. "The first thing Malcolm said to me," Tom said, was, 'I've got this manuscript, and I can't convince your old man, but maybe you'll like it.'" Tom read *On the Road* by Jack Kerouac and did, indeed, like it; in 1957, Viking published this seminal work. "I found a $20 check the other day in a box someplace," Tom told me. "It was from Jack, apologizing, he wrote, 'for last night. I acted like a horse's ass. I don't remember how you got me home.' Kerouac had gone on the Steve Allen television show blind drunk, and they had to hook him off the stage."

Malcolm Cowley was also a teacher for most of his life, which gave him immediate access to prominent new talent. In one of his writing classes at Stanford, he found a writer he thought could go places, and he brought Ken Kesey to Viking. Boom! Kesey's first novel was *One Flew Over the Cuckoo's Nest,* and *Sometimes a Great Notion* came next. Kesey continued to be published in my years at Viking with a fine young editor, David Stanford, at his side.

Tom's apprenticeship ended in 1961 upon the death of Harold K. Guinzburg. He took over his father's house.

IMMEDIATELY, TOM HELD OUT a golden hand, beckoning a new generation of vital young editors to his side. His first editorial hire was Corlies Morgan Smith, who became one of the most loved editors of the Golden Age. Smith, who was always known as Cork, had grown up in Philadelphia, where his father taught English at the University of Pennsylvania and built himself a seven-thousand-volume library. Cork went to Yale and tried graduate school for three weeks, then quit. But he didn't know what to do with his life. On the recommendation of a friend, he applied for a job with the CIA. "What do you think about the significance of the recent French elections?" the interviewer asked Cork. The kid just laughed and said, "I'm sorry, I didn't know they'd had any French elections." Somewhat to his astonishment, he was hired. (The interviewer told him later, "I admired your honesty there.")

When his father quit teaching to open a bookstore in Philadelphia, Cork quit the CIA and went to work in the store. He stayed for three and a half years. Business was not great, so when his father died in 1955, Cork closed down the bookstore.

Then, even though he claimed that he wasn't in love with the idea, he gave publishing a thought. He went to see Pete Martin, a big-name writer at *The Saturday Evening Post,* who had been a customer of the bookstore. "Why don't you go across the street to Lippincott?" Martin suggested to Cork, and he called the person he knew there and said, "I have a bright young man here." Cork went over for the interview and was hired by George Stevens, who had joined Lippincott in 1940 to head the general trade books division.

The J. B. Lippincott Company went all the way back to 1850. In the 1950s it was still a house that mattered. Cork did everything at Lippincott. He read submissions, he wrote copy, he even sold some accounts, which, he admitted, "I was very bad at." Then, in 1959 Cork made the discovery of his life. (Sorry again, Mr. Huebsch.)

The paperback house New American Library, under the creative guidance of Victor Weybright, had since 1952 begun publishing a semiannual magazine of short stories, poems, and other literary pieces, many of them by new authors. Called *New World Writing,* it worked well for a few years, and then began to slacken. In 1959 Weybright decided it wasn't in their interest to publish it anymore. The person in charge of *New World Writing* at NAL was Arabel Porter, a woman with an extraordinary reputation in book publishing. Truman "Mac" Talley, who was Weybright's stepson and who was working there at that time, told me, "Arabel Porter was one of the nicest, gentlest people in the world." ("Mac" Talley is the editor for this book, I might add.) Sandy Richardson, who was working with Cork as a Lippincott editor, was a friend of Porter's. He suggested to George Stevens, "Why don't we try to buy it from NAL?" To everyone's surprise, Stevens said, "Sure, why not? We can use it to get young authors and stuff; it won't cost anything much." In addition to their editorial responsibilities Sandy and Cork became coeditors of *New World Writing.*

The second short story bought for Lippincott's first issue of the magazine was by a twenty-two-year-old writer named Thomas Pynchon. The story was called "Low-lands." The opening sentence of "Low-lands" read: "At half past five in the afternoon Dennis Flange was still entertaining the garbage man." Cork thought, *You've got to read the next sentence, don't you?* And he showed the story to George Stevens. "I don't know what you like about this thing," Stevens told Smith. "I think this guy will be selling used Chevrolets within a year." Cork thought, *What a nice turn—not new Chevies, used ones.* But Stevens allowed Cork to buy it.

When this issue of *New World Writing* came out, Pynchon's agent, Candida Donadio, called Cork. She said, "Tom Pynchon wants to write a novel." She also told Cork that she had an offer from Jim Silberman, who was then at Dial Books, for $1,500, $500 down. "But since you published the story," Candida said, "if you'll match that offer you can have it."

"Well, we like his stuff," Cork said. "What's the novel about?"

"I don't know."

"Have you got anything to show?"

"No, nothing to show."

"Is it going to be a long novel, short novel?"

Candida said, "I don't know."

"Well, what are we buying on?"

"You're buying it so he can get a ticket to Seattle, where he's got a job."

Cork and Sandy went to Stevens and said they'd really love to do this. "Well, I don't think very highly of this guy," Stevens said, "but it's only going to cost us five hundred, and, after all, the purpose of this enterprise is to basically get writers, so go ahead."

Pynchon was working for Boeing in Seattle, and Cork waited for his manuscript. And waited. For about a year nobody heard from him. Then one day a manuscript arrived in a black box, a long novel of about seven hundred pages. Cork read it and "fell hopelessly in love with it."

He and Pynchon worked for about three months on the book, which was called *V.* It sold somewhere between 12,000 and 15,000 copies and received an amazing critical reception. Pynchon's second novel, *The Crying of Lot 49,* was also published by Lippincott, but by that time Cork had moved on.

CORK SMITH

My first couple of years at Viking I was very lucky, because Ben Huebsch and Covici were both alive, and both had all their marbles. I mean, they weren't doddering. I spent a good deal of time with Covici. He was a marvelous man, a very warm fellow. He would ask me to read some stuff, which flattered me somewhat. One day I read a manuscript for him of a novelist—I can't remember his name—which was under option, not yet under contract. I wrote a long, almost a term paper kind of memo about it. Pat called me into his office, and he thanked me, said he agreed with me the book should not be published, it should be turned down. Then he said to me, "You read the book up here, didn't you?" He pointed to his forehead. I said, yes, because I had. "You can't read fiction that way," he said. "If fiction is going to get you, it's going to get you here." He didn't point to his heart. He pointed to his stomach. He said, "If it gets you there, it can get you in your head."

I went to both Huebsch's and Covici's memorial services. Every time I go to a funeral now there are ten speakers, and they mostly talk about themselves. I wind up disliking the person who died.

The first book I did for Viking, not long after I left Lippincott, was Jimmy Breslin's *Can't Anybody Here Play This Game?* What happened was that I got a call from Sandy Richardson. He said, "Look, I just tried to sell people on a guy called Breslin, who's written a piece in *Sports Illustrated* called 'The Worst Baseball Team in History.' I think it's pretty damn good; he's a pretty good writer." He said, "Nobody here wants to publish a book about a team that has lost more than anybody ever had in history. I think they're wrong."

I got the manuscript from Breslin's agent, Sterling Lord. I loved this stuff. Tom loved this stuff, which is what counted. And the rest is history. It sold ten to twelve thousand copies and stayed in print in paperback for many years. It may still be in print.

The decision on what we bought was Tom's. He could say no to anything—except I never knew him to stand in the way of something that somebody felt strongly about. A good example of that is the most controversial thing I did when I was there.

The editorial meetings were held once a week. At the meetings, Marshall Best sat at one end of the table and Tom at the other end. Marshall Best had been with Viking more or less forever. I think he was a very complicated fellow. He was rather cold, rather impersonal, quite shy, but strong. He didn't tolerate nonsense much. He didn't have much sense of humor, or I never saw it. But he certainly knew writing, and he was completely dedicated to Viking; it was his whole life.

Sitting around Tom and Marshall were Denver Lindley, Helen Taylor, Pat Covici, and Malcolm Cowley. Then there were the young ones—me and Catherine Carver and Aaron Asher.

We'd published a first novel by a guy called Leonard Cohen. He was a Canadian, and we had done a book of his poetry. The novel was called *The Favorite Game*. It was okay, it was well written. Tom had bought it in England. I worked with Cohen, and then contracted with his agent, Mike Watkins, for an unspecified novel. We gave him, as I remember, a contract for $3,000; I think for the first book we had paid him $1,500. We didn't know anything about the new one, except that it was a novel. *Beautiful Losers* turned out to be very explicit for the time. There was a jerking-off scene in it, and a lot of stuff. But I thought it was wonderful. Still do— I reread it a couple of years ago. Anyway, there was a sharp difference of opinion editorially about this book. I think I said to Tom in my memo, "There are some issues of faith and morals or something going on here, because it's very, very explicit." We had eight readings. Plus Tom.

So at the editorial meeting everybody—I remember this well enough—was extremely eloquent, with very well-reasoned pros and cons. Marshall was strongly against it. I mean, the opening line in the memo he wrote was, "As far as I'm concerned, this is gilded shit." And Marshall never said "Damn!" He felt that it would be bad for Viking. He was always a defender of the faith here. So the meeting went on for about an hour, and then Tom said, "Thank you for all your opinions. I'll let you know how it comes out." We all trooped out. I went into his office, and I said, "Look Tom, I don't know what you're going to decide, but I promised Mike Watkins I'd let him know something by the end of the day today."

And Tom said, "You'll be able to tell him. Why don't you go to lunch? I'm going to go take a steam bath and come back." A steam bath! I thought that was a bad sign. So I came back from lunch, and I was sitting in my office, which was down the hall at 625 Madison Avenue, and he came by, stuck his head in the door, and said, "Take the book."

That was it. Nobody said anything after that. It was a credit to the people, the naysayers; Marshall and the others never said anything. And, in fact, we sold maybe 2,500 copies. I remember Aaron Asher saying of *Beautiful Losers:* "Never has a book this dirty done so badly."

[In 2006, the same Leonard Cohen, still very much with us, was celebrated with a documentary film titled *Leonard Cohen: I'm Your Man.* It was all about his life as a poet and singer-songwriter. The *Times Literary Supplement* referred to him as "the growling Zen monk and laureate of unrequited yearning." Take that, you naysayers!]

I stayed at Viking throughout the good times. I left in 1984 with no regrets. One shouldn't have regrets. Because whatever you did got you to there. It's like Whistler, when he was being sued by John Ruskin. At some point during the trial Ruskin said to Whistler, "How long did it take you to do this painting, Mr. Whistler?" Said Mr. Whistler, "My entire life." Good answer.

In 1967, Cork accomplished what he always wanted to accomplish: He brought Thomas Pynchon to the house. As with his experience with *V,* he didn't know what the novel would be about. "Candida wanted $25,000 for it, more or less sight unseen," Cork said. "Pynchon got $5,000 up front." The novel came in five years later. "I did nothing on it," Cork said. "I gave them my memo, saying 'I'm not quite sure what this book is about, but it is brilliant from page one to the end.'"

He did more than that. I have a copy of his Editor's Summary, subtitled Full Description of Book. (In parentheses he added—"a very lumpy description.") Referring to it as "this vision, this hallucination of America," he was somehow able to explain the plot of *Gravity's Rainbow*. It is, he said, "one of the most intricately constructed novels ever written. The reader may feel himself flung far away from the narrative path sometimes, but the devious and masterful creator always brings him back."

But how would Viking get people to read it? It was Cork's idea to publish simultaneously a hardcover edition as well as a trade paperback edition, exactly the same as the hardcover except for the binding.

My colleagues at the Book-of-the-Month Club who read *Gravity's Rainbow* (I confess, I hadn't then) raved about it. We decided to use the paperback edition. It's odd, but I still remember what we sold—15,000 copies. Not too bad for a middlebrow audience.

The novel was published in February 1973 and exceeded BOMC's sales, with 45,000 copies in hardcover. The reclusive author sent this telegram to the president of Viking: "DEAR TOM GUINZBURG WHEREVER YOU ARE, I THOUGHT YOU WOULD LIKE TO KNOW I'M NUMBER EIGHT AND MY FRIEND FREDDIE IS NUMBER TWO."

Pynchon was referring to the fact that Frederick Forsyth's second thriller, *The Odessa File,* was No. 2 on the *New York Times* bestseller list and *Gravity's Rainbow* was No. 8. Christopher Lehmann-Haupt in *The New York Times* wrote of *Gravity's Rainbow,* "If I was banished to the moon tomorrow and could take only four books along, this would have to be one of them." In fact, it stayed on the *Times's* list for four weeks. It then went on to share the National Book Award for fiction with a short story collection by Isaac Bashevis Singer.

Viking had one other bestseller in that glorious year of 1973: *Serpico* by Peter Maas. That led me to ask Cork Smith what was his best period during his twenty-two-year life at Viking. He didn't mention Pynchon. Instead, he said: "It was in the seventies, when I was editing Roger Angell—just a collection. Isn't that funny?" he said. "Because I remember at the time thinking—*See, it's not going to get any better than this.*"

AS MUCH AS Cork contributed to Viking in the golden age, it was never a one-person show. Tom Guinzburg's next editorial hire, in 1964, was Aaron Asher, who had established his reputation as a first-rate literary editor at Knopf and then at Meridian Books. It was odd that in this period of high camaraderie "Double A" (Tom's nickname for Asher) would spend five years at Viking, never quite fitting in with the others. He earned a reputation there for being a prickly kind of guy, difficult to work with; yet he was also a person who knew how to think as a publisher. He also translated Milan Kundera's *Book of Laughter and Forgetting* from the French. His wife, Linda, still translates important international literary works. About Aaron, his fellow editor, Elisabeth Sifton, insisted: "We all did better work when Aaron was around."

Asher's last big job at Viking was working with Saul Bellow on *Mr. Sammler's Planet,* which went on to win Bellow his third National Book Award. (Later, Double A was Bellow's editor at Harper & Row for *The Dean's December.*) Asher was on vacation when the second proofs of *Mr. Sammler's Planet* landed at Viking. Cork was the backup editor for Bellow and had to handle the proofs closely. At one point he hustled into the office of Elisabeth Sifton and flung down a piece of paper on her desk. "Look at that!" he said. "Look what that bastard did!" It was a page from *Mr. Sammler's Planet* with a heavy revision and two handwritten lines in the middle of the paragraph. "Look," Cork repeated with some heat. "Bellow took a perfect sentence and made it better!"

When we met, Aaron told me that his Viking period was the best of times for him in his publishing career. And he did enjoy a brilliant career, editing six Philip Roth novels at various houses, Saul Bellow, Arthur Miller, Kundera, and other literary luminaries. Alas, Aaron Asher, seventy-eight years old, died on March 16, 2008.

TOM GUINZBURG made another ten-strike when he hired Elisabeth Sifton in 1968. She was the daughter of the brilliant theologian Reinhold Niebuhr, who, Hiram Haydn wrote, was "as urbane as Talleyrand, hiding his passionate metaphysical ache under an almost suave civility." His daughter was much different. Elisabeth brought little publishing experience with her to Viking, but a vast intelligence. She was the one, for instance, who opened the house to high-category nonfiction. "I very much liked working with the very best journalists," she told me. "The good ones were as scrupulous and intelligent and interpretatively strong as good historians, but they were more fun."

She was thinking about such authors as Victor Navasky, the sterling editor of *The Nation* magazine, whose book *Naming Names* about HUAC's investigation of Hollywood "radicals" won the National Book Award; Peter Maas, with his bestseller *Serpico;* and the three-person "Inside" muckraking team of London's *Sunday Times*—Lewis Chester, Godfrey Hodgson, and Bruce Page (under the supervision of the *Times*'s Sunday editor, Harold Evans). The first book Elisabeth did with them was a Theodore White kind of treatment on the 1968 presidential campaign. Titled *An American Melodrama,* it became a Book-of-the-Month Club Main Selection and a bestseller for Viking. Later, she took over the wonderful Canadian novelist Robertson Davies and Saul Bellow, working with him on *Humboldt's Gift.* "The trouble with Bellow," she said, "was that he liked to revise. He revised famously. Hugely!" (I found that out, too, when I did a turn as Bellow's editor on two of his last three books.) "He liked being copyedited, sort of double-checked," Elisabeth said. "You know, Auden said that love is a form of attention. Saul wanted you to pay attention."

The author she had "the most intense, rewarding, and difficult relations with" was Tom's old friend, Peter Matthiessen. Way back, Harold Guinzburg had said to his son, "Thomas, you know you're going to have to decide quite early on whether you want to publish your friends, or whether you want to keep your friends."

"That's why Matthiessen and I every so often would break up," Tom said. A bit perturbed by the memory, he stared into my face, saying, "You know as well as I do that no book is ever perfectly published; it's impossible by the nature of the game. But I would always try to make sure that Peter got as many breaks as possible on advertising and publicity."

The two had had some disagreements along the way. Once Matthiessen left Viking for Random House, but Tom lured him back in 1976.

"At that very time," Elisabeth Sifton told me, "I went to tell Tom that I was being romanced by Random House. All Tom said was, 'What a pity if you take this job, because I have Peter Matthiessen's new book for you if you stay here.' Well, he knew how to press my buttons." The book was *The Snow Leopard,* which won the National Book Award in 1979 for Contemporary Thought.

In her early years at Viking, Elisabeth was able to understand the past better, because she had made friends with one of the last complex heroes at the old Viking: Marshall Best. By then Best was mostly retired, but would come in three or four days a week, sniffing around the new editors. At first Elisabeth felt negative about Best because he "was always carping," she said to me, "a cheese-paring, carping sort of person. I think it had been his role vis-à-vis Huebsch and Covici, who were swashbuckling entrepreneur charmers. And somebody had to hold the whole thing together and fuss over details. This was Marshall. And then I began to see many of his other great qualities."

She started asking him questions about the past and about some of his own authors. "I liked learning how he had edited Graham Greene," she said. "He told me that he read the manuscripts and sent back to Greene his comments or queries. He would particularly pay attention to phrases and usages having to do with any American character. And very often Greene disregarded them. But Marshall said to me, chuckling, 'I have noticed that when he corrects his proofs, even the second proofs, he sometimes incorporates the changes that I suggested in manuscript—but not until then.' On Marshall's behalf I was furious when I heard that. I said, 'That is so awful! Why didn't he do it when you asked him?' And Marshall said patiently, 'Well, he needed time to make it on his own; which I thought was very wise.'"

IN 1969, UPON a strong suggestion by Cork Smith, Tom Guinzburg hired Alan Williams away from Little, Brown. Lippincott is where Cork first met Alan, and they almost immediately became intimate friends. Williams was originally from Philadelphia, too, and had gone to Yale, but their paths had never crossed. After a while Alan became Lippincott's New York editor. In 1961, when he went to Little, Brown, it was Cork who took his place in New York for Lippincott. Alan was hired as editor in chief.

Williams was renowned for his range in the authors he chose to work with—authors as disparate as Iris Murdoch and Stephen King, for example. Gerald Howard, who started at Penguin in 1978, watched Williams exude his charm one day at a sales conference when he was introducing Stephen King's latest novel, *Cujo,* to the reps. "He presented *Cujo*," Gerry told me, "with some sound effects of a barking dog that at first sounded sort of like a friendly dog and then turned more threatening and feral; and it was like a good radio play, and very funny." At the end of Alan's presentation it was Mark Gompertz's turn to speak; he was then representing the Overlook Press, which was distributed by Viking. "You know," Mark said apologetically, "I've never followed a dog act before."

That was Alan Williams, so versatile an editor in so many ways. "Writers would get a six- or seven-page letter from Alan," Tom said, "after which they wouldn't know whether they'd been accepted or rejected."

With Stephen King, there was never any rejection. In 1979, with King's first novel for Viking, *The Dead Zone*, Alan became Stephen's editor and loved the experience. "It didn't hurt that King, who was in a wilder phase of his life, took my pa to great parties and introduced him to rock stars," said Marjorie Williams, Alan's daughter. (I met Marjorie in the early 1980s when I tried to persuade her to become Book-of-the-Month Club's editorial director. Wisely, she decided to stay with *The Washington Post*, where she flourished as a writer of brilliant political profiles for *The Post* and other national magazines. She also wrote moving essays about family life, including what it was like to be dying young; she died of cancer in 2005 at the age of forty-seven. Her husband, Timothy Noah, put together a superior collection of Marjorie's pieces under the title of *The Woman at the Washington Zoo*.)

The love affair between Viking and Stephen King cooled when Alan Williams left Viking for Putnam's in 1987. He took King with him, and published *Tommyknockers*. Then King returned to Viking, without Alan.

IN 1975, FOUR years before Stephen King began to sweep the boards for Viking, the house endured a most tumultuous year. In the cause of literature, it was all positive. There were three National

Book Awards and a Pulitzer. Roger Shattuck and Lewis Thomas shared the National Book Award for Arts and Letters, Shattuck for his biography of Proust, published by Viking in its successful Modern Masters series (edited by Elisabeth Sifton), and Lewis Thomas for *The Lives of a Cell,* which also won an NBA in the Sciences category." Saul Bellow won the Pulitzer Prize for fiction with *Humboldt's Gift.* And John Ashbery had just finished a book of poetry called *Self-Portrait in a Convex Mirror.* It took both the Pulitzer Prize and the National Book Award the following year.

It was also the year that Tom Guinzburg made two major moves: He hired a new editor, Jacqueline Kennedy Onassis, an inspiring move that began so well, then ended in disaster, and he sold his company.

Aristotle Onassis had recently died, and Mrs. Onassis was back in New York with time on her hands. She and Tom had known each other as children and liked each other, and Tom felt she could become a smart editor. Surely he remembered that his father had warned him about bringing in friends to work for the company, but he went and hired her anyway. "People said to me, 'Tell me why you are doing this? It's just a public relations stunt, isn't it?' And I'd say, 'Well, if the public relations part works out, fine. But that's not why Jackie's being hired.' And they'd say, 'Well, why is she being hired?' And I'd say, 'She's being hired because on any given day she's having lunch or dining with someone who may very well want to write a book.'"

Cork remembers the first day Jackie stepped into the office—all the women at Viking had come in dressed up. "They looked terrific," he said. "And when Jackie came in, and she was wearing slacks, which may have cost $800, and a shirt, which may have cost $300, but it looked like she had just been to Target or something."

She held her own as an editor in her two years with Viking. One day she came over to the Book-of-the-Month Club to show us a book she had found at a book fair. It was titled *In the Russian Style,* and she sold it to us, not because she was who she was or because of her charm at the meeting, but because the book itself was charming. "I did one book with her," Cork told me, "and she was fine. She had a knack for it."

Tom Guinzburg ought to have enjoyed that year with Jackie's exciting entry into the company, as well as the house's literary successes. Alas, it was also the time of a cash-flow crunch for Viking, as it was for many other independent publishing companies. (You have read in these pages of the fate of fine houses like Grove Press, Atheneum, and Scribner's—all occurring in this same period.) In the late seventies, interest rates had pushed as high as eighteen percent, and price-to-earning ratios went down to $7, the lowest they had ever been in United States' history. It was great for stock pickers—they could buy promising companies at that low ratio—but not for Viking. "We were borrowing more money than made sense," Tom said, admitting that "I was the last one to open up to it and understand that we couldn't survive with the imbalance of what was coming in and what was going out." One day he confessed to Rich Barber, Viking's public relations wizard, "I'm just tired of waking up every morning and owing the bank eight or nine million dollars."

It wasn't the state of the economy alone that was striking at Viking's heart. For many years the house finished with good sales, but not such good earnings. Tom wasn't cutting corners much. His offices, for instance, were in the heart of New York's most fashionable thoroughfare, Madison Avenue, whereas most of the other book publishers were downtown where the rents were considerably cheaper. He also, as has been noted, liked to celebrate occasions. "The book of the day gets you excited," he told me, "and getting to No. 1. I mean, we would bring a hot dog stand up to the office, fill it full of Bloody Mary mix and just roll it around the office. We could do that. We were a private company. I mean, you know—'Tom's office drinks again.' "

Parties were held even for books that didn't sell. Both Tom and Cork loved Jimmy Breslin, and in 1973 on the publication of his underrated novel *World Without End, Amen,* about the troubles in Ireland, they held a party "at some joint," as Tom puts it. The show people came, as well as the future governor of New York, Hugh Carey, and Walter Cronkite. Both were seen dancing an Irish jig. Jimmy's retinue was there, too, like Fat Thomas and Marvin the Torch. "At 1:30 in the morning," Tom said, "Marvin the Torch came up to me, eyes glazed, ready to help me if I ever needed help. 'Mr. G,' he said, 'I can blow up swimming pools, too.' Well, that's what he did. He blew things up. I think he was just trying to express his ecstasy at finding himself in the company of Lauren Bacall and Frank Sinatra."

In the fall of 1975, to help ease the financial strain, Tom found what he felt was a proper partner for his company—the huge British conglomerate, Pearson Longman, Ltd., that owned *The Financial Times, The Economist*, and other media companies. Pearson had bought Penguin Books in 1970 after the death in that year of its owner and founder, Sir Allen Lane, and the company was looking for the right hardcover house. Viking looked just grand to them. Tom was excited, and why not? What could be better for Viking, basically a hardcover house, than hooking up with the original and most famous paperback house in the world?

The merger was announced on November 10, 1975. Tom Guinzburg was able to get Pearson to agree to the agreeable new title for the company—Viking/Penguin—"and they gave me pieces of paper that said I could run it forever," Tom announced to the press. "The marriage is ideal. Each partner brings an enviable dowry to the other." What Pearson brought with them, of course, was the money. For Tom Guinzburg, it meant new hope for the house. The only drawback was that for the first time since

1961, when he'd lost his father, Tom had to answer to somebody. "One of the problems obviously in those situations," Rich Barber told me, "was that when you're bought, somebody owns you. And Tom was not used to being owned."

In 1977, Tom Guinzburg was still feeling reasonably good about his company. The capital was there, and while Viking's bottom line was not yet what Pearson hoped it would be, he felt it was just a matter of time for the house to gain traction. So off Tom went to London, seeking bestsellers.

Almost as soon as he landed he got a call from a young agent, Debbie Owen, an American, now living in England and married to David Owen. (In 1977 David Owen became foreign secretary for the ruling Labour party.) "I've got this manuscript," she told Tom, "and I know what you're going to think of it, but I still need a fast response from you."

"I'll read it over the weekend," he said. It was called *Shall We Tell the President?* It was set in 1984, in a fictional future when Ted Kennedy is president, and there is an assassination plot against him. Its plot was much like that of Frederick Forsyth's hugely successful first novel, published by Viking, *The Day of the Jackal,* about a plot to assassinate French president Charles de Gaulle. But *Shall We Tell the President?* was a lot more sensitive for an American audience, as it dealt with the Kennedy tragedies. Tom felt it was kind of smarmy in the use of the president, but the young author, Jeffrey Archer, whose first book had sold well in England, seemed to have talent as a writer of thrillers.

Tom called Cork Smith from London, told him about the book, said that "Debbie Owen would like us to do it, and she'd like you to be the editor. Let me send you the script." Cork read it and thought it was "pretty good, not much better than that, but not a bad story."

Back in New York, Tom went to Jackie Onassis's office and told her, "I have a manuscript and a problem."

"Well," she said, "is it a good manuscript?"

"I think the guy is the best storyteller. He'll write better ones than this, but we can make it work. But there's an editorial problem."

"What's that?"

"It's an assassination plot."

"Of who?"

"Ted Kennedy."

Jackie paled. "The assassination—it doesn't work, of course."

"No," Tom said, "it doesn't work."

"If we don't publish it, will somebody else?"

"Sure."

"Do I have to look at it?" she said. "I mean, do I have to work on it?"

"Of course not. You don't even have to read it."

"You know, I'm no fool," Jackie said. "I know of other books that you've turned down. I know that you've feared for me and my family, and that we're close. It's about time maybe you took one of these things and made some money on it. So if I don't have to have anything to do with it, that's the end of the conversation."

Tom went back to his office and called Debbie Owen. "Let's go," he said. He paid $200,000 for the book.

Shall We Tell the President? was published in October 1977. In the Sunday *New York Times Book Review,* John Leonard wrote a devastating review of the book, laying some blame for its publication on Mrs. Onassis herself. The next day, a Monday, she resigned from Viking.

AT THIS TIME, always a bit of a romantic, Tom felt the house, though not under his full control, was still strong on many levels. The children's division, under the direction of a superb editor, Mae Massee, was capturing more Caldecott and Newbery medals (the premier prizes in children's literature) than any other pub-lishing house. Many became classics: *Ferdinand the Bull* (the one Tom as a child had urged his father to buy); the *Madeline* books; *The Snowy Day* by Ezra Jack Keats, and *Make Way for Ducklings* by Robert McCloskey. The imprint Studio Books, with its outstanding illustrated works, was doing well, too, under the direction of Bryan Holme, whom Guinzburg described as "just kind of a genius."

Alongside the American successes were a terrific number of British literary figures (perhaps too many for the new owners to respect, since they didn't all sell well): Graham Greene, Rebecca West, Rumer Godden, Iris Murdoch, Muriel Spark, Nadine Gordimer (Nobel Prize, 1991), and William Trevor (who, fortu-nately for Viking, is still writing his wonderful stories).

Yet, in spite of these successes, the Pearson people began to make suggestions. A man named Jim Rose, who had married the Pearson chairman's sister, was now in charge of Penguin. "He didn't like me," Tom said, "and I didn't much like him."

PEARSON HELD QUARTERLY meetings with Viking, most of the time in New York. The next meeting was scheduled for Septem-ber 1978 in Viking's office at 10 A.M. But Tom Guinzburg was stuck in bed with what he called "a little blood clot thing in my leg, something I'm prone to." So he asked if the board meeting could be held the same time in his house. The person he talked to said, "Sure."

Right after that, Tom got a call from Jim Rose. "I know we have a meeting scheduled for tomorrow," Rose said, "but can I come in and see you now?" As he was telling me this story, Tom seemed to grow agitated.

"He came in where I was lying in bed and said, 'I'm sorry to tell you that you have been relieved of your duties, and we're ap-pointing a new president tomorrow. *And you will not be at the board meeting.*' " Tom was replaying his humiliation twenty-eight years after the execution, and his eyes still registered shock.

He immediately began calling all his closest colleagues, inviting them to his bedside for a party. "I remember telling the housekeeper, 'Get out every bottle of booze we have, because it's going to be a long day.' " Over thirty members of his Viking family gathered in the bedroom to drink and commiserate with their boss, who would be with them no longer.

I asked Tom whether, before that fatal meeting, he had suspected anything about what would happen to him. He shook his head. "You get spoiled, you know. It's been yours for so many years. Even if you sell the company, you still think it's yours."

LIFE WENT ON at Viking without a Guinzburg there. Irv Goodman, an old colleague of mine—we had both started our careers together in the early fifties, working as young editors on *Sport* magazine—was named its president. Irv would be answering to Peter Mayer, based in London, who was in charge of the Penguin imprint all over the world.

From the beginning, Irv understood that he couldn't run Viking the same way the founder's son had done it, free of corporate responsibilities. Pearson was very corporate, but Irv was used to that, having managed to do okay at Holt, which was then owned by CBS. At Viking, Irv gave his good editorial people more room to do their things. It wasn't how Tom Guinzburg had operated when an editor wanted to buy a book; he would always retain final approval. Irv was more inclined to ask for opinions from the editor and others about a book's possibility. "Well," he'd say, "what do you think?"

At about this time a problem arose with one of Viking's authors: William Kennedy. Bill Kennedy had been a newspaperman in Albany, New York, who later went to Puerto Rico to edit a new newspaper, *The San Juan Star.* He was also trying to write fiction. Saul Bellow also happened to be in San Juan, teaching a course in creative writing. Kennedy submitted his first novel to Bellow, and he was accepted into Saul's course. Bill said, "He told me it was *publishable.*"

His first novel, *Legs,* took place in his hometown, Albany. It was bought and published by Putnam's, but it didn't do much (we liked it a lot at the Book-of-the-Month Club and made it an Alternate selection). Kennedy's second book was *Billy Phelan's Greatest Game,* and Putnam's didn't want to publish it. The book came in to Cork Smith, and he loved it, so Viking published it. It received a lot of good reviews, but it didn't sell more than five thousand copies. Cork had also signed up Kennedy for a third novel, which came in when Cork was on a leave of absence. He openly confessed, "I was drinking too much, frankly." Gerald Howard, a young editor at Penguin who regarded Smith as his mentor, remembers Cork referring to that period as his "dry cleaning."

In Cork's absence, nobody who read Kennedy's third novel, *Ironweed,* liked it enough to recommend publishing it.

Cork talked to Kennedy's agent, the smart and sensitive Liz Darhansoff. He told her, "I don't think we can publish it well. Go find someone else." Liz sent it to a dozen of the finest editors in New York, and nobody was willing to publish it.

Shortly after Cork returned to Viking, in good health, he received a postcard from Saul Bellow. "Bill Kennedy's just been up here interviewing me for *Esquire,*" Bellow wrote. "And he happened to leave a manuscript with me. And I read it." Bellow was enthused enough to tell Cork that if Viking published *Ironweed,* he would say what he thought about the novel. And what he thought was "that the author of *Billy Phelan* should have a manuscript kicking around looking for a publisher is disgraceful."

"So," Cork told me, "I went to Alan and Elisabeth and, I guess, Irv." He also went to the Penguin editor, Gerald Howard, with an idea.

" 'With Bellow aboard,' " Gerry Howard remembers Cork saying, " 'here's what we do. We'll call it some shit like "The Albany Cycle," and you Penguins'—he pointed to me—'will reissue *Legs* and *Billy Phelan* while Viking publishes *Ironweed.* And we'll sort of make an event out of it. It doesn't work unless Penguin plays along. So would you read these?' "

And Gerry Howard did. "I thought *Legs* was pretty good. And then I read *Billy Phelan* and I noticed that a couple of characters that had shown up in *Legs* were also in *Billy Phelan,* and a light went off in my head. I said, 'Oh, I get it. He's doing a Faulkner [with his fictional Yoknapatawpha County] and treating Albany as a place where everything's going to happen. How interesting. And then I went on to read *Ironweed,* which was a stunning book. I thought, *Gee, this guy Kennedy is pretty terrific.*

"So we all said, 'Yeah, okay, we'll go along with this idea.' My own feeling was that there was really no big money in it, but it just seemed the right thing to do. So we did all the covers in a kind of uniform edition. Victoria Meyer, who was head of Viking publicity and a genius—one of the most wonderful and effective publicists in literary terms I've ever run into—went out to the book review editors. She told them, 'We've got something special here, and I hope you will pay attention.' I remember when the bound books came around and I saw them on my desk, and I looked at them and thought, 'Wow, this really looks good. Maybe this thing is going to work.'

"And then a miracle happened. On the week of pub date, the most glorious avalanche of reviews I've ever seen arrived on schedule, saying every possible thing you could ask the reviewers to say. And it wasn't simply that *Ironweed* was an awfully good book. It was that William Kennedy was a major American writer to whom attention had to be paid. And they reviewed the cycle entirely, exactly the way we hoped they would, and the way it was set up by Victoria. To take a terrific guy, whose career was completely dead in the water, and through just an exercise of pace and commitment and, you know, resurrect it completely, was just intensely thrilling."

With Saul Bellow's endorsement, the novel was published in 1981. *Ironweed* won both the Pulitzer Prize for fiction and the National Book Critics Circle awards. A year later Kennedy was named a MacArthur Fellow, which gave him $500,000, handed out over a five-year period, to use as he saw fit.

ONE THING CORK Smith wanted to do by this time was leave Viking (everything had changed since the departure of Tom Guinzburg). In 1984 he became editorial director of Ticknor & Fields, and then, in 1989, he was named editor in chief of trade books at Harcourt. Alan Williams had left Viking before Cork to go to Putnam's, and Elisabeth Sifton had joined Knopf. Viking had lost its three great editors.

IN MARCH 2006 I talked a second time with Tom Guinzburg. Tom came to our apartment, and, aside from a severe limp, which he waved away, he looked as fit as ever. He was wearing white pants and a yellow sweater. His head was now completely shaven, and with his horn-rimmed glasses, he looked a little bit like a Tibetan monk.

One of the things I'd forgotten to ask him at our first meeting was a question, which I asked most of my interviewees: Did he have one single book (other than *Ferdinand the Bull*) that might have been the discovery of his life?

"I think I fall into the Covici camp," Tom said. "It's the book of that day that gets you excited. *Ordinary People* by Judith Guest was a great example." *Ordinary People* came in "over the transom," as they say—unsolicited, not from an agent—and was for Viking the first unsolicited manuscript to be published in twenty-six years.

"I ended up six, seven, or eight months later," Tom said, "calling up Judith in Minnesota, where she lived. 'Listen,' I said, 'I've had to close my office door, because most of the women are sort of wandering around, managing to loiter a bit in front of the door.'

"And she said, 'What are you talking about?' And I said, 'Well, there's a man here in my office who wants to buy your book for the motion pictures.'

"She said, 'There is? What man?' And I said, 'Actually, he's a man who knows exactly what he wants to do with it. Why don't I put Robert Redford on the phone.' That whole experience with Judith and her first novel—that doesn't happen every day."

Tom was quiet for a moment, reliving a scene that has stayed with him ever since. And then he said, almost to himself—not for himself, but for the profession he loved serving every day of his life—*This is the way it should be.*

CORK SMITH ARRIVED at our apartment on a mournful February day in 2004. There was a cold rain, and he came in wearing a light raincoat. I was startled, because his face was clammy and he could hardly breathe. It was emphysema, and I never knew he had been feeling so bad. But once he sat down and sucked on oxygen and began to breathe easier, he spoke, entirely at ease, about his life in publishing. Then we went down to Billy's restaurant, which he'd always loved, as did many other publishing figures; it was on First Avenue, not far from Random House's old offices. Billy's was just steps from our apartment, but the rasping came hard to him again. It was all right, though. Billy's was his place, and he seemed to be enjoying himself.

He died in November 2004, a major loss for the community of

the book. There was a celebration for him at his and Sheila Smith's apartment, and his kids and grandkids and friends who loved him just moved around and talked fiercely with each other, some laughing at memories, some dropping tears. No, there was no memorial service.

7

THE CURIOUS FAMILY
ESTABLISHMENT
Doubleday

You can do almost anything with a book publishing house
if it has a substantial list, provided you are clever
enough to manage it properly.

—F. N. DOUBLEDAY

Ｉt was 1945 and the war had just ended. It was a time when
two ambitious young women were sharing a tiny office at
Doubleday & Company, Inc. Mostly they were reading unsolicited manuscripts, which a Doubleday executive estimated
came to about ten thousand a year. Their names were Judith Bailey, a recent graduate of Bennington College, and Betty Arnoff, a
recent graduate of Vassar. Later, when each had married, the sur-
names changed—(Judith) Bailey to Jones, (Betty) Arnoff to
Prashker. Both Judith Jones and Betty Prashker went on to forge
brilliant book publishing careers. Judith Jones is still an editor at
Knopf with such authors as John Updike, Anne Tyler, and the
late Julia Child. She has also written her own fine book, *The
Tenth Muse,* about her life in food. Betty Prashker became a

powerful editorial presence at Doubleday and elsewhere—all the more remarkable given that she had taken ten years off early in her career to raise three children.

In 1945 they were at Doubleday because there were no men around to fill the positions. But that was all right; they'd gained a foothold to a future in book publishing. They worked hard. After work Judith and Betty liked to play, so they would head down to Greenwich Village, the postwar mecca for fledgling bohemians. One evening Betty met a pop-eyed young black man at a party. He told her that he was working on a novel, and he gave her two chapters to read. She liked the writing and passed the chapters on to a Doubleday editor, Bucklin Moon, who was much higher up in the Doubleday food chain; he was actually allowed to attend the book meetings. Moon really liked the material and tried hard to sell it to his seniors, but he was turned down. Doubleday lost James Baldwin's first novel, *Go Tell It on the Mountain.*

At another Village party, Judith introduced Betty to Gore Vidal. "He was the most gorgeous thing I'd ever seen," Betty remembered. "He came up and said to me: 'Now look at all the people at this party. You are only interested in half of them. I am interested in all of them. So imagine how much more fun I'm going to have in my life than you are going to have.'"

IN 1948, JUDITH left her job at Doubleday and went to Paris, a city she fell in love with. She stayed for three and a half years. By 1950, Judith was doing secretarial work and reading French manuscripts in Doubleday's Paris bureau, which was actually an elegant apartment owned by her boss, Frank Price. One day Price, as he was going off to lunch with a French publisher, handed her a pile of manuscripts. "Here," he said, "would you write the rejection letters?"

"So I did," Judith told me the day I met her at her delightful, homey apartment. When I asked Judith where she was born and raised, she pointed to the floor as if to say—*right here.* It was the truth. Her family had owned the apartment since 1929.

"That afternoon in Paris," Judith went on, "I got to a book on the pile. It was French and it had not been published. I saw that face on the cover and the name of the young author and I started reading it, and I remember reading all afternoon. I just could not put it down. When Frank came home, he was sort of surprised that I was still there. And I said, 'We have to send this book to New York. It is wonderful.' I was in tears.

"He looked at the face on the cover and the name of the young author, Anne Frank, and said, 'What!—a book by that kid?' Fortunately, they knew me at Doubleday. I called New York, left it in good hands. *The Diary of Anne Frank* was published by Doubleday in 1952. Judith Jones returned to New York with a budding reputation.

BETTY PRASHKER'S OWN story may lack Parisian flair; nonetheless, it is filled with incident. She began her decade-long sabbatical in 1950; she was married and went on to have three children. "And after I'd done this for about ten years," she told me, "I suddenly realized I was going insane. I felt that my entire life was constricted by when the man was coming to fix the washing machine, and the logistics of getting children here, there, and everywhere."

In 1961, ready to take on book publishing again, she headed straight for Doubleday. They didn't have a job for her. So she worked for an advertising agency, then became editor of a small house, Coward, McCann and Geoghegan. She arrived at the right time. Jack Geoghegan, the bright owner of the house, had discovered a British thriller writer, and here was John le Carré's third novel, *The Spy Who Came In from the Cold,* flying out of the stores. Two years later, Betty got a call from Ken McCormick, the legendary, longtime editor in chief of Doubleday.

"He took me to lunch," Betty remembered, "and he said, 'You

know, we just had a meeting of all the vice-president heads, and we were addressed by our personnel director' [now most commonly known by the postmodern term *human resources*] 'and he said, "Doubleday doesn't have enough women in top jobs. And if we want to continue to do business with the government, we have got to do something in the way of affirmative action and have more women in our group." '

"And so Ken said to me—he had absolutely no guile—'I tried to think who I might hire, and I called Carol Brandt [a leading agent of those days], and she recommended Betty Prashker.' Of course, Doubleday was where I wanted to be in the first place, so I went back there."

Betty Prashker got into affirmative action, all right, when she heard about a young woman who was writing her Ph.D. at Columbia University on women's perceptions of themselves and how those self-perceptions could be changed. Betty read the doctoral dissertation and immediately felt that it had life-changing possibilities for women. So she bought the book, Kate Millett's *Sexual Politics*. *Time* magazine did a cover story on *Sexual Politics*, calling Millett "the Mao Tse-tung of Women's Liberation," and Betty Prashker had her first big success as an editor.

BETTY PRASHKER

One day—it was in the early seventies—I was a little discombobulated about something, and I was in Sam Vaughan's office. He suddenly looked up at me, and he said, "You know what? I don't know whether you know it, but you're one of the best people we have around here." And this was the first time that anyone had ever said anything like that. And I thought to myself, well, if he thinks I'm one of the best people around here, maybe I should aspire a bit more than I am.

And that was the beginning of my climbing up the ladder to more executive positions.

But when I asked to be a vice president, they said no. So I went to New American Library and accepted the job they had offered me: to be the vice president and editor in chief and all of that. And that night when I went home, I just felt like throwing up the whole night. The next day I said to Sam, "Look, I don't really want to leave. If you can get me a vice presidency and a decent raise, I'll stay." And Sam went to his boss and finally they gave me what I wanted. I think being unafraid is important, because if you're afraid all the time, you never do anything. It's like playing a game not to win, but to lose. You have to make choices.

In the beginning, in the forties and fifties, the editor was at the top of the pyramid, supported by the administration, the art department, the sales department, the promotion department. There was basically no business department; there was someone who said, "You're spending more than you're getting." But there were no people doing financial analyses and P&L's and that sort of thing.

But gradually over the years that pyramid ended, and the editors wound up down at the bottom. They're at the bottom of the pyramid, and they're supporting an infrastructure of business people, financial people, publicity people, human resources. And each one of those departments takes a cut out of the book that you've published. So instead of having to support your editorial staff and a few other people who help launch the book, you're supporting an army. Each book has that burden.

I used to get downhearted about it all, but then—you know what?—a manuscript would come in, or I'd get a review, or

THE CURIOUS FAMILY ESTABLISHMENT

something would happen that would be such a rush, that I'd totally forget about the burden and get all excited again.

I found out that one of the things that was so great about publishing was that it was a constant educational process. I was learning as much as I was giving to other people. More.

Many times I think about my career and Judith Jones's career. Because there we were as baby editors together, and now I'm at the end of my career; she's still in there, but also not planning for the future, I guess. And I see that our roads have separated in the sense that she has remained basically an editor, devoted to her authors. And I became an editor-executive, in which I paid half the attention to my authors that she might have, and more attention to running the show and getting the books out, and having the right people and the right authors and so forth. Sometimes I wonder, would it have been better if I had just stuck to working with authors and forgot about the executive suite and the administration of a department or a company or a list? But, I think, being who I am, I really enjoyed the other part of it as well. I probably would have missed not having that opportunity.

In 1945 Ken McCormick, fresh out of the Army Air Force and now wearing his normal civilian clothes—often a plaid sport jacket, a colorful shirt, and dark brown or light gray trousers fitting his loose, lanky frame—came back to reclaim his position as the guiding editorial light of Doubleday. McCormick, an Oregonian, had begun his career in 1930, working in New York at a Doubleday bookshop before being hired as a reader. Through the years he kept bringing in a stream of bestselling authors, both in fiction and nonfiction. Among his novelists were Nelson Algren (he worked with Algren on *The Man with the Golden Arm*), Noël

Coward, Daphne du Maurier, James T. Farrell, Edna Ferber, and
W. Somerset Maugham. In nonfiction, he edited the memoirs of
Presidents Eisenhower, Truman, and Nixon. In 1942, McCormick
became editor in chief of Doubleday's trade division.

Ken died in 1997, and his widow, Anne McCormick, very
kindly allowed me to read his oral history. I was intrigued by a
scene where Ken was working on one of Nixon's memoirs. He
was at Nixon's home and walked into the kitchen to get a drink
of water.

> Mrs. Nixon was standing in the middle of the kitchen, just
> standing there. I had this funny feeling that she was just as
> if on a desert island. So I asked her pardon for breaking in
> on her, and said I just wanted a drink of water. So she came
> out of a little tremor she was in and showed me where the
> glasses were, and I got a drink and went out . . .
>
> And I thought it then and I thought of it many times
> since. She struck me as a desperately lonely woman who
> saw no exit. All those times you see her listen to her hus-
> band making that same speech, with that eager smiling look,
> it was as though she was hearing it for the first time. I think
> she just puts that look on her face and goes away some-
> where and leaves the look there.

McCormick's editorial soul mate through the years was Lee
Barker, who had joined Doubleday in 1943 after working at
Houghton Mifflin for sixteen years. He became, as he liked to
call himself, the "middlebrow" editor of Doubleday. (Well, they
were all mostly editors of middlebrow disposition; it's what the
Doubledays preferred.) Included in Barker's list were such au-
thors as Arthur Hailey, Leon Uris, the actress Ilka Chase, and
Herman Wouk. Wouk had written his first two books for Simon
& Schuster. Neither one had created a groundswell for the

author, who was then earning a living as a gag writer for the comedian Fred Allen's popular weekly radio show. ("The cannibal had a sweet tooth. He always ate a Good Humor man for dessert.")

The Caine Mutiny was another story. Wouk had given his agent, Harold Matson, about 150 pages from the book; Matson wanted a $20,000 advance for his author. Both Simon & Schuster and Knopf turned it down. At Doubleday, Lee Barker read it with enthusiasm. "I thought it was a gamble," he said later, "but might sell 50,000 in the trade. I was wrong." Yes, he was. *The Caine Mutiny* was a No. 1 bestseller for thirteen straight months. It wound up selling over a million copies in hardcover and winning the Pulitzer Prize for fiction in 1951.

For over twenty years, McCormick and Barker worked side by side as mainstays of Doubleday's trade division. Sam Vaughan, who himself became a major editor for Doubleday in the sixties and the seventies, described them this way: "Lee, dashing, authoritarian, opinionated, distanced, demanding, with the touch of the New England patrician; Ken, open, plainspoken, funny, with a kind of Henry Fonda Americanness."

THE FIRST BOOK I read before I decided to write this one was *The Memoirs of a Publisher* by F. N. Doubleday. Reading it made me feel better about what I was doing. In the late 1920s the first Doubleday had written for his family what he called *A Few Indiscreet Recollections*. In a preface to the original manuscript, the publisher confessed that it "had been entirely composed in an automobile." That was because he found that the automobile offered "relief for nervous chills" issuing from his Parkinson's disease. In 1972, for the company's seventy-fifth anniversary, the last Nelson Doubleday authorized the publication of his grandfather's memoirs (with considerable contributions from Sam Vaughan).

When he was fifteen years old (about 1877), Frank Nelson Doubleday had gone to work for Scribner and Company as a stock boy. He stayed there in a variety of increasingly important positions for twenty years. "I gathered that he left Scribners because my grandfather was too cantankerous," wrote Charles Scribner, Jr., in his 1990 memoir, *In the Company of Writers.* "He would go to my grandfather and say, 'Don't you think this is a good idea for a book . . . ?' My grandfather would cheerfully reply that it was a terrible idea. That happened once too often, and Nelson Doubleday *primus* went off and established his own firm."

But Doubleday *primus* felt he lacked two qualifications for becoming a publisher: education and capital. As to the first, from his Scribner's experience, he finally figured out that "you can do almost anything with a book publishing house if it has a substantial list, provided you are clever enough to manage it properly." As to the second, he asked a dear friend, Andrew Carnegie, how to work a bank for a loan. The steel magnate's reply was, "Pick out the best bank in New York, walk in on your heels and make them understand that you are doing them a favor by borrowing money from them."

"But what if they still wouldn't lend me the money?"

"You could say that Andrew Carnegie would."

Almost immediately, Doubleday became such an overpowering presence in the business that he earned the nickname, "Effendi." That, a play on Doubleday's initials, FND, came from another dear friend of the family, Rudyard Kipling, who knew that *effendi* meant "chief" in Turkish. So there he was, an Effendi who had already sired a potential Effendi II—his first son, Nelson Jr.

When he was nine years old, in 1898, young Nelson had read an animal story in a magazine by "Uncle Rud" Kipling. "Why not have him write more animal stories in one book," he told his father, "like how an elephant got his trunk, how a leopard got his spots and all that?" So his father said, "Why don't you send a letter to him?"

"No, no, no," Nelson Jr. replied. "If I give him the idea, I need to get something from it."

Well, hadn't the father once avowed that "when I make a deal with a man, if I didn't feel later that I got the better of it, then I feel cheated?"

He would not cheat his son. "If he writes this story, and we publish the book," Effendi promised young Nelson, "I'll give you a penny a copy for every copy sold."

Borrowing a five-cent stamp from his father (he eventually repaid him) Nelson wrote Kipling a letter, and the result was the *Just So Stories* that have been popular since they were published in 1902. And the boy cleaned up. His estate was paid a penny a book even after his death.

Then, when he was in his teens, the son came up with another brainstorm.

"He thought he was headed to Columbia University," Nelson Doubleday III told me. "He got off the subway at the wrong stop and enrolled in the wrong university, NYU. He went for about two weeks and then got sick." That was the extent of his college education. He was confined to bed for almost five years by a form of typhoid fever. Occasionally, he was allowed to get up, and he began to spend some of his time observing the local newsstands. "*Why was it,*" he began to ask himself, "*that someone will pay fifty cents for a magazine today and one week later, when it goes off sale, it returns nothing?*" That didn't seem right, and he came up with an idea to make it right.

He told his father what he had in mind, selling the fifty-cent issue to another person for twenty-five. Effendi gave him a $500 loan to start a new business that he came to call "deferred subscriptions." Frank Jr. found his audience by using various mailing lists, and it comprised the beginning of Doubleday's vast mail-order empire, including the largest book club operation in the country.

Young Nelson returned the loan sometime later, and in a letter to his father, he said, "This $500 has had a gay and adventurous career for the past year and will I hope serve you in the future as well as it did me."

In 1928, Frank Nelson Doubleday made this entrepreneurial son president of the company (there was a second son, Russell, who also performed gainfully for the company). In 1934 the father died, it was said, "in some contentment."

The second Doubleday's reign was one of enrichment for his company. He was what he was. "I sell books, I don't read them," he always said, with ardor but not complete accuracy. He did read the books of his authors who were also his friends. One was W. Somerset Maugham.

Nelson Doubleday II owned an 1,800-acre plantation in South Carolina where the family stayed all winter long, Frank himself working there rather than in New York. Early in World War II, Maugham gave up his home in France because he thought the Germans might arrest him for spying and fled to America. (It wasn't farfetched: Maugham had been a British spy during World War I.) Doubleday built a house on the plantation for him. "Then he came to my father," the present Nelson Doubleday told me: 'Look, I need an office.' He had a writing room in his house, but that wasn't working because the maids were coming through and he couldn't concentrate. So my father built him a writing house.

"Two or three days later, Maugham apparently complained to my father that there were no windows in it. My father looked at him and said, 'You're meant to write, not look out the window, Willie.' My father had built the windows, but had purposely covered them up. The next day the windows were in."

According to Nelson Doubleday III, his father was a practical joker of high repute (the son confessed to me that he had inherited the same calling), but he served Maugham well. Willie returned the favor by writing in those war years his most commercially successful novel, *The Razor's Edge* (1944).

By the end of World War II, Nelson Doubleday II had seen to it that his book publishing company was the largest in the world. His competitors tended to disparage that feat. In a wartime letter, Random House's Bennett Cerf wrote to his partner, Donald Klopfer, who was then a major in the Air Force, that there was "no possibility, in my opinion, of [our] ever developing a sprawling and unmanageable menagerie like the Doubleday outfit. I share your abhorrence for impersonal 'big business.'"

That was not Nelson II's take on his firm. When he died in 1949, Pulitzer Prize–winning novelist Edna Ferber, one of Doubleday's most popular authors (and formerly a member of the Algonquin Round Table), said that Nelson's main achievement was in "devising schemes for putting books in the hands of the unbookish." In its obituary, the *New York Herald Tribune* called him "one of the world's leading merchants of books."

DOUBLEDAY HAD THE foresight to pick his successor three years before his death—Douglas McRae Black, who was then executive vice president of the company. Doubleday fully trusted Black, a confidence that was formed in late 1927 when Effendi himself called on the young lawyer to put together the merger of George H. Doran & Company with Doubleday. From that time on, Black's law firm handled Doubleday's major legal affairs.

Black was quite unlike the two Doubledays who preceded him. While the father and son had been big, strong, aggressive creatures, Douglas Black was thin and wiry, but not without his own kind of aggressiveness, and much less conservative than they had been. Douglas Black offered a more balanced philoso-phy about the business than had his predecessors: *"Publishing,"* he declared, *"is a commerce first and a 'noble calling' second."*

Right after the war ended, Black used the noble calling to con-vince Dwight Eisenhower, who was a close friend and soon to be the president of Columbia University, to write a book about his wartime experiences. Black insisted on a "perfect" book with no errors. He called on Ken McCormick to be its chief editor, with help from Joe Barnes, who had been a war correspondent for the *Herald Tribune,* and put four or five others on the Doubleday ed-itorial staff on the project. *Crusade in Europe* was published in 1948 and became a perfect book in sales: 240,000 books sold the first year, and 1.5 million in subsequent Doubleday editions.

There were contrasting views about Doug Black among Dou-bleday employees. "He was an extremely difficult bully," one of them who was there in those years told me. "He was incredibly rude, treated people like serfs. And he drank a lot, and people were terrified by him." Well, he did drink a lot, as did almost all his executive colleagues (and everyone else in those years). It was conversant with the Doubleday tradition.

Eleanor "Elky" Shatzkin, the widow of the legendary Leonard Shatzkin, who went to work for Black in 1950, testified only to the complaint about his drinking.

"The first time I met him," she told me (this was before her death in 2006), "I got a phone call from Mrs. Douglas Black inviting us to a weekend on Shelter Island. We flew there in a pri-vate plane. It was a strange experience for us because we'd never been to anything like this. There must have been twenty or more people for the weekend.

"At the lunch hour there were drinks and I was given a martini, but I really didn't want the damn thing. I thought I had found a place to put it that nobody would notice, which was on a counter in a sort of pantry area between the dining room and the kitchen.

And, of course, Doug Black saw it. At dinner he sat me on his right and he said, 'I notice you don't drink. Would you like some wine?' I said yes, so he kept filling my glass. But he was a jovial, pleasant guy."

Douglas Black had invited the Shatzkins to his home, because he liked Leonard Shatzkin and, most of all, felt that he owed him a debt for the contributions he had made to Doubleday's bottom line.

Leonard and Elky Shatzkin had come to New York from Pittsburgh. They'd met as students at Carnegie Tech's school of engineering. Elky was, in fact, the first woman allowed into that school; she went on to graduate with a degree in physics. In their senior year they married, and after graduation in 1941 they moved to New York.

Len Shatzkin's first job was as production editor of *House Beautiful* magazine. Then, in 1945, he took a job with Viking Press in the production department. "I guess, starting then," Elky said, "Len began to have ideas that were ahead of his time. And he continued having ideas that were ahead of his time almost till the day he died."

Yet, after four years at Viking, Len discovered that maybe he had become too avant-garde for his own good. "You've got big ideas," Harold Guinzburg, the founder of Viking Press, told him one day. "You want to do all kinds of big things. I don't want to do big things. I just want to publish these books, so I think you'd probably be happier someplace else."

Doubleday, the biggest publishing house in the country at that time, was more into "big things." Shatzkin went to talk with the head of manufacturing, Charles Pitkin who, curiously enough, had taught both Shatzkins at Carnegie Tech. "If you have a very hard skin," Pitkin said, "I'd like you to come work with me at Doubleday. But you'll have difficulties; there will be anti-Semitic remarks." Doubleday had about 5,000 employees at that time, yet it was hard to find Jews who worked for the company. Undaunted, Len took the job and stayed at Doubleday for ten years.

As its head of research, he did much for the company, including devising the standardization of trim sizes in the trade division and a new way to determine the quantity of first printings (similar to what the television networks were doing in predicting the results of presidential elections well before the polls closed). And, when he determined that he would never become president of Doubleday, he moved on to other things.

Doubleday also had but one African-American employee. One of Shatzkin's most notable achievements there was to hire a second African-American, who would mean much to the company: Charles Harris.

Harris, whose grandfathers were born into slavery in 1854, was born and raised in Portsmouth, Virginia, one of seven children. In high school he was editor of the school paper and he went to college at Virginia State. In 1956, after a stint in the army, he came to New York seeking a job on a newspaper. He tried them all. No luck. He had also written to the Urban League of New York. He found a person there who was friendly with Len Shatzkin, and he sent Harris to see Shatzkin. Len gave him a job as an assistant to himself and to the number-two person, sales manager George Blagowidow (a mathematics whiz and trained statistician), whom Shatzkin had also recently hired.

"Len was trying to bring a lot of systems of analysis to the publishing business," Charlie told me the day we met to talk about his career. As usual, he was immaculately dressed—double-breasted blazer, a foulard in the outside pocket, a starched white shirt, and colorful blue-red tie. He is a tall, handsome man who had to fight his way to get ahead in a business that had long tended not to see (or employ) minorities. We had become friends years back when I was editing *Sport* magazine. He was a sports fan, too, and later at Doubleday brought in several bestselling sports books. Charlie became the first African-American editor at a major book publishing house.

"I wanted to start in the editorial department," Charles told me, "but Len convinced me that I would learn more about how the publishing business operates because of all the studies that we did, so we were interacting with different departments." Harris stayed with Shatzkin and Blagowidow for four and a half years, soaking up the magic they were creating for the business. And then he moved to the editorial department.

Charlie Harris's foremost achievement at Doubleday occurred in the mid-1960s when he got the two leaders of the company, Nelson Doubleday III and John Sargent, to approve a new imprint for African-American readers. "It was an idea I had had almost when I started at Doubleday," Charlie said, "to do books on American minority groups. They would be for the general trade audience, but at the same time they could be used in the classroom."

"How did you get the name for it?" I asked him.

"I remember that Len Shatzkin once told me—if you name something, make it at the beginning of the alphabet or the end, where it will get noticed. So I was looking at television, and my set was a Zenith—*Zenith*!!!"

Harris invited the noted African-American historian John Hope Franklin to be the general editor of the series. The first book Harris and his small editorial team commissioned was *Worth Fighting For,* about the participation of black troops in the Civil War. The 1989 film *Glory,* starring Denzel Washington, was based on that book. Zenith Books were published both in hardcover and paperback, and were a successful addition to Doubleday's various imprints.

BEGINNING IN 1961 a number of important changes were made at Doubleday. Doug Black was sent upstairs as chairman of the board, and John Turner Sargent, who was Nelson Doubleday III's brother-in-law, became president of the company. Doubleday took the title of executive vice-president, but he and Sargent pretty much stood on equal ground. "He furthered my education and took good care of me," Nelson told me.

John Sargent had come from a privileged background; his father was a partner in a large New York securities firm. John went to St. Mark's School, attended Harvard, but left to go in the Navy and never went back to college. In 1945, when he was discharged, he joined Doubleday as a copywriter in the advertising department. A longtime friend of mine, Vilma "V" Bergane, who started at Doubleday in 1940 and stayed there until she moved to the Book-of-the-Month Club in 1971, remembers John Sargent's first day on the job. "He'd come over earlier wearing his naval uniform," she said, "and that's when the swoon began. And now all the girls wanted to come over to look at him." V also said that she had to write up the details of his hiring. "He was paid $80 a week. I don't think he needed the money," she said with a smile.

Early on, John Sargent met Neltje Doubleday, who was the daughter of Nelson Doubleday, Jr., and sister to the third Nelson Doubleday. (It should be noted that Frank Nelson Doubleday's first wife was also named Neltje.) In 1953, when Neltje was eighteen, they were married. In 1965, Neltje divorced Sargent. "She married a Greek god," Brendan Gill of *The New Yorker* once said, "and she divorced a Roman emperor."

He may have been a Roman emperor, but he ran Doubleday for over a decade with care and unusual editorial clarity for a house that held tight commercial borders. "He was a renaissance type, very well educated, extremely well read," said Anne McCormick, who had come out of the training course to become Sam Vaughan's secretary (and who later married Ken McCormick). Sargent was Theodore Roethke's editor when, in 1965, Roethke won the National Book Award for poetry with *The Far*

Field. They were also close friends. When the Sargents enter-tained, which was often, Roethke, who was a master drinker, would sometimes end up sleeping in the bathtub.

Ed Fitzgerald, who had given me my first job as a junior editor on *Sport* magazine and later steered me toward the book club business, went to work for Doubleday in 1960 running their book clubs. "Whenever I think of the Doubleday years," Ed wrote in his engaging memoir, *A Nickel an Inch,* I think of John. . . . He was born with the kind of confidence that made him certain no airplane would think of leaving without him or club refuse him membership or attractive woman deny him her company—a con-fidence that was foreign to me. . . . I learned a lot from John, in-cluding a few modest lessons in assertion. When he saw a stewardess hurrying into the galley with a half a box of caviar in her hot little hands, he moved out a foot and slowed her down. 'Before you take that home, love,' he said, 'we'll each have a few more spoonfuls. And some more vodka, please. . . .'

"Once while we were having lunch at Lasserre in Paris we dis-covered that it was March 16 and he suggested we fly to Dublin for St. Patrick's Day. It would be hard not to like a man like that."

Sargent, Fitzgerald wrote, was one of the "Holy Trinity." The other two were Nelson Doubleday himself and John O'Donnell, who handled all the financial affairs of the company. "John knew where every dime in that company was," Nelson told me. "I mean he knew manufacturing, he knew money, and he knew about the heritage of the company, and he loved to have fun."

John Sargent, John O'Donnell, and Nelson Doubleday devel-oped a new operating principle for the company, MBP: Manage-ment by Party. The most enthusiastic follower of MBP was Nelson Doubleday; he amended MBP for me by also describing it as "practical jokes."

For instance, he told me about a time in London when, leaving ahead of Sargent, he volunteered to take Sarge's tuxedo back with him to New York; John would need it at the opera when he got back on Saturday. Nelson took it to a tailor he knew and told him sternly to have every seam taken in an eighth of an inch. "Monday morning," he said, "I'm back to work, and I ask, 'Where's Sarge?' 'Oh, he had to get a new tuxedo because he broke a few buttons on his tuxedo at the opera.'"

Another time the trio was flying to Rome for a conference. When the plane landed, they kidnapped the stewardesses and took them to where they were staying. The ride to Rome was in the dead of evening on three "chariots"—well, three wagons. They raced through the mostly deserted streets; the first person to make it to the hotel would win $1,500. There is no record of who won, but they had a stimulating time in the Eternal City.

Nelson was still in his thirties, a hefty man like his father and grandfather. He was happy playing Prince Hal to John Sargent's Falstaff. Unlike Prince Hal, who became Henry V and then turned his back on Falstaff, Nelson III took the throne and allowed John Sargent to supervise the monarchy. "He was great for Doubleday," the late John Appleton, a former Harper's editor and friend of Sargent's, told me. "He made them all richer than they were before."

It wasn't easy for Sargent to play the role of Nelson's foil. Nelson had a volcanic personality and would often blast in on Sargent and stage a tantrum. It reminded me what another head of house, Walter Minton of Putnam's, once said to me about himself: "I've got a nasty streak sometimes." But Sargent was cool. "He would sit there," Vilma Bergane told me, "twirling his cigar and never saying a word to Nelson."

When Nelson and I talked, he had only good words to say about Sargent and John O'Donnell. "We ran that company for about fifteen years, and it didn't matter who was the king. We were the trio. We never had a disagreement. If one of us didn't like something, it didn't happen. And nobody held any grudges. It was that way."

BY THE MID-SIXTIES, Doubleday was a true book publishing giant. It had its own printing plant, its own book clubs (larger than any others in the U.S.), its own religion department, and had bought a textbook publishing house, Laidlaw, that in 1963 earned an income of $13 million. The trade division was flourishing, too, publishing 700 books a year, and leading the pack in bestsellers year after year.

The most esteemed graduate of Doubleday & Company's training program surely had to be Samuel S. Vaughan. Sam came to our apartment in February 2004. He had much to say about his large-scale career.

Sam Vaughan stands six feet three, allowing for a little stoop that seems to afflict all of us of a certain age, but he still makes a compelling presence wherever he goes. Betty Prashker remembers him taking her and Sandy Richardson to lunch in 1966; both had just come to work for Doubleday. "Sam was wearing a white jacket," she said, "and looked dazzling." Katherine McNamara, who interviewed him for her excellent literary online magazine, *Archipelago,* called Sam "a tall, courteous man resembling James Stewart in aspect of voice." I think of Sam's voice as being a little more melodious than Stewart's, but in appearance he does resemble the Jimmy Stewart of *Mr. Smith Goes to Washington.* Sam had gone to the capital often, too, helping Ken McCormick with such authors as Dwight Eisenhower, Harry Truman, Richard Nixon, Hubert Humphrey, Eugene McCarthy, Edmund Muskie, William Safire, and Pierre Salinger. I recently found a memorandum containing "a partial list" of authors Sam had helped over the years. I counted 110 of them—God love us—from Shana Alexander to Yevgeny Yevtushenko.

One of the first things Vaughan told me about his life as a

trainee was that he had held three jobs in his first six years with Doubleday. "I started out as assistant manager of the Doubleday syndicate," he said. "We were a two-man operation, so I was managing myself." Part of his job was to prepare excerpts from books about to be published and take them to newspapers to try to sell the rights to excerpt the books. For instance, in 1952, the year his training began, he went to *The Philadelphia Bulletin* and persuaded the editor there to use an excerpt he had put together from a book he wasn't all that keen on: *The Diary of Anne Frank.* "I didn't understand then," he apologized to me, "that it would become 'a publishing phenomenon.'" That was all right. He went on to sell the same serial rights to a dozen other newspapers.

He worked for the syndicate for two years and was then sent out to the other Doubleday in Garden City, Long Island. "Garden City was a publishing company that flourished during the Depression and during World War II," Sam explained. "They did a great many practical books. They published hardcover reprints, they published crossword puzzle books, and the like." Garden City was completely separated from the Doubleday company in New York, the home of the trade division.

"At some point in the fifties," Sam said, "the company decided that the two things should be put together. So we had an internal merger, with the usual consequences. When you have a merger—either from outside, or from inside—you have two guys for every job. So I was made manager of the Doubleday operation; the other guy became the manager for Garden City.

"I did advertising for two years. I really didn't love book advertising; I've been critical of it ever since. The only advertising manager I've ever admired is Nina Bourne." (His admiration for Bourne is unanimous in the trade. She began her career at Simon & Schuster in 1939, and is still working, for Knopf. You will meet her in chapter 11.)

The next job Vaughan took was as sales manager for Doubleday. It was the time when Len Shatzkin had made a radical recommendation to Douglas Black: Do not cut the Doubleday sales force after the merger with Garden City; rather, triple the sales force. Black took Shatzkin's advice and Doubleday ended up with more salespeople across the country than any other publisher—just at the time when the mass market paperback business became huge.

So Sam found himself looking for extra salespeople. In Detroit, the first man he interviewed had been selling sporting goods. At the end of the day, he came to see his prospective boss. "You know," the applicant said, "I want this job. But there's something that's bothering me, and I have to ask." Sam told him to go ahead. "I'm a Catholic and I take it seriously. What will I do if you guys decide to publish an anti-Catholic book, or a book that the church regards as anti-Catholic?"

"It was a good lesson for me," Sam said. "Mr. Black used to say, 'The books have a lot of religion, the books have a lot of politics, but the house doesn't have any.'" Sam offered the man a job, and he took it. What else he learned from that experience was that though he voted Democratic, it was okay to turn right in pursuit of good books of nonfiction.

In 1958, Ken McCormick promoted Sam to senior editor, which is where he wanted to be. He was in very good company. At the time, the three principal editors in the general trade division were McCormick, Lee Barker, and Walter Bradbury. After Sam had been there a good while, he found a memo in the file. It was an exchange between Bradbury, McCormick, and Barker. "This man, Catton," Bradbury wrote, "has written two books on the Civil War for us, and one sold 2,000 copies and one sold 3,000 copies. He wants to do a third. Do you think we should let him go on?"

"And either Barker or McCormick," Sam said, "wrote on the memo, 'Yeah, let him do a third, he's going to be one of the great ones.'" The third book was *A Stillness at Appomattox* (1953). "All the stars fell on him," Sam said. "He got the Pulitzer and National Book Award, and Book-of-the-Month Club Selection." Sam had the memo framed and given to Bruce Catton.

Some years later Doubleday teamed up with *The New York Times* to do a centennial history of the Civil War. Sam Vaughan was given the job of being Bruce Catton's editor. Before he took it on, McCormick offered him a simple word of advice: "Never write on an author's original manuscript until you know him well. It can be like writing on his skin." (You will see other examples, one in particular, when a writer went berserk over an editor's comments.) Sam stayed with Catton up to the time he died in 1978.

The first book Sam bought on his own he refers to as "an embarrassment. I've always had a soft spot for humor," he confessed. "One of the syndicate operators who knew me from the old days sent me some letters from a niece of his. And he said, 'She writes great letters.' And she did write great letters. So I got in touch with her, thereby learning one of the lessons, which is that great letters don't make great books necessarily.

"Anyhow, her husband had a business in San Francisco selling prepared baby formula to new mothers. Trucks would come to the house or apartment, deliver the formula with bottles and so forth. And she wrote a book about it called *Back Away from the Stove*. The title comes from an incident when all hell was busting loose in the business, and somebody called her up and said, 'I'm having trouble. My nipples are burning on the stove.' To which she replied, 'Back away from the stove.' The author's name was Sue Wenner, a mother of two little kids, one of whom grew up to be Jann Wenner, the founder of *Rolling Stone* magazine."

In 1970, a year before Ken McCormick's retirement, Sam Vaughan was promoted to publisher and president of the Doubleday trade division. By then, Lee Barker had died and Wilbur Bradbury had retired. "The publisher's job at Doubleday was interpreted a bit more broadly than elsewhere," Sam said. "I was in charge of the acquisition of books, to be sure, but I was also in charge of the sales department, the rights department, the publicity and advertising departments." That didn't allow him a lot of time to find authors he would like to work with. But just as he was getting used to his imperial title, he found one he loved, a novelist named George Garrett.

"I had done a book or two of his," Sam said, "but when he called me he said his novel was with another house. 'It's there in three big boxes,' he said, 'and they haven't got anybody to read it.' So I got my hands on it, and was bowled over by it."

Sam had indeed done two books with Garrett. The better one was called *Do Lord, Remember Me.* The author recalled a bit of surgery the editor had performed on his prose, as he told it to Katherine McNamara in a conversation for *Archipelago.*

"Vaughan had seen a 'Rabelaisian scene' that is based entirely on flatulence, and it had to be cut. . . . 'Mr. Nelson Doubleday suffers from flatulence and we don't allow any book published here that has farts in them. It's just a house policy. So you've got to take the farts out.' " Garrett did as he was told, transposing fart into "a very loud sneeze."

The new novel, which was called *Death of a Fox,* was not flatulent at all. It was about the life of Sir Walter Raleigh, and it would become the first book of a trilogy (Sam edited the second one, too). He told McNamara what he said to Garrett once he bought it: "George, the only editing I'm going to do on this— because it's long—is I'm going to draw a pencil line in the margin of any page where I fall off the rails, or fall off my chair, or fall asleep. . . . So that's what we did." Sam called *Death of a Fox,* one of the few literary novels published by the generally middle-brow house, "the finest historical novel I ever read."

LATE IN KEN McCormick's regime, another bright editor was rising from the ranks. Straight from Nina, Wisconsin, and the University of Wisconsin, Lisa Drew had come to New York to seek her future. Her first interview was with an advertising agency. "Do you have a particular interest in advertising," the personnel person asked her.

"No, really not," Lisa said.

"Well, what do you like to do?"

"I like to read," Lisa said.

"Well," the interviewer said, "have you ever thought about publishing?"

"I don't know anything about publishing," Lisa said.

"Doubleday has open interviews. You can walk in off the street on Wednesday." Since the day was Wednesday, Lisa wandered over to Doubleday.

She passed the obligatory typing test, and was offered a job by a woman in personnel named Loretta Lunt. She asked Lisa what salary she wanted. "Seventy dollars a week," Lisa said.

"Why seventy dollars a week?" Ms. Lunt asked.

"Well, because it's halfway between the sixty-five dollars a week I think you'll offer and the seventy-five I'd really like."

"Oh, I like you," Ms. Lunt said. "You're a realist. You're hired."

Lisa spent her first period at Doubleday working on jacket flap copy, also seeing to it that the seven hundred books a year Doubleday was publishing would be properly copyedited and sent to the type house so they would meet deadlines.

A year and a half later, Lisa was called into the personnel department. Fearful of losing her job, she worried, *"Oh, gosh, what have I done?"* Her interviewer this time was Loretta Lunt's boss, Bob Barnes.

"Now when you came to work here," Barnes said, "you expressed an interest to go into the editorial department. Is that correct?"

"Yes," Lisa said meekly. And he asked her if she was still interested. "I guess so," she said, "why?"

"Well, Ken McCormick, who is the editor in chief, has three people working for him. He has an editorial assistant, an administrative assistant, and a typist. Things are quite chaotic in that office. We think he needs another person—a personal secretary to keep him on track during the day, because somebody needs to coordinate that office. Are you interested?"

She actually liked her present job, bearing great responsibility for all those book jackets a year. "I don't know," she said. "What would I be responsible for?"

"My dear," Barnes said with a smile, "you'd be responsible for Mr. McCormick."

She thought about it for a day, talked with McCormick's present assistants, then went to see McCormick, whom she had never laid eyes on. It was a relaxed interview. By the end of it she was calling him Ken and he was calling her "Baby" or "Sweetie," as he called every female at work. And, she thought, how could you not love him. She took the job.

It was demanding. As Ken had explained to her, "I want you to sit in my office with me. I want you to just keep an ear on what dates I'm making and stuff, just so you know what I'm up to." And so she really was his personal secretary. After three years she became his administrative assistant, then his editorial assistant, and then she was promoted to associate editor.

"It was slow going for women then," Lisa told me when we met. "Doubleday was not prone to promoting women into editor's jobs." We were talking in the spring of 2004, two years before she retired from Scribner after forty-five years in publishing, twenty-three of them with Doubleday. Lisa is a cool, classy woman, young in heart and looks, wearing black bangs and horn-rimmed glasses (her easily recognizable look for years), and still involved in some of the social and legal issues that have long bedeviled book publishing, such as the banning of books, the rights of women, and assaults on the First Amendment. She also retains a firm institutional memory about what things were like back then.

"There were only three women who preceded me as editors," she said. "You got to a certain level and then you left. But of course, they hired tons of men out of college, made them editorial assistants, then six months later, made them editors. A year or two later they were gone, because they didn't know how to be editors. So when that all got sorted out around 1970, give or take a year or two—when the whole industry began to change—women, as well as men, began coming in at the assistant level."

Ken McCormick's retirement was a "bonanza" for her, as Lisa put it. "I had worked in one capacity or another with his authors for eight years. They all knew me, and they were comfortable with me—people like Irving Stone and Allen Drury—huge names and bestselling people. And he turned, gosh, probably thirty or forty percent of his list of authors over to me. So I was named an editor one morning, and by the afternoon I had a gigantic list of reasonably well-known, respected writers."

The one who may have meant the most to her was Alex Haley. Lisa and I had Alex in common. When I was editing *Sport* and *Saga* magazines in the 1960s, Alex was writing pieces for us. For *Sport,* we sent him to spend one spring season training in Florida with the black members of the St. Louis Cardinals—stars such as Bob Gibson, Curt Flood, Bill White—who had to live together in a boardinghouse, apart from their white teammates. Haley came back with a hard-hitting story we called *Baseball in a Segregated Town.* For *Saga* magazine, which I also edited, he wrote profiles on Miles Davis and Malcolm X, which led him to writing the autobiography of Malcolm X. The book was bought by Doubleday, but not published by them.

"Alex was actually brought in by Ken [McCormick] in 1962 or 1963," Lisa said. "After reading his *Playboy* interview with Malcolm X, Ken signed him up to do the autobiography. Alex worked very, very hard on it. He did get it done in a timely way and when we were in a stage between a copyedited manuscript and galleys, Nelson Doubleday got involved."

"I was running the publishing division then," Nelson Doubleday told me. "Ken McCormick came up to me and said, 'Guess what? The Malcolm X book is in.' And I said, 'Oh, good.' Later I got to thinking about it and I caught Ken in the hall one day, and I said, 'Ken, can you get rid of that book? I don't really want it.'" This came after the assassination of Malcolm X. "I began to get very nervous about it," Nelson said, "because the Doubleday bookshops were all over the place. I didn't want any of our people to get hurt."

"To Ken's horror," Lisa Drew said, "he had to call Paul Reynolds, who was Alex's agent, and say, 'Nelson doesn't want to publish this book,' and he told him why. So Paul said fine, and then Ken said, 'You can keep the money.'"

But it wasn't over yet. Ken told Nelson that he had to spend more money on Alex Haley. "It's going to cost you $40,000." Ken explained, "The guy wants to write a story about his people and his family, and how he came over here. We've got to pay him $20,000 a year for two years. "Fine, good, I can live with that," Nelson Doubleday told McCormick. "Well," Lisa Drew said, a knowing smile on her face, "that was the birth of *Roots.*"

THE DARK YEARS began to descend on Doubleday's trade book publishing in the mid-1970s, as they did for many other houses throughout the industry. But with Doubleday still making a ton of money from its book clubs and other ventures, the trade division's fate was not as crucial to its business. Doubleday, in fact, continued expanding during that period. They bought Dell Publishing Company for $35 million in cash. Dell had its own hardcover publishing house, but also a hard-driving paperback business. Doubleday had lacked any sort of market paperback presence in the industry. They certainly got that from Dell, and so they started to look at how to make trade books more profitable.

"I was demoted to editor in chief," Sam Vaughan said, with irony in his voice. "They brought in new heads for the division, none of whom survived too long." It was a sobering time, even though the trade division had two big hits—*Roots,* as mentioned, and a novel found by Tom Congdon, a young editor whom Sam had hired from Harper's, and who, Sam said, "was quite a rocket burst as an editor."

It was in 1971 that Congdon read a magazine piece by a writer named Peter Benchley. He liked it so much that he called Benchley to have lunch with him. Over dessert, he asked Benchley if he had any ideas for a novel. To his surprise, Benchley said yes: "I want to write about a great white shark that fastens on an American seaport town in New England and provides a moral crisis." Congdon paid him $1,000 for an initial submission of a hundred pages. That was good enough for Doubleday, and Benchley was paid all of $7,500 as an advance for *Jaws.*

It was published in 1974 and spent forty weeks on the *New York Times* bestseller list. Hardcover sales were about 200,000 copies. Doubleday had exclusive book club rights, and their sales came to just under that, 192,000 copies. Bought by Bantam Books, *Jaws* sold nine million in paperback. *Roots* was published two years later.

"I guess we hit a peak with *Roots,*" Sam said. "The only thing worse than having *Roots* was not having *Roots* the next year. So, we had *Roots* one year, or maybe two, and then we had the *Roots* returns. The *Roots* returns were enough to make a giant bestseller in themselves, because you can't stop a phenomenon in a hurry. So we had some money troubles then, and for the next couple of years we had money troubles. And Doubleday was kind of entering its period of getting a new president every year, and it was very much in a state of flux."

When Sam Vaughan, crestfallen and tired out by all the management changes, applied for early retirement, Nelson Doubleday asked him to stay. "I know I haven't been paying attention much lately," Nelson admitted to Vaughan, which was true. By then he had his baseball team, the New York Mets, to worry about, and he was losing interest in book publishing.

Betty Prashker had finally been granted a vice presidency and had become editorial director of the division, but in 1981 she left Doubleday in disenchantment. She went to Crown as vice president and editor in chief.

In 1982, Sam left Doubleday for Random House, where he spent many happy years.

Also in 1982, Lisa Drew, crushed by the people Doubleday was bringing in to run the trade division, even though she had finally been handed a vice presidency, quit the company to become vice president at William Morrow. The golden age at Doubleday had come to its end.

IN THE LATE SPRING of 2006, Nelson Doubleday invited me to visit him at his office in Locust Valley, New York, not far from Garden City. He had recently come back from Florida, where he lives in the winter, and would soon be heading off to Nantucket, where he spends the summer. Wherever he goes, his golf clubs keep him company. He is seventy-three years old. It was only when we were shaking hands to say good-bye that he told me he'd had a liver transplant in 2000. It had come, he said, about six hours before he would likely have died. That gift of life, it occurred to me, may have softened the disposition of a man who had never really felt comfortable with himself.

Nelson seemed absolutely comfortable when we talked in his large oval office. He is a large man. He was wearing a golf sweater that covered a barrel chest, and his bulky legs were concealed in khaki pants. His assistant, Rose, a bright, attentive woman, worked at her desk on the computer. Nelson's face lit up as he told his stories. The smile reminded me a little of my two-year-old grandson, who would flash a winning smile after he bit you.

We had maybe shaken hands a couple of times in my years at Book-of-the-Month Club. We were rather heavy competitors in those years; Book-of-the-Month Club always seemed to be competing with the Literary Guild for James Michener's next book. I gather he knew all of this, because he had an amusing story to tell me about his father and Harry Scherman, the founder of the Book-of-the-Month Club.

"Harry was a great friend of my family's," Nelson said. "He used to come down to South Carolina because we were trying to sell him books that we were publishing. My father would take him out for a drive in the afternoon; someone would be driving the car and my father would sit there and talk about the book business. And they'd come to some little jerkwater town and my father would say, 'I betcha ten dollars, Harry, that we got more book club members down here than you do.' Okay, so they'd write it down and they'd go on and a couple of towns later—'I'll betcha we have more here.' Harry Scherman never won a bet."

Nelson was fifteen when his father died in 1949. That summer he worked as a messenger in Garden City. His mother was a McCarter, and the McCarters had close ties to Princeton, one of them being the McCarter Theatre, a gift from her family. He went on to graduate from Princeton in 1955; he was in ROTC there, so

In 1946, Roger Straus
gave birth to a
publishing house that
would kick-start the
golden age of the book
in American life.
COURTESY OF FARRAR,
STRAUS AND GIROUX

Though Straus and Robert Giroux (*center*) never loved each other, they worked well as a team because each wanted to find enduring works of literature. In 1981, Bernard Malamud (*left*), then the president of PEN (and a Farrar, Straus and Giroux author) presented Giroux and Straus with their "publishing citation award." © NANCY CRAMPTON

Joseph Brodsky (*right*) was the author Roger Straus held in the warmest esteem. Here they are, hugging, just after Brodsky won the 1987 Nobel Prize in literature. COURTESY OF FARRAR, STRAUS AND GIROUX

In a letter to Barney Rosset (*right*) written on June 25, 1953, Samuel Beckett said that he was sending Rosset his "first version of *Godot.*" At the end of his letter Beckett signed off with these words: "Thanking you for taking this chance with my work and wishing us a fair wind." The wind between these lifelong friends always blew gently. © BOB ADELMAN

Rosset with his devoted editor, Fred Jordan. Rosset once said of Jordan, "A certain sensibility always echoed strongly." COURTESY OF GROVE/ATLANTIC

George Braziller was twenty-one years old when he married Marsha Nash. She worked closely with him when Braziller started the Book Find Club and later the Seven Arts Club. When he went off to war, Marsha held the company together. COURTESY OF GEORGE BRAZILLER

Late in World War II, Braziller found himself in Normandy, serving with the 133rd gun battalion, under the command of General George Patton. Their mission was to shoot down German V-2 rockets, which were wreaking havoc on London.

COURTESY OF GEORGE BRAZILLER

In 1958, Braziller published Nathalie Sarraute's most famous novel, *Portrait of a Man Unknown*. He went on to publish all her works. Here she is with Braziller in 1995, four years before her death at the age of ninety-nine.

COURTESY OF GEORGE BRAZILLER

Thomas McCormack, here in his mid-forties, asked his wife, Sandra, to read a book from a British publisher. She did, and recommended it. Tom persuaded the author, a veterinarian, to revise and expand the work, and in 1972, James Herriot's *All Creatures Great and Small* changed life at St. Martin's Press. COURTESY OF THOMAS McCORMACK

In 1977, McCormack (*right*) hired Sally Richardson to run subsidiary rights at St. Martin's. Here is a rare photograph of them both from that time, with other younger "Saints," including Tom Dunne (*left*), who has his own imprint within St. Martin's Press. © NANCY CRAMPTON

Upon Tom's retirement in 1997, Sally became St. Martin's publisher and president, and as you can see, she seems to be enjoying her work more than ever.
COURTESY OF SALLY RICHARDSON

From left to right: Thomas Guinzburg in 1966, the owner of Viking Press, with his prized authors: playwright Arthur Miller and two Nobelists, Saul Bellow and John Steinbeck. INGE MORATH AND MAGNUM PHOTOS

A wary Corlies "Cork" Smith keeps a watchful eye on his unpredictable author, Leonard Cohen (*foreground*). Smith died in 2006 after a triumphal life as an editor. That same year, Leonard Cohen's life as a poet and singer-songwriter was celebrated in a successful documentary film titled *Leonard Cohen: I'm Your Man.*
COURTESY OF SHEILA SMITH

One of the greatest editors of the golden age was Ken McCormick, who began at Doubleday in the late thirties and flourished in the decades after World War II. Here he is on the right with one of his most illustrious authors, Jacques Cousteau. COURTESY OF ANNE McCORMICK

Ken McCormick
(*right*) with
Somerset Maugham.
COURTESY OF ANNE
McCORMICK

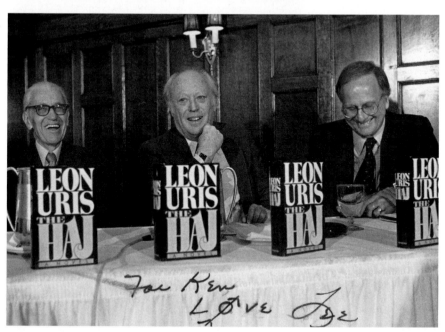

Sharing the podium with McCormick and Leon Uris (*center*), whose novel *The Haj* was published in 1984, is Sam Vaughan, himself an inspiring editor with Doubleday and Random House. COURTESY OF ANNE McCORMICK

In 1967, Genevieve "Gene" Young found herself at the American Booksellers Convention. There, her boss, Cass Canfield (*holding the cigar*), introduced her to Martin Luther King, Jr. Next to Gene is Melvin Arnold, a veteran editor at the company. COURTESY OF GENEVIEVE YOUNG

In the early postwar years, Elizabeth Lawrence was the editor Cass Canfield listened to, especially for her skill at scouting out superior fiction for his house. A fellow editor, Ann Harris, called Lawrence "the most principled woman I had ever known." COURTESY OF GENEVIEVE YOUNG

Father and son. Cass Canfield, Sr., and Cass Canfield, Jr., who loved his editorial life at Harper's. COURTESY OF CASS CANFIELD, JR.

At a Book-of-the-Month Club lunch, sitting between Charles Scribner III and Al Silverman, is P. D. James. She is being honored after the BOMC judges made her 1980 novel, *Innocent Blood,* a main selection of the Club, which catapulted her to literary bestsellerdom. AUTHOR'S COLLECTION

Nan Talese (*left*) was a young and talented editor at Random House before she moved elsewhere. Here she is with Frances FitzGerald, who became one of Nan's authors. FitzGerald's first book, *Fire in the Lake,* was published by Little, Brown and won both the National Book Award and the Pulitzer Prize.

In 1965, Robert Bernstein, sitting between Random House's great publishers, Donald Klopfer and Bennett Cerf (*foreground*), became president of the company. Standing at back is Lew Miller, the sales director. THE NEW YORK TIMES

Bob Bernstein and the "Cat in the Hat," standing over Dr. Seuss (Theodore Geisel, seated) in 1984 after delivery of his newest manuscript, *The Yooks and the Zooks.*

MARTHA KAPLAN

RIGHT: A rare photo of Alfred and Blanche Knopf—rare because Blanche is smiling and Alfred is looking at her in adoration. HARRY RANSOM HUMANITIES RESEARCH CENTER PHOTOGRAPHY COLLECTION, THE UNIVERSITY OF TEXAS AT AUSTIN

BOTTOM: Mr. Knopf was renowned all over the world for the books he and Blanche selected and for the ways they made them into a work of art. Here he is with one of his prize-winning authors, John Hersey. © NANCY CRAMPTON

Robert Gottlieb in 1973, with the smile he's worn all his life. He started at Simon & Schuster in 1955 and became editor in chief two years later. In 1968, he succeeded Alfred Knopf as editor in chief at Knopf. © NANCY CRAMPTON

On April 2, 1962, a party was held at the "21" Club in New York for Katherine Anne Porter, to celebrate the publication of her long-awaited novel, *Ship of Fools*. Talking with Porter is the novelist Glenway Wescott. Listening in the background is Arthur Thornhill, Jr., who would succeed his father, Arthur Thornhill, Sr., as president of Little, Brown. COURTESY OF ARTHUR THORNHILL, JR.

Seymour "Sam" Lawrence (*left*), one of the most important editors of the golden age, at an event in London with Arthur Thornhill, Jr. That's Arthur's wife, Dorothy, next to Sam. COURTESY OF ARTHUR THORNHILL, JR.

LEFT: Herman Gollob in July 1960, age thirty, on his first day of work at Little, Brown. He made many professional moves in his life, but Atheneum became the house closest to his heart.
JOHN CUSHMAN;
COURTESY OF HERMAN GOLLOB

LEFT: Victor Weybright, the guiding genius of New American Library, loved relaxing in rural Maryland. Here, in the mid-1940s, he is about to go out with the Timber Ridge bassets.

COURTESY OF TRUMAN TALLEY

RIGHT: Oscar Dystel (*left*) made Bantam Books one of the greatest mass market paperback houses in the world. Here he is with his early editor in chief, Saul David.

COURTESY OF OSCAR DYSTEL

Ian Ballantine, one of the founders of the paperback revolution, working in his apartment in 1952. Behind him is the cover art for Hal Ellson's *Golden Spike*, one of the Ballantines' first original books.

COURTESY OF BERNICE GALEF AND BETTY BALLANTINE

In 1969, Larry Hughes, president of William Morrow, and his wife, Rose, found themselves sitting with Erle Stanley Gardner on his eightieth birthday. *The Guinness Book of Records* maintained that Gardner, the creator of eighty-two Perry Mason novels, plus forty-five other mysteries, was, at the time, the world's bestselling author. FREEMAN LEWIS; COURTESY OF LAWRENCE HUGHES

The Dream Team: Betty Ballantine and her husband, Ian Ballantine, who brought the first Penguin Books to America when she was eighteen and her new husband was twenty-one. The Ballantines contributed much to the golden age of book publishing in America. COURTESY OF BETTY BALLANTINE

Together at a publishing lecture, Leona Nevler, president of Fawcett; sociologist Ned Polsky, author of *Hustlers, Beats, and Others*; and Aaron Asher (*right*), a distinguished editor of the golden age. © NANCY CRAMPTON

he served in the Air Force for the next two years. And then he started in Doubleday's training program at the shop he owned, and—well, yes—worked his way up. "I was kind of like my father," he said. "I had never really read much, so I never got involved with the books." John Sargent was there for that.

I asked him about the family split that came along in the early 1970s that affected all of the family's lives. Doubleday stock was then owned by only five hundred shareholders. The largest amount was owned by Ellen Doubleday, then her two children, Neltje and Nelson Doubleday, Jr. Nelson came into his full share of the stock in 1973 when he turned forty. "Neltje's stock," it was reported by John Tebbel in *Between Covers: The Rise and Transformation of Book Publishing in America*, "was in a life trust that prevented her from either voting or selling her stock. Neltje wanted Doubleday to go public, and she petitioned the court to replace one of her trustees with a disinterested person who would pursue the idea of going public with her trust." It ended up Neltje versus her mother (Ellen Doubleday died in 1975), her ex-husband, and her brother. When I mentioned the situation with Nelson and his sister, I referred to it as a squabble.

"Yeah," he said, "I mean, I never had a *squabble* with her, except that she kept lobbing grenades at me. My family had taken care of things, so that she could never do anything. But there was no warfare between us. Well, I think she was always unhappy that I didn't fire John Sargent. But I couldn't. There was no way. He was so good at what he did."

"I knew the stresses in the family over the ownership, which were considerable," John Sargent, Jr., told me when I met him at his office in New York's Flatiron Building. Today, Sargent is CEO of Macmillan (whose name was changed from Georg von Holtzbrinck Publishers in late 2007). He sees to the needs of St. Martin's Press, Henry Holt, Farrar, Straus and Giroux, and other

American companies owned by the Holtzbrinck Group of Stuttgart, Germany.

When his father and mother were divorced, life changed completely for John and his sister. They would spend a month in the summer with their father in New York. The rest of the time they lived in Sheridan, Wyoming, with his mother, who was, and is, a rancher and an artist.

After graduating from Stanford and Columbia, young John worked at Doubleday for four years in various positions, but he understood that "being the son of a historic figure on one side of the family, and the nephew of a historic figure on the other side," was not helping him; rather, it was the opposite. "How much that had to do with Nelson, Mom and Dad and their relationship, I never knew and never asked," John said.

In my conversation with Nelson, he continuously referred to young John Sargent as being "a great kid." But when I asked him if he ever thought about this Sargent someday running the company, Nelson said, "I don't think his heart was in it." I wondered if Nelson would have felt differently if he'd had a son. He'd had four daughters from his first wife, and a stepson and stepdaughter. "They didn't want to have anything to do with the company," Nelson said without hesitation. But one of his daughters, I was told, worked at Doubleday and was highly regarded.

In the end, Nelson said with some feeling that selling the company in 1986 to Bertelsmann "became something that I had to do, and it took care of all of the family problems and everything else.

"Now," he said with some contentment, "I just play golf and have a good time, and harass my children and grandchildren—ten of them—and on my way to eleven."

Nelson thought some more about the past, and he said to me, "I can't think of a day that I didn't look forward to going to work. Whether it was because I was going to play a practical joke on somebody, or just see somebody, or just see what the hell happens today, you know, I just loved it."

As I was leaving, Nelson handed me a bumper sticker to put on my car. It read:

"WANNA BANG TONITE? CALL BAY FIREWORKS."

He gave me that mischievous smile. "Yeah, I'm in the fireworks business."

I think he always has been.

8

THE COMPANY THAT WAS ALWAYS ABOUT CASS

The House of Harper

It was a place that really was collegial in the best sense.
It had its pecking orders, but it also did honor to the
craft we were engaged in.

—ANN HARRIS

I t was always said of Cass Canfield that any friend of his—
and he had a wide and influential circle around him—likely
had a book in him. Because of such certitude, he most always
carried in his pocket a blank author's contract with the name and
title not yet filled in. You never could tell.

Cass Canfield's role in life, almost from the moment he joined
the House of Harper in 1924, was to bring in the best books for
Harper's trade division. One of the most effective editors in
Harper's glorious postwar period, Genevieve "Gene" Young, remembers having to do a survey of Harper's one hundred most
successful books. "The terrifying thing," Gene told me, "was that
Cass had brought in, I'd say, ninety-five percent of them."

As the head of the house for thirty-six years, Cass Canfield became the most demanding editorial figure in the modern history of book publishing. He not only led a lively group of editors who came to Harper's, but he himself plunged into the scrum like no other head of house (not even the fabled Bennett Cerf could surpass him), pulling out of his pocket contracts for such eminent names as Eleanor Roosevelt, Sumner Welles, James F. Byrnes, William O. Douglas, Adlai Stevenson, and John F. Kennedy. "Cass was a terrific publisher of living prominent people," said John Appleton, who was an editor at Harper's from 1949 to 1961. "He hardly ever missed with them."

Ashbel Green, a longtime major editor at Knopf who retired at the end of 2007, told me that when Harold Macmillan resigned as prime minister of Great Britain, Alfred Knopf wanted a shot at his memoirs. But he found out, Ash said, that "Cass was on the next plane to London to snag them. I think Alfred envied Cass's connections."

A leading editor of the period, William Targ, drummed out his feelings for the Harper hero: "Canfield was a 'working stiff' with style; he was shrewd, nimble-footed, and nervy, able to make a quick decision or a deal. He worked with duchesses as well as longshoremen, not too worried about ethics or fine points of negotiation. A bookman. A collector of William Blake. A cool man, gifted with humor, taste, and especially a zest for good living."

Canfield was as imposing as Moses on the Mount. Well over six feet tall, with a slightly stooped bearing, he had a long, melancholy, inquiring face, made longer when his hair at an early age began retreating from his forehead. No long white beard, however; a small mustache was centered under his resolute nose, giving the face a certain buoyancy. His smile, when he offered it, was warm, but reserved. He didn't smile often; most of the time he seemed lost in thought. Once he complained to a colleague that the highly attractive Ms. Young never said good morning to him in the elevator. "It was because he always seemed so wrapped up in his own thing," Gene told me, "I felt I didn't exist." This seems rather out of character for Canfield, who was renowned for his taste in pretty women. Was he a chaser? I asked one of Cass's editors. "You bet," the editor replied.

Fran McCullough, another Harper's editor of the time with a mind of her own, spoke not about Canfield's penchant for women but about how he presided over the editorial meetings. "We all sat at this gigantic oval wooden table, junior editors, too, and he, puffing on his pipe, acted like we were all equal, and he would fill us in on what he'd been doing, or what he'd been thinking. Sometimes it was dumb, like once he was just enraptured by ice dancing. 'Say, you know we could do a huge illustrated book on ice dancing. What do you think?' But you always felt like you were on the team."

Fran remembered the evening when she and Cass were coming back from a cocktail party. "All of a sudden, he asked me, 'Say, who do you think is really interesting? Let's say you were just sitting around trying to think who should do an interesting book.' I gave him a few names. He pulled out his notebook and started writing them down. And he said, 'Now, how can I get hold of them, and what do I say when I call?'"

An affable fellow in public, he turned into Darth Vader when he went after a book he really wanted. Another editor, Hugh Van Dusen, former executive editor of HarperPerennial who had been with Harper's for forty-three years when we talked in late 2004, gave me an example of Cass leading the charge. Hugh said, "It was a book called *Leadership* by James MacGregor Burns, already written." Burns was a distinguished historian with two Pulitzer Prizes and two National Book Awards, and he had never been published by Harper's. That bothered Cass not at all. He simply called a meeting with seven or eight of his people who might be involved in the deal. Hugh Van Dusen was one of them. "I was there," Hugh said, "because there might be a paperback sale. The textbook editor was there because there might be a textbook sale. The others who sold subsidiary rights were there. He pulled an old envelope out of his pocket and started scribbling on the back of it.

" 'What do you think you can put up for the paperback rights?' he asked me. I said, '$15,000.' 'Well,' he said to the rights person, 'what can you get from the Book-of-the-Month Club?' 'Wow,' she said, 'maybe $7,500 on a good day.' He went around the table like that and wound up with $90,000. This wasn't just pie-in-the-sky. It was at least a semi-commitment from each of us in the room. He wanted it on the record. And he bought the book for $90,000. We published it in 1978 and it's still in print."

What could William Jovanovich, the hard-driving president of Harcourt Brace Jovanovich, have been thinking when he said this about one of his contentious competitors: "The life of Cass Canfield cannot be emulated; he is the last of his kind and the first"? We shall see.

WHEN I FIRST started thinking about this book, I assumed that my golden age in publishing would not be a perfectly shaped vessel—because women were mostly out of the loop. There was only one major exception, Helen Meyer, who went to work as secretary for George Delacorte at age sixteen, and in the late 1950s became president of the Dell book and magazine empire (see the section on Dell in chapter 13). The others who sought to become editors in book publishing worked mostly as secretaries or readers at minimum salaries. When Gene Young joined Harper's in 1952, they paid her $43.50 a week and called her "Stenographer No. 2." She never found out who was "Stenographer No. 1." These underpaid, overqualified women stayed on for one reason only—because they loved books at least as much as their male rivals did.

The first woman to break through the circle of male bonding at

Harper's was Ursula Nordstrom, one of the greatest children's editors in the history of book publishing—a creative and tough-minded person, you might say, in the Cass Canfield mode. Once she was asked how she could publish for children since she had none of her own. Her answer was that she was a former child, "and I have forgotten nothing." In 1954, she became the first woman elected to the Harper board of directors. She was a fiercely independent board member. At one board meeting, when she was asked to make the coffee, she said she did not know how.

Women got sort of a break during World War II, when they had to fill gaps for the men who had gone off to fight. Harper's relied on Joan Kahn, a dynamic, outspoken person who founded Harper Novels of Suspense, and was almost as tough as Ursula Nordstrom. After the war, when one of those efficiency outsiders, periodically hired by the financial people, came around to see her and asked her, "Where do you find your books?" she said, "On my desk." Joan Kahn spent an entire career at her desk, finding superior mysteries.

Elizabeth Lawrence was made a senior editor not just because the men were away, but because she was such a good reader and editor. It was Elizabeth who convinced a writer named Betty Smith to turn a nonfiction account of her family's life into fiction. *A Tree Grows in Brooklyn* was a major bestseller in 1943 and 1944. Then, in the early fifties through the sixties, came the editors Ann Harris, Genevieve Young, and Fran McCullough, and the gold rush was on.

THE WOMEN WERE there in the golden age all right, but you couldn't find a woman in sight back in 1817, when it all began for Harper's. In fact, it was four brothers who got together—four farm boys from Long Island. "The Brothers Cheeryble," a grandson, J. Henry Harper, called them when they opened up a book printing and publishing operation in New York City. Some thirty years later Harper & Brothers was the largest English-language publishing house in the world, with 350 employees, printing two million books and pamphlets a year, plus a series of popular magazines (*Harper's* magazine is the one that lasted). They had a nonpareil list of British authors—Dickens, Sir Walter Scott, Thackeray, the Brontës, George Eliot, Trollope, and more—but by the end of the century they had fallen into sorrowful times. It was a family-owned business and too many of the brothers' heirs were cashing in their shares in the company. Harper declared bankruptcy. J. P. Morgan, who had saved other WASP publishing houses, put up enough capital for the Harpers to regain their footing. But by the early 1920s, the brothers had a huge indebtedness to Morgan. That's when Cass Canfield decided book publishing might be his thing.

He was born in 1897 on Park Avenue and Thirty-sixth Street. His father, Augustus Cass Canfield, had been brought up in France and then moved to Detroit. He was an engineer, but he never learned how to earn a living. He never needed to. His hobby was designing yachts for himself. Cass's mother, Josephine Houghteling, came from Chicago. Oscar Wilde called Josephine "the most beautiful woman in America." It was a pampered childhood, set in elegant high society.

"The Canfields cut quite a figure," Cass wrote in his charming memoir *Up & Down & Around: A Publisher Recollects the Time of His Life.* Cass's vision of his childhood was remembering his parents' "victoria drawn by spirited chestnut horses with two men on the box wearing cockades and sitting bolt upright." Once, when Edith Wharton was visiting his parents in their Long Island home, she said of Cass, "Josephine's child is a very silent young man, isn't he?" He grew up with that special gift: He became a *listener.* He always listened to what people had to say; something useful might come out of that conversation, and the same was true when he entered book publishing.

Cass enrolled at Harvard, but left in his junior year to join the army. After the war he graduated from Harvard, and then studied at Oxford University. He had a bit of the explorer in him, and when he finished at Oxford, he and a couple of university friends retraced Marco Polo's trade routes, later called the Burma Road, on foot. Back in New York in 1922, he became a reporter and advertising representative of the *New York Evening Post*. Two years later he went to work for Harper's.

He had hardly settled in when he was asked to run the London office. He set out with his wife, Katsy, their infant son, Cass Jr., and a newly adopted son, Michael. Canfield became a refreshing presence among the leading British book publishers, most of whom became his friends and allies in the business. He wanted to accomplish two things in England: scout for British authors and, like Frank Buck, the famous collector of wild animals, "bring 'em back alive," and try to find homes for Harper's books that had not been accepted in the United Kingdom. He had some successes and one notable failure.

That was the day he went to see George Bernard Shaw, who was said to be looking for a new American publisher. Shaw lectured Cass on Harper's mistake in not having a bookstore in the Harper building. Canfield argued that publishing and retail selling were distinct and separate functions. Shaw went to Dodd, Mead & Company.

In this rich period of Cass's life, the new editor in chief of Harper's general books division, Eugene Saxton, came to London once a year to buy books, and he and Canfield immediately hit it off. (Saxton had come from George H. Doran & Company and had also been editor of *The Bookman*.) "He was one of the most considerate and gentle of men," Canfield wrote of Eugene Saxton in his memoir. "Nervous and sensitive, he possessed a delicately ironic sense of humor and combined a flair for publishing with an appreciation of good writing."

Saxton had an interesting way of judging books. He would read a manuscript and then leave it on his desk for weeks. One day Canfield, who moved a lot faster, asked Saxton why he hadn't yet made a decision. "I want to see whether the book sinks in," his editor replied, "whether I remember it. If it doesn't make a lasting impression, I turn it down." A lot of books did sink in between Canfield and Saxton in Cass's London years; authors signed up included J. B. Priestley, Richard Hughes, Harold Laski, and the Huxleys, Julian and Aldous.

It was during his London stay that Canfield was introduced to a young American newspaperman by the name of John Gunther, who had just gone to work for the *Chicago Daily News* as a foreign correspondent. In his memoir Canfield suggested that it was he who had asked Gunther to write a book about "the personalities and events in Europe." He was turned down. But some years later Canfield told the melodramatic story of how he finally persuaded Gunther to do the book—by catching Gunther unawares in his New York hotel room with a terrific hangover, needing to take the next boat to London. In that condition, Canfield intimated, Gunther would sign anything. Out came the contract, and Gunther signed on the dotted line. There was, however, a different story about the origin of the "Inside Classics," this one from William Shirer, Gunther's friend, but also his foremost competitor among American foreign correspondents.

Shirer's version appeared in a profile he wrote on Gunther for the Book-of-the-Month Club *News*. The idea, Shirer reported, came from Gunther's wife, who, like her husband, had global inclinations. Why not, she told her husband, do a "merry-go-round" of Europe? She was thinking of Drew Pearson's and Robert Allen's lively *Washington Post* column called "Washington Merry-Go-Round."

And so he did, and after collecting some 500,000 words he felt that all he now needed was a title. According to Shirer's account,

Gunther was in the dining car of a train taking him from Wales to London. "He sat facing some cold mutton," Shirer wrote, "a glass of lukewarm British beer and the London *Times*. The dispatches in that venerable journal, he reflected, somehow got *inside* a situation. That's what he had tried to do in the book—get *inside* Europe. On the margin of the august *Times,* he scribbled 'Inside Europe.'"

Gunther cabled the title to his publisher, who was indeed Cass Canfield. This was a classic example of Canfield's Fourth Commandment: *Pertinacity*. "The publisher, if he thinks someone can produce a first-rate book, should continue to press for it, just short of making himself a nuisance."

In *Up & Down & Around,* Cass postulated eight such Commandments for book publishers everywhere. His First Commandment, however, was pertinent: *A Nose*. As he explained it, "it is not only a matter of having one for books. For subjects, and for what people want to read, but a nose for authors, for gifted individuals likely to write well, but who haven't yet proven themselves." But pertinacity worked well, too. *Inside Europe* was published in 1936 and sold 150,000 copies in the original edition. Then came *Inside Asia, Inside Latin America, Inside U.S.A.*—eight Inside books in all that sold 3.5 million copies over a span of thirty years.

Canfield returned to New York in 1927, at the age of thirty. In four whirlwind years he became president of Harper & Brothers. And he set out to reinvigorate the trade division. The backlist was wonderful, but Harper's needed new authors who could make a difference. In 1924 the two Harper bestsellers were Mark Twain's autobiography and Zane Grey's western *The Call of the Canyon*. Twain had come to Harper's in 1895 with exotic terms for the time—fifteen percent of list price on the first five thousand copies, and twenty percent thereafter. Zane Grey wrote seventy-eight western novels that were widely read around the world. Harper's published forty of them, nine appearing after his death in 1939. (This "posthumous productivity" caused E. B. White to comment in a P.S. of a letter to Canfield in 1964: "I saw Zane Grey on the street the other day. He looked awful.")

In the 1930s Cass worked hard to bring promising authors to his house. One who became a friend for life was Thornton Wilder, whose novels and plays were all published by Harper's. Then there were E. B. White and James Thurber from *The New Yorker*. As a team, White and Thurber came to Harper's one day to show Canfield and Saxton a book they were working on together. Cass and Saxton accepted it immediately, and *Is Sex Necessary?* became a big hit.

One evening at a dinner party Cass found himself sitting next to Margaret Leech. She had written three novels, and Cass almost immediately asked her if she'd ever thought about trying nonfiction. "My question struck a sympathetic chord," Cass reported. Leech's first nonfiction work (for Cass, of course) was *Reveille in Washington,* about the Lincoln family during the Civil War. In 1942, it won a Pulitzer Prize. Eighteen years later, Leech won another Pulitzer for her biography of President William McKinley. Of course, it hadn't hurt that she was married to Ralph Pulitzer, who was publisher of the *New York World.*

In 1942, at the time of Harper's one hundred twenty-fifth anniversary, Cass received a letter from President Franklin D. Roosevelt. "There are few businesses," FDR wrote, "that are so intimately interwoven with the national fabric as a publishing house. I congratulate you and all your associates on a fine job in keeping your institution so valiantly on the side of civilization."

And then Cass went off to war.

EUGENE SAXTON, ONE of Cass's best men, died in 1943, and that same year Canfield joined the Office of War Information, running the OWI's operation in North Africa and, when it was freed, in Paris. A member of Canfield's OWI team in Paris was a young man named Simon Michael Bessie. "The high point of our day,"

Canfield said in *Up & Down & Around*, "was the cocktail hour when we assembled in the hotel bar. The talk would be lively, particularly when Mike Bessie would turn up to pour out a torrent of words that held the company spellbound."

Bessie was then on leave from the Cowles's newspaper chain and *Look* magazine, where he had worked at the beginning of the war. When I went to see Mike at his home on historic Washington Square—we sat in a living room right out of a Henry James novel—one of the first things he told me was how he wound up at Harper's. "Cass wanted to know what I was planning to do after the war. I said I imagined I would go back to *Look*."

" 'Well,' Cass said, 'why don't you come join us? I think you'd do well in book publishing.'

" 'Cass,' I said, 'why do you think I would be good in book publishing?'

"He said, 'Well, two reasons. You're interested in a great number of things, but not very deeply. I think that will go well in publishing.'

"There was a pause before Cass gave me his second reason. 'You know,' he said finally, 'there really are two kinds of people in the world, some people are both, but some are neither—there are people who are writers and there are people who are talkers, and you are a talker. And that's better for publishing.' " According to Richard McAdoo, who came to work for Harper's after the war (later becoming one of Houghton Mifflin's blue-ribbon editors), "Cass was not a great talker, not particularly articulate, and I think he probably appreciated that in Mike Bessie."

Simon Michael Bessie went to work for Cass Canfield in November 1946. Another promising young editor came soon after Bessie. Evan Thomas was the youngest son of Norman Thomas, who regularly throughout the Roosevelt years ran for president on the Socialist Party ticket. During the war, Thomas drove an ambulance in North Africa for the American Field Service, and later served in the Navy. Bessie and Thomas became one of the strongest teams in postwar publishing. The problem was, they were both after the same goal.

"Cass liked to manage by conflict," said Gene Young, who became Thomas's secretary when she joined Harper's in 1952. "Shortly after I got there, they promoted both Mike and Evan. There was a memo outlining their new duties. Evan showed it to me and said, 'Doesn't this sound like I'm the guy that sweeps out the store?' It was true. Mike had all the glamorous titles and Evan had sort of the housekeeping. Mike was charming—he charmed Cass—whereas Evan was just this kind of really very square, upper-middle-class WASP. But they were both bringing in good books."

A lot of Thomas's serious nonfiction was bought by Canfield and given to Evan to work on, including John F. Kennedy's *Profiles in Courage,* JFK speechwriter Theodore C. Sorensen's biography *Kennedy,* and *The Silent World* by Jacques-Yves Cousteau. In 1967, Edward S. Greenbaum, the lawyer for Stalin's daughter, Svetlana, phoned his old friend Canfield to tell him he could have Svetlana's memoirs, especially if Evan Thomas became her editor. The deal was done immediately.

But Thomas also found his own books. One of the most successful in his early years was Jim Bishop's *The Day Lincoln Was Shot.* John Appleton called Thomas "probably the best nonfiction editor in the business. People, no matter how high their station in the outside world, would be delighted to be turned over to Evan."

He had a lovable disposition, Gene Young told me about Evan Thomas. And one day she learned something else about him. Gene shared an office with Joan Kahn. "There was a window that swung between Evan and Joan," Gene said, "so they could talk to each other. One day I remember Evan leaning into the window and showing Joan something and saying, 'That's what I have.' It was multiple sclerosis, and he fought it for over fifty years."

Simon Michael Bessie, who sadly died in the spring of 2008,

was born in New York City. His father was a family doctor, and that's what Mike originally thought he would be. He got a scholarship from the Harvard Club of New York to go to Harvard. He was on the college newspaper, and after reading Vincent Sheehan's 1935 book *Personal History,* which was all about the glamour of a journalist's activities throughout the world, he decided that journalism was the career for him.

Mike's first bestseller was *Tallulah,* the autobiography of Tallulah Bankhead, the most flamboyant and naughtiest theatrical star of her period. *Tallulah* was No. 1 on many of the nonfiction bestseller lists of 1952. But it has always rankled Mike that some people chided him for the acquisition. When, for instance, one of his old college professors heard about it, he said, "Mike, you're cheapening the Harper name." In 2005, Robert Gottlieb reviewed for *The New Yorker* a new Tallulah Bankhead biography. In it he called the 1952 autobiography "prickly, honest (for its day), and amusing."

Mike Bessie heard no such complaints about his taking on John Cheever. At the time, Cheever was working on his first novel, *The Wapshot Chronicle,* for Random House. In a letter that Cheever's son, Benjamin, wrote for the online literary magazine *Archipelago,* he described his father's state of mind at the time:

"Bob Linscott was the editor. He had not approved of an early version, and the despair my father felt at that rejection was quite genuine. In his journal he wrote, 'Still no word from Linscott. This seems to imply no enthusiasm, and if the work I've sent him is bad I have made some grave mistakes. My eyes are wrong, my heart is wrong, and I have been mistaken in listening for all these years to the rain.'

"'These old bones are up for sale,' Cheever wrote to Bessie, who asked in reply, 'Where should I send the check?'"

"When John gave me that," Mike said, "he had only published stories, mostly *New Yorker* stories. And I realized when I began to read the manuscript that the good Lord had delivered an unusual novel in my hands, an extraordinary novel." He became so excited that he sent an early copy of the manuscript to Ralph Thompson, who was then the editor of the Book-of-the-Month Club (and a gracious mentor to me when I joined the Club). Several weeks later Thompson called Bessie. "I've got good news for you," Thompson said. "We would like to make a Main Selection of *The Wapshot Chronicle*." Mike was thrilled.

"But there's one problem," Thompson continued, chilling Bessie. "There's one word in the book that I'm afraid will have to go, otherwise we can't use it. Book-of-the-Month has never used a book with this word in it." Immediately, Mike knew what the word was. "It's the scene in the book," he explained to me, "in which our young hero, who's a pretty sexy guy, is feeling very randy. And he's trying to get his wife to bed, and she's got something she wants to discuss with him, and she keeps yakking away. And finally her husband says, 'Sister, you just missed out on the greatest fuck of your life.'"

Mike called Cheever to tell him about the predicament. "John," he said, "selection by the Book-of-the-Month Club means quite a bit of money. Could mean $100,000 or more for you, maybe twice that." Cheever said, "Mike, that's the only word that will do in that place."

Not only did the Book-of-the-Month Club relent and take the book with the word intact, but *The Wapshot Chronicle* in 1958 won the National Book Award for fiction (also-rans included Nabokov's *Pnin* and Malamud's *The Assistant*). *The Wapshot Chronicle* has since become a classic.

In 1959, Bessie was lured away from Harper's by Alfred Knopf's son, Pat, who wanted to start a new publishing company. It was what Mike had dreamed of, the chance to own part of a book business. He joined up with Pat Knopf and Hiram Haydn, who had been Random House's editor in chief, as partners in a house that would be called Atheneum. (See chapter 4.)

Because of Bessie's ability to bring in literary fiction, his departure left a hole at Harper's. Cass Canfield seldom kept a contract in his pocket for a novelist. He did sometimes handle literary fiction that was of British origin. In the early postwar years he left fiction decisions pretty much to Bessie and Elizabeth Lawrence, who was a fine editor—Ann Harris calls Lawrence "the most principled woman I had ever known." But she was a Puritan in her tastes, as was Canfield. This reminds me of Harold Ross, the great editor for *The New Yorker*. One day he called Clifton Fadiman, then the chief book reviewer for the magazine. Ross wanted to know what Fadiman was planning to do for the next issue.

"I think I'm going to review Edmund Wilson's *Memoirs of Hecate County*," Fadiman said.

There was a moment of silence, and then Ross said, "I understand that's fairly graphic."

"Oh," Fadiman said, "what do you mean?"

Ross said, "I can't tell you over the phone."

MARION WYETH (better known as "Buz"), who was more open to liberated writers than Harold Ross, spent forty-five years at Harper's, buying and editing a varied list of fiction and nonfiction, including Roger Kahn's baseball classic *The Boys of Summer*. Early in his career Buz was a reader at Harper's when, one day, he received a copy of a first novel by J. P. Donleavy called *The Ginger Man*. "I was very excited by it," Buz told me. "It was full of outrageous characters, but I thought it was a fascinating book." He gave it to Lawrence to read. "She was just negative on it totally," Buz said as if he were still mourning its loss. *The Ginger Man* went elsewhere. It later came to be ranked by the Modern Library as one of the top 100 novels of the twentieth century.

Then along came *Lolita*.

It was Mike Bessie who first received a copy of *Lolita*. He was in Paris at the time and it was sent to him by Maurice Girodias, whose Olympia Press published erotic literature. "Nabokov had been published by Harper's," Mike said. "Cass was his editor, and Cass found him very troublesome; rewarding, but troublesome. I sat up a good part of the night reading that book, and when I went to bed, I was enthusiastic about it. I'd read about half of it. I went back to it the next day and found my interest flagging. And so I said, 'Well, he's been troublesome with Cass, etc., I'll let it go.' So I did."

The book was also read in New York by Elizabeth Lawrence and possibly Canfield himself. They agreed with Bessie. "About six months later," Mike said, "I read it again. I couldn't believe that I had let it out of my hands. If you were to ask me which of the books that I had a chance to publish and didn't that bothers me the most [I had asked him just that], *Lolita* is it." The novel was turned down by a lot of other publishers in New York, but Walter Minton grabbed *Lolita* for Putnam's and was never disappointed by the outcome.

IN DECEMBER 2003, wanting to know more about Cass Sr., I went to see Cass Canfield, Jr., at the company that was now called HarperCollins. I got caught in a cold, driving rainstorm and was soaking wet when I squished up to his office. I gave Cass Jr. a damp handshake and excused myself for depositing soggy footprints on his floor. It was then I noticed that he was in some disarray himself. Almost as tall as his father, and slimmer, wearing the family mustache, he was in his shirtsleeves, surrounded by boxes on his floor, and he seemed flustered.

"I shouldn't have come and bothered you," I said. "Looks like you're doing some end-of-the-year housekeeping."

"No, no," Cass said, a note of resignation in his voice. "You know, this is my last day here after forty-five years."

"Gee," I gulped. "I could have come another time."

"No, it doesn't matter."

Well, of course it did matter. Even before we started talking,

Cass handed me a memorandum he had just sent to his bosses. It began: "I thought some background info might be useful so I enclose same." Useful? Why in the world did Cass think that he had to defend a lifetime of good works? Well, possibly because HarperCollins was a far different house than it had been when he first set foot on the premises.

After attending the University of Chicago and Columbia, Cass sought work somewhere other than at his father's company. "I didn't want to come to Harper right away," Cass told me, "and I think it was because my father was there, obviously. I felt that if I did go to Harper, I wanted to have something under my sleeve in terms of my own experience and accomplishment. I didn't want to go there as just Cass Canfield, Jr."

His first publishing job was with McGraw-Hill as advertising manager in the trade division. Then, one day, he got a call from Walter Minton, the gruff, hard-driving owner of G. P. Putnam's Sons and Coward-McCann. "Hey, we don't know each other, Cass," Minton said. "I'd like to meet you." They did meet and Minton took him on as a senior editor at Coward-McCann.

Soon afterward, Tim Coward, who was running the imprint, died. Cass thought he might have a chance for the job, but Minton gave it to someone else. Cass was upset. "Why didn't you give it to me?" he asked Minton.

"Because one of these days," he told Cass, "your father is going to pick up the phone and say, 'Cass, it's time for you to come home,' and you're going to go." He might not have gone if Minton had promoted him. But it didn't happen, so in 1958 Cass did move to his father's house.

"When I came to Harper," Cass said, "my father hoped I would learn the business and do managerial work. But I wasn't the slightest bit interested in managerial experience. My interest was editorial, and so I became an editor in the trade department."

He developed an interest in trade paperback publishing, and over the years he had much to do with the various paperback imprints established at Harper's. He acquired books, too, becoming a specialist on books pertaining to art and architecture. It was Cass Jr. who also bought *A Hundred Years of Solitude,* Gabriel García Márquez's first novel. And he helped strengthen Harper's reputation for serious nonfiction, signing up Hugh Thomas's well-received history of the Spanish Civil War and Paul Johnson's *Modern Times.* His biggest disappointment by far was losing Márquez in a contract dispute. "He left us and went to Knopf," Cass said as if it were yesterday. "It broke my heart."

As we talked that rainy afternoon, largely about his father, I asked Cass Jr. what he felt the trade book publisher's function was. I'm afraid I caught him at a disappointing moment in his life. "It's an impossible business," he said, a tartness in his voice. "It makes no sense at all. I mean, you have a winner one day, and you've got a loser four out of five days. The book publisher is a vehicle to allow the dissemination of ideas or thoughts or stories—anything. That's all we are—we're a vehicle."

FRAN McCULLOUGH NEVER thought of herself as a "vehicle." She had too much spunk as an editor. In 1965, Harper's poetry editor, Elizabeth Lawrence, announced her retirement. She named Frances Lindley, the company's advertising director, to be her successor. The brawl started when Fran McCullough tried to buy a book of poetry called *Ariel* by an unknown poet named Sylvia Plath.

"Frances Lindley," Fran said, "was determined we were not going to publish the book. So we had a fight, but I got Evan Thomas to sign off on it. He convinced Lindley that Fran deserved "to have her head."

Harper's wound up with a book of poetry that has sold over

two million copies and is still going strong. Later in life I got to know Frances, who had become an editor. She was great fun to be with, had a biting wit, laughed all the time, and worked into her nineties. Jim Fox, who was house lawyer at Harper's for thirty-five years and was highly regarded by the editors, said of Lindley, "Frances is somebody I would put in the top five people in my life. I think of her every day. She was so funny and so insightful."

Because of *Ariel,* Fran McCullough got Plath's *The Bell Jar.* In a classic case of miscommunication, I asked Fran what Plath was like to deal with. "She was dead," Fran said. "But that didn't make her any easier to deal with." That caused both of us to laugh, but Fran was utterly serious because now she was dealing with Plath's "poor agonizing mother" and husband Ted Hughes, "who was consumed with guilt. And part of him," she told me, "would think, let's not publish this book. I said, 'No we can publish it. We can make everybody happy. Let me deal with the mother.'" And she did, and she certainly made Harper's (and untold numbers of readers) happy.

In 1968, Fran McCullough published a first novel by an American Indian, N. Scott Momaday's *House Made of Dawn,* which won the Pulitzer Prize for fiction. She also published Richard Ford's first novel, *A Piece of My Heart.*

An editor from another house whom I interviewed said of Harper's culture, "It never understood itself. It published good books, certainly through the fifties and sixties, but you couldn't tell what it was. It didn't have a profile." I don't think this was quite so. Harper & Row's heart was really pumping from an abundance of serious and important works of nonfiction that Cass Canfield was either bringing in himself or inspiring his editors to do. The kids were also finding new authors of strong commercial fiction that would be around for years. In *The New York Times Book Review*'s selection of 1965's best adult titles, Harper led all houses with fifteen books. That same year Harper's won the American Library Association's selections of Notable Books for the sixth time in eight years.

And in 1970 Genevieve Young produced her own grand slam.

GENEVIEVE WAS ELEVEN years old when she found out that her father had been executed. Her mother, Juliana (who celebrated her one hundredth birthday in 2005), was a famous belle in China. She had her own car—a white convertible. She was driving the car in Shanghai one day when Gene's father saw her and followed her. His name was Clarence Kuangson. He had an advanced degree from Princeton and was one of China's rising diplomats. They were married in 1929. At the time of Pearl Harbor he was the consulate general in the Philippines. When the Japanese invaded the island, his entire staff was arrested, and Gene never saw her father again. "All through the war," she told me as we talked in the living room of her comfortable New York apartment, "we thought they were alive, because there were all these rumors—they'd been seen here, they'd been seen there. We didn't find out until we came to America that he had been killed the April after Pearl Harbor."

Living in an all-female household during World War II, Gene went to a girls' prep school when she came to the U.S., then to Wellesley, an all-female liberal arts college. "I had practically never met a man until I went to work for Evan Thomas," Gene said. "He was to be my first man, as it were, besides my father—he was very generous, very funny, very smart, very open. He let me do everything, except buy a book. I wrote jacket copy, I presented books at sales conferences, I edited books, I recommended books. So I had all the fun without any of the responsibility. And then in 1960, after Mike Bessie had left, Evan had been promoted to executive vice president and he wasn't able to do as many books. He'd come back from meetings with columns of figures, which I didn't know how to file. That's when I said to him, 'Evan, I can't do this.'

" 'Well,' he said, 'you've been here seven years, too long to make you a reader. I guess you'll have to be assistant editor.' So I got promoted."

One of the first books she bought was a serious work of non-fiction, *The Negro Revolt* by Louis E. Lomax. It sold well, is still in print, and, she says, it taught her a lesson. "I probably edited to the point where I wrote it. It was just so much work. It was stupid. In those days I had no sense about how much work you should do. It wasn't until I was maybe ten years from retirement I realized that I didn't have to cut a manuscript myself, I could cut one chapter and say to the author, 'You do the rest.' " Gene had good intentions, but it was a lesson that apparently didn't take. In our conversation late in 2004 she told me that she had just spent a month editing and rewriting a new autobiography by her ex-husband, the brilliant photographer and poet Gordon Parks. (Parks died two years later.) She always believed in her authors and was tough as hell with them to make their books really work.

Gene found her next book in B. Altman's department store. One day, when she was still a secretary, she ran into a friend at that store. His name was Ken Milford, a salesman for Harper's printing company. Ken was in B. Altman's to return his wife's raincoat; Gene was there with a furniture problem. They stood in

GENE YOUNG

I got *Love Story* in 1968. Erich Segal's book *The Death of Comedy* was published by us; an ex-academic named Norbert Slepyan was his editor. Erich's agent, Lois Wallace, and I were having a salad at the Plaza. Lois said, "I've got this problem. Erich has written this screenplay for Bob Evans. It's called *Love Story* and Bob Evans is definitely going to make it, because he wants his wife, Ali MacGraw, to star in it. Erich wants to turn it into a novel, but he doesn't think that Norbert is the right person to do it, because he's too scholarly. So," she asks me, "what am I going to do? Your option with him, you know, is for nonfiction. The easiest thing for me to do is to show it to Bill Targ at Putnam's. He once told me, 'Anything Segal writes, I want.'"

"No, no," I said. "Don't do that." Somehow, Lois did send it to Putnam's. And she sent it to Little, Brown, too, who offered $4,000 for it. So I said to Evan, "Let's blow them out of the water." We offered $7,500 and we got the book.

The next morning, I woke up and I thought, *What have I done?* I called Lois and said, "Lois, we don't know that Erich can do fiction. In case he can't, can we make this a double contract and apply it against his next serious book?" And I remember Lois saying in this snide way, "If he can't write a novel, he'll give you back the money. OK?" Well, that was OK to us.

I read the screenplay, and then I met Erich at the Vanderbilt Hotel. We had coffee. And I said to him, "You can't work up to her dying at the end, that's like grand opera. You've got to kill her off in the first paragraph." That was my huge contribution to *Love Story*. So it took him weeks. He'd say, "I can't do it." And I'd say, "Yes, you can." He finally did that famous sentence: "What can you say about a twenty-five-year-old girl who died!" It took him three weeks to write the first paragraph, and about another three weeks to write the rest.

And we published it. It was real short. We had to stretch to make it 131 pages. Sales people kept complaining to our sales manager, Bill Ashworth. They would say, "Why are we publishing this piece of junk?" I think I published it for all the right reasons. He was obviously a comer, he had a good ear, and it was already about to be a movie, for God's sake.

line together and gabbed about family matters. Gene asked Milford about his wife, "What does she do?"

"She's a graduate student at Barnard [Columbia's women's college at the time], and she's just written her dissertation."

"Oh, on what?"

"On Zelda Fitzgerald."

"Can I see it?" Gene said immediately. She had just read an excerpt in *The New Yorker* from Calvin Tomkins's *Living Well Is the Best Revenge,* about the expatriates Gerald and Sara Murphy and their friendship with Scott and Zelda Fitzgerald and other artists of the Lost Generation. Gene wanted to know more about the Fitzgeralds. And so, she thought, would a lot of other people.

She was disappointed by Nancy Milford's first draft, basically a collage of letters from Scott to Zelda. The Fitzgeralds' daughter, Scottie Lanahan (Frances Scott Fitzgerald Lanahan), had handed Zelda's letters over to her. Gene told Milford straight out: "This is a do-it-yourself book. You can't do that. You have to really write a book."

Nancy delivered a second draft. In return, she received another forty to fifty pages of notes from Gene. The next time around—bingo! After seven years, Nancy Milford had skillfully pieced the letters together, and Gene edited them. "The final product," Gene said, "was really wonderful."

Then the troubles began. Scottie had given Milford the two shopping bags containing Scott's letters under the impression that she was writing her master's thesis. When she received her contract, Gene called Scottie to tell her of the change and asked for her permission. Gene never forgot what Scottie said: "All right, you may publish it. All I want is a chance to read the manuscript and have some say in it."

Gene sent the copyedited manuscript to Scottie, and she could not bear to read it. A Fitzgerald-Hemingway specialist at the University of South Carolina, Matthew J. Bruccoli, agreed to read the manuscript. He sent Scottie an eleven-page report, including suggestions about a possible lesbian affair and a romance with a boy. Scottie, so upset by Bruccoli's conjectures, immediately called Gene Young. "I'm not going to sue you," she said, "but how would you like it if I came in and slit my throat in your reception room?"

She may not have been joking. The Harper & Row lawyers took over, and Gene had to make large cuts. Published in 1970, *Zelda* spent twenty-nine weeks on the *New York Times* bestseller list. Scottie Lanahan's only public act of displeasure was to tell the George Sand bookstore to take it out of their window.

Gene's third 1970 success was *The 900 Days,* Harrison Salisbury's epic history of the Nazis' three-year siege of Leningrad. Cass Canfield had bought the book, having known the distinguished foreign correspondent of *The New York Times* for many years. He gave it to Evan Thomas to edit, which he was doing until he left Harper's and moved to another fine house, W. W. Norton. Gene Young inherited *The 900 Days.*

Gene had gotten to know Salisbury from being Evan Thomas's secretary. She remembers him "as one of the few authors who actually treated women as human beings, greeted me by name, sent me Christmas cards." She read his manuscript. "It was one page for every day, and it wasn't working. So I sent him a huge batch of notes." A few years before Salisbury died, in 1993, Gene ran into him, and he offered her a confession. "When I got those notes from you," he told her, "I threw them right down on the floor. What's this girl know about it? And I was going to call Cass. But then I thought, I've got to read them before I call the boss. So I took them off the floor and read them and I said to myself, 'Oh, all right.' "

Gene spent all that summer editing *The 900 Days.* "I carried a bag around I called 'Old Harrison.' But he did it."

NOT SO SUCCESSFUL for the House of Harper was its involvement with the Kennedy family following the assassination of

John F. Kennedy. The Kennedys felt that the country deserved a magisterial book about President Kennedy. There was as yet no publisher, but Bobby Kennedy invited Evan Thomas and Harper & Row to do the book. Thomas had been an editor for both Jack and Bobby on several of their books, and the family trusted him. In addition, Cass Canfield was a friend to Jackie Kennedy—his adopted son Michael had once been married to Jackie's sister, Lee. Jackie wanted William Manchester to write the book. Manchester's publisher was Little, Brown. "Jackie Kennedy insisted on Manchester," said Arthur Thornhill, Jr., who was head of the house. "Evan Thomas called me to ask what I felt about it. I said, 'Fine.' Later, Evan wrote me and said, 'I will always remember your favor.' "

In those years book publishing was still, among the old houses at least, "a gentleman's calling." Tom Guinzburg, whose father, Harold K. Guinzburg, had founded the Viking Press in the 1920s, remembered when he was a child sitting at his parents' dinner table one night with John Gunther and his wife. "Somehow in the course of the dinner," Tom said, "a book idea emerged. Dad went right over to the phone. 'I'm going to call Cass Canfield,' he said."

Tom heard his father say, "Cass, it's Harold. Listen, I'm sitting here with the Gunthers. Would you consider releasing John for just one book I'd like to do?"

"They talked a bit," Tom said, "and it was done."

Manchester submitted the manuscript of *The Death of a President* in March 1966. All the late president's men read it as fast as they could. There were plenty of revisions. Fran McCullough remembers getting a call at that time to come see Canfield and Evan Thomas. There were three other women in his office. "I have a little job for you tonight," Canfield said. And he handed each woman a copy of the manuscript. "I want you to pretend that you're Jackie, and that you're reading this for the first time. And I want you to tell me in writing anything you might take from it." The women submitted their reports. As a result, changes they suggested were made, but they weren't enough. *Look* magazine was approved to do the serialization, and it was what *Look* was putting into the excerpt that upset the Kennedys the most. After a series of tense meetings between the principals—capped by an injunction against the serialization and the book itself— more cuts had to be made to gain the family's approval. *The Death of a President* was published in 1967 with a 500,000-copy first printing, and a number of the author's findings left out, and it became a huge bestseller.

One day, late in the same year, 1967, Cass Jr. called all his editors together. "My father's had a stroke," he said. "He's not himself. But we're going to keep on going." Cass Canfield, seventy years old, stepped down as head of the executive committee, and changes came about.

IN 1962, Harper & Brothers became Harper & Row, a consequence of a merger with the elementary and high school textbook company Row, Peterson. "It was a huge change," Cass Jr. told me. "We ceased being a private company." Gordon Jones, the head of Row, Peterson, emerged as the largest stockholder of the combined firm, and he began to bring a different culture to the company, one that seemed to Harper's editorial veterans more business-driven than book-oriented.

Mel Arnold, who had headed the college division and started a trade paperback imprint called Torchbooks, became president. "Mel was a brilliant man and loved books," Cass said, "but he was really somebody who should have been the publisher of a university press. He was not very interested or sympathetic about general trade publishing."

"The Big Upheaval" was what Dick McAdoo, the editor in chief of a special trade area for Harper's doing social and economic books, called that period. He soon quit his job and ended up happily at Houghton Mifflin. And then a severe blow was dealt to the company: Evan Thomas left to become editor in chief at W. W. Norton, where his career would flourish. Cass Jr. took his father's place on the board of directors and also ran the trade department for a year.

Jay Iselin, who had been at *Newsweek,* was hired to run the trade division. There was an immediate uneasiness among the editors. One of the first editors Iselin faced was Gene Young, who wanted a raise. As managing editor, she got to see the raises other people in the trade division were getting. A new editor at Harper's, Tom Congdon, received a $3,500 raise. "I stormed into Jay's office, and I said, 'I think I should be making as much as Tom because I'm contributing a lot more.' And I remember what Jay said: 'Have a heart, Gene. He's got three kids.' That's what he said. So I was sulking about that." That's when she decided to go to work for Lippincott. But before she could leave she found herself embroiled in another gender battle.

"We were holding our sales conference at the Arley House," Gene said, "which was a conference center outside of Washington, and Iselin decided to take all but three editors. He said he would leave Ann Harris, Fran McCullough, and another woman editor, Virginia Hieu, at home."

As Fran McCullough remembers it, what he told them was, "Now, I'm sure you're all going to make a big deal of this. But the fact is you have children, you have things you need to be doing here. It's not going to be fun. I know it sounds great, but we're not going to actually have a good time. We're going to be busting our balls, in fact." Gene saw it another way: "He didn't want them to come because he essentially didn't like their books, and he didn't think they would sell. So I told him, 'You can't do that. You can take a few people and leave the bunch, but you can't take everybody and leave three.'" But Iselin went ahead and announced it at a meeting. Gene remembers that she and Fran McCullough were standing outside the door, when Fran said, "This is a bad day all around because as I was leaving the house, a pigeon shat on my head." Seeing what was going on, Gene Young took off for Lippincott.

The women decided they would all stay at home for a day. Fran McCullough drafted a letter to the management saying why they were staying home from work, and she passed it around to all the editors, men included, who added their versions. Most of them stayed away, too.

The New York Times covered the story and said it was a women's movement strike. But it wasn't even a strike. "We worked at home," Ann Harris, one of the left-out threesome, told me, "but we would be available. Our assistants would be in the office and doing their work. It's just that we needed to register what an intolerable and irresponsible situation it was."

Ann remembers the time she rode home on the subway, inadvertently, with Jay Iselin. This was well after the strike, at a time when Iselin was being replaced at Harper's. "We were crammed in a packed subway car," she said. "He was bewailing the unfairness and ignominy of his situation. All I could think about was that before Iselin, Harper's was a place that was really collegial in the best sense. It had its pecking order, and it had its politics—it certainly had strong politics—but it also did honor to the craft we were all engaged in. It was a wonderful house."

At a subsequent sales conference, Ann Harris was invited to attend. This time, she was presenting a novel called *The Exorcist.*

"THE EXORCIST," ANN Harris told me, "was the first big book I did myself—I mean, for which I got upfront credit. At that point I'd been in and out of publishing for twenty years. I had kids, I took summers off, I worked on this part-time schedule, I did all these things, and I did other people's books. And I was very happy doing it. It was a heady thing to have a great big bestseller.

From the beginning I knew absolutely that it was going to the top of the list. And I knew that I could make it happen."

So she did. William Peter Blatty came to New York, and he and Harris holed up in a hotel and worked every day for six weeks to get the book into shape. It was published in 1971 and became the biggest-selling novel of the decade. Marc Jaffe told me that the book sold four million copies for Bantam before the movie and four million copies after.

The Exorcist was handed to her, but *The Thorn Birds* was a book Ann Harris found on her own.

"In 1974," she said, "I had bought a first novel by an Australian writer, Colleen McCullough, called *Tim* that I thought had some very special qualities. It wasn't going to sell a helluva lot, but it was good quality. It did modestly well. Then she started to work on this other book, and I could see it was going to be something.

"Colleen McCullough was working at Yale—she had come from Australia several years before—and she'd come down to New York, and we'd work on *The Thorn Birds* together, and she'd stay in our apartment. And we nursed it along for whatever time it took—but I knew what we were going to have. The novel just sold all over the world."

For the next McCullough novel, Ann spent six weeks with the author in Norfolk Island, which was a thousand miles off the coast of New South Wales. *An Indecent Obsession* was published in 1980, the year Ann left Harper's.

Ann continued, "At that point, Harper's had begun to change. It had been through a succession of publishers and editors in chief and difficult times." She felt that it was time for her to leave. "But every now and then," she said to me, "I get into a reminiscent mood about the good fortune of the old days. I see friends from other houses and we talk about what it was like to be working in that kind of atmosphere, the way Harper was in its glory days."

Fran McCullough left in 1980, too, for pretty much the same reasons as Ann Harris. She calls her Harper years the best years of her life. "The Harper people were so identified with the company," she said. "I remember talking to some muck-a-muck when I was leaving. I said to him, 'You think you're running the company, but five years from now nobody's going to know who you are or what happened here.'"

There was much love between all these editors. Every one I spoke with, men as well as women, mentioned the dinner party they held each year at Christmastime. A family they are, right up to this day. "This company was about the authors," said Fran McCullough. "We were all just nuts. We thought we were doing one of the most creative things you can possibly do."

CASS CANFIELD DIED on March 27, 1986. The headline in *The New York Times* read, "Cass Canfield, a Titan of Publishing, Is Dead at 88." Gene Young remembers that after his stroke, Cass became lively, even eccentric. He gave parties all the time because he loved to dance, and he danced his time away. There was the evening that both Cass and Gene Young were heading for the New York Public Library. Cass said to Gene, "Let's skip along." She said okay. So there they were, the two of them skipping their way through the streets of New York and not stopping until they came to the place where the books were.

9

GIVE THE READER A BREAK

Simon & Schuster

There was a lot of freedom at S & S. It was like a loose ball on
a football field. Whoever picked it up could run with it.

—SEYMOUR TURK

Robert Gottlieb sprung to fame on an unsuspecting book
publishing industry almost before he wriggled out of
knee pants. It all began in July 1955, when he took his
first real job in life as an editorial assistant at Simon & Schuster.
Two quick years later he reached manhood.

Gottlieb affirmed all of this to me one morning when we met in
his spacious living room that overlooked the Turtle Bay Gardens,
only a step away from Katharine Hepburn's townhouse. Turtle
Bay Gardens, it must be said, was also where Maxwell Perkins—
the Babe Ruth of book editors until the Gottlieb Revelation—had
lived. From the tone of our conversation I couldn't help but feel
that Bob had always set his sights on busting Perkins to Numero
Duo in the Book Publishing Hall of Fame.

Our meeting took place on my birthday in April 2005. Bob
provided me with a wealth of birthday gifts consisting of his
firmest convictions about the art of book publishing. He was

wearing his usual postmodern uniform—an open-necked sports shirt and corduroy pants—and was still flicking that forelock off his forehead, as I remember him doing in the 1970s and 1980s when he was cajoling us at the Book-of-the-Month Club, with much success, to buy his books. He still looked to me almost younger than springtime but—ah!—I came across an early photo of him in Peter Schwed's *Turning the Pages,* Schwed's stiff but chatty history of Simon & Schuster (Schwed had been a key ex-ecutive with the company for almost forty years, including those uncomfortable competitive years with Gottlieb). It is a head shot that must have been taken in 1955 or '56, when Bob was still an apprentice at Simon & Schuster, because he was wearing a white shirt and a tie, possibly for the last time in his life. He seemed to be making up for that sartorial lapse by the teasing smirk on his face that might be saying, *You understand that I know much more than you do.*

Bob was very obliging to me that morning, even offering me a pillow for comfort; his pillow collection, along with vintage plas-tic handbags, had become famous as Gottlieb's fetishes. Through his large horn-rimmed glasses, the frame as black as his hair, his reflections often expressed gentleness as well as self-satisfaction. I could understand why so many youngsters, trying to break into book publishing, told me how welcoming he had been to them and how much they valued the time he had given them.

One of the first questions I always ask the heroes in this book concerns their early lives, including whether they had read a partic-ular book as a child that still affected them as grown-ups. "Were you ever taken by an author?" is the clumsy way I put it to Gottlieb.

"I was taken by every author," he said.

As a child Gottlieb claimed to be obsessive about various ele-ments in book publishing. "One of the things I got interested in very early," he said, "were bestseller lists, and I kept charts and followed them very carefully." When he was about sixteen years old he started going up to the library at Columbia University to read through issues of *Publishers Weekly,* studying bestseller lists back to 1895 and, he said, "reading the books themselves." For my benefit, I suppose, he cited one such book, *Lolly Willowes,* a first novel by Sylvia Townsend Warner that in 1926 became the first Main Selection of the Book-of-the-Month Club. Bob never saw that one on any bestseller list and it didn't make a nickel for the Club, but the judges loved it. One of them described *Lolly Willowes* as "one of those wise simple books that are so easy to read and so true to human nature that the reader does not at first realize how much quiet humor and how much rare life he is encountering."

From his precocious literary exploits through college at Columbia and two years at Cambridge University (the poet Ted Hughes described Cambridge as "a ditch full of clear water where all the frogs have died"), Bob claims he felt not the slightest interest in being a publisher. I asked him whether it was because he didn't know what he wanted. "No," he said. "I didn't want to do anything at all." However, he came back from Cambridge with a wife and a baby and knew that he had to find a job. "But nobody much wanted to hire me because I was a very arrogant and scruffy young man."

In July 1955, scruffy or otherwise, Bob found a job working for Simon & Schuster's legendary editor, Jack Goodman. Goodman had been only twenty-four years old when he was hired by Dick Simon in 1933 to write jacket and advertising copy, immediately becoming the first boy wonder of the company. Not only was he a whiz-bang at writing copy, he was a man at home in Hollywood as well as on Broadway, and brought in books by celebrities. Bob Hope's *I Never Left Home* was one of Goodman's, which became the No. 1 nonfiction bestseller in 1944.

So there was Bob Gottlieb, at age twenty-four, working directly with Goodman's premier authors—S. J. Perelman, James

Thurber, Romain Gary, Meyer Levin, Herbert Block (the mighty *Washington Post* political cartoonist better known as Herblock), and dozens of others. Gottlieb was also discovering he had the stuff to collect his own authors. And, all of a sudden, he came to love the act of publishing.

WHEN TWENTY-FOUR-YEAR-OLD RICHARD Simon and twenty-seven-year-old Max Lincoln Schuster came together to start a new publishing house in their names, they didn't know the first thing about the business. But they knew they wanted to be a part of what they felt was an ideal profession. Both men were graduates of Columbia, and both came from well-off families. (You may be tired of hearing about "well-off families" by this point, but then as now, if you choose to start at the top in book publishing, you'd better have inherited a lot of money.) They had met in 1921 when Simon was working as a salesman for the publishing house of Boni & Liveright and Schuster was editing a trade magazine. They were vastly different personalities. Simon, a burly six feet three, was an outgoing person with dozens of interests, including tennis, contract bridge, photography, and especially music. It is said that he might have been a concert pianist; two of his children, Joanna and Carly Simon, became divas, Joanna in opera, Carly in pop music.

Max Lincoln Schuster was a head shorter than Simon. He wore thick glasses, severe clothes, and tended to be uncomfortable in the presence of other people. He was also a learned man, more properly headed toward academic publishing—except that he had populist impulses. And so he spent much of his free time at home reading the daily newspapers and plucking from them ideas for books. He would come to work every morning with actual color-coded cuttings from the papers, and his hard-pressed secretaries would have to file them. Once, when he tore out a front-page photo showing a mother screaming for a child who had just died in a tenement fire, he told his secretary, without compassion: "File under Grief."

For a savant, Schuster was accomplished at one-liners. When he began to feel comfortable as a publisher, he wrote a manifesto to everyone in the new company: "One thing we're not going to have around here is a hardening of the categories."

One person who was soft and smart was Richard Simon's aunt. She gave her nephew and Max Schuster a perfect first book for their company. A crossword puzzle fanatic, she told Dick Simon that she would love to have more such puzzles to work on. Simon went right ahead and persuaded three crossword puzzle editors at the *New York World* to produce such a book. Four months into 1924, after they had rented a small room in midtown New York and set their desks facing each other, they published their first book: *The First Cross Word Puzzle Book.*

With each copy of the first printing of 3,600 copies, Simon, displaying his skill as a marketer, offered an attached rubber eraser–topped pencil. Then, further displaying his skill for writing copy, he placed a one-inch ad near the *New York World*'s crossword puzzle. Just like a newspaper's front page, it read: "Out Today! *The First Cross Word Puzzle Book*!"

In three months the book, priced at $1.35, sold over 100,000 copies. Three more puzzle books followed the first one. By 1925, Mr. Simon and Mr. Schuster had sold more than a million books and made *Publishers Weekly*'s bestseller list. Not a bad return on their original investment of $3,000 each.

Their timing had been exactly right to start a book publishing house. If the middle 1920s had a distinction beside prosperity, it was that a brigade of talented wordsmiths had figured out how to prosper by serving the middlebrow culture of America. In 1922, DeWitt Wallace and Lila Acheson Wallace founded *Reader's Digest.* In 1923, Henry Luce and Britton Hadden started *Time.* In 1924, Henry Seidel Canby became founding editor of the *Saturday*

Review of Literature. In 1925, Harold Ross created *The New Yorker*, while Harold Guinzburg created the Viking Press. And in 1926, Harry Scherman invented the Book-of-the-Month Club.

Dick Simon was different from those other pioneers. He may not have invented the way books should be marketed, but no American book publisher of the time could match Simon's abundant flair and originality for selling a book. He taught and inspired a family of the like-minded—most notably his successors at S & S, Jack Goodman and Nina Bourne. It was Simon who dreamed up the slogan for the house—"Give the Reader a Break"—and he made brass paperweights for his editors imprinted with that motto. He not only wanted the reader to buy a book that was well manufactured, with simple, clean typography, but he also wanted to price the book as low as possible. Above all, he wanted a book that was easy to read. Max Schuster agreed with that, having once said that a book should be like a woman's dress: "long enough to cover the subject, but short enough to be interesting." The downside was that these strictures made it difficult for the house to bring in literary fiction. In effect, fiction that might be called highbrow, or even high middlebrow, became a rarity at "Essandess," as the house came to be called.

The Messrs. Simon & Schuster stuck to their strengths. But they couldn't do it all by themselves. In 1927, Max Schuster interviewed a recent Columbia graduate, Clifton Fadiman, who was teaching at the Ethical Culture School in New York. At Columbia, Kip, as Fadiman was called, had run with a first-class crowd of his peers: Lionel Trilling, Meyer Schapiro, Mortimer Adler, Mark Van Doren, and Whittaker Chambers.

The first thing Schuster said to Fadiman at their meeting was, "I understand you would like to have a job with us." Fadiman reached for his folder. "I have typed out one hundred ideas that I think might make books," he said.

The most helpful of the one hundred suggestions was this

one: "I believe an intriguing and successful book could be compiled out of a selection of the Robert Ripley cartoon features for the Hearst papers: *Believe It or Not!*" Instantly, Schuster believed in Kip Fadiman and made him a major editor in the new company. The book version of *Believe It or Not!* went on to sell 200,000 copies in its first year, and thirty million copies throughout the world since then.

Kip was that kind of an idea person. I can't help remembering those times in his Book-of-the-Month Club years, which numbered fifty-seven, when we called on him to give us an idea or two for a project we wanted to pursue. He would unfailingly drop fifty or more on us. "You may," he would say gravely, "find one or two that would be helpful."

Max Schuster felt that he had a counterpart in Fadiman, another discoverer of topics that could be turned into books. "The sheer exquisite excitement of taking the editorial initiative and discovering needs yet to be met by books yet unwritten," Schuster said, "was an unforgettable experience."

The same year that Fadiman was hired, Schuster was discovering the Little Blue Books. Published by Haldeman-Julius, they were pamphlets that sold for ten cents a copy. Will Durant, a professor at Columbia University, had written eleven of them on various philosophers. Schuster read them and immediately thought, *Why not a basic book on the lives and the wisdom of the great philosophers?* He met Haldeman-Julius for lunch one day and proposed that Durant consolidate his essays into a Simon & Schuster book that would be titled *The Story of Philosophy.* In 1927 it became the No. 1 nonfiction bestseller. Many years later, Durant would say about his publishers, "Perhaps half the books they have published originated in their own brains." In the history of Simon & Schuster, Will Durant was the shining example of the partners' wizardry.

For soon after the original publication of *Philosophy*, Durant and his wife, Ariel, began a fifty-year undertaking to do nothing less than *The Story of Civilization*. In the preface of the first volume, published in 1935, Will Durant wrote: "I wish to tell as much as I can, in as little space as I can, of contributions that genius and labor have made to the cultural heritage of mankind. . . . I do not need to be told how absurd this enterprise is . . . and have made it clear that no one mind and no single lifetime can adequately compass this task." Yet Will Durant and his wife of sixty-eight years completed an astonishing eleven volumes. The last volume, *The Age of Napoleon,* was published when he was ninety years old.

Over the years, the life work of the Durants was both a blessing and a curse to those who worked with the single-minded couple. During the decade when the first volumes began coming out, Clifton Fadiman was their house editor, trying to help, even "in a small way," as Kip modestly put it, with the early volumes. Later, when Fadiman became a judge for BOMC, he had to help decide whether the Club should take a volume. "I found it hard to separate affection from judgment," he said. Still, all eleven volumes were taken by the Club as Main Selections. By the time of its sixtieth anniversary, the Club had distributed over nine million copies of the Durant books to its membership. Many of these sales were popular "premiums"—books that could be had for a minimal price by anyone willing to enroll in the Club. Eventually, we offered the entire set as one premium.

Although it may seem that Fadiman was mostly engaged by the Durants in his years at S & S, he also moved in other directions. In 1928, for instance, after Dick Simon had come back from a trip to Europe with a book by an Austrian author, Felix Salten, Kip gave it to Whittaker Chambers to translate. The book was *Bambi: A Life in the Woods,* which not only sold zillions of copies, but also became Simon & Schuster's first Main Selection from the Book-of-the-Month Club.

So the partners were doing all right. But since neither of them had much interest in dealing with managerial problems, especially those involving money, they sought expert help. In the second year of their existence they found someone who had the skills they needed, even though he was only seventeen years old.

AS YOU MUST know by now, this modest book of knowledge favors the editors who, bless them, open up their authors with a dazzling display of show and tell, and a modicum of wit. If you want to know about the bookkeepers who were marvelous at their jobs, you will have to go elsewhere—with one notable exception. Leon Shimkin had come to work for Dick and Max in 1924, and they knew right away that they had someone special when this kid, who had started going to night school at New York University, refused to take the job unless he received the same $25 a week that the founders were then paying themselves.

Right off, he solved a money problem for his bosses. The crossword puzzle books had done so well that S & S reinvested the profits for new books. But come the tax season, they received an unexpectedly high income tax bill and suddenly didn't have enough money left over to meet their obligations. Shimkin immediately understood this tax liability and persuaded the IRS to adopt a new rule that would allow all book publishers, not just S & S, to reinvest such earnings for the benefit of future books. Not long after that coup, Dick Simon came to call Leon Shimkin "Our Little Golden Nugget."

What "Essandess" didn't find out until some time later, to their joy, was that Shimkin was an idea person too, one of those at S & S who knew how to run with a loose football.

"Leon was always involved in self-improvement and self-help," Seymour Turk told me when we talked not long ago. Shimkin had hired Sy Turk in 1951 as a junior accountant. By 1973, he served a short term as president of the company. He and

I became friends when, in my last years at the Book-of-the-Month Club, he came on board as senior vice president and general manager, doing what he had been doing all his life—keeping publishing houses out of financial trouble. He's still at it today, working his magic as a consultant for several small publishing houses.

Sy knew a lot about Shimkin's editorial triumphs. "In the early 1930s," he said, "Leon had an accountant named Irving Stein. He asked Stein to write an income tax guide. The first two volumes didn't work; they just weren't right. So Leon called up a tax authority he didn't know, but who he'd heard a lot about: J. K. Lasser. He asked Lasser to do the third tax book." Shimkin's advice to Lasser was right out of the Simon & Schuster playbook: "Keep the guide simple and readable. Write short sentences and use one-syllable words whenever possible." This time J. K. Lasser's *Your Income Tax* took off and in its heyday was selling a million copies a year.

That was a book you would expect a person like Shimkin, with his extraordinary mind for figures, to dream up—but not the next one.

"Leon was very shy," Sy Turk told me, "and he went to a place to conquer his shyness and to become better as a business executive." It was a fourteen-week course on public speaking offered by a man named Dale Carnegie. Shimkin loved the course, and he thought, *Why not get him to write a book on the subject?* It happened that Carnegie had once approached S & S about doing such a book, but never heard back from anybody. So, still in a fit of pique, Carnegie told Shimkin he was too busy to undertake such a project. Shimkin held his ground and said that he would have a stenographer take notes of the lectures from which the material could be organized and edited. Fortunately, Carnegie agreed. What emerged was Dale Carnegie's *How to Win Friends and Influence People*. It was the No. 1 nonfiction bestseller in 1937, still on the list in 1938, and wound up the biggest bestseller in the company's early history.

Mr. Simon and Mr. Schuster were more than pleased with Shimkin and offered him a $25,000 bonus. Shimkin turned it down. What he wanted was a third of the company. He got it. Add another S to Essandess.

"He was my mentor," Sy Turk told me. "I think Leon was brilliant and underrated. For one thing, he came from a lower-class family, nowhere in the league with the Simons or the Schusters. Secondly, he was an East European Jew in an industry that at that time had mostly German Jews." As a consequence, he was not always treated as well as his "betters." Schuster's wife, Ray, who was a trial to almost everybody at S & S, landed on Shimkin. She once referred to him as a little bookkeeper who "belongs on Seventh Avenue selling *schmattes.*" Another time, in an act of pure malice, she invited the Shimkins to a dinner party but neglected to tell them that it was black tie.

It is somewhat ironic to think that Leon Shimkin's last notable acquisition before he rose to the heights, in a firm where non-German Jews had trouble getting executive positions, came right after the war. He persuaded Joshua Loth Liebman, a rabbi from Boston whom he had heard preach, to write an inspirational book based on his sermons. *Peace of Mind* it was called, and it was a major nonfiction bestseller for three straight years—1946, '47, and '48. It's still in print.

IT WAS JACK Goodman, above all others, who was adored by almost everyone in the company. He adored most of his coworkers, too, but his closest friend of all was Albert Leventhal. "Jack and Al were childhood friends from the day when Harlem was white and Jewish," Tony Schulte, who came to S & S in 1957, told me. "And they were a team. Everything good that happened at S & S, they did."

In the decade before Jack's death in 1957, with both Dick Simon and Max Schuster in failing health, Jack and Albert were literally running Simon & Schuster—Jack as editor in chief and advertising director, Al as executive vice president and chief operating officer. A year after Goodman died, Leventhal left the company.

IT WAS THE first working day of 1939 when twenty-two-year-old Nina Bourne, wearing little ribbons in her hair, came to work for Simon & Schuster as an assistant to Albert Leventhal. Nearly sixty-seven years later, in December 2005, Nina Bourne and I went out for an early-evening drink. I met her in the huge lobby of the huge new Random House building on Broadway that houses Knopf, "little" Random House, Bantam, Doubleday, Dell, etc.—all formerly independent houses now gathered together by the German publishing giant Bertelsmann. Nina came out of the elevator with a little smile on her face. It had to be her. Looking closer, I saw that her face was absolutely untouched by age. She was wearing a light suit and large eyeglasses that looked a bit odd on a woman who only weighed eighty-five pounds. She had a small hat over small bangs, giving her that Anita Loos look. But she was prettier than Loos. Eighty-nine years old, she was still working for Knopf four days a week, doing the same work she had done for Simon & Schuster way back when—reading manuscripts, writing flap copy, helping with the ads, originating book titles, fighting for the books that she thought must be acquired. Alice Quinn, a one-time senior editor at Knopf who later became poetry editor for *The New Yorker,* claims Bourne is "a great, great mentor to me and to many other people." She referred to Bourne as being "sort of the furnace of the firm."

Nina was cool and composed in the comfortable bar she chose for our interview. She ordered an old-fashioned as we settled in to talk.

"My earliest days at S & S were magic," she told me. "It started the first working day of 1939. I was so taken with the snazzy ads written by Dick Simon. We called him 'Boss,' because he didn't have to please anybody. He just wrote. And his ads were complete and straightforward and conversational and factual, and terrific." "It was a style," Jonathan Eller wrote in his definitive essay, "Catching a Market: The Publishing History of *Catch-22*," "that had been learned from Dick Simon himself—the idea of bringing the reader inside the publishing house to learn the story of the novel."

Nina mentioned how Simon & Schuster early in its life had cleverly introduced an advertising column called "The Inner Sanctum," one to be placed in *The New York Times,* the other, more specialized, in *Publishers Weekly.* Both versions contained bright little excerpts about what was happening not only at S & S, but elsewhere, too. The items were separated by the small figure of the sower taken from Jean-François Millet's painting *The Reapers,* which had become the S & S logo. The Inner Sanctum (also the name of the company's mystery line back then) was first written by Max Schuster and Dick Simon, and later continued by Goodman and Bourne. In his book *Turning the Pages,* Peter Schwed remembered one column that had nothing to do with book publishing. "It was devoted to the art of flipping playing cards into a hat set on the floor eight feet away." It had to have been written by Jack Goodman, who, Schwed reported, was "the uncrowned world's champion at the art."

"He wrote the most elegant and charming ads," Nina said of Goodman. And then, thinking of those days, she said, "It wasn't that everything was sweetie pie there, but there was nothing hidden."

It seemed that wherever Nina was needed, she was there. An important S & S book was to be published in 1961. William Shirer had been working on it since 1955, the time that Joe Barnes, an editor and former foreign correspondent, had suggested it to him. The title of the book was *Hitler's Nightmare Empire,* and nobody liked it much. Its subtitle appeared in small letters at the bottom of the jacket. Nina took one look and said, "Why not use the subtitle as the title? The new title became *The Rise and Fall of the Third Reich.*

Nina's life came to a kind of completion when Bob Gottlieb came to town. "Within twenty-four hours of our meeting," Bob told me, "we became the closest friends, and we still are. My children grew up with a Mommy and a Daddy and Nina. They're with her all the time. Nina and I flung ourselves into working together. She can still tell you which of us put in which words in the jacket copy for *Eloise.* Whoever did it, it was perfect." The copy read: *"A book for precocious grown-ups."*

SIMON, SCHUSTER, AND SHIMKIN had created Pocket Books. In 1944 the team, with Robert de Graff, sold that giant along with Simon & Schuster to Marshall Field III, a liberal newspaper tycoon based in Chicago. Pocket Books was sold to Field outright, but S & S was sold with the right to repurchase.

After the death of Marshall Field in 1956, followed by the death of Jack Goodman and the retirement of Dick Simon (who died in 1960), Max Schuster and Leon Shimkin bought out Simon's shares. Now hardly on speaking terms, they bought back S & S. And Shimkin, with the help of an investor, James J. Jacobson, bought Pocket Books for $5 million. So there were now two distinct owners: Schuster had S & S, and Shimkin had Pocket Books.

AS HAS BEEN noted, throughout Simon & Schuster's early history, serious fiction—whether literary or commercial—had never been a staple of the list. That's because Dick and Max didn't know how to invent novels. Despite this, three middle-brow novels did make it in the 1940s and early fifties. *Gentleman's*

Agreement by Laura Z. Hobson was considered a daring novel at the time for the lash of anti-Semitism it revealed. A different kind of religious novel in 1950, Henry Morton Robinson's *The Cardinal,* was published simultaneously as an experiment in hard and softcover. It became a No. 1 bestseller in 1950 and 1951, mostly in paper. S & S published a half-dozen other novels in both hard and softcover, but none worked and so they abandoned the idea.

The third novel had been acquired by Dick Simon. It was written by Sloan Wilson under the original title of *A Candle by Midnight.* Simon didn't invent the theme of the novel, but he knew how to put the right title on it—*The Man in the Gray Flannel Suit.* It became a bestseller and was critically well received, for the novel seemed to sum up the suburban innocence of the 1950s. *Gentleman's Agreement* and *The Man in the Gray Flannel Suit* became first-rate films (both starring Gregory Peck) that you can still Netflix today.

WITH THE DEATH of Jack Goodman and the retirement of Dick Simon, Robert Gottlieb became the taste-master of books, and a new wave of fresh air swept through the company. Everyone benefited from the Gottlieb touch, especially the novelists.

"It was gone with the wind in 1957," Bob Gottlieb told me, as we talked in his house. "So six of us who had been juniors found ourselves running Simon & Schuster because Mr. Schuster did nothing but hide in his office."

Besides Bob Gottlieb, the other new leaders of the company were Peter Schwed with a new title, vice president and "administrative editor," also a member of the editorial board (along with Schuster and Dick's brother, Henry Simon, a donnish editor, then mostly with Pocket Books); Nina Bourne, who took Goodman's place, flying rapidly above the advertising and copy geniuses of the era; Seymour Turk, the treasurer; a new editor, Michael Korda, who came on the scene in 1958 as an editorial assistant for

Henry Simon, and, later on, would become a reigning editor in both fiction and nonfiction; and Anthony (Tony) Schulte, a young S & S salesman from Chicago who took Dick Grossman's place when Grossman (whose specialty was marketing and photography books) left for Viking. Schulte also handled book club and paperback subsidiary rights before becoming the company's sales and marketing director.

TONY SCHULTE

I was thinking about book publishing, I guess, while I was at Harvard Business School after Yale, before the army— thinking, maybe I should try it and see if I like it. I got out of the army in the summer of 1955 and sent letters to a whole bunch of publishers. Eventually I was offered two jobs, and I had to choose between them.

One of them was from Macmillan, where I would be assistant to the sales manager. I was interviewed twice, and then a half a dozen of them took me to lunch. They wanted to see the cut of my jib, I think, and I made quite a point of letting them know that I was Jewish. They said, "Oh, that'd be all right. You know, we don't really care." I'm not so sure that they didn't.

The other job offer was from Simon & Schuster, after being interviewed by Albert Leventhal. It turned out that Albert knew my mother, which I hadn't even realized. He said to me, "Why in hell did you write all those letters around? Why didn't you just call me up?" I said, "Mr. Leventhal, I didn't know you." They wanted me to start out as the sales rep in Chicago, so they could bring their junior sales rep there back to New York.

I didn't know which job to take. I'd had an introduction to a man named Alan Ullman, who was in charge of the book publishing they were doing at *The New York Times*. I'll never forget what Ullman said to me. He said: "Would you rather be in the starting lineup of the Philadelphia Phillies or come off the bench as a utility player for the New York Yankees. And without making anything of the fact that I was a Yankee fan, I said, "I guess I'd rather be with the Yankees." He said, "Then take the job at Simon and Schuster." So I became the utility infielder in Chicago.

Thanks to being in Chicago, I also became Shel Silverstein's first publisher. We had been in the army together and Shel was now hawking peanuts at Comiskey Park, where the White Sox played. Sometimes we'd go to a ballgame together. I was there when Shel got his first check from Hugh Hefner, for a Silverstein racy cartoon. Hefner was trying to make a go of it with a new magazine called *Playboy*. Shel was desperate to get the check in the bank and cash it before the bank closed that afternoon, because he thought Hefner's check probably would bounce.

When I came to New York to work—it was right over the Fourth of July weekend of 1957, and Jack Goodman had just died, which shook up the whole structure of Simon & Schuster—we published two cartoon collections of Shel's. Then he came around with his children's book. We did the first book of children's poetry, with my son's picture on the back cover with a little girl. They were sitting with Shel, while Shel was reading to them from His Uncle Shelby's ABZ—otherwise known as *Don't Bump the Glump*. And then we sold Golden Books, and he came around with his next children's book. And I said, "Shel, we're not going to do any more children's books." And he said, "Well, you should do this one, at least, because I'm your author." I said, "I don't think that they'll buy it." And

I couldn't make them buy *The Giving Tree* all by myself. It went on to sell seven and a half million copies. Ursula Nordstrom at Harper's took Shel over and never let him go.

Not long after Jack Goodman's death, Bob Gottlieb marched into Goodman's office and claimed it for himself. The twenty-six-year-old Gottlieb began to create a ten-year mini golden age for the house.

Bob still had to obtain permission from Schuster to buy books. "I made Max very nervous," he said, "because I didn't take no for an answer. I spoke up. I was arrogant, a real pain in the ass; he couldn't deal with us so he would basically say anything to get rid of me. A perfect example of a book Schuster would not approve of was John Lennon's first book, *In His Own Write*. We published it in 1964, and it became a bestseller.

"So I said to Max, 'I have to have a title because I'm not just an editor.' So when it was 1964 or '65—by which time I was in my thirties—I was made editor in chief." He paused a moment in a lucid soliloquy that suddenly turned confessional: "The reason I wanted to be editor in chief is I didn't want anyone else to be editor in chief." I wondered, *could it have been because he was nervous about the entrance of Michael Korda to the mix?* Bob had only the nicest things to say to me about Korda. And in his book, *Another Life,* Korda had only the nicest things to say about Gottlieb. Still, there seemed to be a slight competitive edge in their comments.

"Michael was a wonderful hands-on editor," Bob said. "He was eventually more attracted to a different kind of commercial fiction, the Irving Wallace thing."

Korda said so many endearing things about Gottlieb in *Another Life* that it was easy to slip in, here and there, certain negatives about his rival's personality. "The truth was," Korda wrote in a section where he was trying to determine Bob's psyche, "that Bob's character disguised not only his ambition but a certain steely authoritarianism. He wanted to run things by himself, in his own way, but in spite of this need to dominate, he always wanted to be loved."

Another potential rival to Gottlieb at the time that I'm sure Bob didn't overlook was Justin Kaplan, a young man with a scholarly reputation. He had been hired by Max Schuster to help him edit Bertrand Russell and Kimon Friar's translation from the Greek of Nikos Kazantzakis's 333,333-line epic poem *The Odyssey: A Modern Sequel.* In *Back Then,* a lovely book about the 1950s, mostly in downtown Manhattan, coauthored by Kaplan and his wife, Anne Bernays, Kaplan only mentions Gottlieb once in passing. But he did refer to S & S at that time as being "like a summer camp for intellectual hyperactive children." Kaplan decided finally that he would prefer to be a writer than an editor. A writer he was and is. His first book, *Mr. Clemens and Mark Twain,* was published by S & S in 1966 and won both the National Book Award for Arts and Letters and the Pulitzer Prize.

Mostly, among Gottlieb's junior editors, it was pretty much true love. Connie Sayre, one of the youngest of them—she started at S & S in 1966 when she was twenty-one—suggested to me that Bob sometimes could be divisive, but she quickly added, "He also pulled you together. He got everybody excited about books. You know, today we take word-of-mouth as the best way to sell a book. Bob, as far as I'm concerned, invented it. He had everybody reading everything.

"I remember when *True Grit* was published," Connie went on. "It was a book I had read in manuscript and didn't much like. But when I moved into rights and had to sell it, it ended up being *the greatest book ever written* as far as I was concerned. Bob had us all raving about it and he did it better than anyone."

Gottlieb couldn't have been in a better position in those years because of the structure of the company. "S & S was in no way a typical firm," he said. "It was the opposite of a stifling bureaucracy. It had no apparatus. It was an amazing place to be, because it was absolutely free. You could do anything you wanted. When you came in as a cabin boy everybody stood around applauding and assuming you'd one day be admiral."

Bob supplemented what Justin Kaplan called "the firm's rich history of improvisation" by bringing in contemporary quality fiction and upper-level middlebrow fiction. Bob lovingly rattled off the names of some of the books he had acquired in the period "that reflected what I was": Chaim Potok's *The Chosen;* Robert Crichton's *The Secret of Santa Vittoria;* Charles Portis's *True Grit.* He and Nina Bourne worked closely together on Jessica Mitford's *The American Way of Death,* which became a No. 1 on the *New York Times* bestseller list. And, of course, there is the book that Bob and Nina both treated as an obsession: *Catch-22.*

IN THE EARLY spring of 1962 I invited Joseph Heller to lunch at Tim Costello's saintly landmark pub. At that time I was the editor of *Saga* magazine, a men's salty adventure magazine, in addition to editing *Sport.* The invitation was to celebrate a two-part excerpt from *Catch-22* that we had bought from S & S for $500 each—big money for us to pay in those days. The first one, "The Death of Kid Sampson," would appear in the July 1962 issue of *Saga.*

Heller had a pleasing smile on his face when we shook hands. I had asked my colleague at *Saga,* Berry Stainback (who later became a strong magazine editor on his own, as well as an author of popular nonfiction books), to bring the proofs to lunch. And here Berry was, sitting on a barstool at Costello's, pulling the six pages out of the tube and laying them on the bar. Heller took one look—we had commissioned a full-page 4-color painting of Kid Sampson, naked on a raft, the propellers from a plane looming toward him—and Joe's striking blue eyes began to glow.

He was an amusing guest—a handsome, stocky thirty-eight-year-old with hair full of curls—as he talked with us about his book and his war background. That day he seemed both ecstatic, and a bit nervous, because he still wasn't sure what was going to happen to his novel. *Catch-22* had been published in the fall of 1961 to mixed reviews, some really great, some disappointing. The book hadn't yet taken off.

Bob Gottlieb and Nina Bourne, in the tradition of Simon & Schuster, had staged an extravagant worldwide blitzkrieg on *Catch-22* that included numerous brilliant ads over the months, all written by Bob and Nina as they tried desperately to elevate the book to the must-read category.

When I called soon after reading an advance copy of the book and falling in love with it, I told the person on the other end of the line (it may have been Gottlieb himself or possibly Candida Donadio, the agent) that I wanted to buy two excerpts for *Saga,* I heard reluctance in the person's voice. It turned out that Donadio had tried three times to get *Esquire,* the elite men's magazine of the time, to buy it. In the end, according to Jonathan R. Eller in "Catching a Market: The Publishing History of *Catch-22,*" Gottlieb and Bourne were frustrated. They tried one more time on their own to convince Rust Hills, the book editor of *Esquire,* to take a chapter. Hills later told Eller, "Harold Hayes [the editor of the magazine] and I didn't think it was all that great. . . . It might have been my worst mistake as an editor."

Well, there was that energetic tug of war going on between the committed and the naysayers. In our July issue, I gave *Saga* readers my opinion of the book: "It is a wild, funny, tragic, somber, upside-down novel in which the author slices through all hypocrisy." Anyway, I was glad to pay the tab at Costello's.

Neither Gottlieb nor Bourne would give up on the novel. They had worked compulsively for eight years on *Catch-22*. "Joe Heller is the only writer I've ever dealt with," Bob told me, "where it was really like two surgeons working with a patient on a table under anesthesia; he was a completely disinterested observer. We just went back and forth, diagnosing and doing what had to be done, amputating, or whatever."

Bob Gottlieb described the "amputation" in his "Art of Editing" feature in the Fall 1994 issue of *The Paris Review*. This was a different kind of Q and A for the *Review* in that it was not one person asking the author all the questions; it was many of Gottlieb's authors interspersing their own comments about their editor between Gottlieb's own flights of wisdom.

"Just before *Catch-22* went to press," Gottlieb said, "I was reading it again. I came to a chapter I'd always hated. I thought it was pretentious and literary. I said to Joe: 'You know, I've always hated this chapter,' and he said, 'Well, take it out.'" Many years later *Esquire* made up for its original sin by publishing this "lost chapter of *Catch-22*."

By that time *Catch-22* was in the literary canon all over the world. The book was an instant bestseller in England, but it never became a hardcover bestseller in the U.S. The U.S. paperback version was another story. Bought by Dell for $32,500 and under the guidance of Dell's brilliant publisher, Don Fine, it took off immediately. In less than a year, Dell had sold one million copies. The eventual super success of the novel around the world did one other thing for its editor—it made Bob Gottlieb's reputation.

By 1974, when Joe Heller's second novel, *Something Happened*, was published, *Catch-22* had sold six million copies. Heller and I met that year at a Book-of-the-Month Club lunch to celebrate the novel's selection by the Club. He looked great, his hair a little grayer, but he was comfortable and cool and happy about his new success. Bob Gottlieb was there, enjoying himself,

I think because he always felt that *Something Happened,* which Bob published at Knopf, was Heller's best book. Yet there is *Catch-22.* Since the book's publication in 1961 the term "catch-22" has entered the language; it's defined in *Random House Webster's College Dictionary* as "a frustrating situation in which one is trapped by contradictory regulations or conditions."

Catch-22.

IN 1966, MAX SCHUSTER, not in good health, nor on talking terms with Leon Shimkin, decided to retire. On his last day in the office he asked Sy Turk to walk around the office with him so he could say good-bye to people whose names he did not know. Sy always liked Schuster and used to have lunch with him every Monday, but now it was lunch every Monday with Leon Shimkin at the Rockefeller Center Luncheon Club. For on the retirement of Schuster, Shimkin seized complete control of both S & S and Pocket Books. He merged the two companies and named the new company Simon & Schuster, Inc. Max Schuster died four years later, in 1970.

The rise of Leon Shimkin to the top aroused no flag-waving among his soldiers. Shimkin was ascetic with other people's money, particularly tightfisted about salaries. When, in the early thirties, Clifton Fadiman asked Max Schuster if he could work one less day a week because of his *New Yorker* book review commitments, Schuster said okay. But in his next paycheck Kip found that the treasurer, Shimkin, had lopped off a day's pay from his salary.

BY 1967 THE GOTTLIEB team began to feel restive, and they thought of moving on. For one, they didn't like the way Pocket Books, under Shimkin, seemed to be taking over things rather than S & S trade books. Tony Schulte thought about finding a company to buy. He was saying to himself, *I'm thirty-seven years old and if I'm ever going to do it, now's the time.*

That was the year Elliott Macrae, one of two brothers who owned the E. P. Dutton publishing house, died. Tony called the lawyer who was handling Macrae's estate. "I had a conversation or two with the lawyer suggesting my interest in buying Dutton," Tony told me. "The lawyer said, 'Well, if you think you can raise some money, make an offer.'

"I said, 'Well, I'm going to do so only if my friend Bob Gottlieb will come along to be editor in chief, and Nina Bourne, too."

The Dutton thing was still a possibility, until Tony discovered that Gottlieb was being pursued aggressively by Robert Bernstein at Random House.

Bernstein, a tall, imposing, freckle-faced young man, had come to work for Simon & Schuster in 1946, "lower than anybody had ever started," he said. "I was hired to take the place of an office boy who was being promoted to a reader. So I was 'Office Boy in Waiting.'"

A better title for him might have been "President-in-Making," somewhere. Over a ten-year period, he rose quickly at S & S. But it ended with him being fired by Leon Shimkin (it was a money thing between them). And then, at the end of 1956, he was almost instantly hired by Bennett Cerf to become sales manager at Random House. This time he moved fast up the ladder; in 1966, he succeeded Cerf as president.

I met with Bernstein twice, since his tendrils had spread wide between S & S, Random House, and Knopf. He had a lovely office high up in a building off Park Avenue, with a close-up view of the Chrysler Building's magnificent art deco topping. The first thing I wanted to hear about was his involvement with Gottlieb, Schulte, and Bourne.

From the moment that Jack Goodman died, Bob Bernstein, secure in his job at Random House, had fixed his eyes on the threesome. He told me that he had already gotten to know them so well that he said to them: "You have an open invitation to come to

Knopf." And he continued his wooing. Bob recalled, "We would get together for sandwiches every six or eight months. I think it was ten years later, we were having sandwiches at this little apartment Bennett had gotten me, when I told them that Alfred Knopf was planning to retire, and that I had to find somebody to take his place. So I said to Bob and Tony and Nina, 'Other people can offer you a job. I can offer you a publishing house. If you come, the three of you can run Knopf.' "

Just before the New Year's Eve that would turn 1967 into 1968, Bob Gottlieb and Tony Schulte took Peter Schwed, who was now the publisher of Simon & Schuster, to his favorite restaurant, P. J. Moriarty's, for lunch. They told Peter that they were going to leave. "Peter nearly died at the table," Tony remembered.

In April of 1968, Gottlieb, Schulte, Bourne, and a fourth favorite, Toinette Lippe, who was selling rights, formally began their career at Knopf. For Nina, it was the most radical of happenings. Years later she told a story to Jane Friedman, who today is CEO of HarperCollins, but had spent happy years at Knopf.

"The most amazing thing happened to me, Jane," Nina said. "One day I went downstairs for a pack of cigarettes at Simon & Schuster, and by the time I got upstairs twenty-nine years had gone by."

In 1970 both Max Schuster and Henry Simon died. In 1974 the lone survivor, Leon Shimkin, moved to chairman of the board. In January of 1975 Shimkin sold the company to Gulf + Western. Some months later, he retired and Richard E. Snyder became its head. For the next two decades, Dick Snyder and Michael Korda, working in tandem, would remake the company in nobody's image but their own.

THE LAST IMPORTANT book Gottlieb and Bourne worked on before they left Simon & Schuster was Chaim Potok's first novel, *The Chosen*. It had been around for several years, but no one wanted it. Bob Gottlieb set new eyes on it, as only he could do, peering around the edges, pulling at its center, finally deciding that it had the essence he wanted. "Look," Bob told me, "we all take on authors whom other publishers failed with and then have huge successes. We all let go of authors whom we didn't do very well by, and then other people did very well by. We can see something that nobody else saw in a book, as I did with *The Chosen,* because many people had turned it down for different reasons."

He was willing to take *The Chosen* if Chaim Potok would do one thing—cut the second section, which was 300 pages long. "Chaim had finished the book without knowing it," Bob said. "The second half of the manuscript was like a second book." Potok, a man of faith in his editor, agreed to make the change.

Bob couldn't wait to give Nina Bourne the manuscript to read. He told her it was a book he was absolutely crazy about. "Then came another perfect Nina moment," Bob said. "She took it home that night and the next day she came in and said, 'I read it last night. It is so wonderful and it was so frustrating because I wanted to tell somebody about it. It was too late to call you. But I had to tell somebody about it. So what I did was, I made myself a cup of tea, and I sat down and I told myself about it!'"

Bob looked directly at me, saying nothing for a moment or two, then his voice softened.

"That's the publishing impulse: the desire to make public your enthusiasm for a book. That's what it is, whether you're an editor or a publisher or a salesman. It doesn't really matter—you want to grab the next person you see and say, 'You've got to read this.'"

INTERLUDE: PUBLISHING WAS

IN HIS VEINS

"YOUNG CHARLIE," AS he was always called, was the fifth Charles Scribner, and the last one in the book publishing profession. His father had sold Scribner's to Macmillan in 1984. When, later, Macmillan was bought by Simon & Schuster, Scribner's became a valuable imprint for S & S's trade publishing program. In his last years with Scribner's, the handsome young Charlie, now in his mid-fifties, called himself "the curator of dead authors." His main chores were to look after the Hemingway and Fitzgerald estates (Scribner's, and therefore Simon & Schuster, has them for the life of copyright). Today he writes and lectures on art history.

CHARLES SCRIBNER V
I tell people when they say they want to start a publishing company: You'd better do what my great-great-grandfather did—marry a girl who's the daughter of the richest man in America at the time. The first Charles Scribner's father-in-law was a man named John I. Blair. He owned more miles of railroad track than anybody in the world. (This was pre–robber barons, before the later generations of the Vanderbilts, Astors,

Rockefellers, and the Belmonts, with their huge fortunes at the end of the nineteenth century.) So my great-great-grandfather, in 1846, started our publishing house.

My father was only thirty years old when he took over in 1952. Had he a choice he probably would not have chosen to go into book publishing. He did it out of a sense of duty. His real avocation was physics and higher mathematics. He used to sit at the desk in the evening after dinner—he had no interest in food—so he would eat dinner quickly. He would then sit at his desk and work on Einstein's equations.

His close author friends were P. D. James, C. P. Snow, Marjorie Kinnan Rawlings, author of *The Yearling,* and, of course, Hemingway. When I was eighteen months old he wrote to Hemingway and said that I was pulling the books out of the bottom shelf of the bookcase. Hemingway wrote back, "What young Charlie's trying to do is get the deadwood out of publishing." Classic Hemingway.

My father's dealings with agents and the new breed of novelists that came in after the war were often a burden to him. The last author whom Maxwell Perkins brought in—he died in 1947—was James Jones. When, in the mid-1960s, James Jones was taken away by Delacorte for a novel called *Go to the Widow-Maker,* a reporter at *The New York Times* asked my father how he felt losing the author of *From Here to Eternity*. His comment was: "My disappointment is under control."

I was trained to be an art historian, and I really thought that between my master's and doctorate degrees I would be coming into book publishing only temporarily to help my father and get some experience. And then I would go off and teach. But it stretched out to almost three decades, and there were some good years. I don't regret any of them. I really loved our experience with P. D. James; we were all so happy when she broke through with *Innocent Blood.* Later, I commissioned August Heckscher's biography of Woodrow Wilson and Louis Auchincloss's book of essays, *The Vanderbilt Era,* to which he added a dedication I shall always treasure.

My father, who was always so deeply involved in Scribners, looked at his profession in a bemused way. He once said to me, "Publishers have got to remember that the business is really like that of an obstetrician. The job of a publisher is to deliver another person's baby. But it's not our baby, it belongs to the author. Of course, if something goes wrong with the delivery, it's the obstetrician's fault."

I never trained to be an obstetrician. Now I'm able to do things I was trained to do. So, no regrets.

10

THE PLACE THAT RAN
BY ITSELF

Random House

Each editor was like a little imprint. You just pressed your
own case, and when you succeeded, you succeeded. I was
surprised to learn that at other companies the editors didn't
have that kind of freedom.

—TONI MORRISON

Jim Silberman, who was once editor in chief of Random
House, came to our apartment on February 23, 2005. This
was three days after Hunter S. Thompson, the creator of
"gonzo" journalism ("eccentric, druggy commentary," just like
the man who coined the word) had shot himself to death. Since
Silberman had been Thompson's principal editor over the years,
it seemed logical for him to open the conversation about the person called by Tom Wolfe, in his obituary for *The Wall Street
Journal*, "the greatest comic writer of the twentieth century."

The way it all began, Silberman told me, was in the early
1960s, when he read a short piece on Thompson in *The Nation*
magazine about his experiences with the Hell's Angels. It piqued

his interest so much that he determined to meet Hunter Thompson on a trip to see his Random House authors in San Francisco. And meet him he did, in a saloon in North Beach. "He was sitting at the bar," Jim said, "and we talked, and as we talked he kept looking out the window. Finally, I asked him, 'Hunter, what are you looking for?'

" 'My Harley's out there,' he said, 'and I want to be sure no one steals it.' He told me to come along with him to his apartment because he had a manuscript he wanted to show me.

"When we got out on the sidewalk, Hunter said, 'Get on the back of my Harley.' 'No thanks,' I said." It wasn't that Silberman lacked a sense of adventure—in his later life Jim had learned how to fly solo in an airplane. "The reason I didn't want to ride with him," he explained, "was that shortly before then, a writer, Richard Fariña, had been killed on publication day of his novel riding on the back of a motorcycle." So Jim grabbed a cab. "Follow that motorcycle!" I said.

In Thompson's apartment Jim met Hunter's then wife Sandy and their baby boy, who was sleeping in the crib. "I took the manuscript away and read *Hell's Angels*. "It was messed up," he said, "but it was very good."

The book, he found out, had already been bought by Ballantine, one of the leading paperback houses of the time (later to become part of Random House). Jim acquired the hardcover rights for Random House. "I did some editing," he said, "and so did the editors at *Rolling Stone*." Hunter and Jann Wenner, the owner of the magazine, were close friends. *Hell's Angels* was published in 1967 and it became a legend.

The two worked together on other books, though working with Hunter Thompson was often a walk on the wild side. "He was totally unpredictable," Jim said. "One day, he came in to Random House, and stood in my doorway. He pulled out what looked like a can of shaving cream. It was a Marine warning signal that you could hear twenty miles away." The noise rattled off the walls at Random House, interrupting everyone's slumber, but what could you do? It was the gonzo way. Silberman actually enjoyed working with this renegade journalist, and he published Thompson's most famous work, *Fear and Loathing in Las Vegas.* "When the going gets weird," said the central figure in the book, "the weird turn pro." It was always true of Thompson.

JAMES H. SILBERMAN, not then a gonzo follower, was never sure about book publishing as a profession. A native Bostonian, he graduated from Harvard in 1950 and thought about going to law school. But his mother, who, he said, "liked books better than life," was a strong influence on him. Another influence was a friend of his father's, Angus Cameron, who had been editor in chief at Little, Brown since 1943. With Cameron's help, Silberman got a job writing copy in Little, Brown's advertising department.

He stayed a year and a half, then moved to New York. His girlfriend, Leona Nevler, who had also worked at Little, Brown, was already there (they married in 1960).

In 1953, Jim found a job at Dial Press and stayed there for ten years, starting in publicity, and eventually switching to editing. He worked his way up to editor in chief. Among his authors were James Baldwin, Herbert Gold, Thomas Berger, and Vance Bourjaily. In 1963, after a shakeup at the top level of the company, Jim decided to move on. He was negotiating an offer from McGraw-Hill when the Dell switchboard operator rang him: "Bennett Cerf is on the phone for you."

Guess what? Jim took the call.

"I understand that you're thinking about leaving Dial," the founder and president of Random House said. "I'd like to talk to you."

"Well, Mr. Cerf," Jim replied, "I ought to tell you that I have practically taken a job elsewhere."

Cerf answered crisply. "Well, I don't want you to do anything until you talk to me." Recalling this conversation, Silberman gave me his Cheshire cat grin and said, "I didn't know that the fact that I was unavailable would spur him to go on. It was later I learned that Bennett wanted to have *everybody,* and he wanted to publish *everything.*"

Jim was invited by Cerf to stay overnight at his Mount Kisco estate, and meet his wife Phyllis and their two boys. He had a wonderful time, just as Hiram Haydn had had when Cerf was wooing him. (See chapter 4, on Atheneum.) Jim slept fitfully that night, thinking, at Random House I will be surrounded by all these famous editors—Albert Erskine, Joe Fox, Harry Maule, Bob Loomis, Jason Epstein. How would I do?

The next morning he got into Bennett's private railroad car and on the ride to New York the two worked out all the details of the job. There was only one thing bothering Jim. He would be taking a step down from editor in chief to senior editor, and he asked his prospective boss if he could do better than that with his title. "He fixed me with a terrifying stare," Jim recalled, "then said, 'If you're as good as I think you are, you're going to do very well at Random house.'" Soon enough, Jim Silberman became editor in chief. But what he didn't know at the time was that Bennett allowed his leading editors to buy books without having to get the editor in chief's approval (they still of course had to deal with Cerf himself). It was a civilized way to run a trade division, and Bennett Cerf was a most civilized person.

WHAT BENNETT WAS not was shy. He had full confidence in himself. He always believed that his intelligence plus his persona—a sharp, quick-witted quipster with a million-dollar smile, a razor-sharp mind, and a need to be loved—would take him places. But as he was graduating from Columbia University's School of

Journalism in 1920, he never dreamed that he would become the most famous book publisher in the history of American publishing, or that he would become a Class A American celebrity who even judged Miss America contests.

After college Cerf seemed to be heading toward a career in finance. He started with a job on Wall Street while at the same time writing a column for the *New York Tribune*'s financial page. He was also cleaning up on the crazed stock market. But he soon found himself wanting something other, something more. He thought about his college friend, Dick Simon, who was working as a salesman for the vaunted Boni & Liveright publishing house. One day in 1923, Simon told Bennett that he was leaving Liveright to start his own publishing house with Max Schuster. He urged Bennett to go see his ex-boss, Horace Liveright, who was looking for a replacement for Simon.

What Cerf ran into was a man of stupendous charm and egocentricity—the Bennett Cerf of his day, and then some. "Liveright was utterly ruthless and completely self-centered," said Donald Friede. "He was also a magnificent host, and an irresistible force as far as women were concerned." Friede was one of those who had become an immediate vice president of the firm in exchange for a $110,000 "loan" to his boss.

It was also said of Liveright that he never read a book he bought, but that his sense of smell was superb. So here he was, with the likes of Upton Sinclair, Robinson Jeffers, Eugene O'Neill, and Theodore Dreiser in his stable. Dreiser, who had a fierce temper, once got into a fight with Liveright over money. The fight ended when Dreiser threw a cup of hot coffee into Liveright's face.

Needless to say, when Bennett Cerf was invited to have lunch with Liveright at the Algonquin, he, too, was swept up by the host's munificence. The wily publisher introduced the young man to such members of the Algonquin Round Table as Dorothy Parker and

Robert Benchley. Figuring he had dazzled Cerf, Liveright expressed how much he liked the young man, would make him a vice president, offered to give him an eighth of the business—in return for a loan. So Bennett drew $25,000 of his stock market winnings to help Liveright avoid bankruptcy and joined the company as a vice president.

Cerf all his life was a noticer. It was one of his traits that carried him to the top. In his two years with Liveright he noticed that the only imprint really working was The Modern Library of the World's Best Classics. It had been conceived in 1917 by Alfred Boni when he agreed to merge his publishing house with Liveright's. (Boni and Liveright flipped a coin to see who would run the house; Liveright won.) There were over one hundred classic books, all in public domain, all being under-published. Bennett immediately sensed an opportunity.

When Liveright came to Cerf early in 1925 asking for another loan, Bennett offered him not a loan, but $200,000 to acquire the Modern Library. With reluctance, Liveright agreed to the deal.

Now Bennett needed a partner. The first thing he did was call his friend, Donald Klopfer. He had met Klopfer, a tall, handsome, thoughtful young man, at Columbia. Even though Klopfer spent only three months at Columbia—he moved to Williams College the next year, then quit to go into his family's diamond-cutting business—Cerf liked him very much, believing their ambitions matched. Donald was the exact opposite of Cerf: quiet, deliberate, smart, humane, and always on top of things. "Donald was the rock of Random House," wrote Bob Loomis, who himself would become a fifty-year editorial Gibraltar at the company. "He was the sort of person whose simple presence could help you solve your problems." Bennett Cerf put it more simply in his luscious memoir, *At Random:* "There was a bond between us that I can't describe."

Klopfer was happy to join Cerf. He paid $100,000 to become his partner, a partnership that lasted harmoniously for fifty-five years.

They opened for business in August 1925. The partners immediately set about to make the Liveright Modern Library into a more presentable package. Upon reviewing the titles, they cut the losers from the group and added many winners. In three years they recouped all of their original investment.

At that time, Cerf and Klopfer never really thought about becoming conventional book publishers. They enjoyed picking up titles at random, starting by publishing deluxe one-shots— coffee-table books for wealthy book buyers. Their first offering was a new translation of Voltaire's *Candide* lavishly illustrated by Rockwell Kent. They published several other "limited editions," as they were called, including Dante's *Divine Comedy* and Whitman's *Leaves of Grass*, and kept looking for others to publish—*at random.* By 1927, they decided to include fresh, young, promising authors. Their little venture came to be appropriately called: Random House. Rockwell Kent drew the original house that has been the colophon ever since.

WHEN THE STOCK market crashed in 1929, Cerf and Klopfer lost their market for selling fancy books. A lot of other publishers, in fact, went belly up, including Horace Liveright, who died in 1933 at age forty-seven. Bennett Cerf immediately went after Liveright's premier author, Eugene O'Neill.

Bennett had gotten to know O'Neill during his Liveright days. He also knew that a host of publishers would come after the great American playwright. Right off, he flew to Sea Island, Georgia, where O'Neill lived with his wife, Carlotta. "We took long walks on the beach," Bennett wrote in *At Random,* "and talked and came to know each other." They came to know each other well

enough for O'Neill to sign a contract with Cerf. The one thing
that O'Neill insisted on was that his editor, Saxe Commins, come
with him (shades of James Joyce and Ben Huebsch—another editor's clause that enriched the promising new publishing enterprise). For twenty-five years Saxe Commins, one of the century's
most brilliant American editors, served Random House well beyond the call of duty.

ONE DAY IN the late spring of 2004 I drove to Woodstock, New
York, to visit Betty Ballantine and learn more about her husband
Ian's uncle, who was Saxe Commins. I found her at age eighty-
three to be in sparkling health. She lives alone in her home with a
swimming pool that she uses almost every morning in the summer. She also does volunteer work in Woodstock and vicinity for
environmental and arts organizations. And she reads—all the
time. Her two-story house is filled with books, and she worries
that the upstairs floor, loaded with books, might someday set off
an avalanche into her living room.

In the course of hearing about Saxe Commins, I learned a lot
about her husband, Ian Ballantine, and how she and Ian, two
young arrivals from their native England, took Commins as their
mentor.

"He was Ian's literary father," Betty told me. "I remember sitting at lunch with Saxe and his wife when I was getting really interested in editing. And I said to him, 'What do you think is the
single most important factor in editing?' And Saxe said, *'Well, it
will sound very simple: You have to help the author say what he
wants to say in the way he wants to say it.'* "

That's exactly how Commins worked over the years with his
Random House authors such as Dreiser, Gertrude Stein, W. H.
Auden, Sinclair Lewis, William Carlos Williams, Irwin Shaw,
Walter Van Tilburg Clark, Richard Tregaskis, Isak Dinesen, and
especially Eugene O'Neill and William Faulkner. In his late years

at Random House, he was particularly close to Faulkner. In *What Is an Editor: Saxe Commins at Work,* Dorothy Berliner Commins's fascinating book about her late husband, she recalled the time when Saxe brought Faulkner to their home after a drinking episode that had left him unconscious. When Faulkner recovered, he came forward and said to Saxe's wife: "Dorothy, I've misbehaved again." In forgiveness, she clasped his face with her hands.

Saxe Commins died in 1958. Dorothy Commins remembered that William Faulkner had given her husband the first copy of the Nobel Prize acceptance speech (1949), which, Dorothy Commins wrote, "turned out to be a brief but eloquent plea for the values 'of love and honor and pity and pride and compassion and sacrifice.'"

IN 1942, WHILE Bennett Cerf minded the store, Donald Klopfer, age forty, enlisted in the Army Air Force. He was stationed in England as an intelligence officer for the Air Corps. For two and a half years of separation, the partners corresponded with each other diligently, Cerf writing about what was happening at Random House, Major Klopfer describing his wartime adventures. Klopfer also sought answers to questions that came up in Bennett's letters and worried him. In 2006, Random House published *Dear Donald, Dear Bennett: The Wartime Correspondence of Bennett Cerf and Donald Klopfer.* The loving letters for the book were selected with much care by Bob Loomis. They provide clues as to what each partner was thinking and feeling about their company.

Klopfer, for example, stressed his anxiety about the future of the house. In one letter he asks plaintively, "Will Random House be any fun at all as a 'big business' instead of our own very personal venture?" A few days later he repeats this refrain in another letter: "Is it any fun anymore, or are you just developing a big audience like Doubleday or S & S? We've had so damned much fun out of the business that I hate to think I'm a stranger to this new phase of it."

It was true. When Bennett's son Christopher was asked what he wanted to do when he grew up, the nine-year-old boy said, "I want to be a publisher." Why is that? the man asked the boy. "Because all they do all day long is laugh and talk."

Bennett answered Klopfer quickly: "The setup can remain a simple one, right under our control, and with no possibility, in my opinion, of ever developing into a sprawling and unmanageable menagerie like the Doubleday outfit. You know that I share your abhorrence for impersonal 'big business.'" But after the war Random House did become big business—the ultracompetitive Cerf wouldn't have it any other way. But while Cerf was still in control, the company certainly remained personal.

"You'd start off every day with a joke from Bennett," Charlotte Mayerson, who became a senior editor at Random House in 1968, told me with a broad smile. "He would stop by every morning. And I would dine off that joke at night. But I think it's important to say about Bennett, who sometimes gets bad-mouthed for being frivolous—he was frivolous in certain respects—that he had a very sharp, keen eye for literature."

In 1934, Cerf and Klopfer took a large risk—going after an unsurpassed work of twentieth-century literature, James Joyce's *Ulysses,* so that it could be read in the United States without the reader going to jail. *Ulysses* had been published almost everywhere else in the world, but was not allowed in the U.S.A. because it had been deemed "obscene." Cerf and Klopfer mailed a copy of *Ulysses* to themselves in New York, hoping it would be confiscated by customs officials. It was. They then hired Morris Ernst, a noted civil rights lawyer who had become famous for defending censored books, to pursue the battle. And he won when Judge John M. Woolsey made a landmark ruling case, declaring the book *not obscene*. Even in the appellate courts, this verdict was upheld. *Ulysses* surprised Bennett and Donald by becoming a moneymaker. Perhaps because of its notoriety, *Ulysses* sold 60,000 copies in the trade edition, and later, as a Modern Library paperback, it continued to sell hundreds of thousands of copies.

The next thing the partners vowed to do—perhaps the smartest act of their professional lives—was to surround Saxe Commins with a fraternity of creative editors—"editors," as Cerf put it, "whose taste and judgment we could trust." Charlotte Mayerson told how Bennett would often say: "This company is a success because we have editors who could be heads of their own companies."

Here's how Cerf and Klopfer strengthened their editorial department.

In 1936, Robert K. Haas was brought in as a third partner after Random House acquired his small publishing house, Smith & Haas. Haas brought with him, among others, William Faulkner, Isak Dinesen, Edgar Snow, André Malraux, Robert Graves, and Jean de Brunhoff, author of the *Babar* books for children.

In 1939, Harry Maule, fifty-three years old, was encouraged to join Random House after he had been urged to resign by Doubleday. He brought with him Sinclair Lewis and Vincent Sheehan.

In 1944, Robert Linscott, who was a leading editor at Houghton Mifflin and ready for a change, was hired by Bennett. Linscott didn't waste a lot of time making an impression. He was tipped off about a manuscript written by an unknown midwestern writer named Mary Jane Ward. After reading her novel about life in a mental institution, Linscott recommended it to Cerf, who agreed to publish *The Snake Pit*. It became a 1946 bestseller and a Book-of-the-Month Club selection.

Soon after that, Linscott read a short story in *Mademoiselle* titled "Miriam." He called the author, whose name was Truman Capote, to come meet him and his boss. If Bennett didn't immediately fall in love with this teeny baby boy who wore bangs, then his wife, Phyllis, did. "One sees a beautifully modeled head," Harper Lee described Capote in a Book-of-the-Month Club *News* article, "with sensitive hands, a graceful carriage, blue eyes behind thick glasses." Linscott worked with Capote on his first novel, *Other Voices, Other Rooms,* which immediately established his reputation as a writer, as well as a larger-than-life personality.

When Linscott retired in 1954, it was Joe Fox who took over Truman Capote. Fox thought Capote was a bit of a burden, but he knew how to handle him. One day Joe came back from lunch and found Truman in his office, his face beet red. "Joe!" he screamed. "I don't think it's funny! I don't think it's funny at all!" Joe laughed. He was aware that Truman would occasionally go through his desk drawers. So Joe had put a note in one saying, "No, Truman, stay out of here!"

Joe worked heroically with Capote on *In Cold Blood.* When Capote turned in the manuscript, Joe saw that there was no ending. Bennett wanted to know what was going on. "When is he going to finish it?" Joe shrugged. "I don't think Truman is going to finish this book until the guys are executed."

In the movie of *In Cold Blood,* we see William Shawn, the editor of *The New Yorker,* accompany Capote on several trips to Kansas. In real life Shawn never left his office, except to walk a few steps to the Algonquin for lunch. It was Joe Fox who made those trips with Capote. After the executions, when they were coming back to New York, Truman held Joe's hand all the way and just sobbed and sobbed.

Joe Fox had other authors who also really delivered. He worked with Philip Roth on Roth's first full-length novel, *Letting Go,* as well as *When She Was Good* and *Portnoy's Complaint,* which was the country's No. 1 novel in 1969. Among his other authors were Peter Matthiessen, Stanley Elkin, David Halberstam, and Alison Lurie. In 1995, after an outstanding career, Joe Fox died at his desk.

In 1947, the true successor to Saxe Commins, Albert Erskine, came over from the book publishing firm of Reynal & Hitchcock. After Saxe Commins's death, Erskine inherited not only his office, but also his author William Faulkner, whom he served as editor and life preserver as Commins had. Erskine also handled all of Faulkner's money for him. Somehow, he still had time to work with other notables such as Irwin Shaw, John O'Hara, James Michener, Ralph Ellison, Robert Penn Warren, Eudora Welty, and Cormac McCarthy.

Robert Bernstein, who in 1966 would succeed Cerf as head of Random House, remembers the time when Erskine came into his office. "Look," Erskine said, "I'm Cormac McCarthy's publisher. I know his last three books have flopped. I'm just telling you, Bob, that if you don't sign this contract for the fourth book, I'm leaving Random House."

Bernstein, not at all hostile to Erskine, said, "Albert, what are you so aggressive about? You want to publish a book, you know I'm going to publish it. That's why you're here."

"I know. I'm just telling you he's going to be a great author."

"He never realized how right he was," Bob told me. "He died just as Cormac was breaking out." McCarthy, the author of such novels as *Blood Meridian,* National Book Award winner *All the Pretty Horses,* and *The Road* (which in early 2007, courtesy of Oprah, became a huge paperback bestseller), remains one of the great American novelists of the twentieth century.

Behind Erskine, Random House's quarterback, were these All-American teammates: Fox, Epstein, Loomis, Silberman, and Hiram Haydn for four years (before he was lured to Atheneum). Watching these hard-hitting editors at work in those years was also a determined young woman, Nan Talese, who had come to Random House in 1954 and felt that she had been dipped into "an amazing man's world."

In the summer of 2006 I met with her in her office at Doubleday, where she serves as editorial director of her longtime imprint,

Nan A. Talese/Doubleday. What the title means is that she is her own editor and publisher. She finds the books *she* wants to publish and sees to it that they are published well. As usual, Nan looked dazzling, beautifully dressed and the person whom one of her prime authors, Ian McEwan, calls "the jewel in the crown of American publishing." One story she told me seemed to exemplify the discomfort she and other talented women were feeling back in those days: The period I call a golden age was not, for the most part, an idyllic time for women.

"I got this proposal for a book: *Male Chauvinism, How It Works* by Michael Korda. I read it and I thought, *I don't believe this. This man is so secure, or he doesn't care.* I gave it to Jim Silberman to read, saying that I'd like to publish it. 'Nan,' he said, 'I don't think so. It never does any good to publish a colleague.' Well, I didn't know until then that Michael Korda was in publishing, working at Simon & Schuster. I didn't know anyone in publishing, except my little Random House group. And so I went back to my desk, and I thought, *This is really too good.* I went back to Jim again and said, 'I really think we should publish this.' And he said, 'Why don't you give it to others in the office and see what they say?' He recommended Anne Freedgood, who was an editor there, and Selma Shapiro, who was publicity director (Selma and Jim later married). So I gave it to them to read.

"Another person I gave it to was Toni Morrison, who was then an editor at Random House. I said, 'Toni, I really think this could be a terrific book. And it's all true.' Toni read it, said it was terrific, and we sort of forced it through. It may have even gone to Bennett." *Male Chauvinism* did well, and it is still being read. This successful fight for the book ignited Nan's ambitions. She realized she was a serious editor, and she wanted more work.

NAN TALESE

I came into publishing through a young man named Gay Talese, who was at *The New York Times*. I was beginning to fall in love with him, and I was at *Vogue* magazine, assistant to the Accessory Editor. I spent my days running around bringing gloves and jewelry and handbags and scarves to the models at fashion shoots. After about six months I thought this was a bit silly and said so to Gay.

He had noticed I read all the time and usually carried a book with me and he knew an editor at Random House who was interested in his writing a book; he suggested I go see him. Quite frankly, I never connected in my mind books and a job. The editor I first met was Paul Lapolla, who introduced me to the editor in chief, Albert Erskine. Albert was a handsome Virginia gentleman of few words, very soft-spoken, with a sort of devastatingly wry sense of humor and observation. He brought me back three times for interviews because I had no credentials whatsoever. They were looking for a real copy editor with experience. Also I had graduated from the Manhattanville College of the Sacred Heart College, which I think made my taste suspect.

I remember Albert warned, perhaps thinking about my education, that I would be reading manuscripts of all types and would have to make recommendations on them. I think I quickly responded by saying I had written my thesis on existentialism, a philosophy frowned on by the Church, and I doubted he would have to worry about any moral censorship on my part.

In those days, after Gay and I were married in Rome, I just thought of myself as a wife and eventually a mother with a job. Senior editors let me work on their manuscripts, but acquisitions were made only by them. A friend and fellow *Times*man of Gay's, Philip Benjamin, had written a first novel about Antarctica, *Quick Before It Melts*, and Philip wanted me to read it. I thought it was awfully good and gave it to Joe Fox for a confirming opinion. The next thing I knew he had called the agent and bought the book for his list. I confess my nose was out of joint, but along with Albert, Joe became my mentor.

My great learning experience came when Robert Penn Warren delivered his novel, *Flood,* which was a very perfect manuscript. Michener's *Hawaii* had just been sent to Albert and needed enormous editing, and thus Albert asked Warren if it would be all right if I did the line editing on his book. And because Red Warren was a very secure and gracious man, he said that would be fine. I went through the novel page by page, going over all my queries to see if they were worth asking, and I remember that sometimes when a word didn't seem right, I would think: How do I dare ask the poet and the author of the glorious *Brother to Dragons* and *All the King's Men* if that was the word he really meant? But I did, and the two of us went through the book, going over the queries together.

Partway into the novel a character seemed to suddenly appear and in the margin I had written, "Would you identify him? Who is he?" Warren said, "He is introduced in the second chapter." Of course, I just blushed and thought, "Oh God, I have failed the exam." He saw immediately my embarrassment and said, "No, no. If you don't remember him, it means I either have to introduce him more strongly at the beginning or reintroduce him here." He was so gracious all the way through, and he gave me the confidence to ask writers questions—not thinking it was about me—but I was just a reader who might be puzzled. I think that is what an editor does: sees the manuscript afresh, asking the questions before it is printed so the reader will follow smoothly.

The prototypical Random House editor was—and is today—Robert Loomis. In January 2007, Random House held an elegant fiftieth-anniversary black-tie dinner to honor him. And why shouldn't they have? Robert Lescher, an agent for many years (and, before that, an editor of distinction), singled out Loomis as "a born editor. I think he is able to look at material and see what it can become."

In the spring of 2006, Bob Loomis and I had lunch together, and I mentioned what Lescher had said about him. Without guile, Bob confirmed that judgment call. "I think I *am* a born editor," he said. "Because, you know what? A lot of people don't figure out what they can do."

Growing up in Plain City, Ohio, population 12,000 (his father served as mayor of the town for a minute or two), Bob remembered that he just wanted to be a writer. "But I realized in school that I wasn't as good at that."

School for him was Duke University, which was then crowded with World War II veterans able to go to college because of the government's GI Bill. Among them was a group of promising young writers. One was Peter Maas, who wrote *Serpico* and many other works. Another was Mac Hyman, whose novel *No Time for Sergeants* was a bestseller for two years at Random House. A third was William Styron, who became Bob's closest friend; when both came to New York they roomed together, and Styron was Bob's best man at his two weddings.

When Hiram Haydn (an older Duke alumnus who had convinced Bob to come to Random House) left the company for Atheneum, Bob took a last look at Haydn's office. "He had left it empty," Bob said, "except that in his wastebasket was the framed Paul Bacon jacket for Bill [Styron]'s *Lie Down in Darkness*. I pulled it out. It's still on my wall."

Loomis's first job was at Appleton-Century writing ads. "It was horrible," he said, "writing copy for books I hadn't read." In

1950 he became an editor at Holt, Rinehart & Winston. "The first Book-of-the-Month we had was Martin Russ's book, *The Last Parallel: A Marine's War Journal.*" I asked him, needlessly, whether that was one of his books. "Yeah," he proudly remembered. "It was a big celebration, because it was like $60,000 from the Club and, you know, that's like $200,000 now."

Loomis came to Random House in 1957. Bennett Cerf was happy to have the young, already prominent editor on board.

Six months after Bob took the job, he and his first wife, who had been renting in Greenwich Village, found a one-bedroom apartment that they liked. But it would cost them $8,000 to buy. "It doesn't sound like a lot," Bob said, "but I had nothing."

The next thing he knew, he was called into Bennett Cerf's office. "He and Donald Klopfer were sitting there," Bob recalled, "and Donald said, 'We hear that you want to buy this apartment.' And I said, 'Yeah, well, eight thousand dollars. I don't have any money at all.' Donald pulled out a checkbook and wrote on it *eight thousand dollars.*

"I said, 'How do I pay this back?' Bennett said, 'You'll pay it back.' We didn't sign a piece of paper; there was no interest, nothing." He paid it back the Loomis Way—with fifty years of creativity and devotion to the company, and by becoming one of the greatest editors of the age, both in fiction and nonfiction. His authors over the years have included Styron, Maya Angelou, Daniel Boorstin, Edmund Morris, Neil Sheehan, Pete Dexter, Jonathan Harr (Loomis calls the author of *A Civil Action* "maybe the best narrative writer I've ever published"), and John Toland— all of whom have won various literary awards. Bob Loomis's effort with John Toland on his book *The Rising Sun* exemplifies the way in which Bob collaborates with his authors.

He had bought Toland's book on the Battle of the Bulge, but this next one, on the history of the Japanese war machine in the 1930s and forties, was met with little enthusiasm in the house.

THE PLACE THAT RAN BY ITSELF

Toland had spent a lot of time in Japan, and had even ended up marrying his translator.

"He had all the material," Bob said, "and he wrote it. He always wrote it from the point of view of the person he interviewed, which often was not the point of the scene. I met with him twice a week for thirteen months. That was maybe the most arduous time I had with a book, and, actually, I enjoyed it. He would write a chapter, I would rewrite the next one, and he'd revise it. We just kept going. At the end of the year, though, I had no other books on the list. But *The Rising Sun* won the Pulitzer Prize."

ALL THROUGH THE reign of Cerf and Klopfer, their prime editors were doing the job. So the founding fathers were able to continue to conduct their personal business as fun. But when they decided to extend themselves, the fun began to lessen.

In 1959, Random House became the first trade publishing house to go public. Two years later, much to Cerf's satisfaction, his firm's name was traded on the New York Stock Exchange.

In 1960, they took over *three* publishing houses. The one that attracted the most attention was the purchase of the most respected publishing house on earth—Alfred A. Knopf. (See next chapter.) The day after the sale, April 17, 1960, *The New York Times* made it a front-page story: "Knopf, Random House in Publishing Merger." The reporter who broke the story was Gay Talese. Nan Talese blushed as she told me how he got his scoop.

"I had been at Random House a very short time. I came home one day and said to Gay, 'Oh, God, it's the end of publishing.'

" 'Why do you tell me that?' he said.

" 'Well, I heard a rumor that Random House is buying Knopf. And if that happens, the whole sky is going to fall.' "

"Gay said to me, 'What's Bennett's phone number?' 'I don't know,' I said, 'and it's only a rumor. You're just going to get me fired.'

"Gay tracked down Bennett's number, and got Bennett, who was not saying anything. But he kept at it and finally got him to admit that this was true. It was a triumph for Bennett."

Also that year Random House bought the distinguished Pantheon imprint, which had been founded in 1942 by Kurt Wolff and Helen Wolff. Bennett had assured both Alfred Knopf and the Wolffs that they would be editorially independent. And so they were in those years.

Finally, late in 1960, Random House went into the textbook business, buying the L. W. Singer Company of Syracuse, New York, founded in 1924. At that time the magic word among book publishers, who were gobbling up other publishers, was *synergy*. The word later spread throughout the business world and became one of the primary concepts behind any kind of merger/acquisition. The irony of the Singer sale to Random House was that synergy did work, but in a most unlikely, most remarkable, way—it led to a Nobel Prize for the acquiring company.

FOLLOWING THE ACQUISITION, Bob Bernstein visited L. W. Singer in Syracuse several times a year for Cerf to keep an eye on a thriving business. He got to know a lot of people who worked there. "I'm walking around talking to the employees," Bob told me, "and I came to this young woman in the college textbook department whom I'd never met before. I said, 'What are you working on?' She told me she did literature anthologies for schools and was working on a book of African folktales. Our conversation was sparkling, and I said, 'Jesus, what are you doing in Syracuse?'

" 'I got divorced,' she said. 'I have two children. I didn't think New York was so safe. I thought I'd bring them up in another place, so here I am.'

"I said, 'Well, what would you like to do now that Random House owns you?'

'I'd like to be an editor at Random House,' she said. And so it was that this editor, born Chloe Anthony Wofford in Lorain, Ohio, moved closer to her destiny. At the time Bernstein met her, she was calling herself Toni Morrison.

A graduate of Howard University, Toni went on to Cornell to receive her M.A. by writing her thesis on suicide in the works of William Faulkner and Virginia Woolf. She taught English at Texas Southern University and at Howard University before taking the job at Singer in 1965.

The one thing she hadn't told anybody was that she was working on a novel. She sent it around personally to various publishers—she had no agent—but nobody was interested. She then sent it to an editor at Holt, Alan Rinzler, on the advice of Claude Brown, a student of Toni's at Howard University (Brown also wanted to marry her); Brown's autobiographical novel, *Manchild in the Promised Land,* had been bought by Rinzler. I spoke with Rinzler, who had had a long career as a *Rolling Stone* editor and who now runs the Jossey-Bass nonfiction imprint in San Francisco (a division of John Wiley & Sons). "Toni showed me the book," Rinzler told me, "and I thought *The Bluest Eye* was great." Aaron Asher, Rinzler's boss at Holt, was equally taken by the novel. Holt published *The Bluest Eye* in 1969. Although it didn't sell many copies then, the reviewers took notice of this new writer. So did some people at Random House, namely Tony Schulte.

When Tony Schulte came into Toni's life, he was the executive vice president for trade books at Random House, Knopf, and Pantheon. He met Toni while attending a publishing conference in Jamaica.

"I think you should be in trade publishing," Schulte told Toni. "Wouldn't you like to be in trade?" Toni said she would. "And," Schulte said, "you can choose Random trade or Knopf trade." Toni thought, *Ah, this is like a dream come through.* So, at Schulte's suggestion, she went to talk with Jim Silberman, the editor in chief of Random House, and with Bob Gottlieb, the editor in chief of Knopf. "Bob Gottlieb had told me when I visited him," Toni said, "that he thought *The Bluest Eye* was 'a perfect book, like a poem.'" But when she talked with him about coming to Knopf as an editor, he was plainspoken. "He told me," Toni remembered, "'I have to be able to fire you if you work for me, and I don't want to do that. I'd much rather be your editor than your boss.' You know, Bob ran a tight ship.

"So then I talked to Jim Silberman. He wanted to be my boss. It was for me a perfect marriage. I got Bob Gottlieb as an editor for my next book, and I got to work in trade at Random House, which was very "loose" in those days—loose meaning the really great thing was that I would acquire something, and while I had to get approval from the editor in chief, there was no committee. You just pressed your own case, and when you succeeded, you succeeded. I was surprised to learn that at other companies the editors didn't have that kind of freedom."

Toni later became the first black woman to hold a named chair at an Ivy League university. I went to visit her at Princeton in December 2005, where she has been the Robert F. Goheen Professor in the Council of Humanities since 1989. We had lunch together at one of her favorite restaurants. Toni Morrison is a presence. She came in with a flowing gown, assertive dreadlocks, and a queenly smile. Everyone in the room knew who she was, but no one peeked or peered. She and I talked about the past, remembering when we first met in 1973. She had come over to the Book-of-the-Month Club offices with the galleys of a book which she hoped would be of interest: *The Black Book*. It consisted of news clippings, photographs, songs, advertisements, and recipes that echoed the black experience in America. Toni took us through the book, speaking in that soft, purring, melodic voice of hers. We decided to buy *The Black Book* as an Alternate and it did very well for us.

Four years later she was back at the Club, this time in a more significant role: Toni was honored at a luncheon to celebrate *Song of Solomon* becoming a Main Selection, the first for an African-American author since Richard Wright.

I remember the judges' meeting we held in May of 1977. There was a long discussion about *Song of Solomon,* one of three Selection candidates (the judges could say no to all the candidates if they didn't find one they liked). Mordecai Richler's is the only name I'm going to reveal. Richler, a Canadian with a rich sense of humor and a large list of marvelous novels to his name (*The Apprenticeship of Duddy Kravitz* was his most popular novel), opened the discussion saying about *Song of Solomon,* "I'm afraid I was very taken with this novel. Not since Cheever's short stories or *Lancelot* [a novel by Walker Percy] have I been so taken with a book. This is the kind of novel that may get major attention. I was overwhelmed by the writing and the narrative drive."

One judge replied: "I decided three-quarters of the way through that I was being mesmerized and didn't like it."

A second judge said: "I was worried about its self-conscious symbolism." To which Richler, in his deep, authoritative voice, observed: "This is almost like an early Chagall. I thought it was powerful."

A third judge asked: "What I really wonder is, what does it mean?"

Richler conceded: "I don't perfectly understand it, but reading it was such a magnificent experience."

Then things began to turn Mordecai's way. I always thought it was amazing the way one judge, with a strong feeling about a book, could get his or her colleagues to come around to his point of view. It started with one judge saying: "Its beginning is wild. I would allow her that." Immediately, another judge backed in: "It held me three-quarters of the way." A third clinched it for Mordecai: "For the most part I did like it."

At our lunch for Toni she was pretty happy. At one point she spoke about her mother's influence on her. Her mother had been an avid reader, even joined a book club, Toni said, giving me a sly look at that moment. "Not the Book-of-the-Month Club," she said, "but the Literary Guild." Well, why not? The Guild always found "good reads." That certainly was true. They did have many more women members than we did.

As an editor, Toni Morrison fit right in at Random House even though she agreed with Nan Talese and other female editors that it was mostly a boy's club. She told me that Albert Erskine may have been an exception. His office was next to hers. "I used to smoke a pipe. He and I would have pipe and tobacco conversations."

One of her first assignments was to help edit Muhammad Ali's autobiography, *The Greatest: My Own Story*—not so much to edit the writing as to keep Ali in line. The book was being written by a Chicago writer, Richard Durham. It had been brought in by Charles Harris (whom you met in chapter 7, on Doubleday). Ali and his entourage came over for a morning meeting; their next stop would be Simon & Schuster. There was no next stop.

"Bennett came in to see him," Charlie told me. "He knew Ali because the champ had been on TV's *What's My Line?* You know how corny Bennett can be; both of them were such hams. So we just sat there while Bennett told one story, and Ali would tell another one."

They finally hammered out a $250,000 deal. Ali asked if he could get half of the advance immediately. He did.

Jim Silberman did most of the editing on the book (Charlie Harris had since left the company), and Toni saw to it that Ali would behave once the book was in the stores. "When I first met him," she said, "I was sitting in a room with all these big white salesmen. If I asked Ali a question, he'd answer one of the men. At first, I thought, *Oh, God, it's very difficult being a girl with these guys.*

"What I learned about Ali was interesting because the way he related to me was to flirt. And I had to giggle, but then I remembered that Ali had enormous respect for older women. So I would go in and cross my arms and tap my foot and say, 'Ali, get out. You have to be over there'—you know, take on a motherly, grandmother role. I took myself out of the realm of a girl."

Mostly, Toni enjoyed finding and acquiring books by new African-American women, among them Toni Cade Bambara, Gayl Jones, June Jordan, and Angela Davis. I asked whether it was helpful for her as a writer to be a good editor or vice versa. "I think that editing probably helped my writing," she said. "But the process of writing was never helped by editing—because you can't teach that thing. You just have to go through it, and each person is different. You have to find out what you need to make it work for you. And different people need different things.

"As Bob Gottlieb always said, 'Well, it's just a conversation, you know. It's just talking, finding the right thing to say.' And in a way it's true. But for me, I always thought I was really, really good as an editor for fiction writers because I was one, and I wasn't in competition with them. I knew what the problems were."

Toni said an interesting thing when she was on *First Edition*, a half-hour television show we produced for a couple of years at the Club. Each show featured an interview with a major writer. "I don't want to close the reader out," she said during her interview. "Provide less information, you get more truth. I don't want to read a book that's just received information."

She also talked about Gabriel García Márquez. "You go and drink from him. I have been seduced by that echo I found in Márquez, which was the extraordinary combination of that magic and information in one beat."

Her eyes lit up that day in Princeton when she told me, "I liked the part of the job that has no respect now," she said, "which is line editing. When I was able to do that with writers whose work was really interesting to me—that's when I was happy."

While she was still working as an editor, she wrote *Sula* and *Song of Solomon* under Gottlieb's protectorate. She kept working at Random House until the moment Gottlieb said to her, "One of these days you're going to have to figure it out. Are you a writer or not? Are you an editor who also writes, or what?"

"So I said, 'You're right, so let me just go and do the writing thing.' In 1983 she left Random House to write full-time. Ten years later, she became the first African-American (and the first woman since 1938) to win the Nobel Prize for literature.

JIM SILBERMAN ENJOYED having Toni Morrison around. He was pleased with the books she brought in, and especially pleased with how she taught Muhammad Ali about manners. And Jim was still enjoying his role as editor in chief, even though it was without full portfolio. His executive obligations in the trade division never stopped him from buying good books. In 1968 he edited and published *The Money Game* by Adam Smith, which became a bestseller. He also bought and edited the surpassing bestseller *Future Shock* by Alvin Toffler; *Beggars in Jerusalem* by Elie Wiesel; and E. L. Doctorow's critically acclaimed third novel, *The Book of Daniel*. He signed Doctorow's next book, which turned out to be *Ragtime*. Jim wasn't there when *Ragtime* was published; he had been wooed by Dick Snyder to Simon & Schuster in much the same way he had been wooed by Bennett Cerf to Random House. At Simon & Schuster, he started a new imprint called Summit Books, and made it a big success. Meanwhile, Milly Marmur, the house's mighty subsidiary rights director, sold the paperback rights of *Ragtime*, a critically acclaimed literary novel, to Bantam Books for an extraordinary $1,850,000.

THE MONEY GAME in book publishing was being played at higher and higher stakes. What a difference there was in the mid-1970s from in the early 1950s when the paperback revolution was just getting traction. But back then, aware that a revolution was simmering, Bennett Cerf made the two appointments that came to mean so much to his house. He hired Jason Epstein, who at Doubleday had founded a literary paperback imprint called Anchor Books. And he hired Robert Bernstein, whose most recent job had been at Simon & Schuster, where he was unhappy. Cerf made Bob Bernstein advertising manager; he figured Bernstein was a young man who might play an important role in the company's future. Besides arriving at Random House at about the same time, at the beginning of 1957, Bernstein and Epstein had very little in common, except high intelligence.

One day, early in his tenure at Random House, Bob Bernstein's mother attended a popular literary luncheon sponsored by the *New York Herald Tribune.* "My mother was a rather pushy lady," Bob told me, "and she pushed her way up to see Bennett Cerf, who was speaking there. He was then more famous for his light books full of puns and his television appearance on the program *What's My Line?* than as a book publisher.

"So my mother says to Bennett, 'I'm Bob Bernstein's mother. Do you know him? He works at your place.' Bennett says, 'Of course I know Bob. We hired Bob and Jason Epstein at almost the same time. We call them *Mass and Class.*' My mother says, 'Which is Bob?' Jason had founded Anchor Books and I had founded *The Shirley Temple Story Book.* I don't remember my mother being upset by having a son who dealt with mass culture."

Jason Epstein's nearly half-century at Random House was never without incident. That may have been why Cerf, in *At Random,* called Jason "the cross I bear." Jason, a counterpuncher at heart, countered: "Bennett is the bear I cross."

In the fall of 2006 I went to see this demon barber of book publishing in the golden age at his gorgeous downtown apartment in the Edwardian beaux-arts Police Building. Hard by City Hall, it had been transformed from police headquarters in 1987 into lavish condominiums for well-to-do personages (another resident there is Toni Morrison). Jason opened his door—the building, true to its name, seemed to be full of solemnly dressed security guards—and escorted me through a warren of large rooms until he seated me in what must be his favorite room: the kitchen. Being a well-known chef de cuisine, the kitchen seemed to be the natural sanctuary for him to talk about his life at Random House.

First, though, he wanted to tell me about his latest and most novel approach to book publishing, the Espresso Book Machine. A piece of it was there on his kitchen table. He had a smile on his face that frightened me as he fingered it, trying to explain its magic to me. *Brrr!* A year later, in June of 2007, it actually came to life.

In this corner, standing eight feet tall, weighing in at 1,660 pounds, was the heavyweight contender, the Espresso Marvel, ready to print books on demand! Jason is in this with several partners. The hope is that eventually a lot of publishing houses would be willing to buy it for a company's exclusive use. The cost now would be around $100,000. Solemnly, Jason told the world that it is nothing more or less than "the future of publishing."

Then I got back to asking him my usual question: As a youth, was there any one book that had captured his heart? "No," he said. "What changed my life was that I went to see a movie on lower Fifth Avenue. It was called *The Scoundrel,* starring Noël Coward, and it was almost exactly based on the life of Horace Liveright. 'That's for me,' I said. 'I think I'm going to do it. I think I'll be a publisher.'"

Maybe that's why Jason said to me, "I was only incidentally an editor. The deal I had with Bennett was that I would do my books with no other responsibilities, and I would be free enough to start my own companies. When I left Doubleday, I did not want to go back to work for anybody else. I knew I had this entrepreneurial edge, and the idea of just being an editor didn't appeal to me. So it was a wonderful arrangement. What could have been better?" Horace Liveright would have approved.

Sam Vaughan, who spent many years at Doubleday before coming to Random House, remembers Jason Epstein very well. "I was the Doubleday sales manager, and he would come into the sales department every day and check on the sales of his infant line, Anchor Books. I remember thinking, 'This guy is not an egghead; he's not just a brainy intellectual, he's really a publisher. He had the greatest entrepreneurial spirit, I think, of any young editor I knew. He's an enormous pain in the ass but he's always very funny in his curmudgeonly way. I learned things from him from just watching him."

Why had he left Doubleday? I asked Jason. He said it had to do with Douglas Black, who was then president of the company. "I was on very bad terms with him. For some reason we got on each other's nerves. Anchor Books, which I started, was bringing in lots of money, and he wasn't paying me nearly enough. But what really troubled me about Black was *Lolita*."

Wait. *Lolita*? What was this all about?

He told me, "My wife, Barbara, and I had spent a Thanksgiving weekend with Edmund Wilson in Wellfleet. We'd become friends. And on the Sunday that we were leaving, he took me into his study and said, 'Here's a novel by my friend, Vladimir Nabokov. You might want to read it. You'll see why when you read it.' I thought it was terrific, and I wanted to go with it. I was not upset by the story.

"So I took it to Doubleday, and Ken McCormick, who was editor in chief and a good friend, read it, and I think he was a little nervous about it. 'Well, there's reason to be nervous about it,' I told him. 'It could get us in trouble. You better show it to Black, and see what he says.'"

Sitting at his kitchen table in his denim work shirt and dungarees, Jason's face turned dark. "Black wouldn't read it," he said. "He wouldn't read it! And the tension between us became intolerable. I finally said to myself, *I've had it with this place. I'm going.*"

Go he did. He and his wife, Barbara Epstein, went to London for three months. It wasn't exactly a honeymoon. It was a three-month buying trip. He went to see Allen Lane, the founder of Penguin Books, hoping that Lane would sell Penguin to him.

Lane had other ideas. He knew what Jason had done when he converted classic books into lower-priced classic *paperback* books. Anchor Books became a triumph for Doubleday. Allen Lane asked Jason if he would like to run his Penguin business in the U.S. Jason said no. He was in the middle of running Anchor Books and didn't want to abandon that business. A man of sharp opinions about people, Jason wondered about Lane. "I didn't quite like him," he said. "Something about him made me nervous."

While Jason was still in London, he got the call from Bennett Cerf in New York. Bennett asked him: "Do you want to come to work here?" Jason said, "'No, I want to start my own business.' So that's how I got involved with him. I liked Bennett. I can think of a lot of reasons not to have liked him. But I think if you look at him in perspective, and in the right context, I mean, he was a great publisher. He was also a super-egomaniac."

I have to say that Jason Epstein—and this is a compliment—reminded me of Glenn Gould, the brilliant but highly eccentric concert pianist. Once, when Leonard Bernstein, then conducting the New York Philharmonic, allowed Gould to be soloist in Brahms's Second Piano Concerto, Gould instantly became Bernstein's cross to bear. He deigned not to follow Bernstein's baton; wherever it was going, he was going his own way. When it was over, Bernstein said he'd never allow Gould to play with him again. Bennett Cerf was quite a bit more conciliatory with the cross he bore.

And so Jason brought fabulous publishing ideas to life: *The New York Review of Books* (started by him and his then wife, Barbara Epstein, and Robert Silvers); the Library of America, and *The Reader's Catalogue*, two thousand pages with more than forty thousand titles that could be bought over the telephone—a precursor to the Online Nation. Whatever he was assigned to do at Random House, however, suffered not only from his prickly personality, but also from his benign neglect.

When I talked with Charlotte Mayerson, I asked her which of the Random House editors she liked the most. She said, "I loved Joe Fox. I still dream about Joe sometimes. He was a wonderful person. And Jason. He was, of course, a difficult person, but he was always very good to me. When my son got sick, it was Jason who took care of me." (Charlotte's son, Rob, died of AIDS.)

The other editors felt that Jason had no time for their books; he was only interested in his own. Well, perhaps it was because he was working with interesting writers—Nabokov, Roth, Mailer, Doctorow, Gore Vidal, even a commercial novelist, Robert Ludlum. He was also trying to make his Vintage classic paperback line competitive with Anchor Books.

It got worse for Jason when, in 1976, Jim Silberman moved to Simon & Schuster. "It was Bob Bernstein who called me, about becoming editor in chief," Jason explained, "and said, 'Will you do this?' And I said, 'I'll do it until you find someone.' But I didn't want it. I knew I'd be terrible. I was going to take that job for two weeks. I just wasn't good. I hated doing it."

Milly Marmur gave me an example of Jason Epstein at work. "We were publishing one of Michael Korda's books, *Success*. Our publicity director, Carol Schneider, came in and said there was a problem. The problem was that Korda was in Chicago, and he wanted to come home for the weekend. But he had a major TV appearance in Chicago on Monday at 9 A.M. Carol didn't know what to do. It was a Friday morning and, of course, Jason was in his house in Sag Harbor. So I called Jason. I figured he was the one person who could talk to Michael.

"When I got him, I said, 'Jason, it's Milly. We've got a serious problem here.'

"And Jason said, 'You have exactly two minutes to talk or my mayonnaise will curdle.' "

Jason stayed on not only because he continued to do the things he wanted to do, but also because the culture of the company appealed to him. Like so many Random House editors I talked with, Jason said the beauty of Random House was that "the place ran by itself. I was too young to appreciate it at the time." He claims he never thought of it competitively. "We were very collegial, we were all friends, but we didn't work together." He felt, maybe because Bennett Cerf almost never had meetings, that it was all right *not* to work together. Most of his other colleagues felt differently about that.

"Still," he said, "I just thought it was a dream to be there. The authors would hang around with us. Auden would come in his carpet slippers with his big manuscript and would put it on my desk and would say with a chuckle, 'I'd like to have my money right now.'

"I was too naïve or too stupid to know that it was extraordinary. But that's what life is like. I had no idea that it was not going to last forever."

IN 1965, BENNETT Cerf and Donald Klopfer sold their company, including Alfred A. Knopf, to RCA for $27 million dollars. When I was talking with Gloria Loomis, a leading literary agent since the 1970s, about her ex-husband, she gave me a very simple explanation for the sale: "A day came when Bennett and Donald said, 'We have kids. We don't know what the company's worth.

We're going to sell to RCA.' They were going to take their wealth and pass it on to their children."

The other thing was that Bennett didn't want to report to anybody, it wasn't his style. When the sale to RCA was finalized in December 1965, Bennett, then sixty-seven years old, simplified his life. He moved up to chairman of the board and appointed Bob Bernstein president of Random House. Bernstein could deal with RCA.

Bernstein was a different kind of person from either Bennett or Donald, but he tried to run the company in their manner. At his twenty-fifth anniversary celebration, a "Hail to Our Chief" gift was presented to him by perhaps Random House's biggest star, Dr. Seuss:

Since that memorable day
back in Nineteen Five Seven,
most witnesses long since
have packed off to heaven.
But to those who still breathe
the great memory's still fresh
of the wild wind that blew
with a woosh and a wesch
when Bob Bernstein showed up
in the fine freckled flesh.

Bennett Cerf was packed off to heaven on August 27, 1971. The obituaries were long and lavish on his publishing career. One of the obits got it right, stating, "He gave full measure to his profession." But Bennett Cerf was not just a great and legendary book publisher. He was an icon of the age, a television personality whose smile told his friends watching that they could count on him in a pinch. Ah, he would have loved reading his last reviews.

One still thinks of Bennett and Donald Klopfer, who died in

1986, hand in hand, doing it all together. A photograph of Gertrude Stein hung in Bennett's office for years, with an inscription that read: *For Random House, which is Donald and Bennett, the nicest, the sweetest, the kindest and the most spoiling of publishers.* That tells it all.

11

LIVING IN A DREAM WORLD

Alfred A. Knopf, Inc.

I have to tell you—and this is where it sounds very
arrogant—but we paid no attention to anybody. I think
everybody paid attention to us.

—JANE FRIEDMAN

Robert Gottlieb had hardly settled into his new chair,
having departed from Simon & Schuster in December
of 1967, when in early March of 1968, he read a letter
from a student at the University of Michigan. Daniel Okrent
wanted to know all about book publishing. Bob typed a letter
back on Knopf stationery, which he was just getting used to.
There was the illustrious title at the top: *Alfred A. Knopf Incor-
porated*. Under that came *Publisher of Borzoi Books,* with a
picture of the Russian wolfhound that had been chosen by
Alfred Knopf's wife, Blanche, to become the colophon of the
company.

About getting into publishing, Gottlieb said in his reply to
Okrent, "There's no given way, as you've probably guessed. Actually, what happens is this: you meet someone or know someone
who takes enough of an interest to send you on to someone else at

another house, etc. etc. until you happen to arrive at the right desk on the right day, and then you are in publishing."

One of the gems Gottlieb revealed to the kid from Michigan was how he hired beginners: "I pick people on the basis of a little talk and a lot of impulse. . . ." He also mentioned that it was important to find young people who might make excellent editors. Bob went on to tell Okrent that if he ever came to New York, he should come to see him.

That was all the eager student needed to hear. Within a week, he flew into New York. When he arrived, he called Gottlieb's office and got Toinette Lippe, Bob's assistant. "My name is Danny Okrent," he said, "and I'd like to see Mr. Gottlieb."

"Well," she asked, "do you have an appointment with him?"

"No," he said, "but he told me if I was ever in New York, I should give him a call." Toinette advised Dan that Mr. Gottlieb was very busy, but maybe he could see him sometime next week.

"Well, I'm just a student," Okrent said, with some panic in his voice, "I have to go back right away." She put him on hold. Moments later, she told him to come on by.

"It was late afternoon, maybe five-thirty," Dan remembered, "and we talked for two hours. And that's how it happened."

In April 1969, Daniel Okrent went to work for Gottlieb and spent four and a half happy years at Knopf. He loved working for the editor who was so kind to him.

DAN BEGAN HIS story as we sat in his home on Manhattan's Upper West Side. "I had seen a piece by Josh Greenfeld on the cover of *The New York Times Book Review* about Joe Heller and how, since *Catch-22* had been published, it had established Heller as a leading American novelist. Robert Gottlieb was Heller's editor. I was a kid from Detroit and I had never heard of book editors. I didn't even know they existed. Bob was so great to me."

Dan's first acquisition at Knopf, he told me, was a book called

Defending the Environment, written by a University of Michigan law professor, Joseph L. Sax. It was way ahead of its time and almost immediately became an environmental classic. The day that the book was being talked about among the editors, Alfred Knopf walked into Gottlieb's office. He had heard about the book and liked its title; he was always looking for sound environmental works. "Maybe we should sign this person up," he said to Bob. "Let's ask Okrent," Bob said. "Who's Okrent?" said the reigning figure in the world of book publishing.

Dan remembers Bob Gottlieb pointing to him. "You know, I had hair down to my shoulders, and Alfred comes over to my desk, which was out in the corridor, and says, 'Good work on that Sax book. Good work!' Then he walks away, and two editors, Herbert Weinstock and Jane Garrett, who had adjacent offices, come out and said, 'We've worked here for years, and he's never said anything nice to us.' So I became an editor, too."

In 1973, things changed. While Bob was working in London, Okrent was offered a job by Richard Grossman, who had his own imprint at Viking Press. "Dick wanted me to be his deputy at Grossman," Dan told me. "He said that he was thinking of retiring, and if he did, I would succeed him." When Bob Gottlieb came back home, Okrent told him about the job offer. Bob asked for specifics, and Dan told him. " 'You know,' Bob said to me, 'if you take that job, I'll never speak to you again.' I was stunned. The next day when I told Bob that I was taking the job, I was in tears in his office. It was just awful."

It was Bob Gottlieb's disposition to surround himself with loyal colleagues—people who loved him as he loved them and who would stay with him forever. Look at how many Knopf loyalists, who started back then at the beginning of the Gottlieb regime, are still there today: Judith Jones, Toinette Lippe, Victoria Wilson, Nina Bourne, Kathy Hourigan, among others. (They are now, of course, working for Sonny Mehta, who succeeded Bob at Knopf in 1987, and a perfect successor Sonny became.) "When Bob went to *The New Yorker,*" Okrent went on, "I was in the magazine business by then. I sent him a letter of congratulation. In it I said, 'Welcome to the magazine business, it's no better than the book business.' He did write me a letter back, a very nice 'thanks for the note.' And he went on to say, 'The only thing I can imagine worse than the book business today is the book business tomorrow.'" That marked the end of it between the teacher and his pupil.

In his years at Simon & Schuster and Knopf, Bob Gottlieb always made blue-ribbon choices for assistants, almost all of whom went on to bigger and better professional lives. Okrent's predecessor, for example, was Richard Locke, who later became an important editor at *The New York Times Book Review.*

Twenty-six-year-old Lee Goerner came to work for Gottlieb after Okrent. Katherine McNamara was married to Goerner until his death in 1995. In one issue of her online literary magazine, *Archipelago,* she wrote about how Lee came to edit Michael Herr's *Dispatches,* the great American book about the Vietnam War: "When Michael Herr turned in the manuscript, no one at Knopf knew how to edit the hyped-up, rock-and-roll language. Lee hovered in the hallway by Gottlieb's office, his face glowing. Gloria Emerson, the war correspondent and a friend of Bob's, was there. She watched him and finally said to Gottlieb, 'Give it to that young man.' Bob did, and it was Lee's first big book."

In 1983, Lee Goerner was given the Spanish-language edition of a novel written by an unknown Chilean author, Isabel Allende. When he finished reading it, he went to Gottlieb and said, "I don't know anything about her, you don't know anything about her, but this is the book we have to publish." Bob looked at me and blinked. He said, 'Well, OK.'" Goerner wasn't happy about the translation, and he retranslated much of it himself. *The House of the Spirits* became a bestseller, a Book-of-the-Month Club Main Selection, and marked the beginning of a brilliant authorial career for Allende.

Katherine McNamara offered an interesting notion about the Gottlieb-Goerner relationship that could have applied to any of Bob Gottlieb's "finds." "Powerful older men," she said, "often thwart gifted, rising young men—the young bucks who challenge the alpha stag, but cannot (yet) vanquish him."

Bob may have been an alpha stag of sorts, but he was also extraordinary when it came to dishing out help for others who craved to be editors. Gerald Howard, later of Viking and W. W. Norton, who now runs Doubleday's Broadway Books imprint, remembers when he was first looking for a job in book publishing. He said he wrote letters to all the big guns. The one who wrote back immediately was Gottlieb. "I want to say here," Gerry told me with startling vigor, "that Bob Gottlieb—who doesn't remember this, I'm sure—was exceptionally generous in answering my doubtless silly and embarrassing letter, giving me an hour of his time, letting me rattle on about Don DeLillo, who was my great obsession, and who Bob was publishing at the time. I've always been grateful to him for giving of himself, and I try to do that for other people."

Well, that was what Bob Gottlieb brought to Knopf. Seeking love from those around him—once their talent was proven—he offered them full devotion in return. Unlike the difficult and sometime malevolent founders, Father Bob took the chill out of the house.

IT HAS BEEN said of Alfred A. Knopf that he was irascible at his best, and cruel at his worst. I never did hear anyone excuse his behavior as being merely a kind of defense mechanism or that, in truth, he was secretly kindhearted and sweet. All the evidence I have acquired indicates that his irascibility was genuine, along with a resolute egotism.

In that respect, he was not unlike other masters of his period—people like Cass Canfield, Bennett Cerf, Henry Holt,

Alfred Harcourt, William Jovanovich, and Roger Straus. They, too, possessed major egos yet managed to sublimate them in their quest for success. Knopf, certain that success was his birthright, took the highest road. He was the publisher of the time—no one could wear purple shirts and green ties, or vice versa, like him.

I only met Alfred Knopf once in my life. It was during a luncheon at his country home in Purchase, New York, which someone early on had named Hovel; it was anything but a hovel for almost everyone but Blanche, Alfred's wife. She hated the country, preferring to stay in her own apartment in New York. We were guests of Alfred and his second wife, Helen, a personable woman who seems to have given Alfred, in the twilight of his life, a warmer personality. When Blanche Knopf died in 1966, Helen, who'd had a novel published by Knopf in 1941, sent him twelve red roses. She and Alfred married the next year.

The other couple for lunch was Warren Chappell and his wife, Lydia. We actually first went to their home in Norwalk, Connecticut, because Warren was eager to show Rosa his studio. For years Chappell had served Alfred as a master draftsman, a designer of type, a designer of books, an illustrator—who, one of his closest friends said, "could translate thoughts into drawing." I was lucky that when Warren sent me letters (we worked together for many years at the Book-of-the-Month Club and became friends), there was always a drawing in full color. One that I cherish shows an obstetrician, masked in goggles, pulling a newborn baby out of an inkpot. Chappell titled it "Birth of an Editor."

During the lunch, Alfred reminisced about his friendship with Harry Scherman and his wife, the founders of BOMC, and talked a bit about the Club's service to publishing, particularly to his company. After all, that was the reason we were asked to have lunch with the old master: The Knopf books were at the head of the class. My wife and I left that pleasant afternoon wondering what Alfred Knopf had been truly like when, at the top of his game, he was a force unlike any other in book publishing.

HE WAS BORN in 1892 into a privileged household in New York. His mother, Ida, had died when he was four years old; as a consequence, his father, Samuel, a successful advertising executive, paid close attention to his son, who was known to be bashful and timid around outsiders. "S.K.," as his father was called, was a tough businessman, but made friends easier than his son. One of his closest friends was H. L. Mencken. "S.K.," John Tebbel wrote in *Between Covers,* "may have been one of the few men alive who could outtalk Mencken."

One thing father and son had in common was they both felt that the language of God was music, and they attended every concert they could. (Later in life, Alfred brought the most extraordinary musicians into his Fifth Avenue home when entertaining.) At the age of thirty-four, Alfred and his eight-year-old son took piano lessons from a leading musicologist, David Mannes.

In 1908, Alfred entered Columbia College, attuned especially to history and literature. On his graduation in 1912, like many children of the very rich, he was given a summer on the Continent. While writing a paper on John Galsworthy for a class at Columbia, Alfred initiated a correspondence with Galsworthy, one of the grand British novelists of the era. Galsworthy invited Knopf to visit him in his Devonshire cottage on the edge of Dartmoor. It was a visit that changed his life.

Galsworthy talked to Alfred about books and the writers who should be read in America; he showed particular fondness for Conrad and W. H. Hudson. He spoke to the young man with such passion that Alfred became infected. "I came home," he said, "determined to be a publisher and not a lawyer as the family intended."

Alfred's father didn't mind at all. Right away, he persuaded his friend Frank Nelson Doubleday—Doubleday the First—to give him a job, and Alfred was immediately hired as a junior account-ant. Could that have been the moment—a move by the most sig-nificant figure in book publishing then—that marked the beginning of the ascension of Jews in book publishing? In En-gland, the Jewish interest about getting into publishing had al-ready become a subject of discussion. A British publisher wrote about Knopf: "He is one of that small and choice group of pub-lishers of other than Anglo-Saxon extraction, who has liberated publishing in America, and even exacted a broadening influence on British publishing."

Alfred gave Doubleday more than just accounting services. He found himself involved in manufacturing, advertising, and sales. "I was able to frequent the composing room," he said, "play with cloth, sample books and try to improve the looks of binding."

That wasn't all. Joseph Conrad's new book, *Chance,* was to be published by Doubleday in 1913, and Alfred put together an 18-page evaluation of Conrad's novels as a promotion pamphlet. It must have helped, because *Chance* sold over 50,000 copies, in addition to also improving sales of his previous Doubleday titles.

"I suppose the biggest thrill in my Garden City days," Knopf said, "came with the arrival of Conrad's first letter to me." Con-rad told the youngster: "If you had not happened along, all these books would have remained on the back shelves of the firm, where they have been reposing for the last ten years." Alfred was not only thrilled, he was inspired by Conrad's words. He began thinking about his future.

IN 1911, KNOPF met a seventeen-year-old green-eyed girl, Blanche Wolf, who also came from a wealthy family. She was exotic, out-spoken, and worldly, having been raised by French and German governesses. Once they got to know each other better, she found herself sharing Alfred's enthusiasm for book publishing as a trade. She even invested some money in the firm of Alfred A. Knopf, Inc., when it came into being in 1915, the year before they married. Another investor was Alfred's father, who became treasurer of the company and served his son well until his death in 1931. By 1921, Alfred was president of his company, and Blanche was a director and vice president. In effect, the Knopfs became the first married couple to own and run a book publishing house together.

From the beginning, Alfred Knopf took his firm in different directions than his competitors. First of all, unlike other American book publishers of the time, he made the physical design of the book beautiful for his readers. His first published book was *Four Plays* by Emile Augier, which was translated from the French. Knopf had the book bound in orange and blue, and his advertisements stressed not its content, but its imprint. "The fundamental trouble," he once said, "is that people concerned with books—and I mean publishers, booksellers and authors—have never succeeded in gaining from the general public the kind of fundamental respect for the book that it deserves." He was out to gain that respect for all the works he published.

Second, he and Blanche decided, perhaps because of John Galsworthy's influence, to go after literature that had been published in other countries. (They did not buy works by authors who had never been published. They didn't have the editorial talents to do that.) In his first year the Knopfs published eleven books, seven of them by Russian or Polish writers. In 1916 they found their most successful book so far from an Englishman: *Green Mansions,* a novel by W. H. Hudson, whom Galsworthy had recommended to Alfred. It wasn't a new book; the novel had been published in 1904 by Putnam's, without success. But due to a contract error, *Green Mansions* was now in the public domain. Knopf published a new edition. John Galsworthy wrote the introduction. This time the book worked.

One other guiding principle for the Knopfs was to only publish books that commanded their interests: for Alfred, historical scholarship, music, gastronomy, conservation; for Blanche, the great French authors (Camus, André Gide, Jules Romains, and Jean-Paul Sartre), as well as the writers of hardboiled crime and detective novels. It was Blanche who brought to Knopf the best of this genre— Dashiell Hammett, Raymond Chandler, and James M. Cain.

In 1921 the Knopfs made their first trip to Europe, spending three months in pursuit of literature. They visited France, Germany, Denmark, Norway, and Sweden. One of the first authors they brought back was Norwegian novelist Knut Hamsun, publishing his book *Hunger* in 1920, an opportune time: That year Hamsun won the Nobel Prize for literature.

Other books came to the Knopfs from writers they had befriended. It was Witter Bynner, a Knopf author, who introduced them to an unusual fellow then living in New York, Kahlil Gibran, who had moved to America from Lebanon. Gibran gave them his summary of the book titled *The Prophet:* "The whole Prophet is saying one thing: 'You are far greater than you know— and all is well.'" They published *The Prophet* in 1923, but all wasn't so well. They sold only 1,300 copies in its first year. This magnified the Knopfs' embarrassment at publishing a book they felt was beneath them. But two years later, all was really well. *"The Prophet,"* wrote John Tebbel, "is said to have earned more money for the firm than any other book, much to Alfred's personal mystification."

As all of this was happening, Alfred Knopf's ego was beginning to inflate. His frequent use of the first-person singular soon became his coat of arms. Listen to three of the Nine Commandments in his *Borzoi Credo*:

I believe that a publisher's imprint means something and that if readers paid more attention to the publisher of books they buy, their chances of being disappointed would be infinitely less.

I believe that good books should be well made, and I try to give every book I publish a format that is distinctive and attractive.

I believe that I have never unknowingly published an unworthy book.

When the House of Knopf stood on stronger fiscal ground, Alfred felt even more self-satisfied, saying, "I think I benefit the art of letters and serve the American reading public, which has backed so generously—most of the time—my sincerest enthusiasms."

Many of his sincerest enthusiasms did indeed take off. Knopf's first *Publishers Weekly* bestseller came in 1926, third on the fiction list for that year: *Sorrell and Son* by Warwick Deeping. A Scotsman who wrote sixty-five novels in his lifetime, Deeping published six other bestselling novels with Knopf over the next few years.

In 1931 the Knopfs scored their first literary bestseller, Willa Cather's *Shadows on the Rock.* The novel finished second on the year's fiction list, behind Pearl S. Buck's *The Good Earth. Shadows on the Rock* sold 120,000 copies, plus 45,000 copies from the BOMC, whose judges had made it a Main Selection.

The fascinating element about the Cather experience was that she had pursued Knopf. "His early books looked very different from other books that came out at the same time," Cather once said after an examination of Knopf titles. "I was convinced that he had set out to do something unusual and individual in publishing. That's why I went uninvited to call on him."

Right away she asked "the young man" (they were born the same year) if he might consider becoming her publisher. He might indeed. They stayed together for twenty years. In all that time, Cather never asked for an advance. In fact, with Knopf's major writers of this period—Mencken, Carl Van Vechten, Joseph Hergesheimer, Sigrid Undset, Katherine Mansfield, Gibran—an advance was "never ever a consideration."

Those were the years when Alfred and Blanche relied on international scouts to find books for them. In addition, there were those friends in the know. One of their closest friends was Carl Van Vechten, an important literary figure of the 1920s. Between 1922 and 1933, Knopf published seven Van Vechten novels (*The Tattooed Countess, Firecrackers, Spider Boy,* etc.). In return, Van Vechten gave back by suggesting they take on the poets Wallace Stevens and Elinor Wylie. And so they did. (Some years later in a meeting, Knopf complained venomously about Wallace Stevens: "It took me thirty years before I made a dime on him.") A patron of the Harlem Renaissance, Van Vechten was friends with Langston Hughes and introduced to the Knopfs' list works by Hughes, James Weldon Johnson, and other African-American authors.

Another staunch member of the Knopf brain trust was H. L. Mencken, the sturdy friend of Knopf's father and, in turn, a steadfast friend of the son. In 1921 Mencken wrote Alfred Knopf with a suggestion: "If you can get *Buddenbrooks* at a reasonable price, grab it." They did, and Thomas Mann was on the list. Knopf was so taken with Mencken that in 1924 he funded a new magazine for Mencken and the theater critic George Jean Nathan to run. *The American Mercury* was one of the liveliest intellectual magazines of its kind and elegantly designed. It lasted until 1934, when the Great Depression and Alfred's loss of interest killed it.

Looking at all the feverish activity going on at Knopf in the years before World War II, I find it odd that there was never a mention of the word *editor*. Knopf showed his essential feelings about the breed in an interview he gave to *The Saturday Review* in the mid-1970s. Talking about changes in the book publishing business, he said: "The most fundamental one was the increased importance of the editor. *In the early days, things were quite simple. The book came in, we published them as written."* (Italics mine.)

Alfred Knopf would find many changes taking place in the world of book publishing at the end of World War II. Hardly any of them would give him peace of mind.

THE KNOPFS' ONLY child never saw much of his parents in his early years. With Blanche and Alfred immersed in the razzle-dazzle of book publishing, Alfred Jr.—everybody called him Pat—was passed over to a nurse. Blanche made little time for child-rearing, preferring to live in her own world. She pretty much lived in her own world anyway. When the Knopfs married, she was attractive if somewhat plump. Gaining weight didn't much bother her until the night that she and her husband held a party at their spacious New York City home, complete with a Hollywood-type staircase. As Blanche made her entrance, coming down the stairs in a Chanel suit, Joseph Conrad, one of their guests, was heard to say, *"Quelle belge!"* (an unkind allusion to her appearance). For the next thirty-five years Blanche kept to a starvation diet. Such deprivation gradually took its toll. In her last years she lost her eyesight, but never let anyone become aware of it. She faked it. One day at a luncheon, she picked off the floor what she thought was her bag. It was her Yorkshire terrier.

As he got older, Pat Knopf was allowed to participate in his parents' social gatherings. There is a charming photograph taken by Alfred Sr. (a capable portrait photographer) of guests at Pat's tenth birthday party in Purchase on June 17, 1931. He shared the day with Carl Van Vechten and James Weldon Johnson, both also celebrating their birthdays. In the photograph you can see Van Vechten and Johnson standing in the back, and young Pat in a suit and tie kneeling in front along with his mother, her spindly arms in front of her, but with a rare hint of a smile on her face.

Things never seemed to be quite right for the son. In an interview

Pat once gave to Herbert Mitgang of *The New York Times* (the first *Times* reporter to cover what came to be called "the book beat") Pat said, "I have a very talented mother and father. I hope I wasn't adopted." Mitgang took it as a joke, which it probably was, except that it cut to the bone. Pat's parents didn't much treat him as a son.

In March 2004, Pat and I met for lunch to talk about his early life. He seemed very relaxed; he had been retired for a number of years, did a lot of traveling with his wife, Alice, kept up with book publishing gossip, and devoured books, especially serious works of nonfiction. Pat has the same sharp nose as his father, but his style of dress is a lot quieter. And though he carries his father's weapon of sarcasm, he is more careful about displaying it.

He seemed pleased to answer my questions about his wartime experience, which was obviously one of the fulfillments of his life. In July 1941, when he was twenty years old, an aviation cadet examining board came through Schenectady, New York. Pat told me that two or three nights before, he had watched a movie about Air Force pilots with a beautiful Hollywood star in it. The motion picture was all he could think about. "So when that board came through," Pat said, "I went in and took the exam. Three or four weeks later, I got a notice saying that I had been appointed as an aviation army cadet to the United States Army Air Corps. There was small print at the bottom of the page that said, 'If you are currently in college, sign here and you will not have to report to duty until further notice.'"

Further notice came for Pat on December 7, 1941. On the afternoon of Pearl Harbor he heard from the Air Force. He was told to report to the Albany, New York, railroad station at 5 o'clock the next afternoon. Twenty-four hours later he was in Montgomery, Alabama, and spent the next eight months learning how to fly.

He pinned on his wings, went overseas, and became a B-24

pilot and squadron commander. Captain Knopf flew forays into Germany night after night. "I was very lucky," he said. "I was never shot down."

"Was your plane ever hit?"

"Yes," he said, "but so was everybody else's."

The high spot of his bombing runs came the night he was approaching home with only three engines running. "It was raining," he said. "I was down below ten thousand feet, my radio wasn't working, and I was getting low on gas. I figured I had better land at the first field I could find. I was flying over a part of England where there were a lot of U.S. bases. I flew down and landed on this field. I shut the engines off, let the kids get out.

"I was on the wing when I saw this guy in the rain on a bicycle pedaling toward me. I jumped off the wing. A word came out of my mouth and a word came out of his mouth almost simultaneously. I said, "Klopfer!" And he said "Knopf!" He wasn't flying, but Donald Klopfer was an intelligence officer and this was his base (see chapter 10, Random House). For Pat Knopf, "It was just one of those war stories that I'll never forget and neither will he." But it was more than that. For, as Hiram Haydn wrote in his memoir, "Donald Klopfer was Pat's dream father."

With the war over, he was discharged late in 1945. When he got back to New York, free at last from military service, he dashed over to the offices to see his parents. His Knopf colleagues were delighted to see him, but Blanche and Alfred were in a meeting and didn't come out for thirty or more minutes. Soon after that punctured reunion, the Knopfs made an announcement: Pat Knopf would become secretary of the company and trade book manager.

THE WARTIME EDITOR in chief at Knopf was Harold Strauss. He had come to work for the company in 1939. His specialty was Japanese literature. With the publisher's reluctant approval—over the years, Strauss was ground down by Alfred Knopf—he arranged many translated works by some of the best Japanese novelists of the time: Yukio Mishima, Yasunari Kawabata, and Junichiro Tanizaki. "He deserved the gratitude of everyone connected with modern Japanese literature," said Donald Keene, who, in his role as translator, was the greatest twentieth-century ambassador to Japanese culture and literature.

But Strauss didn't get much gratitude from Alfred Knopf. In 1957, when Judith Jones came to work for the company, Alfred took her around to meet people. She remembers Alfred stopping in front of Strauss's office and sneering, "That's Harold Strauss. He calls himself editor in chief."

Judith Jones was the company's first great postwar editor, which is particularly impressive given the fact that publishing was still a male-dominated profession. She had lived in Paris for three and a half years. There she read French manuscripts, and she and her husband, Evan Jones, a novelist and respected nonfiction author, discovered the glory of French cuisine.

When Judith came back to the States to live, she went job-hunting. For a while she worked part-time for an agent, Ivan von Auw, of Harold Ober Associates. One day, she got a call from William Koshland, a gentle administrator at Knopf. "Ivan von Auw has recommended you."

"For what?" Judith asked.

"Blanche is looking for an editor."

"So I went to meet Blanche," Judith told me, "and we had a talk. I told her about some of the things I had done, including the Anne Frank thing. [Judith had discovered *Anne Frank: The Diary of a Young Girl*; see chapter 7 on Doubleday.] I think that just did it. She hired me on the spot."

. Judith shared a small office and telephone with Aaron Asher. It was Aaron's first job in publishing—working, he told me, as

Alfred's "gofer." "We were so afraid of them," Aaron said, "that we were even chicken about who was going to answer the phone. When it rang I'd say—'You take it, Judith.'" Aaron managed to survive his trial and quickly moved on to another house and enjoyed a masterful career in book publishing. Judith stayed.

"I would never have survived," she told me, "if I hadn't been sort of a pawn between the two. I mean, when Blanche wouldn't speak to me, Alfred was supporting me. She was impossible, really. One false step and out. The only time we were kind of friendly or intimate was when we had our sales conferences at the Harvard Club. In those days, women had not passed the threshold. When we had to go to the ladies' room, they took us to the men's room—with guards standing outside."

That reminded Judith about Blanche in the office. "You see," Judith said, "she wore open-toe shoes, and when we were in the ladies' room, you always knew when Blanche was in there with you because you could see the red toenails under the stalls. So if we were gossiping, suddenly a silence would fall—*here come the red toenails.*"

Judith's main task in those days was to read the books that came from France, untranslated, and write reports on them. She was also given permission to work on two novels by the British novelist Elizabeth Bowen, a major literary figure of the period. "I would go in," Judith said, "write a report or something about the novel, and give it to Blanche. And then, of course, Blanche would write my recommendations as hers." When, one time, Bowen came over from London, Alfred took her to lunch, and he invited Judith along, which annoyed Blanche greatly.

"I had never met Bowen. I was totally anonymous. All of a sudden, when we were putting on our coats in the coatroom, Bowen looked over at me quite fiercely. She had this stutter, and she said, 'Y-y-you're the one.' I said, 'What?' She said, 'You're the one that's been editing, aren't you?' She knew, because she knew that Blanche was always quoting somebody. And she said, in a whisper, 'Let's have lunch.' The next day we snuck out and had a three-hour lunch together. I just adored her."

Judith also remembered when, in the spring of 1960, a huge manuscript came in to Bill Koshland. It had been sent from Cambridge by Avis DeVoto (the wife of historian Bernard DeVoto), who was one of Knopf's scouts. It was a treatise on French cooking by two French authors—Simone Beck and Louisette Bertholle—and one American author nobody had ever heard of, Julia Child. It had been turned down by Houghton Mifflin, who didn't believe that many Americans would want to know all this about French cooking.

Judith was asked to look through it. She was excited. "It was a book that translated the mysteries of French cooking into terms that Americans could understand." Although she recommended the book, Judith wasn't allowed to sit in the meeting that would determine its fate. But she heard all about it.

"It was really Angus Cameron who stood up for me," Judith said. "Cameron had recently been hired as an editor by Alfred, and he was a foodie. He had worked at Bobbs-Merrill when they published *The Joy of Cooking*. He made a good case for the book." But in the meeting Blanche threw a fit. "What does this woman know about French cooking?" she said. When her husband said that the book should be bought, Blanche rose from her chair. And when he said, "Let's let Mrs. Jones have a chance," Blanche Knopf stomped out of the meeting. "She didn't want to give me a chance," Judith said. "She wanted to keep her French editor."

Mastering the Art of French Cooking was published in the fall of 1961. "If you can sell a book with that title," Alfred told Jones, "I'll eat my hat." Chomp, chomp. Before Christmas Knopf did a second printing. Within a year Julia Child—after she had begun wowing television audiences with her very American savoir faire—became a stalwart household figure in American kitchens. It was the beginning of a lifelong relationship between Jones and Child, as they worked together on all of Child's subsequent books. Judith worked on other cookbooks over the years but never became immersed in the subject. She still made time to take on other prominent authors throughout her sunlit career. She was Langston Hughes's last editor and still holds on to Anne Tyler and John Updike.

ONE OF JUDITH JONES'S closest friends is Stanley Kauffmann, who came to Knopf in June of 1959 and lasted to the fall of 1960. In that short period of time, Kauffmann did brave battle with the House of Knopf.

I visited him not long after I had seen Judith Jones. He lives in Greenwich Village with his wife, Laura, in a warm and comfortable book-lined apartment. Kauffmann is a person I've always admired, and I was pleased by this opportunity to talk with him. For years he has written theater, film, and literary critiques for magazines, mostly *The New Republic*. He has also written plays and published seven novels. Now, in his late eighties, he writes a weekly column for *The New Republic* and teaches drama at Hunter College. In the 1950s he took a hiatus from most of his own writing to conduct a ten-year flirtation with book publishing. It was, for him, like a marathon runner thinking that he could run forever, only to discover, after a decade was up, that his knees were failing him. With Kauffmann, it was Alfred Knopf who had failed him.

For much of his brief publishing career he had worked in paperback publishing, with Bantam Books and then Ballantine. He had heard that Knopf was looking for an editor who could bring in quality fiction from American writers. All these years Alfred Knopf had been the recipient of literary treasures from around the world—an early form of globalization, you might say. Now he wanted to buy American. After a taxing interview with both Alfred and Blanche, Stanley was offered the job. I asked him whether he was truly comfortable being in book publishing. "I loved editing," Stanley told me. "I loved working with authors." Then he admitted, "I hated the scrapping for manuscripts. I was no good at it. I felt like a beggar. Working at Knopf soured me on the idea of being in publishing. I was sort of glad they fired me."

"What went wrong?" I asked. "The pleasure," he said. "The pleasure was soured by Alfred himself. Alfred, as I'm sure you heard, was an extremely complex character, who had, I would say, as close to no taste in literature as a leading publisher could have. He was very worshipful—that was his dramatic side—of anything academic. He loved history books, he loved all kinds of books that didn't require real literary insight."

Another thing about Knopf, according to Stanley, "was his attitude toward his editors. He wanted them to fail and succeed at the same time." That would allow Alfred to maintain his hold on the throne.

About a week into the new job, it looked like Stanley was sure to succeed. He went to see an agent, Elizabeth Otis, who, he felt, was a discreet and well-bred woman. He asked her to please not send him anything that had been shopped around awhile. "At that time, the New York agents were mailing me all these dog-eared manuscripts for this new fellow to read. I told her that if she did send me a manuscript, let it be one she believes we ought to publish. She promised she would." About a week later she sent him a manuscript.

"I took it away for the weekend, and I began to read it," Stanley said, flattering me by saying that I would know what it was like to discover "a *wonderful, wonderful* writer." Of course, that is the ultimate gratification for all book editors.

Reading the first page," Stanley said, "was like looking into a lighted room with life in it."

The manuscript was called *Confessions of a Moviegoer,* written by a new author, Walker Percy. "The book went halfway along," Stanley said, "and I began to see that while he had the voice of an angel, he didn't know how to construct the novel. As it went on, it got very flabby and floppy and I couldn't publish it—it was *fatty.* "

He sent it back to Otis with a long letter, hoping that she would send a copy of the letter to Percy. "I expected never to hear from him again," Stanley said. "Why should he take my suggestions?" In mid-July of 1959, just about a month after he had started at Knopf, Elizabeth Otis called Stanley and told him that Percy was planning to work on the book. It came back three months later. The editor felt it was much better, but still needed work. It was January 1960 before Percy returned a second revised manuscript. Not quite good enough yet, Stanley thought, but he asked two Knopf editors to make suggestions. One of them was Henry Robbins, who would have an enduring career as an editor before his untimely death in 1979.

Walker Percy did a third revision, and this time Kauffmann, after showing it to Alfred, told him it was a go. The novel, now simply called *The Moviegoer*, was published in May 1961, six months after Stanley Kauffmann had been fired. "It was published with some enthusiasm," he said, "but it didn't seem to amount to anything."

Walker Percy came to New York some months later, and he and Kauffmann had lunch together. Stanley spent the time trying to cheer up his author. He even quoted Browning's line, "There shall never be one lost good."

Well, maybe. A. J. Liebling read it. *The New Yorker*'s boxing and gastronomic specialist felt it was a book that deserved literary recognition. He told his wife, the novelist Jean Stafford, that she should read it. It just so happened that she was one of the fiction judges that year for the National Book Awards. Knopf had never submitted *The Moviegoer* to the judges. She read it, loved it, and passed it on to her fellow judges. *The Moviegoer* was awarded the prize for fiction, beating out an astonishing group of novels that included *Catch-22* and *Franny and Zooey.*

Judith Jones was in a room with Alfred Knopf when he heard about the award. Alfred was confounded. "He may have read the book at some point, but he had never expressed any feelings for it," she said. Besides, Knopf had submitted one novel for that year's National Book Award, *The Château* by William Maxwell, which would have been nice for Knopf if it had won, considering that Maxwell was a highly regarded *New Yorker* editor. But more than anything, Knopf didn't appreciate being upstaged by an editor he had fired. What he said, Judith remembered, was, "They're running that prize into the ground."

However, a day after the award ceremony for *The Moviegoer,* Stanley Kauffmann received a one-sentence note from Alfred Knopf on his luxurious private stationery that read: "I want to congratulate you, even at this late date, on the early confidence you showed in Walker Percy." It was a rare thing for Knopf to put to paper his feelings for a book that he had misjudged.

Why then was Kauffmann fired? Because he and Alfred Knopf disagreed about books that Alfred liked and Stanley did not. Because Stanley was never frightened of Alfred Knopf as so many other Knopf editors were. Because, without his knowing it, Stanley had been hired to compete with Angus Cameron, another new Knopf editor, for the editor in chief's job. Leave it to Alfred to let others make decisions for him.

In 1987, Kauffmann published a fascinating essay in *The American Scholar.* It was called "Album of the Knopfs" and it was an unsparing account—though thoroughly objective in many ways—about Alfred and Blanche and their quixotic personalities. He summed up Alfred this way: "Aside from his experience, I saw that his own chief resource was not great taste or intellect, but huge ambitions to be a great publisher. Still, that combination of experience and ambition made him powerful."

It's too bad that Stanley Kauffmann came to Knopf when he did. Blanche died in June 1966. Soon after, the Knopf reign came to an end, to be replaced by a Restoration that I think would have pleased Stanley.

IN THE SPRING of 1967, Alfred Knopf married Helen Norcross Hedrick, a widow and author whose book he had published decades before. One day Knopf and Helen were on their way to visit John Hersey in Martha's Vineyard. Hersey was one of the founder's literary heroes, having given the house *A Bell for Adano* (Pulitzer Prize, 1945), *The Wall,* and other novels as well as such brilliant works of nonfiction as *Hiroshima.* On their way to LaGuardia they opened *The New York Times.* When he reached the airport, Alfred immediately called Robert Bernstein, who was the person responsible for the new order at the company. "I want them fired," he told Bernstein.

Alfred had thrown his fit over the Knopf ad appearing in the paper for the book of Joseph Heller's play, *We Bombed in New Haven.* Alfred hadn't even yet met Robert Gottlieb, Nina Bourne, and Tony Schulte, who would carry the house's fortunes for years to come, if they survived Alfred's demand.

As Tony Schulte tells the story, Bob Gottlieb, in one of his first acts for the new firm, a symbolic one, for sure, published Joe Heller's play in a hardcover edition. Hadn't *Catch-22* been their singular triumph at Simon & Schuster? Nina Bourne's monstrous sin was that she had included in the Knopf advertisement the S & S *Catch-22* graphic—a figure in red with a soldier's hat on, dangling like a puppet in the air. What Nina—who would become Knopf's great advertising director—had failed to do was to make room for the Borzoi logo that had appeared on every book and in every ad that Alfred and Blanche had ever published. In Alfred's mind, the newcomers were guilty of treason.

"What happened," Tony said, "was that Bernstein somehow smoothed it out. He persuaded Knopf that he ought to get over his animosity and pretend that we didn't exist. It was agreed that we would meet Alfred and Helen at the pool room of the Four Seasons for lunch to see whether we could all get along. Bob Gottlieb spent the entire lunch talking with Alfred about Ivy Compton-Burnett, an author whom Alfred also liked. Alfred decided that Gottlieb was really okay in his literary tastes. And Nina and I spent the whole time talking to Helen about the old days in Oregon, when her family went out there on the Oregon Trail and planted pears." Tony said the verdict was "not guilty" and they all went back to work.

I doubt that it was quite that easy. Alfred, having sold his company to Random House in 1960, no longer had any real power to change things. When he originally signed the deal with Bennett Cerf and Donald Klopfer, he negotiated for complete editorial control, which included the right to veto other editors' manuscript selections, but only for five years. Now he was defanged.

The Missing Borzoi Incident didn't bite into Bob Gottlieb's faith in himself. In my long conversation with him at his home, he elaborated on his relationship with Alfred Knopf and his editors, mentioning Nina's early take on the situation: "It was as if the three bears had landed on their heads from outer space."

Bob refers to Knopf at that time as being a house nobody was running. "Alfred was still there on the premises—a presence," Bob said. "And there was nobody strong enough who had ever grown up under Alfred to run Knopf. And anybody who Alfred and Blanche could put up with couldn't possibly run anything."

As for recently published authors, Bob waved his hand dismissively. He mentioned only John Updike and Julia Child, "whom they had blundered into."

I wouldn't say that blunders occurred with either author. You have been told how Judith Jones and Julia came together. It was Pat Knopf, the son of fractious parents, who, before he left to start Atheneum in 1959, delivered them the author who would remain with Knopf forever.

Harper's had published Updike first—a book of poetry called *The Carpentered Hen.* Then Pat's friend John Hersey gave Pat a tip. "There's a wonderful young writer at *The New Yorker,* John Updike." Pat had heard of him. Hersey told Pat that Updike wasn't happy at Harper's, didn't at all like someone telling him how he should write his first novel. Pat immediately passed on the information to Sandy Richardson, a bright, sophisticated young Knopf editor. Sandy went zooming after Updike and brought *The Poorhouse Fair* to the house. As was Knopf's bent, he fired Richardson soon thereafter. So Judith Jones, feeling like a woman who suddenly found herself a benefactor in Scrooge's will, inherited Updike with Alfred's blessing.

Hearing all these things about Alfred Knopf's idiosyncrasies, I asked Bob Gottlieb how the two of them got along. "Alfred at first was suspicious and wary," Bob said. "When we would do things he didn't approve of, he would issue a memorandum that nobody paid any attention to. But within a year or two he had turned around completely, and he would suddenly send me wonderful little memos about things he assumed I had done—because at heart he was a publisher. And when he saw good publishing, he loved it. That was the saving grace of Alfred. He in many other ways was an impossible person."

I asked him who he reported to at his new house. "I never reported to anybody in my whole life. My view was, it's nobody's business what I do at Knopf as long as it is profitable. But I got along wonderfully with the head of Random House, Bob Bernstein. The only time he ever complained to me during my nineteen years at Knopf was that my expenses were so low they were skewing the company. I had stopped having lunch—I was too busy. "You know," he went on, "I loved it all. I loved reading manuscripts. I loved editing. I loved talking to salesmen because I loved sales. I even loved meetings. In other words, I loved publishing."

AND BOB BROUGHT people into his green garden who felt the same way.

In 2006, Jane Friedman was named by *Publishers Weekly* as the "Publishing Person of the Year." For eleven years Jane has been the CEO of HarperCollins. Before that she worked at Knopf, where she had spent twenty-nine happy years. I met her in October 2006 in her large orchid-filled office. She was as relaxed as Bob Gottlieb, and she seemed to enjoy talking about their past together.

"In 1967, I came in as a temp at Random House," she said when I asked how she got her start. "I walked in off the street and said, 'I want to be a publisher.'"

I was impressed. "What made you say that?" I asked. "Because I had thought of two things I always liked. I liked reading, and I liked the stock market. I worked one summer while at school for a financial house and I didn't like it. So I said, 'Okay, there goes one thing. Now I'm going to be a publisher.'"

In March 1968 she moved from Random House's rights department to the Knopf publicity department. She would work for William T. "Bill" Loverd, who had a long and distinguished career at Knopf as head of publicity. "I remember Bennett Cerf used to walk around the floor," she said. "I had very, very long hair, and I was sitting in the hall as we all were as young assistants. And he would come over and pull my ponytail." The first author she met was Joe Heller, and she felt like she was "in the middle of heaven."

At the outset she didn't see many authors because, she said, "most of Knopf's authors were dead. But Bob and Tony and Nina were bringing in all the living, breathing authors."

WELL, NOT QUITE. Along with Judith Jones, who is still there, was Ash Green, a consistently valuable editor over the years. Ashbel Green came to Knopf in 1964 after a four-year stint at Prentice Hall, where he worked in the publicity department. The first thing I asked him when we met in his office on the Knopf floor was where he got his name. "Oh," he said wryly, "I come from a long line of Presbyterian ministers."

He told me that working at Prentice Hall was okay, but he was looking for a place with a broader list of books. He secured an interview with Harding Lemay, who was then the publicity director at Knopf. (Lemay later wrote a memoir, *Inside, Looking Out,* in which he referred to his bosses as "veterans of decades of flattery from those who worked closely with them and victims of the inflated vanities such flattery breeds.") That interview went well for Ash. Then came Alfred Knopf. "After about ten minutes," Ash said, "he offered me the job as manager. What I later discovered was that the managing editor had resigned the previous morning and I was perhaps the warmest body."

When Gottlieb was announced as the new head of Knopf, Ash was nervous about the change. He and Gottlieb had once been in a class together at Columbia, but that was all. "I'll never forget what Bob Bernstein did for me," Ash said. "He called me a day or two after the Gottlieb announcement and said, 'Look, I hope this is going to work for you. But if it doesn't, I'll make a place for you at Random House.'"

It worked for him. I asked him what his new job consisted of. Ash gave me a simple, sensible description of a managing editor's duties: "The basic job is shepherding books from editorial through production." From 1964 to 1974 Ash did just that, but he also became an acquiring editor. One of the first authors Alfred turned over to Ash was Ross Macdonald. It became a turn of fortune in Ash's career.

"I had a lunch date with John Leonard," he told me, "who was then the editor of *The New York Times Book Review* (a lot of old-timers in book publishing, including myself, felt that Leonard was the greatest of the *Book Review*'s editors). "I mentioned to Bob Gottlieb that I was having lunch with John. Bob said, 'I've never met him, do you mind if I come along?' I said no.

"At lunch we talked about this and that, and I mentioned that we had a new Ross Macdonald novel, *The Goodbye Look,* and Leonard said, 'Oh, I'm a great admirer. We're going to have to do something about that.' And he did. Leonard commissioned William Goldman, a novelist and playwright, to write the review, in which he called Macdonald's oeuvre 'the finest series of detective novels ever written by an American.' So we had a bestseller on our hands."

Another job for Ash as managing editor was to look at the slush pile. "One Friday, I picked up a manuscript. It was covered with a two-page letter. I read the first page and decided to take it home over the weekend. I gave it to Bob on Monday, and he came back a couple of days later—he was very quick—and he said we should do it." The book was *The Friends of Eddie Coyle* by a Boston assistant district attorney, George V. Higgins, bought by Ash for two thousand dollars. Norman Mailer gave the book a quote: "What I can't get over is how so good a novel is written by the fuzz." The book was a bestseller, as was Higgins's second novel, *The Digger's Game.*

As Ash's career went along, he bought a ton of good books for the company, fiction and nonfiction. In 1970 he had two National Book Award nominees in history and biography. One was *Zapata and the Mexican Revolution* by John Womack, Jr. The other was T. Harry Williams's biography *Huey Long,* which won the award. Both books are still in print.

Ash was also the one responsible for taking Gabriel García Márquez away from Harper's. He had heard that Márquez's agent, Carmen Balcells (whom some called "the Beast of Barcelona"), was having difficulties in negotiating with Harper's for his next book, *Chronicle of a Death Foretold.* Ash wrote the agent and told her, "If you're ever looking for a new publisher for García Márquez, we'll honor a great tradition of Latin American publications here; we'd love to be considered." Six months later a deal was made that also included Márquez's backlist.

JANE FRIEDMAN AND Ash Green became friends; she enjoyed working for one editor, she said, who was not eccentric. Meanwhile, she was earning a reputation as a live wire in publicity and marketing, presenting lots of books at the sales conferences. She, of course, became one of Bob Gottlieb's beloveds.

The first live author she met and worked with was John Updike on his novel *Couples.* She says she will always remember the date of publication, April 15, 1968, because Updike was one of the few people in her life who made her tongue-tied. "I was just so rattled by meeting the great author of *Rabbit, Run,* and now here was *Couples.*" But she encountered immediate trouble with *The New York Times Book Review.* "They didn't want to take our ad because Nina had a man who was naked in the ad, and we had to cover him up." She put it in perspective: "Those were the days when you had to cover up organs." Such a cover-up didn't hurt *Couples.* It became the No. 2 fiction bestseller of 1968.

I asked Jane, who had come to work at Knopf about the same time as the Gottlieb-Schulte-Bourne trio, how the Gottlieb culture had developed. From the first, she said, "It was totally familial. And I'm not trying to give lip service to the fact that it was a family. It had all the dysfunctions and all the functions of the family. I mean, being in the middle of the group, it was kind of hard to see that anybody was outside the group. And our lives were so totally full.

"I have to tell you," she said, letting her feelings flow out, "—and this is where it sounds very arrogant—but we paid no attention to anybody. I think everybody paid attention to us. And that was where Knopf was so special. If Bob Gottlieb decided that the flavor of the year was British women writers, the next thing we knew we had everybody from Stevie Smith to Doris Lessing and Antonia Fraser. If we decided that we wanted to publish popular fiction, but do it in a way that we never let on that we were really a bestselling house, the next thing you knew, we had Thomas Tryon, Michael Crichton, John le Carré. If he wanted to publish celebrities, they were real celebrities: Liv Ullmann, Margot Fonteyn, Lauren Bacall, Brooke Hayward, Sidney Poitier, et cetera. And don't forget *Miss Piggy's Guide to Life*. Bob knew trends before we ever had heard the word *trends*. He decided to publish *Miss Piggy's Guide to Life* because she fit into his very special celebrity status, and of course we went on to sell 500,000 copies."

She remembers her friend Steve Rubin, now the president and publisher of Doubleday, once saying to her: "You at Knopf, you all live in a dream world." She said, 'So?' "

"You all think that everyone wants to be published by you."

"They do."

"You all think you know how to publish better than anybody else."

"We do."

"You all seem to think that financially, you're always profitable."

"We are."

Jane conceded a little, admitting, "Of course, he was right. It was a dream world. I will never say that we lived in a perfect time, because we didn't, and there was internecine warfare, and people guarding their books, and it wasn't always, you know, one happy family. But Bob held us together."

She says she has remained very close to Bob to this day. "I still feel that very strongly because I was not an editor. I mean Bob's an editor. He connects with words in a way that a great editor has to connect with words."

ROBERT GOTTLIEB

Books come out of nowhere. That's what's so thrilling. That's what's really exciting in the business. The fact is that books are not predictable. You can't stage-manage publishing the way you might want to. See, businesspeople don't really understand that. Or a lot of them don't. They think that you can write the rules. But, finally, on the whole, readers know best. Sometimes books you have high hopes for just don't work. Others succeed beyond your expectations. Like *Up the Organization*—a perfect example. This came in and Tony Schulte and I really liked it.

Robert Townsend, who had been the head of Avis, wrote it. We bought it for a modest amount of money. Our biggest worry was the title. We couldn't think of one we liked. I thought *Up the Organization* sounded cheap, didn't mean anything, and nobody would know what it was. We spent about four months looking for a title, but nobody could think of anything that wasn't worse. So finally we called it that.

And I saw something I've never seen before or since in publishing. An excerpt ran in what was then called *The Atlantic Monthly*. The day after it came on the stands, we had people coming up the elevator to the Knopf floor asking the receptionist if they could buy this book, not yet in the stores.

The book had struck a chord. It said all those amazing, outrageous, funny, accurate things about business that nobody had ever said before in such a lively and amusing and intelligent way. And we sold over 300,000 copies, which would be like selling a million today.

337

As for editing, sometimes it is intuitive. Sometimes it's not intuitive, and on a large scale sometimes, it's scissors and paste. I once said to Len Deighton, "You have a problem here, Len, because this character is shot and dies on page 44, and he's at a cocktail party 200 pages later." And Len, who was not a rewriter, rewrote it to say he was shot and almost died. John le Carré, on the other hand, loves rewriting and will take an idea or suggestion and run with it.

Sometimes, you suddenly get an idea that a writer could or should write a book on a particular subject. I remember proposing to Antonia Fraser that she write about the six wives of Henry VIII, and she leapt at it. Where does intuition come from? It comes out of knowing the writer, or empathy or sympathy with the writer. But then there is just intuitive editing, the application of common sense to written material. And taste.

Editing is not something you get better at. You either have that application of your taste, your energy, your judgment, and your grasp to written material, or you don't. That doesn't get any sharper. If anything, it gets less sharp. As you grow older your focus wanders far more than when you were young.

Sometimes you're nervous about intervening. Take John Cheever. I didn't do his early books, but we worked together on his last half dozen or so. When I read the manuscript of his final novel, *Oh What a Paradise It Seems,* I felt that the ending wasn't right. But I also felt, who am I to be telling John Cheever there's something wrong with his book? Because he was so delicate and so withheld and private, I really wrestled with myself about it, and then I forced myself to tell him. Because I thought—you know, they don't pay me all that money to keep my mouth shut. What's more, he came

> to Knopf because he wanted to be with me. So I spoke up, and he solved the problem brilliantly.
>
> The only time we weren't in accord was when I said to him, "I think it's time to do a huge collection of your stories." He said, "I don't see why you want to do that; they've all been previously published in books." And I said, "That's my worry." He gave in, and *The Stories of John Cheever* became a big bestseller and won the Pulitzer Prize for fiction.

The peerless editor of the golden age left Knopf in 1987 and became editor of *The New Yorker*. When I asked him about his leaving he said, "Oh, I never left. Well, I went to be the editor of *The New Yorker*. I had a lot of fun there, but I went on editing certain writers for Knopf, like Barbara Tuchman and Robert Caro." Gottlieb also edited Bill Clinton's bestselling memoir, *My Life* (2004).

"We all thought that he was irreplaceable," Jane Friedman told me. "I like to tease and say, to replace the Jewish prince, they had to go and find an Indian maharaja."

His name is Sonny Mehta, and it was Bob who recommended him. He came in from England, where he was king of the paperbacks. But he had never published hardcover books. It didn't seem to matter. Even though the golden age of book publishing was past, Mehta became a superb head of house. Still is. Everything *has* changed in book publishing, except maybe at the house of Knopf. Sonny has kept his fingers in the dike and won't let the Bertelsmann waters come rushing in. "The one thing that has never changed," Ash Green told me, "is that no one has ever told us to publish a book or not to publish a book."

I asked Ash how he would compare Gottlieb and Mehta. He cavalierly dismissed the question, saying, "Shakespeare said comparisons are odious." He paused before adding, "I've often said that Sonny is very different from Bob, as Bob was very different from Alfred and Blanche. But they've all been involved in quality publishing."

Go take a look at a Knopf book today. See the Borzoi dashing across the spine and title page, never knowing what it is to grow old.

12

A FATHER AND SON STORY

Little, Brown

Editorially, we want to present a diverse list. If you strive
for the best possible books in all genres, inevitably
you're going to be successful.

—ARTHUR THORNHILL, JR.

I t was almost noon when the son heard the father talking on
the telephone. The son had occupied "the front office," as
they reverently called the best seat in the house, since 1962,
when he replaced his father as chief executive officer of Little,
Brown and Company. But the father still came to work every day,
dispensing words of advice to all those who sought it, or who he
felt needed it, from his long, happy, and successful life with the
company he'd always loved.

The front office had a swinging door. When somebody went
through the door and it opened, the son could often hear his father
in his small office off to the side. "Hello, Ralph," is what he had
heard his father say late that morning over the telephone, "how
are you doing today?" He knew his father was talking with Ralph
Thompson, the editor of the Book-of-the-Month Club. But it was
all his son heard because the swinging door had shut. The other

thing he knew was that, within seconds, his father would be out the door on his way to Locke-Ober for lunch.

A short walk from Beacon Street through the Boston Common, Locke-Ober was then one of the most favored restaurants in Boston. His father liked "Locke's," as the gentry called it, liked its scrod, also its Canadian Club on the rocks, with a dash of water. The waiters knew when to put the second drink before him and then, when they handed him the menu, the third one. That day he was lunching with Little, Brown's editor in chief, Eliot Fremont-Smith. Fremont-Smith remembered that the father had just started his first cocktail, and he was "very chipper."

As it happened, more often than not, the son was also going to Locke-Ober for lunch, on this day with Fred Hill, head of advertising and publicity in the sales department. Father and son always sat two tables away from each other in Little, Brown's power center.

As he was putting on his overcoat this freezing cold day of January 9, 1970, the phone rang. He picked it up hurriedly, aiming to tell the caller that he would call back. But it was from a woman at Locke-Ober with a message that smashed the son in the face: "Your father has just had an attack. You'd better come quickly."

He and Fred Hill ran to the restaurant. Hill remembered seeing that the father's table had been removed, "and Arthur was on the floor." Eliot Fremont-Smith was sitting at the bar, dazed. The son tried mouth-to-mouth resuscitation. It didn't work.

Just then a police wagon arrived, not an ambulance. It was apparently the best Boston could do for one of its anointed at that moment. In the back was a fireman wearing his rubber boots. While the driver rushed father and son to Massachusetts General Hospital, the fireman tried administering oxygen.

In the emergency room they found that it was all too late. Arthur Thornhill, Sr., had died. The son, Arthur Thornhill, Jr., was now alone in the house his father had helped build for the last fifty-six years.

I HADN'T EXPECTED this impermanent book of mine to give so much attention to the relationships between fathers and sons—to Alfred A. Knopf and Pat Knopf, a chilling relationship at best; to Cass Canfield and Cass Jr., not what the father and son would have wanted; to Nelson Doubleday, a regimented relationship extending over three generations; and to Harold Guinzburg and Tom Guinzburg, different personalities in almost every way. This relationship between Arthur Thornhill, Sr., and Arthur Thornhill, Jr., was perhaps the most comfortable because the two had been totally intertwined for twenty-two years, from 1948 to 1970—the best of times, as we have said, for book publishing in America.

Arthur Jr. was my first eyewitness to that golden age. We had known each other for a good stretch of time, especially after the Book-of-the-Month Club was bought by Time Inc. in 1977; Time Inc. had acquired Little, Brown in 1968. So there we were— Little, Brown and BOMC—the central pillars of what was known in the corporation as "The Book Group." Those were the years when we were both able to operate independently, in the sense that all the decisions about running our companies were ours and ours alone. Peace reigned into the early 1980s, ending only when Andrew Heiskell, the brilliant and comforting president of Time Inc. retired, allowing his retinue of MBA foster children to fight it out for control of the company. That contest soon smothered our independence.

Arthur Jr. was in New York for a few days in the fall of 2003, when we spent a relaxed afternoon seeking out the past. It was a pleasure to see Arthur and his wife, Dorothy, again. He was dressed as his father had taught him years past. For almost every day of his life the elder Thornhill came to work in suits designed by his exclusive Boston tailor. The suits fit perfectly over a starched shirt, a linen handkerchief in the breast pocket, and, during the summer, a bachelor button from his garden in the lapel. Arthur Jr. followed the leader, except that he bought his suits on Savile Row in London.

This Boston publishing house was very different from those in New York. "There was a lot of formality still very much in evidence there," Joe Kanon told me. Joe had gone to work for Little, Brown in 1973, the beginning of his outstanding publishing career. He is now a first-rate suspense novelist (*The Good German,* for one). "In those days," he said, "Little, Brown was still a company where in the summer some of the executives really would wear white shoes and seersucker jackets and bow ties." It seems the only man who wasn't called by his last name was Jimmy the Handyman. Arthur disputed this a bit. He told me that after his secretary had been with him for a few years, she called him by his first name.

Arthur seemed completely relaxed that afternoon we spent together, as thin and as dapper as ever, with the expression on his face of a younger man now reasonably comfortable with himself. His smile still seemed halting and reserved, the smile of a careful man, of one who was sometimes called "gloomy" by his underlings, but who really wasn't.

One of the first things I asked Arthur was how he and his father got on after he was made president, since Arthur Sr. still came in every day in his lesser role as chairman of the board. "Obviously, a father-son relationship is relatively sensitive," Arthur said, "and after he gave way to me in 1962 he was always very careful to keep a certain distance. We did have differences in ideas and philosophies. There were cases where we would simply disagree about things. I wanted some younger people on the executive board, and I was very anxious for us to build more toward the future. But once I took a position, my father never interfered.

He gave me the utmost cooperation. I have a letter from him, which I prize. In the letter he said—this was back before I was president—'I now understand what you're trying to do with certain things.' And he said, 'I really think you're setting the company on the right course.' I was so appreciative of how he treated the situation, which could have been different."

He looked at me, with that sort of tentative smile on his face. "The gestalt theory is my old favorite phrase," he said. It is as the dictionary says: "A configuration, pattern, or organized field having specific properties that cannot be derived from the summation of its component parts." For the gestalt theory as applied to book publishing, Arthur told me, "It simply means that you do a balanced list, and then you do not have to analyze each title. I always had great pride in publishing a book well written, well produced, and well presented."

One of Little, Brown's finest editors of the period, Roger Donald, had come to work for the company in 1968, six years after Arthur Sr. had stepped down. "Arthur Jr. had a rough time there for a while," Roger said. "But I think, in the final analysis, he was a better publisher than his father. He expanded the place in so many ways. I mean, the old man was great fun. If you wanted to have lunch with somebody, you wanted to have lunch with the old man. When we first became friends, he would take me to lunch. He'd have his Canadian Club and I'd have a martini on the rocks. He'd order a second Canadian Club and wouldn't ask me, so I'd just say to the waiter, 'I'll have a martini.' And Arthur would look at me, and he'd have three and I'd have three. All the time he would be telling me stories. And at the end of each story he would throw his arms out, look me flush in my eyes and say, *'And that's the truth, Roger.'*" Other people have said the same thing to me about Arthur Sr.: that *that's the truth* was his mantra in life.

Comparing father and son, Roger thought that "Arthur Jr.

didn't have the ability to marry the authors to him the way the old man did. But what he did, which I think was better than the old man, is that he *built* the backlist. He *built* the college division up. He *built* the medical division up. He *built* the legal division up."

Little, Brown's ancestors would have agreed with that, as you will see.

"THE UNDERSIGNED have formed a co-partnership, under the firm of CHARLES C. LITTLE & CO., for the purpose of Publishing, Importing and Selling books, and have taken over the old stand of Hilliard, Gray & Co., No. 112, Washington Street, and purchased their Law, Foreign and miscellaneous stock." It was signed *Charles C. Little* and *James Brown*. This notice appeared in the *Boston Daily Advertiser* on June 29, 1837.

That was exactly what the Messrs. Little and Brown did: they became the world's largest publisher of "law books" at the time. They also wanted to sell foreign books. For that goal the partners offered a succinct mission statement: "We will sell and publish standard works of a high grade, books of a grave, solid and substantial character."

James Brown died in 1855 and Charles Little in 1869, but they left a solid, growing operation. They also left a young man, James McIntyre, who would begin to sculpt the company with deft strokes in thoroughly modern directions.

Born in 1848, McIntyre became an apprentice at Little, Brown at age sixteen. He was given the responsibility of running the firm's Washington Street bookstore. He then did a stint as a salesman, finally working up to his most challenging position—editor in chief of the publishing division.

In 1896 he was responsible for Little, Brown's first two bestsellers. One was also the company's first acquisition of a novel not yet under contract in the U.S. The author was a Polish journalist, Henryk Sienkiewicz, who had begun to write historical novels.

McIntyre agreed to publish in translation his first two novels. Neither book sold more than 2,500 copies, but McIntyre stayed with him. Sienkiewicz's third book, *Quo Vadis,* set in the time of Nero, complete with violence and steamy sex, sold 600,000 copies in its first eighteen months and has never stopped selling to this day. It has also been adapted three times for Hollywood films. In 1905, Sienkiewicz was awarded the Nobel Prize, according to the citation, "because of his outstanding merits as an epic writer."

The other new work McIntyre championed was altogether different from *Quo Vadis,* although it was also meant for an epicurean audience: Fannie Merritt Farmer's *Boston Cooking-School Cook Book.* Little, Brown made Fannie Farmer a household name.

One of the house's most notable assets late in the nineteenth century, and continuing into the twentieth, was its ability to find good authors who, indeed, were regularly ringing Little, Brown's doorbell with new offerings. Take Francis Parkman, who gave the house a distinguished seven-volume history of the French colonies in North America. In 1903 it was James McIntyre's turn. He signed a contract with E. Phillips Oppenheim, an English novelist who would go on to write 134 mystery thrillers for Little, Brown (*The Vanished Messenger, An Amiable Charlatan,* etc.). And in 1910, McIntyre listened to a Little, Brown salesman's excitement about a New England children's writer named Thornton W. Burgess. Burgess would write more than sixty Peter Rabbit stories for Little, Brown.

But it was in 1898 that McIntyre performed the coup of his publishing life. He bought the Roberts Brothers publishing company, a once distinguished house that was stumbling, with more than 900 tiles on its list, three times the quantity of Little, Brown's. Among the authors Little, Brown inherited were Emily Dickinson, Louisa May Alcott, Christina Rossetti, Algernon Charles Swinburne, and George Sand. I remember one visit I made to Little, Brown's headquarters at 34 Beacon Street, where I was shown a framed note from Louisa May Alcott. It read: "Will you give my Pa $50 from my account?" Sure, why not? By the early 1900s the author of *Little Women* had earned $200,000 in royalties. McIntyre and his fellow directors were so happy about what they had just accomplished at the end of '98 that they gave every male head of household in the company a ton of coal for their cellars.

COULD ARTHUR JR.'S grandfather have been one of those recipients? It's possible. Joseph Thornhill had gone to work for Little, Brown sometime in the late 1890s, and he seems to have flourished there. "It was my grandfather," Arthur told me, "who arranged for his son to come and work in the shipping room, which in those days was in the back part of the building at 34 Beacon Street." Joseph's son, Arthur, was said to have worked twice as hard as the other stock boys, and he was offered a full-time job at $10 a week. Eight years later, Arthur Jr. told me, "He had an opportunity to become a salesman. So he went out and carried a bag and sold books and traveled all through the country." Another colleague said of Senior: "He could have sold anything, but books were his religion."

Arthur Jr. was stirred by the memory of his father on the road all the time, leaving his wife and only child alone in the house. And he was caught by a remembrance. "When I was only six or seven, my father took me with him when he called on the manager of a bookstore in Falmouth, Massachusetts. He was an awful nice man, this Mr. Cole. He gave me a boat, a lovely little boat, and I never forgot that gift."

In 1913, the year that Arthur Thornhill, Sr., joined Little, Brown, editor in chief James McIntyre died. His son, Alfred McIntyre, became general manager that same year. He was unlike his father and Joseph Thornhill, who had not gone to college and had entered the job market as teenagers. Alfred McIntyre had graduated from Harvard, though nobody held that against him when he joined the firm in 1907. He and Arthur Thornhill worked side by side for the next forty-one years, transforming Little, Brown into their image of what a book publishing house should be. "He was disciplined in many ways," Arthur Jr. said of McIntyre, "soft-spoken and very correct. He was really of the old school, but he had a brilliant sense of literature and books, and he worked extremely well with authors."

In his lively publishing memoir, *Two Park,* Paul Brooks described how his friend and rival Alfred McIntyre judged a novel: "He would take the manuscript home, and after dinner sit down in comfort with a scotch and soda. If, after a second highball, it brought tears to his eyes, he would recommend publication."

WHILE McINTYRE WAS doing wonderful things for Little, Brown, Paul Brooks was his lively competitor at Houghton Mifflin as editor in chief for twenty-five years, and the battles between these two preeminent Boston houses were fierce. "It was like two clubs at Harvard, old WASPy houses, old WASPy clubby things," Bill Phillips told me. Bill had joined Little, Brown in the latter years of the era and came of age in the follow-up years as Little, Brown's editor in chief throughout the 1980s and '90s. "There was the gentleman's agreement: the unspoken word was that nobody hired anybody from each other's house," Bill said. No poaching on authors, either, I was told by several who worked at both houses.

At the end of each year, the kissing cousins held a grand banquet—for men only in those years—to give each other awards recognizing the company that had sold the most copies of a novel, a first novel, nonfiction, first nonfiction, "juveniles," as children's books were then called, and so on. The scene, as described by a latter-day onlooker, consisted of "bizarre people, mostly guys, sitting there, getting absolutely shit-faced drunk in their tuxedos, eating awful club food, and checking on their wagers." During the evening there were also a lot of side bets made on small contests like who would get national coverage for the greatest number of publicity releases. And they got sillier and sillier as the contestants drank on.

Some say the highlight of the evening was a rather outrageous award that was given for the most outrageous behavior on the part of an author. It was named for J. Randall Williams, Joe Kanon told me, "because Randy always thought that dealing with authors was impossible." I didn't recognize even one author I knew on that exalted list.

Yearly dinners still go on today.

I learned something about the differences between the two houses from Harry Houghton. His full name is Henry Oscar Houghton, identical to that of his father and his great-grandfather, who had founded the company in 1864. In September 1955 young Harry, not long out of the army, was looking for a job. "I was walking on Beacon Hill one day," he said, "and I saw the name plate on this building—LITTLE, BROWN. I said to my dad, 'I wonder what goes on at Little, Brown.' I knew one place that I was not going was Houghton Mifflin."

"You are a Houghton?" I asked him.

"Yes," he said.

"Who was your father?"

"My father was just a guy that traded on his name and worked for Houghton Mifflin for many, many years, till he retired. He was basically a nonfactor."

So Harry's father did go ahead and call the sales manager at Little, Brown, whom he knew, and said, "I want you to take a look at my son. He's just come out of the army and is looking for a job."

He went for the interview and apparently did well, because the next person he met with was Arthur Thornhill, Sr. "He looked me over," Harry remembered, "and then said to me, 'All right, if we should offer you a job, what guarantee do we have that you won't jump ship and go to Houghton Mifflin?'

" 'They've got too many Houghtons there already,' was my answer. The next thing I knew he'd offered me a job as a salesman for New England."

Harry spent the next few years selling books in other parts of the country. He ended up in New York City, working out of the New York office where Arthur Sr. ruled. This Thornhill treated Houghton like his own son. He helped train him to participate in the subsidiary rights game, teaching the kid how to deal with the paperback houses and book clubs. At lunch Harry would sit quietly with his boss while revered paperback oracles such as Oscar Dystel of Bantam Books and Victor Weybright of New American Library babbled on about deals. "Arthur Senior," Harry told me, "would have his Canadian Club. When the third one came around, he would tell the waiter, pointing at me, 'my friend will pass.' "

I found Harry Houghton to be one of the straightest guys to deal with; no malarkey from him. We did a lot of business together, and became friends—some might say the hard way—at a Book-of-the-Month Club luncheon honoring a Little, Brown Main Selection. (I believe it was for the first volume of Henry Kissinger's memoirs.) In the middle of the lunch I noticed Harry turning distinctly red; he had something caught in his throat. I hustled him to the men's room, gave him the Heimlich maneuver and a piece of steak dislodged from his throat. I'd also broken at least one of his ribs.

One day, when we were having lunch together, I asked Harry about his father's house and what he thought the difference was between Houghton Mifflin and Little, Brown. "Houghton Mifflin," he told me, "rested on their laurels. They had this giant textbook division that carried all the freight. I guess because of that Houghton

Mifflin's trade had this country club atmosphere, while Little, Brown was like being in basic training for the army. It was pressure, pressure, pressure. And that's why we were more successful—because the heat was always on. Houghton didn't have that kind of pressure. It was so laid back and half the guys that worked there had huge trust funds and didn't give a damn about what kind of salary they made. It was a very genteel place." He thought a moment, and then added, "But they did do some wonderful publishing."

We noticed the differences when a few of us from Book-of-the-Month would come up to Boston once or twice a year to see what was going on at both houses. (We also went over to Harvard to visit Arthur Rosenthal, who was always cooking up something as head of Harvard University Press.) At Little, Brown we had cordial and businesslike meetings with them, and then we were marched off to lunch at—where do you expect?—Locke-Ober. When we walked 250 yards to visit Houghton Mifflin, and stepped into their rickety nineteenth-century elevator, we had our tennis rackets with us.

I remember the first time I visited Houghton Mifflin. Lovell Thompson, the company's highly regarded editor, opened a desk drawer and let me hold a cigar cutter, which, he said, had belonged to the poet Amy Lowell. Both Boston houses, WASPy to the core, cultivated an aura of Henry James respectability that none of the New York houses possessed. This must have appealed to Henry Kissinger, who chose Little, Brown from among half a dozen suitors to publish the first volume of his memoirs, *The White House Years* (1979). "It was like choosing between ancient Rome and Athens," was how Kissinger saw it. As one of his associates observed, "The publishers in New York represented Rome, where everything must be done *today*, and Boston represented Athens, which produced less of immediate moment but more of enduring value." This was the value of Little, Brown, created by Alfred McIntyre, enabling the house to compete with the biggies of book publishing.

ONE OF MCINTYRE'S special qualities as head of the company—he became president in 1926—was to work closely with his editors in chief. His first editor in chief was a dedicated fellow named Herbert Jenkins, who had been with the company since the early 1900s. One day in 1929, Jenkins went to McIntyre. He had just read in a British newspaper about a war novel recently published in Europe that was doing very well. Jenkins thought perhaps the horror of World War I was beginning to recede, allowing the reading public to now buy books on war. Jenkins felt that this particular novel would be a good gamble for the house. McIntyre read it and agreed. Before any other publisher could act, Jenkins cabled the London literary agent and offered a thousand-dollar advance. The agent immediately accepted the offer. *All Quiet on the Western Front* by Erich Maria Remarque was published in 1929 and quickly became the No. 1 fiction bestseller of the year, accounting for 20 percent of the company's trade sales that year.

The biggest move of McIntyre's publishing life—with an impact similar to that his father had achieved by buying Roberts Brothers—came in 1924. The prestigious *Atlantic Monthly* magazine, founded in 1857, was owned early on by Houghton Mifflin. But in 1908 it was bought by Ellery Sedgwick, its publisher and editor, and in 1917 *The Atlantic Monthly* began to publish books. It dawned on McIntyre that somehow a connection could be forged between Little, Brown and their neighbors down the street. He talked with Sedgwick about the possibilities. They came to an agreement in which Little, Brown would publish books under the title of "Atlantic/Little, Brown books." (On the title page the book was identified as "An Atlantic Monthly Press Book/Little, Brown and Company • Boston.") This is how it worked: *The Atlantic Monthly* would take the books they wished to publish to the

Little, Brown editorial board. If the board agreed, *The Atlantic Monthly* would buy the books and do all the editorial work. Little, Brown would then manufacture and sell the title, and pay royalties to *The Atlantic Monthly* for all copies sold. If, however, Little, Brown said no to a book, the magazine could still go out and publish it on its own, without help from the stepfather.

The results over the years were extraordinary, benefiting both organizations. During the 1920s and '30s, Atlantic Monthly Press contributed to the Little, Brown catalog such bestsellers as *Mutiny on the Bounty, Good-bye, Mr. Chips, Drums Along the Mohawk,* and *Captain Horatio Hornblower.* It was just what McIntyre envisioned. "We thrive on bestsellers and languish without them," he once said.

THERE WAS NO languishing at Little, Brown in 1937, the year it celebrated its one hundredth birthday.

Considering that 1937 was the second year that *Gone With the Wind* was ranked No. 1 on all bestseller lists, it was somewhat incredible that other fiction was selling well too, but here was Little, Brown with three novels on the bestseller list: A. J. Cronin in third place for the year with *The Citadel;* Walter D. Edmonds (an Atlantic Monthly/Little, Brown book) in fifth place for *Drums Along the Mohawk;* and James Hilton in tenth place for *We Are Not Alone.*

But this was just the icing on the cake. In 1937, C. S. Forester's first Captain Horatio Hornblower novel, *Beat to Quarters,* was published, and led to a rich series of Hornblower novels over the years. It was also the year when the eleventh edition of *Bartlett's Familiar Quotations* was published, the edition first having been put together in 1855 by a literary wizard, John Bartlett.

It is fascinating that over the years the masters of Little, Brown seem to have ignored what so many other book publishers cherished: literature. The McIntyres, father and son, tended to embrace the Lawrence Welks of their time, comfy popular novels that were full of romance and decorous plots. There was no influential editor in the early years of the house's life with avant-garde sensibilities. But in 1937 an author of literary bent did finally come around: John P. Marquand from Newburyport, Massachusetts.

Marquand found that storytelling came easy to him. Before he was thirty years old he was earning $30,000 a year, much of the income coming from *The Saturday Evening Post* for his short stories and easy-to-read novels. The *Post* published his novels in serialized pieces over two or three issues, in the same way Charles Dickens had done it in England. Marquand was no Dickens, but as he went along he felt he could be doing more serious works. He looked at his successful contemporaries such as Sinclair Lewis, whose cutting novels about American society—its main streets and businessmen, doctors and clergymen—had shaken up the feelings of readers who'd never thought of American life as quite that shallow and dispiriting. Millicent Bell, Marquand's astute biographer, referred to his literary yearnings as "unconscious compulsions that more decisively attached him to the efforts of literature."

It was Roger Burlingame, a former Harvard classmate, who brought Marquand to Scribners. The two had worked together on the Harvard *Lampoon,* and Burlingame, now a Scribners editor, felt Marquand might become a first-rate novelist. Scribners published Marquand's first novel, *The Unspeakable Gentleman.* It sold six thousand copies—not bad—so Marquand sent Burlingame his second novel, *The Black Cargo*, about the derring-do in a colonial seaport. Burlingame's editorial boss, Maxwell Perkins, decided to read it. (Roger Burlingame, by the way, wrote a centennial history of Charles Scribner's Sons, published by Scribners in 1946, titled *Of Making Many Books: A Hundred Years of Reading, Writing, and Publishing.*)

"After studying Marquand's manuscript carefully," Millicent Bell reported, "Perkins wrote Marquand a long letter in which he pointed out 'that the plot had flaws of carelessness and contrivance.' It was the first time that Marquand had ever received genuine literary judgment, and by *the* literary editor of his time. Later, he and Perkins had long face-to-face talks about the author's efforts."

"Without being a writer himself," Marquand wrote, "Perkins could speak the language of writers better than any editor or publisher I ever met. He could make you feel that he understood everything about your individual work and your problems, and what is more, he actually did understand. He also gave you a feeling of complete confidence in his suggestions and advice. The best thing about him was that he gave advice seldom and his suggestions were few, but somehow after an hour or two with Max, you went away with more confidence in yourself, and with a feeling that he and you both knew what you were trying to do, and with a burning desire to do it better."

With an advance of $250, Charles Scribner's Sons published *The Black Cargo* in 1925. It got some good reviews but sold only three thousand copies. This caused Marquand, despite his love for Perkins, to move to Little, Brown. Alfred McIntyre and Herbert Jenkins bought Marquand by paying an advance of $1,000 and a "decent royalty," and in 1928 they published his novel *Warning Hill.*

Later in his life Marquand would tell a friend, "I thought it was fair to make a complete break with Scribners without telling them I had a higher offer and giving them the opportunity to equal it." Fair it was, and the Marquand approach has since become a live and kicking authorial weapon.

In 1934 he was working on a satire on the life and letters of a Bostonian. Feeling unsure of himself, almost panicking, he wrote McIntyre: "I, personally, have enjoyed writing it, and think it's amusing. . . . I certainly don't want to go ahead with the thing, however, if you don't think it holds any promise, and if it's not any good. . . . I know you will tell me frankly just how it strikes you, and its fate rests largely in your hands. Tell me quickly."

McIntyre did write back quickly, telling Marquand, "John, I personally think it is swell. I can't tell you whether it will sell more than 2,000 copies—it may be too highly specialized. But we think this may very well be a remarkable book and of great interest in Boston."

On January 4, 1937, John Marquand's *The Late George Apley* was published. Millicent Bell called it, "Marquand's ambiguous masterpiece." After three weeks in the stores, 20,000 copies were sold. In Boston it was outselling *Gone With the Wind.* By the end of the year, *The Late George Apley* had sold 32,700 copies. The following April the book won the Pulitzer Prize for fiction. It is still in print.

Little, Brown had found its own Sinclair Lewis, its own John O'Hara—authors who wrote bestselling novels of manners. Marquand's next six novels from 1941 to 1951—*Wickford Point; H. M. Pulham, Esquire; So Little Time; B.F.'s Daughter; Point of No Return; Melville Goodwin, U.S.A.*—were all novels of manners, and all were bestsellers.

These successes made Alfred McIntyre feel good about his house. Finally, he had a literary novelist with a popular fiction taste. Meanwhile, he kept looking for books that would capture the middle course in American life. And he thought that his new editor in chief, Angus Cameron, would be just the person to cast a line in that direction.

A TROUT FISHERMAN from way back, Angus Cameron was born in 1908, raised in Indianapolis, and after college went right to work with Bobbs-Merrill, an Indianapolis publishing house of national renown. He started as a promotion manager but soon became an editor. His biggest acquisition was *The Joy of Cooking* by Irma Rombauer, which became a lifetime bestselling cookbook. Cameron moved to Little, Brown in 1938 as the New York editor and in 1943 McIntyre brought him to Boston.

He was happy there, seeking out fiction of all kinds, as well as significant nonfiction projects. It was Cameron who developed, with historian Dumas Malone, the first two volumes of what would be a six-volume biography of Thomas Jefferson, a Little, Brown treasure. In fiction, Angus enjoyed a big success editing Samuel Shellabarger's bestselling *Captain from Castile* and *Prince of Foxes* (it was McIntyre, his boss, who had been given the first seventy-five pages of *Castile* from an agent, and passed it on to Cameron with his blessing). Angus admitted that "I was one of those guys who's very good at picking commercial winners. There was a period when everything we touched turned to gold."

Angus's Midas touch began to tarnish in 1947 when historian Arthur M. Schlesinger, Jr., wrote a biting letter to Alfred McIntyre: "Each day increases my sense of shame at ever having been associated with your house." His Little, Brown book *The Age of Jackson* had won a Pulitzer Prize in history. "I would never have signed up in 1939 if one of your leading members had been an active pro-Nazi," Schlesinger wrote McIntyre, "and I have no intention of being published by Little, Brown when one of your leading members is pro-Communist." Schlesinger was referring to Angus Cameron. McIntyre never responded to the letter. In November 1948, McIntyre, the soul of the house, died unexpectedly. Not just Little, Brown, but the whole publishing community mourned his passing.

In 1948, Cameron worked on the Henry A. Wallace presidential campaign. Wallace, vice president of the United States in Franklin D. Roosevelt's third term, was a left-winger who felt he was a valid candidate to run against Harry Truman and Thomas Dewey. To Senator Joe McCarthy, anyone who supported Wallace was suspect. When the Wisconsin senator started his rampage against Americans he scorned as communist sympathizers, or worse, Angus Cameron felt the lash.

So did Little, Brown. In August 1951, *Counterattack,* a magazine beloved by McCarthy, accused the house of publishing "thirty-one" books by communists and supporters of fronts. Angus Cameron was named as one of those responsible for such "reprehensible actions." Little, Brown, defending its own, immediately fought back. The directors sent out a missive titled "To All Who Are Interested in the Publishing of Books." "No author of spirit," it stated "would tolerate a publisher's inquisition into his private views. The publisher must make his judgment on what is in the book itself if the tradition and right of freedom to publish are to remain bulwarks of freedom in America."

But when, a month later, Angus recommended that Little, Brown publish *Spartacus* by Howard Fast, who had once joined the American Communist party, it was too much for the company's now beleaguered board to swallow. Even though the house had previously published an historical novel by Fast, *The Proud and the Free,* the board said no to *Spartacus.* It was later published by a house put together by Fast—because no other major publishing company would touch it—and it became not only a bestselling book, but also a blockbuster movie starring Kirk Douglas.

What caused the final rupture between Cameron and Little, Brown was his being told that as a member of the board, he would have to obtain approval of his outside activities, as did all board members. He was an editor, he said, and that required some freedom. He took his freedom and spent a decade effectively blacklisted.

Cameron and his wife, Sheila, moved to the Adirondacks and started their own small publishing house. They loved the pull of the wilderness. They fished for trout, hunted for game. "Woodchuck is the very best tasting game animal," Angus proclaimed with reverence. In 1983, Angus wrote with Judith Jones a book that found a delighted audience—*The L. L. Bean Game & Fish Cookbook.*

Arthur Thornhill, Jr., told me that in one of Cameron's exile years he had had lunch with Angus. "It was most enjoyable," Arthur said. "We talked about publishing at one point. I couldn't resist expressing regret over the breakup. Angus said, 'Forget it. For God's sake, it's ancient history.'"

One day in 1960, Alfred Knopf was talking with his Canadian associate, Jack McClelland, the fiery publisher of McClelland & Stewart, a man always larger than life. "I'm looking for an editor," Knopf said. "I know one," Jack said. "Angus Cameron." So it was Knopf who delivered Angus from the wilderness, making him a senior editor at his grand house. Cameron's exile had ended.

THE UNHAPPY EVENTS of 1951 were offset that year by glorious good karma that electrified Little, Brown—the publication of a first novel that would become one of the most influential literary works of the twentieth century: *The Catcher in the Rye.*

As you'll recall from chapter 1, because of Robert Giroux, J. D. Salinger was supposed to sign with Giroux's house, Harcourt, Brace. But Harcourt's leading editor, Eugene Reynal, never liked or understood the character of Holden Caulfield. Meantime, Little, Brown's New York editor, John Woodburn, had met Salinger, and the fussy author apparently liked Woodburn. So Salinger's agent, Dorothy Olding, awarded *The Catcher in the Rye* to Little, Brown.

"That rare miracle of fiction has again come to pass: a human being has been created out of ink, paper and the imagination," wrote Clifton Fadiman in the Book-of-the-Month Club *News*; the BOMC's judges had made *The Catcher in the Rye* a Main Selection. In the same issue of the *News* appeared an interview with Salinger by William Maxwell, his editor at *The New Yorker*. Salinger modified Fadiman's feelings about the rare miracle of fiction: "I think writing is a hard life," he told Maxwell. "The compensations are few, but when they come, if they come, they are very beautiful." Compensations came to him.

The Catcher in the Rye never made any of the bestseller lists in its first year (it also flopped at the BOMC), but nevertheless, it began to catch on all over the world. It has been estimated that sixty million copies of the book have been sold since first being published in 1951. And the paperback edition today still sells about 250,000 a year.

The Salinger novel created possibilities for Little, Brown. The house that had always seemed to be playing close to the vest in its choice of fiction now began to loosen up. Little, Brown began to take risks outside the safe bestsellers being written by good old boys like James Hilton and A. J. Cronin. With the Atlantic Monthly's help, Little, Brown began to take on bright new works—fiction and nonfiction, many even literary—that almost lived up to Arthur Thornhill, Jr.'s favorite word, *diversity*.

A NEW EDITOR, thirty-four-year-old Seymour "Sam" Lawrence, was hired in 1954 to follow the path to diversity. Young, brilliant, eccentric, Lawrence would show the way.

In 1955, Houghton Mifflin had turned down a novel by a young Rhode Islander, Edwin O'Connor. Sam Lawrence pounced on it. *The Last Hurrah* was scheduled to be published by Atlantic/Little, Brown in 1955, but Arthur Thornhill, Sr., who was entranced by the book and became a close friend of its author, postponed the publication because he thought he could get the Book-of-the-Month Club to pay attention to the book. Arthur made a persuasive case, and BOMC made it a Main Selection. *The Last Hurrah* was published in 1956 and was *Publishers Weekly*'s No. 2 fiction bestseller that year. Five years later, O'Connor's novel *The Edge of Sadness* was No. 8 on the same bestseller list. J. D. Salinger's *Franny and Zooey* was up in second place, but O'Connor won the Pulitzer Prize that year.

One day Arthur Thornhill came to Sam Lawrence, asking him to focus his attention on an acclaimed short story writer on the Little, Brown list, Katherine Anne Porter. She had been working on a novel for over twenty years, but nothing was happening. Sam seemed to be just the kind of editor she needed. "He had infinite patience," Joe Kanon said, "and what he did was become a presence in her life. That was his style with all of his authors. He would go down to Annapolis, where she was living at that point, and say, 'This is nonsense. You have really been working on it for twenty-five years, you haven't been doing anything. It's time to finish this.' The next time he visited her he'd say, 'How much have you done this week?' This went on for a long time. And Sam was crowned in glory."

The glory came with the publication of Porter's *Ship of Fools,* the top bestseller in 1962. And then Hollywood came around, paying $400,000 for the movie rights.

Sam Lawrence, as sharp as he was, created problems for the house. One colleague called him "the laziest editor ever to be in the business." He was also completely egotistical. "It was always, it seemed, 'Katherine and I' in those days, said one of the Atlantic editors. "Whenever he was crossed," another editor said, "you knew it; his face turned beet red."

The guiding principle for Sam Lawrence was his passion for publishing with standards of excellence. He once referred to the period he played in as "the Golden Age of Pericles." And maybe it was.

Lawrence left Atlantic in 1966. Ostensibly it was because he wasn't allowed to buy J. P. Donleavy's wild and, some said, blasphemous first novel, *The Ginger Man.* The truth was he was tired of Boston and he'd gotten a good offer from Knopf, but only stayed there for half a year. Then he joined Delacorte, where the first book he published was the unexpurgated *Ginger Man.* This was also about the time that he found another author, who, he felt, would do great things for American literature: Kurt Vonnegut, Jr. Lawrence and Vonnegut became a powerful editor/author team.

SAM LAWRENCE WAS GONE, but Arthur Thornhill had another ace up his sleeve: Roger Donald, who had become the New York editor in 1969. Arthur brought Donald to Boston as his editor in chief and immediately gave him an author to look after: Lillian Hellman. "Lillian had been published all along by Random House. She was very sensitive and temperamental to a degree," Thornhill explained in his understated way. "She always felt slighted when certain things happened to her. And she was slighted by the fact that Bennett Cerf had come to Martha's Vineyard one time and didn't come to see her." When Arthur found out that Hellman was thinking of leaving Random House, he commanded one of his editors, Stan Hart, to go see her. He surely picked the right man. In his kiss-and-tell book, *Fumblefinger: A Life Out of Line,* Hart writes, "We'd take a taxi back to her place, where we'd fall into bed."

That may be how Hart also got Hellman to agree to a contract calling for a $60,000 advance—$20,000 per year for three years. Arthur then turned her over not to one editor but two, Roger Donald and Billy Abrahams, the latter a superb freelance editor then living in California. As for Roger Donald, Arthur Thornhill was specific about his assignment: "You're in charge of Lillian Hellman, but not editing; don't touch her manuscript. Billy Abrahams will do that. Just make sure that everything goes right."

Between Billy and Roger, it all worked out. In 1970 her memoir, *An Unfinished Woman,* won the National Book Award for Arts and Letters. Then she turned to work on a second memoir, which would be called *Pentimento.*

"She gave me unbelievable hell," Roger told me. Working for Hellman was not exactly what he had expected when he began his publishing career in 1960. The son of a lace curtain Irish mother and a father who, he said, was mostly broke, Roger and his brother became the first ones in the family to go to college. Roger turned out to be an academic wizard, and the heavyweight champion of full scholarships. He went to prep school at Andover for two years on full scholarship, to a boarding school in England for a year on full scholarship, to Yale for three years on full scholarship, and to Cambridge University for two more years on full scholarship. "I figured out," Roger told me, "that some very nice, very rich people put about a quarter of a million dollars into me in today's dollars." Almost everyone thought he would be an academic for life; instead, he accepted a life sentence in book publishing.

Today, Roger lives on a ranch in Montana. He has that rancher look—a full, muscular chest and a cowboy's air of disdain on his lips. He and his wife, Diana Vandervlis, who was an actress, had once vacationed on a ranch in Wyoming and loved it. In 2001, after Diana died, Roger decided to make Montana his home. In December 2005 he came to New York to visit his son, and that gave him time to talk with me. He seemed completely relaxed, his face warming as he told stories in his deep, stentorian voice. There was also a lot of laughter as we went along.

His first job in book publishing was at McGraw-Hill. He got the job because he was dating the daughter of the chairman, Curtis Benjamin. "She dumped me," Roger said, "but Benjamin and I became good friends." Benjamin himself, as a result of his mighty thirty-eight years with McGraw-Hill, became an icon and ambassador for the book industry.

The first thing Benjamin asked Roger to do at McGraw-Hill was to analyze the company's trade division. Roger said, "I wrote a one-line memo—'Put your money in the passbook savings'— which caused everyone to laugh. Curt Benjamin took me to lunch. 'Son,' he set me straight, 'you never met a poor publisher. There's no such thing as a poor publisher.' He went over the list: What kind of car did Alfred Knopf drive? Who had a penthouse?

Who lived on Park Avenue? Who was on Fifth Avenue? Now, you don't think they got that way by putting their money in passbook savings, do you?

" 'So let's figure out how they *did* make their money. Book publishing is like playing poker. You know how much money you got, and you know you gotta go home. You need gas money or subway money to get home. So you bet what you can bet, always keeping enough. This is the name of the game: You're in the trade business—you break even, you make, what, two percent? It's all right. Then you get *Gone With the Wind.* You don't build no factories, you don't hire nobody. You just pick up that telephone and call Margaret Mitchell and say—keep writin', keep writin',—and the money just rolls in. And if you're smart, you don't go on a binge and spend it. You invest it properly in your business.' "

Not long after Roger Donald analyzed the economics of trade book publishing, McGraw-Hill pretty much killed its trade list. And in 1969, after short stops at *Reader's Digest* and World Publishing, Roger landed at Little, Brown. He moved fast. As editor in chief, he wasn't a big acquirer himself, but he found himself nurturing Little, Brown's major league authors such as Norman Mailer, Peter De Vries, William Manchester, William Shirer, Herman Wouk—and Lillian Hellman.

They actually became close with each other. She liked gossiping with Roger. For instance, she told him about the day that her lover of thirty years, Dashiell Hammett, was having lunch at the 21 Club with William Faulkner.

"They were not eating; I mean they were drinking lunch," said Roger, expanding on Hellman's story. "And then Bennett Cerf came in with a bunch of people, and he saw William Faulkner. He went over to talk to him. 'I didn't know you were in town, Bill,' Cerf said. 'I'm having a dinner party tonight. Will you come?' 'Hmmm,' said Faulkner. Cerf took it as a yes, and he went off.

But he didn't invite Hammett, who was also a Random House author. The two of them got drunker and drunker and decided they would both go to the party.

"When they arrived, they saw that everybody else was in dinner clothes. It was a sit-down dinner.

"At one point Hammett is sitting on the sofa and he falls forward onto the floor, and he's passed out, and Faulkner's sitting next to him. And Cerf says something like 'It's such a waste. The man has some talent, but this is ridiculous.' And Faulkner, the little, tiny fucker, stands up and says, 'I wouldn't want to eat dinner with someone who insults my friends.' He then steps over Hammett and leaves."

Roger came to understand the power of alcohol in his industry, so he was prepared to handle it on the day he and Lillian and her agent, Don Congdon, went out to lunch at the Four Seasons.

ROGER DONALD

Very soon, Hellman dismissed Don Congdon, and we stayed drinking. " 'Cause I told her I had grown up in New Orleans, and so had she. We're both drinking stingers the whole afternoon. And, God, can she drink! And she told me two things. She said she'd only once had good editorial advice and that it came from Arthur Senior. I forget what book she was talking about, but she said that she had sent it in, and Arthur said, "I'll read it right away. I'll call you tomorrow and I'll tell you." And he didn't call her. And she said, "I finally called him, and I said, 'Well, what did you think?' And he said, 'Lilly, of course anything you do is very worthwhile, very worthwhile. But let me tell you—I never went to college, I'm really not a cultivated man, I'm not an educated man, so you know, all I'm doing is telling you my reaction. . . . I don't know how seriously you should take it, but I found it very easy to go to sleep during chapter five.'

"I told that son of a bitch," Lillian said to me, " 'Of course, you didn't go to college, you couldn't get in a goddamned college, you uncultivated stupid bastard!' " And she hung up on him. And then she said, "That evening I read chapter five and he was right. So I went and rewrote it."

Then she began talking to me about how editors are useless. "You don't need them," she said, "you need editors for people who can't write. You people haven't the slightest idea of how to keep good writers happy." And I said, "I guess not. You want to give me a hint?" And she said, "Sure. Whatever they send in, tell them it's terrific, and when they arrive, whether by train or plane, greet them with a limo and a bunch of flowers and take them to a good dinner. That's all you need to do. I mean we sit there in front of the blank page. We don't know if it's any damn good. Of course, we insist it's good, but we don't know. We just want somebody to pet us. That's all you gotta do. Do you think Alfred Knopf does anything except give those guys good wine?"

IN ALL OF the publishing houses I have covered on these pages, there is only one in which a particular author matches up with a head of house. I'm referring to Peter De Vries and Arthur Thornhill, Jr. I felt that these two, in their inner lives, were oddly alike in their mind-set. Arthur, buttoned-down even in conversation, always chose his words carefully, seeking the least provocative combination. De Vries, who, if not "one of the saddest men I ever met," as Roger Donald characterized him, was at the least, skeptical of life—"Like the cleaning lady," one of his characters said, "we all come to dust." "Theories of comedy," he once told

David Willis McCullough, an editor at the Book-of-the-Month Club and later one of its judges, "are like a woman squeezing into a girdle that's too small. There are not many things to laugh at, nothing fits. There's always an overflow."

Early in 2007, I was delighted to read a review in the *Times Literary Supplement* by Christopher Hitchens of an autobiography that had nothing to do with De Vries, but opened with a fond remembrance: "The great Peter De Vries, when asked about the nature of his ambition, replied that he yearned for a mass audience that would be large enough to despise." De Vries always did brood over his failure to "break through." Still, he spent over forty years, happy ones I have heard, with *The New Yorker* as poetry editor, writing short stories, and fixing up cartoonists' punch lines.

Little, Brown published twenty-one of De Vries's twenty-two novels (there were three earlier novels that De Vries disowned), all in the time zone of the golden age. I started reading him in the early 1950s after I had disowned the hero of my youth, Thomas Wolfe. My first De Vries was *The Tunnel of Love,* and I couldn't wait for the next one to show up. In my years at Book-of-the-Month Club, I read his works in galleys under the pretext that I was trying to decide whether we should take on his latest novel, when really I just wanted to get at him. We did take most of his novels. While we didn't exactly find a mass audience for his brilliance as a humorist and a parodist, many of our members seemed happy inviting him into their homes. We were also fortunate to have one of his children, Jan De Vries, as a regular outside reader for the Club. It is no surprise that she was one of the best. My continuous frustration is that De Vries has never been honored with a reconsideration or rediscovery of his works that might firmly establish his position in the pantheon of modern American satiric literature.

This is the way he was. One night when De Vries and his wife, Katinka, were having dinner with the Donalds, out of the blue Peter said, "You know, I can tell when one of my readers dies."

"Really?" Roger said.

"Yes, because I always sell eight thousand, four hundred and seventy-six books, and if it's eight thousand, four hundred and seventy-five, I know one of them has died. And Roger, I'm going to sue Little, Brown and I'm going to sue you."

"What for?"

"Fraud."

"Why?" Roger said.

"I have never yet met a person who has not yet read all of my books and loved them. And last week I counted how many new people I met, all of whom had read all of my books and loved them all. And this has been going on for twenty years. So I multiply fifty-two times this number times twenty. I should sell a hundred thousand of each book because everybody I've met has read all of my books and loves them all."

In the best of times Little, Brown might sell 30,000 copies of a De Vries novel; more often, the sales were closer to 20,000. De Vries never came close to his dream of that mass audience.

However, there did come the moment when Roger Donald heard from De Vries's agent, Gloria Loomis. " 'Okay,' she said to me. 'Peter wants a hundred thousand dollars for the next book.' I told her this was crazy. She said, 'Well, that's what he wants.' "

Roger found out that Gloria actually did have a $100,000 offer for his next book. It came from Alan Williams, who had moved from Viking to Putnam's taking Stephen King with him. He also wanted De Vries to come along. Little, Brown's customary De Vries advance was $50,000 for each novel, which enabled the house to almost earn out. Much as they wanted to, they couldn't handle a 100 percent hike.

So the deal was made. De Vries immediately called both Roger Donald and Arthur Thornhill. "It's not Gloria," he said. "It's me. I'd never ever in the world wanted to leave Little, Brown, but Katinka has been very ill and the bills are piling up."

Peckham's Marbles was published by Putnam's in 1986 and sold under ten thousand copies. In the novel, Earl Peckham, having recovered from a bad case of hepatitis that tended to make him "look on the world with a jaundiced eye," has been trying to find the three people who bought his last book. De Vries described his character Peckham sitting in the Algonquin Hotel lunching by himself: "Of everything on which he has eavesdropped as he sipped his martini or partook of his meal, he has heard only one thing he truly wishes he had said. A man at the next table remarked to his lady companion, 'My last book sold a hundred and ninety-seven thousand copies.'"

"It was very sad losing him," Roger Donald said, "because there was enormous affection for Peter." Arthur Thornhill told me he was heartsick not to have published what turned out to be his last book, and that the two of them never stopped talking to each other. De Vries died in 1993. Fortunately, many of his books are still in print.

BILL PHILLIPS HAS distinct memories of the past at Little, Brown. The more he spoke of the old days, the more his face seemed to light up. It was the late 1970s and early '80s, when the house was "on a roll" with fine authors. Some of their preeminent fiction writers at that time included Ellen Gilchrist, whose short story collection *Victory over Japan* won the National Book Award; Martha Grimes's first novel, *The Man with a Load of Mischief* (the book was pulled out of the slush pile by a young Little, Brown editor named Ray Roberts); and Bill Phillips's discovery, James Carroll. I remember how much we at BOMC liked Carroll's first novel, *Madonna Red.*

Little, Brown's nonfiction list was powerful, too: William Shirer for *The Nightmare Years*, bought by Roger Donald for only $25,000; James Thomas Flexner for his volumes on George Washington (volume four won a National Book Award for biography in 1973); Tracy Kidder's *The Soul of a New Machine;* and Frances FitzGerald. Her *Fire in the Lake,* about the Vietnam war, won both a National Book Award and a Pulitzer Prize that same year and has never stopped selling.

"When I look back on that time," Phillips said, "the mere fact is that it's the only place I ever worked for. It was a remarkable place. It had its problems, of course; they were maybe a little slow bringing in new blood, and some of the new ones hired were a mistake. But it had stability and a continuity that was really quite wonderful."

We were talking early in 2007 in his artistic home in Belmont, Massachusetts. He was sixty-four years old but seemed much younger as he told me about some of the things he had brought in. One was *Crockett's Victory Garden,* which became the start of a publishing program with WGBH, the Boston public television station. "It was a breakthrough book in all sorts of ways," Bill said, "because it was given the high-end treatment to a prosaic category of books: the 'how to' books. It became the glossy dream/wish book, and it sold a million copies in the mid-seventies." After that one came *This Old House* books, the basis for another successful public television series.

Bill retired from Little, Brown in 2001, but he still does freelance editorial chores for them. In recent years he edited Malcolm Gladwell's *The Tipping Point* and a comic memoir from Steve Martin.

"Publishing," he went on, "has always been made up of some incredibly flamboyant egos who thought the business was *them,* and not their people—which is really what it's all about." He told me a story he had heard from Doris Kearns Goodwin about a function she attended one night. "She was sitting next to Dick Snyder of Simon & Schuster. All he was talking to her was about himself—blah, blah, blah." And then another night she sat next to Arthur Thornhill—"and all he talked about was his authors."

"Bless his heart," Bill said. "Arthur, at the end of it all, who didn't understand me, nor I him, grew enormously proud of me, and, I think, still is. And it's been one of the lovely parts of my life—to have had that late but nice relationship with him."

WHAT PHILLIPS WAS doing was what Arthur Thornhill, Jr., wished he could do if he didn't have the whole company to worry about. He controlled his company tightly, but was also able to extend his reach in editorial activities. Two bestsellers in the mid-sixties that would probably not have been approved in Alfred McIntyre's time won Thornhill's support: William Howard Masters and Virginia E. Johnson's *Human Sexual Response,* and Gore Vidal's satirical *Myra Breckinridge,* his 1968 novel about a man-hating transsexual. Arthur saw to it that the Masters and Johnson book would be treated as a medical breakthrough. Insisting that the book was meant mostly for an academic audience, Fred Belliveau, the creative and astute head of the medical division, sent reviews of the book to the medical journals and other serious medical media. But the general reader, too, wanted to see what the fuss was all about. In 1966, *Human Sexual Response* nestled between No. 1, *How to Avoid Probate,* and No. 3, *In Cold Blood,* on the *Publishers Weekly* yearly bestseller list.

Gore Vidal's *Myra Breckinridge* was in the middle of the top ten novels of 1968. Bill Phillips, whose first job at Little, Brown was in the publicity department, had the pleasure of accompanying Vidal on a road trip in the Midwest. "We hit it off right away," Phillips remembers. "He was one of those rare authors who really wanted to know about someone else. He had known my father, Wendell Phillips, in his work as an actor. There was a cancellation in Chicago from one of the bookstores, and we stayed up all night drinking and talking in the Pump Room of the Ambassador East Hotel. He told me one juicy story after another about the beautiful people he seemed always to deal with."

Little, Brown lost Gore Vidal to Random House after he had

asked his editor, Ned Bradford, if Little, Brown would buy a house he owned in upstate New York. "We didn't want to be real estate agents," Arthur told me, "and Random House came along."

In 1969, Arthur, still looking for big names, signed up Norman Mailer, Little, Brown's first million-dollar contract, for a series of books, of which five were published. One of the five, published in 1979, was Mailer's brilliant work, *The Executioner's Song,* which won a Pulitzer Prize. Roger Donald worked with him on that one (Ned Bradford had edited the earlier Mailer books at Little, Brown). Like J. P. Donleavy, who never allowed Sam Lawrence or any editor to touch his work, *not one word,* Mailer was a bit difficult to work with. "You couldn't get in with a pencil and do anything," Roger said. "Norman would simply say, 'Don't ever put a pencil on my manuscripts. You can talk to me and I'll listen to you.'"

Mailer did listen to his editors. After his death on November 10, 2007, Charles McGrath, of *The New York Times*, said of him: "Mr. Mailer belonged to the old literary school that regarded novel writing as a heroic enterprise undertaken by heroic characters with egos to match."

In 1983, Roger Donald published *Ancient Evenings,* Mailer's Egyptian novel of heroic length (709 pages) that people were talking about before publication. "It was a great disappointment," Arthur Thornhill said, "a real financial bomb." Roger looked at Mailer's next novel, *Tough Guys Don't Dance,* and thought it wasn't for them. Mailer went back to Random House.

BUT THERE ALWAYS seemed to be someone else out there to grab, if you were willing to pay the money. Arthur would pay the money for Herman Wouk. He'd found out that Wouk, who had always been published by Doubleday, was no longer happy with the way Doubleday printed his books; he was concerned about the quality of the production. Wouk set out to find a house that would publish a better-looking book. There was a scramble among the publishers, and representatives had to come to Wouk's agent, Harold Matson, for discussion. It was there that Ned Bradford read the new manuscript, *The Winds of War*. Bradford came home to Little, Brown, thumbs up. "Then Wouk came to look us over," said Arthur Thornhill. He apparently liked what he saw because Little, Brown got two masterful World War II novels, *The Winds of War* and *War and Remembrance.*

In nonfiction, Arthur went after Henry Kissinger for his memoirs when almost everyone in the house advised him not to—especially Roger Donald. "I had edited a book of Kissinger's when I was at McGraw-Hill," Roger said. "It was part of a series for the Council of Foreign Affairs, and it was an incredibly dull and boring book. So I said to Arthur, 'You're making a big bet on this Kissinger.' And Arthur said, 'Look, there hasn't been anybody in the twentieth century like this man. You're really talking about one of the great nineteenth-century diplomats. This is a man who is remaking the world. It's very important to get his memoirs.' And I said, 'Arthur, you know you're absolutely right, and if Bismarck were alive, we would certainly want Bismarck's memoirs for that very same reason. He was an important man. On the other hand it wouldn't sell, because Bismarck either wouldn't tell you the truth or he'd be boring.'

"Arthur gave me a look. 'Are you telling me that Kissinger won't tell the truth and that he's boring?' I said, 'Both. I've edited him. He'd send my stuff back and ask for rewrites and stuff like that. The guy's speech is better than his writing.'

"Well, wrong again, Roger. What could I say? Kissinger had learned exactly how to write this, and wrote brilliantly." So Arthur went into the chase, competing with Harper's and Random House and others. The advance money went up and up. Arthur did it alone and never stopped until the book was his. Kissinger's *The White House Years* was a major bestseller in

1979. Afterward, Roger told Thornhill, "Okay, I owe you a case of champagne."

There were lots of other authors that Arthur Jr. befriended, but never in the manner of his father, with hugs and kisses. One fine relationship was with William Manchester, who published with Little, Brown such works as *The Last Lion,* the first volume of a biography of Winston Churchill; *American Caesar*, a biography of Douglas MacArthur; *Goodbye, Darkness,* about Manchester's own World War II experiences; and *The Glory and the Dream*, a narrative history of the United States from 1932 to 1972. Bill Phillips, in his youth, took Manchester on a book tour to the Washington, D.C., area to promote his 1968 book, *The Arms of Krupp.* "He gave me an inside tour of Washington and Georgetown," Bill said. "He talked about his difficulties with the Kennedys on his 'authorized' Kennedy book, *The Death of a President* (see chapter 8 on Harper). He took me to see where Jackie was living at that time and spoke about the hours and hours he sat in a room with her as she poured her heart out. It was absolutely clear to me," Bill Phillips added, "that he was madly in love with this person."

It was Ned Bradford who, on one of his trips to England, brought back John Fowles's *The French Lieutenant's Woman.* It became the No. 2 fiction bestseller in 1970. Fowles followed with *The Magus* and *Daniel Martin,* powerful literary novels that made him one of the most distinctive authors of the period. And he and Thornhill became good friends. Arthur showed me a letter Fowles had written him shortly after his wife, Elizabeth, died in 1990. "Please let Eliz stay in your memory," Fowles wrote. "Such is the only life after death."

ARTHUR THORNHILL, JR., WAS the only head of house of my period whom I had gotten to know well and work closely with. That was when our companies were both owned by Time Inc. I would love to have nestled with some of the other publishers, but I think the Thornhill experience was essentially not so unlike those other heads of houses, even though they all had different personalities, different working conditions, and different philosophies about their children. All of them, it might also be said, had the same sense of loss when the new owners of their company told them that their time was up.

I REMEMBER the memorial service for Arthur Thornhill, Sr. It was held at King's Chapel in Boston, attended by a packed crowd of mourners. The first speaker was Ned Bradford.

"Arthur Thornhill's life and work and legacy," Bradford intoned to the overflow audience, "can be characterized by a simple statement which many of my colleagues and I heard him make repeatedly over the years. He would say, 'I want to be a part of something that's *good*.' It was an unaffected comment he was in the habit of throwing out in the context of discussions about the occupation he loved—the occupation that was his daily tonic." What Thornhill meant by *good,* Bradford explained, "had to do with something . . . that is real, satisfying, joyous, truly productive and, by virtue of its intrinsic merits, as permanent as can be in this impermanent world."

You can almost hear the old man coming close to Arthur Jr., who was sitting with Bradford, and whispering: *"And that's the truth!"*

INTERLUDE: MAKING MEMOIRS

For eleven years, from 1953 to 1964, Robert Lescher was an editor. He worked nine years for Henry Holt and Company, which, in 1960, became Holt, Rinehart and Winston. Starting out as a textbook editor, he ended as the editorial head of the trade division. The next two years were spent with Houghton Mifflin. He then decided to become a literary agent. Among his first clients was Calvin Trillin; he still serves Trillin plus other major writers. A literary agent of the first rank, he carries home almost every night two large bags of manuscripts and galleys to read, sometimes with delight.

ROBERT LESCHER

One day at about 5:30 P.M. in April of 1957, I was asked to go see Edgar T. Rigg, chairman of the board at Henry Holt. He offered me a drink and couldn't have been nicer. Then he pushed forward a manuscript, and he said, "This may be the greatest work we'll ever have published at Holt." I said, "Oh, what could that be?" He said, quite proudly, "The memoirs of Bernard Baruch."

Well, Mr. Baruch, who looked like a tall Huck Finn, was probably the most prominent Jewish man in America. He had retired when he was only thirty-two, already a millionaire, and gone into public service. Over the years he served as an adviser to five presidents.

I booked a room at the Algonquin Hotel, and told my wife that I was going to stay uptown because I had to read Bernard Baruch's memoirs and I wanted to do it overnight. I finished around five or six in the morning. I came into the office with a sheaf of notes, and I told Mr. Rigg's secretary I had read the manuscript and would be pleased to see Mr. Rigg whenever he wanted.

But I waited all day. I managed to do some stuff, and at five-thirty or six she came by my office. "Bob, are you free now?" I smiled at her.

The first thing Mr. Rigg said to me was, "What do you think?" Well, I'd had a chance to look over my notes and think about them all day. "Look," I said, "it's going to be a fantastic book. But, as they say, it needs work." "Tell me more," he said.

Over the next thirty minutes' time, without once referring to my notes, I was able to tell him virtually everything chapter by chapter—what hadn't been established, what had been shortchanged, what was cluttered, what characters hadn't been deeply enough portrayed. I did it all, by rote practically.

"That's wonderful," he said. "It's your book. You do just what you think. The only thing I should tell you is that we're going to publish in August; that's his birthday, August 19." I had just four months to produce the book.

I remember when I met Mr. Baruch for the first time. I tried to make him understand that the book could be wonderful, but that there were certain things that had to be done. As an example, you couldn't write a memoir devoting two paragraphs to your wife and two chapters to Clare Boothe Luce. He understood.

I told him I was willing to commit myself full-time. He had two people helping him—Sam Lubell, an old-time political writer, and a very gifted secretarial assistant named Harold Epstein. For the next three months or so I went into the office every morning at nine, and I left at ten to go up to Baruch's office to work with him or his two assistants. Because of what needed to be done, they had to restructure everything. But the core of the book was there.

Baruch: My Own Story came out in August, and there were three or four stories in *The New York Times* on his birthday: One was a book review, which was stunning. One was an editorial on Mr. Baruch. There was also an interview. The book ended up on the *New York Times* bestseller list for thirty-eight straight weeks, No.1 for nineteen of those weeks.

Because of that, I was handed a lot of memoirs to edit. One was Sheilah Graham's *Beloved Infidel,* about her love affair with Scott Fitzgerald at the end of his life. Another was by Major Donald E. Keyhoe, who was known as an expert on flying saucers. That one was *The Flying Saucer Conspiracy.* After reading his manuscript, I told him it lacked continuity— one paragraph was great, the next paragraph didn't follow. He invited me to work with him at his home in Virginia.

I remember when he pulled into his garage and he locked the door. Then he unlocked the backdoor of the house so we could enter. I was going to be sleeping in a bedroom upstairs. So he unlocked the door upstairs, and we went up and I put my bags in the room. Then we came down again and he locked the door, and he said, "Do you want something to eat?" I said I'd

THE TIME OF THEIR LIVES

just as soon take a look at the manuscript he'd begun to revise. He said, "It's downstairs."

He unlocked the door to the basement and there was a pool table, and on the pool table there had to be a thousand pieces of paper. It was his notion that we would reassemble them and write transitions. It took me two days to help the major reorganize his book.

I still wince when I think of it.

Part III

SWIRL

The Paperbound Rush to Life

If there is any period one would desire to be born in, is it not
the age of Revolution; when the old and the new stand side
by side and admit of being compared; when the energies of
all men are searched by fear and by hope; when the historic
glories of the old can be compensated by the
rich possibilities of the new era? This time, like
all times, is a very good one, if we but know
what to do with it.

—RALPH WALDO EMERSON,

"THE AMERICAN SCHOLAR," 1837

13

BALLANTINE, AVON, POCKET BOOKS, DELL

Ballantine

Books have been my life. I don't remember a time when I couldn't read. My father taught me to read when I was three, as he taught all of us four kids. This was out in India, when my father was a British Colonial officer. He was a scholar, too.

For a long time I thought the stories in books were real. I could not tell the difference. Tarzan was a real person to me, as was every character in the Dickens books. It took me quite awhile to sort out that this is fiction, and these people didn't exist! And it bothered me at the time because, you know, Tarzan was my friend.

Ian Ballantine was the cousin of a girl, Enid Ballantine, with whom I went to school in the Channel Islands in England. . . . She called me up one day to say her American cousin was coming over, and would I come and meet him? She was going to give a beach party. . . . We went to the beach party, and I met Ian, and we walked off together and talked for three hours solid, and I don't know what we said to each other. . . . I have a letter Ian wrote to his professor at Columbia, announcing that he was getting married and bringing his wife with him. . . . At the end of the letter he says, "I intend to change the reading habits of America." That's what his ambition was. And he did.

—BETTY BALLANTINE

W hen Allen Lane, the founder of Penguin Books, was introduced to Ian Ballantine, he was immediately impressed. At the time the United States, Germany, and Italy were the only countries where Lane's books were not really acceptable. (Hard to believe that the United States had this in common with the fascist Axis.) Lane hired Ballantine, then studying at the London School of Economics, to bring Penguins to the Pilgrims.

The next thing the eighteen-year-old Betty Ballantine knew was that within twenty-four hours they had married and acquired passports. And here she was, helping her twenty-one-year-old husband carry a load of books on board the *New Amsterdam*. They landed in New York on the weekend of July 4, 1939, and the boy publisher was ready to establish Penguin Books in America.

IT WAS THE opening shot of what came to be known in America as the Paperback Revolution, the time when softcover books were swirling around madly, offering enticing opportunities for hardcover book publishers to get in the game.

There was nothing new about paperbacks. They had always existed in one form or another. In 1782, 190 paperback volumes of John Bell's British Poets series were introduced along the Eastern seaboard of the United States. They sold for eight shillings. In 1831, the Boston Society for the Diffusion of Useful Knowledge diffused liberally in a paperback line known as The American Library of Useful Knowledge. Titles included *An Universal*

History by Johannes von Muller, *Discourses on the Advantages of Science*, and *A Treatise on Hydrostatics and Pneumatics*.

In the post–Civil War period, paperbacks in various shapes and sizes were published again, north and south. But toward the close of the century, when business flopped throughout the country, paperbacks mostly disappeared—until the mid-1930s. In the new century the opportunity for mass-market paperback books emerged again as a result of the introduction of the high-speed roll-fed printing press. Then came the introduction of mass-market channels of distribution, successfully established for the magazine industry, which could, and would serve the paperback industry.

"These Penguins are the means of converting book-borrowers into book-buyers," Allen Lane had written in 1935. And now the Ballantines had arrived in town, ready to convert the reading public. "We are starting an office with the barest minimum necessary—a secretary (my English wife) and a stock boy," Ian Ballantine wrote to his Columbia professor Louis Hacker. "The entire firm is housed in one room halfway up a skyscraper." He had $500 to start with—a gift from his wife's father—to open the American office. After bringing in their first 25-cent Penguins by ship, World War II erupted, causing huge import difficulties. Oftentimes the Penguins didn't make it to shore or, if they did, the paper used for printing abroad was so bad that the books quickly deteriorated.

"So we had to manufacture here," Betty Ballantine said, a bright smile on her face. "We were very successful right from the beginning, and we already had an accumulation of cash."

Good for the Ballantines, maybe, but not so good for Allen Lane. He had become unhappy with the Penguin U.S. operation. For one thing, he didn't like pictures on the covers. For another, he didn't agree with Ian Ballantine's choice of books. And so their partnership came to an early end. For one dollar the Ballantines sold their 49 percent interest in the company back to Allen Lane.

Now operating on their own, the Ballantines swiftly filled in the gaps. Kurt Enoch, a German immigrant publisher new to the United States, joined the Ballantines as "our production man," Betty said. And Kurt Enoch was smart enough to know that if you're going to have a successful mass-market publishing house, you needed to have an American point of view. So he and Victor Weybright got together and made New American Library" (see chapter 14).

In August 1945 Ian approached the people who were running Grosset & Dunlap to convince them that they should have a paperback arm. You may remember that one of the five Grosset owners was Bennett Cerf, whose editor in chief, Saxe Commins, was Ian's uncle (see chapter 10, on Random House). Ian was very persuasive, and Cerf admired Ian's get-up-and-go attitude. So they did, indeed, hire Ian to be their trusty shepherd.

All they needed now was a name for the company. Along came a young Grosset editor, Bernard Geis, who would later in life run his own commercial fiction house and publish authors such as Jacqueline Susann and Helen Gurley Brown. (I came to know Bernie in the seventies, when he had a two-story office with a fireman's pole that would get you downstairs quickly. I slid down that pole once, hanging on for dear life.)

Geis said to the Grosset owners: "How about Bantam Books?" They liked the name, so Bantam Books, Inc., it was.

The Ballantines hired a bright young man they had heard much about, Stanley Kauffmann, to be their editor. When we met, he told me much about his paperback years.

"Ian was a vital, energetic, ambitious person," Stanley said, "who thought of himself and publishers in general, not as publishers, but as *communicators*. He felt that paperbacks were the great new means to spread the word, the *good* word. He had some of the fire and zeal of an apostle. His interest was chiefly in education through books. At one time, for instance, he had a plan—it never went far, by heaven—to publish a set of six or seven books by experts in six or seven fields. With those books on your shelf, you were quick to deal with the modern world."

The more Stanley thought about Ian, who died in 1995, the more he found to say about him. "He couldn't understand why so many fine novelists didn't write more optimistically about America. And I tried to tell him, without much success, that it wasn't necessarily the job of an artist to be optimistic; it was to illuminate the verities of life in America or anywhere else. Ian always saw books in the best sense—as utilitarian, as helpful."

With that, Stanley gave me a perfect example of what he called Ian Ballantine's "quasi-evangelical impulse in publishing."

"He had seen the original production of *Death of a Salesman*. He went mad about it, bought the paperback rights to the book published by Viking. Then he read the play, and he was worried that it would be difficult for a reader—a nonprofessional—to follow it on paper. 'You've worked in the theater,' he said to me. 'Please go and ask Miller to write some filler material for the book.'

"I felt that was like asking God to add on to one of his commandments. Well, I made arrangements through somebody to get an appointment. Arthur Miller was then living in Brooklyn Heights with his first wife—a lovely woman—and I went to see him. He greeted me, and we went up to the workroom on the top floor, where he showed me the new Japanese edition of his novel *Focus*. 'I can't even find any typos in it,' he said. And we talked, and I knew the moment was coming when I was going to have to ask this man, who was a little holier than the Pope, to make some additions. I expected to be thrown out of the window of the third floor. I took a deep breath, and I told him the story—that a little addition here or there would explain a transition, or a fade-out would make it much easier for 'the lay reader' to follow it on paper.

"I finished my little speech and waited, expecting catastrophe. And Miller said, 'I *wanted* to do that! They took the play out of my hands and rushed it into print before I had a chance to do that.' And he sent me some material of about five thousand words to be pieced in here or there, and I have a copy of that version. Viking is still publishing the original unextended version."

Soon, though, it began to get sticky for the Ballantines. By 1951, Ian hadn't persuaded the Grosset owners that the new paperback house was working well enough. Their complaints came during a volatile period for paperback publishing. Too many of the books were flooding the market with titles that nobody wanted. Returns were stacking up in warehouses all over the country. Besides that, Grosset executives felt that Ian had been taking too many chances, raising cover prices too high. "Ian did want to go to fifty cents," Betty said. "Thirty-five cents then was a great price for a paperback, but you could not do a book of more than 160 pages. That meant you were limited as to subject matter. And this is not what we wanted to do. We wanted to expand the subject matter, do bigger books. And that became a huge battle."

At the same time Betty admitted to me, "Ian was not the easiest man in the world to work for. He was demanding. He wanted the best from everybody. And I guess he had a disagreement with some of the employees, and backstabbing conspiracies were formed among some of them, which made it extremely difficult for us to work."

The day after a major meeting of the board of directors, Betty remembered, "he came marching into our apartment. 'Well,' he said, 'I got fired.' His mother hugged him, saying, 'Congratulations, my son,' which I thought was wonderful."

The Ballantines came up to their house in Woodstock for the George Washington weekend of 1952 with one of Ian's best-loved editors, Bernie Shir-Cliff. Bernie had also been fired after Ian left. They both spent the weekend skiing. "Ian broke his leg," Betty said, "and Bernie sprained his ankle. And that month, with his leg in a cast, Ian dreamed up the creation of Ballantine Books."

THE DREAM CAME true that same year, 1952, and Ballantine Books, under the humane care of husband and wife, lasted into 1974. (It continues to this day as an imprint at Random House.) Early on, Ian came up with a fascinating idea: to hook up with one or two hardcover houses and publish the paperback edition *simultaneously* with the hardcover. Betty described how it would all work. "The hardcover publishers would do their own edition, but also put up the money for the paperback. They'd get all the profits on the hardcover, and 25 percent of the profits of the paperback. They had to follow our terms, as far as the authors were concerned, which included the authors' receiving all of the hardcover royalties and all of the paperback royalties. We simply would not divide the paperbound royalties. But the profit was something else. So we were able to put titles on our list funded by the hardcover publishers, which meant that we only had to come up with the money for one of our own titles. It would be published as a Houghton Mifflin/Ballantine book, or a Farrar, Straus/Ballantine book."

Stanley Kauffmann moved with the Ballantines to what was now Ballantine Books, and he worked closely with hardcover houses on joint projects. He almost nailed one author the house would have loved for its list: Georges Simenon. "I knew an agent named Max Becker, who was Simenon's American agent," Stanley told me. "Simenon was then living in Connecticut. He published so many books a year in France that no American publisher could keep up with him. Becker arranged for me to come and meet Simenon on one of his New York visits, and maybe pick up the books that the American publishers wouldn't touch.

"Simenon, as you would expect, was a dynamic man. I remember asking him, 'How long does it take you to write a novel, Mr. Simenon?' He didn't say 'about' or 'usually.' He said: 'Eleven days.'

"I told him of the Ballantine plan of doing simultaneous editions, and he thought it was wonderful. He said he was a partner in a French publishing firm that was founded to do exactly that. I said, 'They will sell like donuts here.' We ended up doing nothing of his, because Harcourt, Brace, who owned Simenon here, was furious when they found out that we wanted a Simenon book."

That was all right. The first Ballantine book, published on November 10, 1952, was a dual selection of Houghton Mifflin and Ballantine Books: Cameron Hawley's *Executive Suite*. Houghton Mifflin sold 22,000 copies in its first printing. Ballantine sold 470,000 in paper. The book is still in print.

It was a successful first year for the Ballantines and their editors, Kauffmann and Bernie Shir-Cliff. So they began bringing in new kinds of books to the field. Shir-Cliff latched on to the *Mad* magazine craze and did a whole series of *Mad* laughers. On the other side of it was the Ballantines' continuous fascination with science fiction. This led to a whole series of Ballantine books that opened up science fiction in all directions, including galaxy novels, and what Ian called adult fantasy titles.

Stanley Kauffmann made a direct hit when he acquired and edited *Fahrenheit 451,* Ray Bradbury's chilling novel about censorship and thought control (451 degrees Fahrenheit is the temperature at which book paper catches fire and burns). Published in 1953, it became a cult book and has never stopped selling.

Still, it was rough going again for the Ballantines, because they never had enough money to operate properly. They found themselves owing their printer $600,000, and another large sum of money to Houghton Mifflin. Fortunately, both the printer and the publishing house said to them, "Pay it off when you can." So Ian and Betty cut back to publishing only two books a month, staying alive long enough to pay off Houghton Mifflin. Their printer eventually wrote off $100,000 of what was owed.

Somehow, they survived. They started going heavily into illustrated books. "We did the Sierra Club books," Betty said, "beautiful reproductions at $3.95." And then along came a very special book. David Brower, the executive director of the Sierra Club, urged a Stanford professor of biology, Paul Ehrlich, to write his prophetic book, *The Population Bomb.*

It was published in 1968, and Johnny Carson brought Ehrlich on his show and left him on for an hour. The book took off. "That's where Ian's strength was," Betty said. "He really knew how to sell books, and he also knew how to get them created in the first place. It was a wonderful combination." Suddenly, Betty had a second thought about her husband. "He was a very interesting man." We both laughed.

Soon another opportunity came to the Ballantines. "What happened," Betty said, "was that our switchboard operator, a very nice person by the name of Mary, came to me one day with this red hardcover book and said, 'Mrs. Ballantine, I think you'd be interested in this. Ballantine Books should really publish this book.' So I read it: *The Hobbit.* And I took it and the whole lot of Tolkiens to Bernie Shir-Cliff and said, 'Hey Bernie, take a look at this. See what you think. I think we ought to be doing it.'

Houghton Mifflin had had the Tolkiens in hardcover for a long time. We made an offer for paperback rights—$2,500 for each of the four books of *The Lord of the Rings*. They said, 'Thank you very much, but no thank you.' Their hardcover edition had been selling steadily for years. They imported sheets from England, so they didn't want to reprint competing editions."

A couple of years later Houghton Mifflin came back to the Ballantines in horror: Ace Books, a latecomer to the paperback business, was pirating the Tolkiens. Ace's argument, based on their reading of U.S. copyright law, was that importing sheets from another country nullified the copyright. Technically, these books were now in the public domain. (Later, that glitch in the copyright law was thrown out by the U.S. government.) The Ballantines said to Houghton Mifflin, "Okay, our offer is still good, and we will publicize the fact that Ace is not paying royalties." "And we did put a little statement on the back covers," Betty said, "saying that Ace was not paying royalties to Professor Tolkien, and everybody who admired *Lord of the Rings* should buy only our paperback edition.

"Well, everybody got behind us. There was literally no publication that did not carry some kind of outraged article. And of course, the whole science fiction fraternity got behind the book; this was their meat and drink."

IN 1969, IAN and Betty noticed that the nature of the business had begun to change. "One day Ian and I kind of looked at each other and said, 'We're like a boutique publisher surrounded by monsters.' Well, we hadn't accumulated any money. So we said, 'Hey, we've got to do something about the future. We better sell.'"

They sold Ballantine Books to a firm called Intext. After months of negotiation, the papers were signed and an exchange of stock took place, which would give them some three million dollars. "The week after we signed the papers," she said, "Intext stock dropped from $43 to something like $1.50. We were wiped out." Random House came along and bought Ballantine from Intext.

For eight months the Ballantines worked as consultants to Random House. "They really wanted a big paperback house," Betty said. "We found, as we should have known, that it didn't work for Ian. He could not be told what to do. In August of 1974 we said to each other, 'Let's get the hell out.' We went to Bob Bernstein, who was our boss. We said, 'Forget your employment contract, we'll leave.' He was very sweet and he said, 'You're making it easy for me.'"

They did leave, becoming consultants to Oscar Dystel at Bantam. Both Ian and Betty proceeded to have fulfilling years, helping to create the books they loved.

Betty is alone today, but not really alone, because she has all those books surrounding her. The Tarzans in the books she reads still seem like real persons to her. For Betty and Ian Ballantine, their lives never lost its sweetness.

Avon

Some of the most brilliant people worked at paperback
publishing, and some of the most hidebound people worked
in hardcover publishing, and they almost lost the game.

—PETER MAYER

Pearl Harbor was a month away when a mass market paperback house that called itself Avon Pocket Size Books pushed into the new arena of book publishing.

The company was established by one of those magazine distribution hopefuls, Joseph Meyers, of the American News Company.

These distribution firms fervently sought the marriage of paperback books to a magazine distribution system. All of a sudden, it seemed that every Tom, Dick, and Harry distributor was rushing to print an old title in a new package—a 25-cent paper book. Many of Meyers's competitors from the magazine world as well as the book publishers were doing the same thing: feasting on old genre books—mysteries, westerns, and novels with a big name attached to them—and paying $250 to $500 to the copyright owner for the privilege of reprinting. They would then slap on a (usually) garish cover and hope for the best. Avon's first book was Sinclair Lewis's *Elmer Gantry,* the cover a close-up of a man in a severe western hat wearing a string tie and a sinister smile on his face. Their second book was the *Rubaiyat of Omar Khayyam.*

Avon in those early years existed in a half-world without a real editorial presence, making little progress as a paperback publisher. But in 1959 the Hearst Corporation bought Avon Publications, Inc., and in 1963, turned it over to Frank Taylor to run. "Frank was kind of a fancy person," someone who worked with him told me. He also had a solid editorial background. In 1941 he was an editor at Reynal & Hitchcock, and by 1944 had become editor in chief. One of the books he brought in was an interracial love story that has never gone out of print, Lillian Smith's *Strange Fruit.*

After the war Taylor became a roving editor at Random House. He also spent time playing in Hollywood. In 1961 he produced a hugely talked-about film, *The Misfits*, written by Arthur Miller, directed by John Huston, and starring Clark Gable, Marilyn Monroe (Arthur Miller's wife), and Montgomery Clift. It was the last performance for both Monroe and Gable, and a critical disappointment. In later years, though, it became a cult favorite.

Taylor then came back to New York, where he and Allan Barnard, one of the finest paperback editors of all time, worked together on Dell paperbacks. It was Frank Taylor who brought in a newcomer to book publishing, a gorgeous young fellow with curls, Peter Mayer. Almost immediately he was pegged as a genius. He was also sometimes called "a raging egomaniac," but nonetheless, one who possessed a complete and total dedication to whatever he was doing. (I have to come clean again: Peter Mayer and I have been friends ever since I found my way into book publishing. When I left Book-of-the-Month Club, he was head of Viking/Penguin all over the world, and it was Peter who invited me to join Viking as an editor. I spent nine wonderful years there in his custody.)

In January 2006 I went to see him at his SoHo office, where he now runs his own company, the Overlook Press. He was on a walker then, having had his umpteenth surgery, this time for a badly broken ankle. But this bionic wonder continues to do what he always did—smoke, yell at his associates, smoke some more, yell some more, and, every once in a while, come up with some revolutionary new way to make money in book publishing. His first such strike was when he discovered that there was money to be made recycling forgotten or neglected books of literary value.

After graduating summa cum laude from Columbia, Peter spent five years driving a taxi. One evening a fellow cabdriver, Eddie Adler (who, it happened, went on to have a novel published by Knopf), told him: "You know, Peter, there's this great novel written about 1934, *Call It Sleep* by Henry Roth." Peter knew nothing about the novel but went to the New York Public Library where, prohibited from taking it home, he read forty or fifty pages a day. He found it a breathtaking reading experience. When he came to work for Avon in 1963 to be "Education Editor" (the title meant that he was expected to find "the *better* books to choose"), he had already found a best book.

"I was allowed to buy any book for up to $2,500 without having to ask anyone's permission," Peter told me. With Allan

Barnard's help (Barnard was a stalwart mentor to Peter, as well as a great acquiring editor in those years), they found the person who owned rights to Henry Roth's *Call It Sleep,* and they bought paperback rights for $2,500. When *Call It Sleep* was published in the fall of 1964, *The New York Times Book Review* raved about the novel on its front page. Before Mayer knew it, Avon had its first million-copy sale.

In our conversation, Peter spoke about his paperback colleagues, trying to match them up with the more generally favored hardcover gentry. "Some of the most brilliant people," he claims, "worked at paperback publishing, and some of the most hidebound people worked in hardcover publishing, and they almost lost the game."

Those were the years Peter speaks of as "guerrilla publishing." At Avon he had only one salesman for the imprint, but he had Allan Barnard, and he also began to bring in and develop smart and ambitious youngsters: Paula Diamond, who would edit and handle subsidiary rights; Nancy Coffey, a young woman who had a perfect instinct for women's commercial fiction; and Robert Wyatt from Miami, Oklahoma, a young man with original tastes.

Wyatt had been working nights as a reporter for the *Tulsa Daily World.* But he wanted more out of life. "A Greyhound bus brought me to New York on Labor Day, 1962," Wyatt once wrote. "But it wasn't a bus that drove me to the city. It was that subtle combination of ignorance and curiosity that always has served me well."

Bob's first job was as a clerk for Doubleday's flagship bookstore on Fifth Avenue and Fifty-seventh Street. Because he had had the largest library of paperback books back in his hometown in Oklahoma, his Doubleday boss assigned him the upstairs area, where rested the remainders and the lonely paperbacks. "A customer named Peter Mayer came upstairs nearly daily," Bob said. "I did not know what he did for a living, and I did not care as long as he bought the books I suggested. I was smitten some by what Avon was starting to do—bringing Susan Sontag, Michael Gold, and a collection of criticism, *On Contemporary Literature,* edited by Richard Kostelanetz, into mass-market publishing."

While *Call It Sleep* was exploding all over the literary marketplace, Peter offered Bob Wyatt the Education Editor post. Frank Taylor had left the company, and it was now Peter Mayer's to run. Allan Barnard had also moved on to Bantam, where for years he pulled winners out of his hat. Wyatt came to Avon filled with enthusiasm about the future. Watching the way Peter Mayer and his gang were promoting *Call It Sleep,* Wyatt was knocked for a loop. "The book even got on the front page of the *Daily News,*" Bob said. "There was a plane crash, and a copy of *Call It Sleep* was found in the wreckage." I asked Bob if anyone had ever accused Peter of sabotaging the plane. "No," he said, "you're the first person to mention that. You understand him very well, I can tell."

Bob was happy at Avon, except that he was still earning only $11,000 a year. Along came Delacorte Dell, offering the youngster $22,000 a year to become editorial director for books for younger readers. Bob had to take the job, and Peter wept. But Peter had a growing reputation as one of the leading Scrooges of the publishing industry. In this case, after Wyatt spent twenty-two months at Dell, Peter brushed away his tears and told Bob to come back. Bob said, "At an appropriate salary."

Bob Wyatt flourished at Avon. He gathered together, for the first time in paperback history, books on gay and lesbian subjects. He also brought in collections of plays, as well as a large number of works from South America translated from the Spanish and Portuguese.

IT WAS AROUND this time that Peter Mayer began to segregate paperback titles into A-to-F categories. " 'Bard, B' was going to

be quality fiction," Peter explained. " 'Camelot, C,' was children's books. 'D' for 'Discus,' was quality nonfiction. 'E' for
'Equinox' was serious trade paperbacks, and 'F' for 'Flair,' was
mass-market paperback category for popular subjects."

With almost every book on earth encapsulated into the Avon
stable, Peter was ready to strike with his second big discovery—
the first since he had found with *Call It Sleep* that it could be profitable to republish forgotten or neglected books of literary value.

Mayer's new discovery was that you could blow away the
competition by paying top dollar for a book purchased *ahead of*
its hardcover publication, *if* you knew in your gut that it would
take off in paper.

It began with a novel called *Up the Down Staircase* by Bel
Kaufman. Peter called it "a weird novel, written as letters and
memos about the New York City public schools." It had been
picked up by *The Saturday Review of Literature* in a series of hu-
morous columns. But other publishing houses had read those
columns, too, and were ready to get into the bidding game.

Peter was able to offer Prentice Hall, the hardcover publisher,
his largest advance to date—$152,000, which was "as much as I
was going to get out of the Hearst Corporation," he said. "I told
Prentice Hall I wanted to come over and talk to them. They said
okay." He collected a copy of every newspaper and magazine
that Hearst published, and he drove to Prentice Hall's offices in
New Jersey. He claims that the whole management of Prentice
Hall was out on the front steps to see him take all the stuff out of
his Volkswagen. At the meeting he offered the $152,000 and said,
"All I can tell you is that the Hearst magazines will back it. Avon
may be little, but I've got a mighty company behind me."

Back in the office, at 5 P.M. Sam Cohen of Prentice Hall called
Peter. He said, "You have the second-highest bid. Dell has bid
$172,000. But the management of Prentice Hall wants *you* to have
this book." When, if ever, had Peter heard such rapturous words?

"Nobody has ever come here and done a performance like that," Cohen went on. "We think that if you have this kind of energy, you'll sell more than Dell." Bob Wyatt said that when it was published in 1965, *Up the Down Staircase* sold 135,000 copies, and "many millions of copies after that."

Hearst suddenly loosened up. Peter bought two books in a row for a million dollars each. One was *Jonathan Livingston Seagull,* a No. 1 hardcover fiction bestseller in 1972 and 1973. "You know," Bob Wyatt told me, "we were going back to press for a million copies a week on *Seagull.*" The other was Thomas A. Harris, M.D.'s *I'm OK—You're OK,* a fourth-place hardcover nonfiction bestseller in 1971 and No. 2 in 1972.

Then came Mayer's third big discovery. For years each of the paperback houses would feature one blockbuster novel that became its leader for the month. Almost always it had been a big book the house had bought from a hardcover publisher. Peter changed all that, not going after the rights to hardcover titles, but publishing blockbuster originals in paperback. He outlined an idea for a novel to an author-friend, Burt Hirschfeld. *Fire Island* became the first original work to be a lead title in paperback publishing.

Then came a book that Nancy Coffey, who had been a fourth-grade schoolteacher in New York City, pulled out of the slush pile. "It was a very long book," Wyatt said, "written by a woman whose name you couldn't pronounce: Kathleen Woodiwiss." The novel was called *The Flame and the Flower.* Nancy went to Peter Mayer. "I've got a very unusual novel, more a woman's book," she told Peter. "I think I can get it cheap." Peter said, "Let's do it."

Nancy bought *The Flame and the Flower* for $1,500 and a four percent royalty. "I don't know what our first printing was," Bob Wyatt said. "It was a lead title so it was several hundred thousand copies, and the women of America embraced it and it was huge." The book was published in 1974, and by 1977 it had sold 2,580,000 copies. It was the first of a new genre of romantic novels for women, commonly called "bodice rippers." Avon cornered the market, and it took quite a while for other houses to catch up with Avon. When Kathleen E. Woodiwiss died in 2007, her thirteen novels had more than 26.7 million copies in print.

"The Avon years between 1964 and 1975—Peter Mayer's time there—have been regarded by historians as among the most fruitful in original American publishing," Bob Wyatt said, "a feat made more remarkable by the fact that Avon had no traditional means of hardcover exploitation and issued most of its books in mass-market formats."

IN 1976, AFTER a disagreement with Hearst (they wouldn't allow him to start a hardcover imprint and run it himself), Peter Mayer left Avon. He moved to Simon & Schuster and Pocket Books.

Pocket Books

I'm the product of the paperback revolution. Ordinary readers
can see in me some day somebody they can identify with.
I'm for the underdog. The average man is always in a state of
supreme distress because life is all complications with no
conclusion. In my books he sees people get out of trouble.

—ERLE STANLEY GARDNER

Erle Stanley Gardner, you could say, came to town in 1938 when the first two Perry Mason novels were published: *The Case of the Substitute Face* and *The Case of the Shoplifter's Shoe*. Their original publisher was William Morrow.

In May 1939, Robert Fair de Graff, as highborn as his name, had lunch with Dick Simon of Simon & Schuster. De Graff, who was a blood cousin to Nelson Doubleday, had been running Garden

City's hardcover reprint companies (a division of Doubleday), one of which called Blue Ribbon Books. He quit Garden City in 1938 and traveled to Europe, where, in Germany and England, he noted that cheap paperback books were doing well. Over a second martini, de Graff told Simon that he wanted to start a paperback house in the U.S. One wonders whether, during that lunch, de Graff might have been thinking about what an Erle Stanley Gardner might do for the company he was proposing to establish.

"Simon was instantly interested," recalled Seymour "Sy" Turk, who was treasurer of S & S at that time. "De Graff wanted to do a paperback book that had the same dimensions as the original hardcover. And Dick said, 'No, it has to be a twenty-five-cent book.'

"'You don't understand, Dick,' de Graff answered. "I'm proposing a dollar book in paperback.'

"'*You* don't understand, Bob," said Simon. 'The only way we're going to do it is if it's a twenty-five-cent book.'"

De Graff finally said okay to that, but in the negotiations between him and Leon Shimkin, the master builder for Mr. Simon and Mr. Schuster, one problem came up. De Graff was afraid that any agreement with S & S would make it tough for him to go to other hardcover publishers to get books for his paperback line. Shimkin, of course, had the answer to that.

"Although de Graff and S & S had agreed that each would provide a share of the capital," Turk explained, "de Graff was allowed to have a 51 percent share in the corporation, so, when dealing with other companies, he could call himself the owner of the imprint."

Shimkin also devised the most important element of the new business. "He figured out that it was really a 'book-a-zine,'" Sy said, "and therefore he insisted that its paperbacks must be distributed not through book distribution servers, but through magazine distribution."

Shimkin fell in love with de Graff's idea. He was convinced that the new business would be a bracing tonic for the book industry. And he wanted in. So Dick Simon and Max Schuster divided the company in two—a hardcover house and a softcover house. The split-level company began to look like Masterpiece Theatre's *Upstairs, Downstairs*, with the successfully established hardcover house upstairs on the twenty-eighth floor and the poor paperback relations down on the twenty-seventh.

That didn't bother de Graff, who came up with the perfect name for the imprint: Pocket Books. No competitor could then, or ever, use it as a title or in any official context. His colophon idea wasn't bad, either—Gertrude the Kangaroo (she was really a wallaby) carrying a book in her pouch.

De Graff almost immediately brought in Freeman "Doc" Lewis, who was a nephew to Sinclair Lewis, to be the executive director. The two had worked together at Doubleday and de Graff had high regard for Lewis. His first contract for Pocket Books was for Pearl S. Buck's *The Good Earth.*

In its first year under Doc Lewis, Pocket Books published thirty-four titles and sold 1,508,000 copies. Among those first paperbacks, readers could find, in addition to *The Good Earth,* James Hilton's *Lost Horizon*, Emily Brontë's *Wuthering Heights, Five Tragedies* by Shakespeare, Thornton Wilder's *The Bridge of San Luis Rey,* and Felix Salten's *Bambi* (first published in 1928 by Simon & Schuster in a translation from the German by Whittaker Chambers). And in 1940, along came Erle Stanley Gardner.

Lee Wright, one of the first important female adult editors in the industry, slid downstairs from Simon & Schuster to Pocket Books, bringing Gardner along with her. Twenty years later, in a list of Pocket Books' twenty bestsellers of those years, five of them were Perry Mason mysteries. It was said that for each one of these mysteries (130 total), Gardner purchased a new gun.

He felt he needed to have an authoritative serial number for use in the fictional courtroom.

Seven more of those twenty bestsellers had in their titles these words: *The Pocket Book of . . .* They included *The Pocket Book of Short Stories, The Pocket Book of Verse,* and *The Pocket Book of Cartoons,* which was inevitably edited by Bennett Cerf, who loved serving other houses as long as his name went along with his freelance activities. But the grandest and most popular title of them all was *The Pocket Book of Baby and Child Care* by Benjamin Spock, M.D.

Bob de Graff was responsible for bringing in Dr. Spock, who was at the time a pediatrician of a friend of Bob's wife. Somebody said to the de Graffs, "We have this pediatrician, and he's written this book." De Graff said, "Well, gosh, we don't publish hardcover books." But after he read the book, he went to the publishing house Duell, Sloan and Pearce and said, "You do a hardcover edition, and we'll do the paperback." According to *The Guinness Book of World Records,* Dr. Spock outsold all other books in the nonfiction category, except the Holy Bible.

IN 1949, Bob de Graff was "moved up" to chairman of the board. This same year a Yale graduate named Lawrence Hughes came to work for Pocket Books. We got to know each other in later years when Larry was CEO of William Morrow & Company, and I was at Book-of-the-Month Club. More recently, we have become closer friends, perhaps because I always seemed to be pestering him for help with this book. And he has always come through for me. The truth is, Larry's whole publishing career has been filled with good deeds.

"I always wanted to get into something that had to do with the written word," he told me. "I wasn't sure what. I got out of Yale in January 1949 [he had served as a marine in World War II], and I was married. Somehow or other I got an interview with Mr. de

Graff, who I found out wanted to start a training program at Pocket Books." So Larry became one of the first trainees for Pocket Books; they started him in the mailroom.

"It was in such a horrible physical location," he said "and so dingy and terrible and everything else that people kept quitting all the time. Well, I didn't want to quit—I was a *trainee,* you know [Larry made it sound like a badge of honor]. So I ended up running the mailroom."

A crisis turned into opportunity for Larry between Christmas and New Year's, a time when wholesalers returned a lot of books. They were supposed to be sending them to the Pocket Books warehouse in Buffalo. But some of them were sending books back to New York. "And of course," Larry recalled, "they came to the mailroom, and we threw them into what used to be a coal bin down there. Finally, I said to the guys, 'Come on, we've got to clean up this mess and put some labels on these packages and send them up to Buffalo, where they can be counted and credited, and all the rest of it.'

"The deeper we got into the pile," he went on, "there was this terrible odor; I mean it was a smell like you've never smelled in your life. So we dig around in there, and we discover there's a package from a wholesaler in Kansas City who had sent our boss, Doc Lewis, a turkey for the holiday. That damn box had gotten in there and had been in there for probably a month and a half.

"And I'm thinking, 'Oh, gee whiz, what are we going to do?' I've never met Freeman Lewis because he's over in another building. But I have to tell him that he should write the wholesaler and thank him, and all that. I wrote him kind of a letter—it was a little smart-aleck. I remember it said something like, 'I know that not all the books we publish are great, but when I approached this box, I didn't know we had any one that smelled that bad.'

"The next thing I know he's asking, 'Who is this guy?' I figure I'm going to get fired for not finding the turkey sooner." Instead, when we meet, he says, 'Oh, no, no, no. I was very amused by your note. Tell me about yourself. What do you want to do?' I told him that my ambitions were editorial, so he says, 'Well, one thing we've got to do, we've got to get you out of that mailroom, get you doing other things.' And because of that smelly turkey, I was on my way."

Larry Hughes moved from the mailroom to the sales department, "pushing books in Far Rockaway," he said, "dressing up the racks and other stuff. I was one of the Stoop, Squint and Squat people."

In the early 1950s, Larry was finally moved to the editorial department, where he began to be a reader for Herb Alexander, a larger-than-life editor in chief in every way.

In his amusing book *Another Life,* Michael Korda described Alexander as "a big man with the build of a wrestler, broad shoulders, a massive chest and a full belly. He had a big head, too, crowned with a crew cut, and wore tinted aviator's goggles." There was of course more to the man. "Herb was modest and never showed his brilliance," Larry Hughes said, "but he was a brilliant person. He was extraordinarily well read and he had a photographic memory. The trouble was that the people at S & S thought the people at Pocket Books were a third-world country."

One of those upstairs denizens that Herb Alexander resisted was the boss of bosses, Leon Shimkin. He thought Shimkin was two-faced about things. Herb Alexander once told Larry Hughes, "I hope Leon is as good at doing his job as he thinks he is at doing mine." Herb Alexander was responsible for many of the best reprints Pocket Books bought, including *The Diary of Anne Frank* and *Profiles in Courage.* He was also responsible for the well-being of Simon & Schuster's biggest author of the period, Harold Robbins. In 1961, Alexander's troupe founded a new hardcover imprint, Trident Press, just for Robbins. By 1967, *The Carpetbaggers,* his first book for Trident, had sold 5.5 million copies. Other Robbins hits were *79 Park Avenue* (originally bought by Pat Knopf for his father's house, a purchase his father and mother never authorized), *Never Love a Stranger,* and *The Adventurers.*

Robert de Graff retired in 1952. Pocket Books was now in the hands of Shimkin, Doc Lewis, and Jimmy Jacobson, who handled administrative matters. "It was never really a cohesive team," Larry Hughes said, "because Lewis, a well-read and literary person, was on one side, and Leon and Jacobson were very much on the commercial side."

In 1959, Larry moved to William Morrow. The reason for the move, he explained, was the close relationship between Morrow and Pocket Books, thanks to Erle Stanley Gardner. In 1965, Larry, no longer smelling a rotted turkey, became president of Morrow and a part owner of the company.

AS THE YEARS went on, given the conflicting management strategies and strong competition growing from the established paperback houses, and some new ones, Pocket Books' profits declined. Change came in 1975. At the beginning of that year, Simon & Schuster was bought by Gulf + Western Industries, and handed over to the hard-driving Richard E. Snyder to run. (By this time, Leon Shimkin had been kicked upstairs.) In 1976, Snyder brought in Peter Mayer to overhaul Pocket Books. And that he did.

ONE OF Peter's great strengths was finding the right people for the job. Carole Baron, an enduring editor of the golden age, at home both with hardcover and paperback publishing, was at Pocket Books when Peter arrived. "The truth is," she told me, "I wanted to find out about paperbacks, so here comes Peter Mayer—Mr. Paperback. This cannot be a bad thing.

"Peter came in June of 1976, and then he kept going into the hospital—he had a severe lung problem—and I kept organizing everything. Then one day he called me [from] the hospital, and he said to me, 'How would you like to be executive editor?' I told him, 'I don't want to be executive editor. I make a decent salary, I get to tell people what to do, I get the overview (I always liked the overview).' He said, 'I'll give you executive editor and you'll run the department.' And my husband, Richard, said, 'You gotta do it.' So I finally said, 'All right.' " She says that Peter taught her a lot about negotiating contracts, about export royalties and advances, etc. "And he taught me how to support an author. A paperback house isn't just a reprinter."

The last thing Peter seems to have done at Pocket Books was to let Carole and her gang buy the paperback rights to a book about to be published by Dutton. Richard Marek, then the editor in chief of Dial Press, remembered going to the Bread Loaf Writers' Conference in Middlebury, Vermont. There he met a fellow named John Irving, who was on the Bread Loaf faculty. They became friends. Subsequently he was offered the chance to buy Irving's third novel, which was called *The World According to Garp*. The author wanted a $14,000 advance so he could repair his roof. His agent only had the first chapter to show people. Marek read the chapter and didn't like it. A week later Marek met Hal Scharlatt, an editor at Dutton. He told Dick that he had just bought *The World According to Garp* for $14,000. Marek said he winced when he heard that.

John Irving's first two novels had been reprinted by Peter Mayer at Avon. Marty Asher, working with Carole at the time, says that both of them wanted *Garp*. "We thought we'd discovered the best thing since sliced bread." (Marty Asher later helped BOMC nourish our new book club, QPB—Quality Paperback Books—and is now editor in chief of Vintage Books.)

But every other paperback house in town was after *Garp,* and Fawcett offered $100,000. "Peter had said no at a hundred," Carole told me, "and it was Friday afternoon. I went back to Dutton's subsidiary rights person, and I said, 'Listen, I can't get you any more money.' And he said, 'Well, if I give you the weekend, do you think you can come back to me?' He really seemed to prefer selling it to us. So I said, 'Fine, let me see if Peter is in a better mood. On Monday morning I pulled him out of a meeting, and I went on and on about how we had to have the book. He just laughed at me and said, 'Okay, bid one ten.' And the rest is history."

Pocket Books was rich with editorial talent and commercial success. In the short time that Peter Mayer was there it broke new ground in the publishing industry. Carole Baron was its editor in chief; Susan Peterson was its advertising director. Claire Ferraro was Peter's secretary. Mary Hall, who would soon become Peter's wife, was the publicity director. And Ann Patty was the editor who bought a book for $7,500 on the strength of a twenty-five-page proposal. The book was *Flowers in the Attic,* a gothic novel by V. C. Andrews that sold zillions of copies to the women of the world. Pocket Books was truly *The Women's Room* for these talented book publishing figures—all of them stars together, at that one time in Peter Mayer's galaxy.

And Pocket Books was reborn.

Dell

I liked many things about Helen Meyer. We would have "austerity drives" when things weren't so good in the company, and she would cut out all the taxi expenses. She always walked from the bus station to Third Avenue, where we lived. And I thought, This is a woman who asks no more of herself than anybody else.

—ROBERT WYATT

When Richard Baron was selling most of his publishing house, Dial Press, to Dell Publishing, he met for the first time its president, Helen Honig Meyer.

"I hear you're a playboy," Ms. Meyer said to Baron.

"I hear you're a bitch," he replied.

The truth was that, indeed, Richard Baron did like women, and Helen Meyer—the first female to become head of a book publishing house—did sometimes bare her teeth.

You've met Helen Meyer earlier, at a Dell sales conference, scaring the hell out of a young sales force fellow, Nat Sobel. Helen Meyer could do that. She had to be a force in a male-dominated industry where a lot of hard men were working for her. Men such as Don Fine, a bristly editor with a marine's haircut and an attitude of hostility toward everyone, but also the knack of finding the author that mattered; Edgar Doctorow, an editor at Dell Press who admitted to me that he was afraid of Mrs. Meyer; and Seymour Lawrence, who landed at Dell from Atlantic/Little, Brown with his own imprint given to him by "the Empress," as he always called Helen Meyer to her face.

The women I have talked with all seemed to have up-and-down feelings about the woman who more than anyone else opened up book publishing. Esther Margolis, who spent only one year at Dell as assistant to the sales director, recounted the time when people just disappeared: "I worked in sales next to the magazine promotion department. I came in on a Monday morning and that department was gone—I mean totally. Helen had a thing about getting rid of people on Friday afternoons, telling them not to come in on Monday. She went through a lot of purges." But as we talked, Esther kept telling me how important Meyer was in her life when she became a powerful woman at Bantam and later founded her own company, Newmarket Press.

My agent, Robin Straus, paints a slightly different picture of

Mrs. Meyer, noting that it was Helen who smoothed the way for her first job in publishing. "My father was in the advertising business," she told me, "and I said to him, 'Do you know anybody in publishing? Because I loved to read and thought, 'Gee, this would be a good way to spend the summer, possibly leading to some sort of career.' And he said, 'Well, there's this nice woman I commute with. Her name is Helen Meyer, and she's at Dell, or some place like that. Give her a call.'

"So I called this nice lady who said, 'Come in, I'd like to meet you.' And I met this woman who had incredibly smart eyes, and she said, 'You want a job in publishing?' I said yes. 'Okay,' she said, 'go talk to the personnel department, they may be able to help you.' And I was hired to split my weeks [it was the first summer job Robin had while in college] between Dial Press and Delacorte. It was really a very instructive, interesting summer because I got to see two different publishers doing essentially the same kind of work. By the end of the summer, I was able to understand quite clearly why one, Dial Press, was far superior to the other, in terms of what they were doing, and how they did it."

Robin's parents lived in New Jersey, as did Helen Meyer. "I was commuting back and forth, and occasionally I would sit next to her—this delightful older woman who was chatty and warm—and we'd talk about her grandchildren and what books we were reading.

"When I was working there, I'd heard stories about this Dragon Lady, who was so fearsome, and this did not jibe at all with the woman I got to know."

HENRY MORRISON, ONE of the hard-bitten agents of that time, found dealing with Helen Meyer the sweat of his life. He told me about the time he challenged her dead-on, when he asked her to give his prime client, Robert Ludlum, more money.

"It happened in the mid-seventies," Henry said. "She had just bought a new novel from Ira Levin, *The Boys from Brazil.* And she paid $800,000 for it. And Dick Marek, who was Ludlum's editor at Dial Press, said to me, 'She can damn well pay it for Ludlum.'

"I said, 'Fine, go talk to her.'

"Dick said, 'I can't, I'm the employee, you're the agent. You go talk to her.'

" 'I'm afraid of her,' I said.

"He said, 'So am I.'

"Ludlum was then getting $350,000 to $400,000 a book, hard and soft. I mean, we were looking for a jump. I called her up and invited her to lunch, and she said no. 'What's this about?' she asked.

" 'Well, I want to talk about the next Ludlum book.' And she said, 'I'm not paying you any more.' So I went up to see her. I told her what I wanted. And I explained why.

" 'No, you're wrong,' she said. 'Ira Levin is worth $800,000 because he's the author of *Rosemary's Baby,* and that sold four million, five million copies. And Ludlum isn't up to that.' Then she said something along the lines of 'Well, I think we're done here.' Whatever it was, I was dismissed.

"I leave her office and go to Dick Marek's office on another floor at Dial Press. I told him what had happened. He said he would have a talk with her. He came back with her report—that I was being supercilious, I was being greedy, I was being stupid, and Robert Ludlum deserved a better agent.

"A couple of days later, Helen and I were talking about something else, and Helen says, 'Would you take $700,000 for the book?' I, very stupidly, said no. And she says, 'Well, you're making a mistake, and you ought to find another publisher.' "

Henry knew that Bantam would be very interested in Ludlum, because he'd get calls from them about Ludlum every few months. "This time, I called and told them to come over to talk about Robert Ludlum. So Oscar Dystel and his colleagues began to hammer out a deal with me. They said, 'We don't want to just buy one book, we want to acquire the author.' I said that would be tricky because he's being published by Dial Press, and that's Helen Meyer. Oscar, I think, said, 'Let me worry about Helen. Just let's make a deal.' So we made a deal for either two or three books, whatever it was. I reported back to Dick: 'We got the money, eight hundred.'

"Dick and I were having lunch the next week, and I get to the restaurant, and Dick's already seated at the table and there's a piece of paper on my napkin on the plate. I figure it was a letter from Helen Meyer excommunicating me. I look down, and it's a check made out to Henry Morrison, Inc., for $540,000, and that was the biggest check I had seen to that moment. It was royalties from whatever Bob's previous book was.

"Later she told Dick, 'You tell Morrison that he should have taken the seven hundred thousand. He would have gotten the eight hundred on the next one.' And she was right. It was stupid in hindsight, but we were so bound and determined."

I sniffed a scent of male chauvinism. *Would it have happened, I wondered, if Morrison and Marek had been dealing with a man?*

When Dial's contracts with Ludlum expired, Henry Morrison moved Ludlum to Putnam's for the hardcover and Bantam to paperback.

For Helen Meyer, it was an unfortunate turn of events, but she shrugged her shoulders and went on doing what she had always done for the company that made her an empress.

GEORGE T. DELACORTE, JR., knew what he wanted from the beginning. He wanted to build a magazine empire for the country that would attract nonreaders. He founded his company in 1921, a time when increasing numbers of Americans were living on easy street—or at least moving closer—and were open to experiences that would make their lives even more joyful. Delacorte's pulp magazines provided pleasure enough for both old and new readers—*Inside Detective, Modern Screen, Modern Romances, Ballyhoo,* and the like. I know all about the craze because in the first phase of my life as a wage-earner, I was employed within the Bernarr Macfadden empire. Macfadden was on the same level as Delacorte, but he was much more exuberant. He was sort of the Charles Atlas of magazine publishing, with rippling muscles on both arms, like Popeye, the guru of physical culture, once walking five miles to his office in Manhattan while carrying a forty-pound bag of sand. In all of his magazines there was invariably a photograph of Macfadden, bare-chested, offering readers an arm muscle as knotted as the roots of a California redwood tree. People took him seriously. George Bernard Shaw once wrote an uplifting piece for Macfadden's *Physical Culture* magazine.

My job was with a mild-mannered magazine called *Sport,* but we were encircled by Macfadden magazines bursting with emotion such as *Photoplay, True Story, True Romance, True Detective,* and on and on. I remember once offering a laurel leaf to Al Govoni, the editor of *True Detective,* for the best cover line I'd ever read—*I Dismember Mama.* It didn't matter that he had written that line before he found someone to do the dismembering.

If Delacorte and Macfadden were competing with each other, the competition ended in the early 1930s after Delacorte brought back from Hollywood *Looney Tunes* and all the other Warner Brothers characters, thus becoming, according to the *Dictionary of Literary Biography,* "the world's leading publisher of comic books."

From the beginning, George Delacorte had a reputation as a frugal individual. One of his close associates, Carl "Bud" Tobey, put it this way: "George, when he shaved in the morning, lathered only one side of his face, and then took what shaving cream was left and lathered the other side." He found a person who would understand his ways when, in 1923, he hired a sixteen-year-old girl, Helen Honig, already bursting with frugality. He knew that she'd done well at a job handling complaints for a company that distributed magazines. He hired her for $20 a week. It was an extraordinary situation for a young woman to have convinced a tough businessman that she could be of help to him. No male chauvinism there.

One of my interviewees was an old friend and colleague, James O'Shea Wade, who knew both Helen Meyer and George Delacorte. When I first came to Book-of-the-Month Club, he was one of our most felicitous outside readers, particularly for nonfiction that had a military ring to it. Jim went on to a varied and storied career as an editor for various publishing houses. One was Dell, where he made a co-publishing arrangement with Dial and Dell—and made friends with both Delacorte and Meyer. He even told me how Helen had met her beloved husband, Abe.

"She was off on the road somewhere, and she was in this railroad car, and the car was almost empty. And a man came along and said to her, 'Is this seat taken?' It was not. He sat next to her and that was the beginning of a great romance and a wonderful marriage."

As for George Delacorte, Jim said, "At some early point George recognized, 'I have someone with terrific talent and energy here.'"

Indeed. By 1942, she was in charge of everything, including the birth of Dell's entry into the paperback world. It should be added that through her whole career working with George Delacorte, Helen Meyer never called her boss anything but Mr. Delacorte.

IN HIS TWO YEARS at Dell in the late sixties, Bob Wyatt was never quite as sure about Helen Meyer. "At five o'clock," he said,

"I was the only one there, and I knew it was an unhappy company. Helen did her best to make it a happy company, but she came from another generation of paperclip savers. The big deal at Thanksgiving and Christmas wasn't a bonus. People got a turkey. But I liked many things about her."

Richard Marek gave me a different sighting about Meyer: "She was totally brilliant. I can talk about Helen Meyer forever." I asked him where her brilliance came from. "She had a real commercial sense," he said, "of what would sell and what wouldn't." She chose to hire Marek to run Dial, when she found out that it was he who had made Ludlum's first novel publishable.

But Dick also saw the other side of Meyer. "She was very tough, very cruel to people who didn't stand up to her," he said. "But from the beginning, I felt . . . it's stupid to say . . . a sexual attraction to her. She was considerably older than I was, and, God knows, we never . . . you know. . . . I kissed her on the cheek once."

One of her troubles was that Meyer had all these client states around her: Delacorte Press, Dell Books, Dial Press, and, in 1965, Seymour Lawrence coming along with his fabulous imprint that included Kurt Vonnegut, Jr. She also supervised all kinds of different children's paperbacks. She had to govern them all with discipline. Henry Morrison once heard her hollering from her office as he was walking by, "No! No! NO!—a 73 percent sell-through is not acceptable." "You know," Henry said, without irony, "if you sell 51 percent of your run today, you're looking good."

Meyer knew how to drive a hard bargain all right; she understood how many books should be printed, and what exactly all the other departments—sales, marketing, and the like—were up to. But she never said, "Why don't we do this one? Why don't we do that one?" because she knew her limits. She did read books—she loved to read as a child—but she understood her one weakness, that she lacked the intuitiveness for discovering the undiscovered. Although she found the right people to do that brilliantly for her, they didn't have the clout to compete with the paperback houses being run by editorial discoverers such as Peter Mayer and Victor Weybright. So, as the years went on, the Dell paperback operation found itself sunk below the two great houses of the period: Bantam and New American Library.

IN APRIL OF 2007, I met Edgar Lawrence Doctorow at his new New York University office in Greenwich Village. Since 1982 he has occupied the Glucksman Chair in American Letters. Edgar (his father named him after Edgar Allan Poe) was dressed for the campus in a blue shirt and red sweater, and he had the furrowed forehead of an academic. His beard was a little grayer than I had remembered it when, in 1975, the Book-of-the-Month Club held a luncheon in his honor, celebrating the Club's choice of his novel *Ragtime* as a Main Selection. As we talked about his life as an editor, his voice sounded the same, too, a hum of low electric current, with pauses to find the right word, and sly smiles along the way as he thought about his kinship with mass-market paperback books.

"When I was seven or eight years old, I fell seriously ill with a burst appendix. Peritonitis set in. The doctors told my parents that I had only a fifty-fifty chance. What ended up saving me was the first wonder drug, Sulfanilamide; before that, people who had peritonitis usually died.

"When I was in the hospital, my father brought me a new kind of book that could fit into your pocket—an idea that the Americans had stolen from the Europeans: *pocket books.* I remember this being placed on my bedside table by my worried parents almost as amulets to see me through my illness. There were five of them from Pocket Books' first list, twenty-five cents each. I still have them: *Wuthering Heights, Bambi,* Frank Buck's *Bring 'Em Back Alive, Lost Horizon,* and *Topper* by Thorne Smith. Wasn't it interesting," he said with a touch of applied irony, "that I grew up and somehow gravitated to mass market publishing?"

Edgar spent ten years as an editor, his first five at New American Library. He might have stayed there longer if NAL had remained what it was—a dominant independent house. But it had been sold to the Times-Mirror Company, and before you knew it, outside consultants were coming around, picking through the wastebaskets for NAL misdoings. "It had been a great place to work," he told me, "but I knew I'd have to leave." It was Richard Baron who hired Doctorow to be his editor in chief at Dial Press, and later, when Baron gave over his company to Dell, Doctorow also became Dial's publisher.

"Mailer was there, Jimmy Baldwin was there. Tom Berger was there," Ed said. "But things were not going well. What I had to do was find some way to sort of kick-start everything. And we came up with some good stuff."

One of them was a manuscript by an unknown writer that had been gathering dust. "I read it," Edgar said, "and it was an intense detective story by Roderick Thorpe. I bought it and called it *The Detective.*" And we sold it to Peter Mayer, who was then at Avon, for about $250,000."

Edgar was joined by some fine editors. Christopher Lehmann-Haupt, who later became the lead book reviewer for *The New York Times,* Don Hutter, Bill Decker, and Joyce Johnson, who had connections to the downtown radical bohemian community and who brought to Dial Abbie Hoffman's first book, *Revolution for the Hell of It.* Edgar published William Kennedy's first novel, *The Ink Truck;* he published Ernest J. Gaines, who wrote *The Autobiography of Miss Jane Pittman;* and he prevailed on Jules Feiffer to write the introduction for a luxurious four-color reproduction of the original comic strips of Superman and Batman. This was the first serious hardcover recognition of these graphic sagas, and it became a bestseller.

"The great fun" for Edgar was dealing with James Baldwin and Norman Mailer. "Richard [Baron] and I would make a lunch date with Jimmy, and he'd come in at eleven o'clock in the morning and chat with everyone in sight. Then we'd go to lunch and that would take three hours, and he'd come back with us, say three or three-thirty and hang around, and then we'd all go out for a drink at five that went on into the late hours and that would turn into dinner. Or he'd go off to live in Europe for a while, and I'd send him his galleys, and I'd say, 'We need these back at such and such a date.' And then we wouldn't hear from him. He was basically saying, 'It's all yours. I don't want to look at it again.' "

Norman Mailer was a lot easier to deal with. "You know, he had this reputation, and as a young editor, I thought, how am I going to deal with this guy? But he turned out to be an absolute pro—thoughtful, considerate; he listened."

It wasn't all that easy for Doctorow because Dial had to compete with Don Fine's Delacorte Press, also owned by Dell—two hardcover houses butting heads. A battle ensued when Dial started bidding against Delacorte for James Jones's next three novels. Doctorow remembers Helen Meyer saying to him, 'Look, you're betting against me with our own money. This is impossible. What do I have to give you to get lost?' Well, by that time I'd reassessed Jones. I began to get the feeling that the books he wanted to do were really not his métier. I decided the deal was too much money and very risky. I got some budgetary concessions by pretending to withdraw gracefully."

When Richard Baron left, Edgar became publisher. "Suddenly it was a matter of how many carloads of paper should I order," he said, "and the personnel problems." He had also been working hard on his new novel, *The Book of Daniel*. He requested a three-month leave so that he could devote more time to it. "People who take leaves usually don't come back," Helen Meyer said to Edgar. "So I'm going to pay you three quarters of your salary while you're on leave, just to keep you." He thought that was extremely generous of Meyer, and he told her so. But at the end of the three months he asked her for another extension. "She was getting a little upset with me at that point," Edgar said, "and she said, 'You must promise that you're coming back.' And I said, 'Of course.' And then six weeks later I resigned. I was so desperately in love with my book and obsessed with it, that it was the only thing I could do."

Edgar had told an agent, Don Congdon, that he was planning to resign. Don had a writer, Oakley Hall, who was at the University of California, Irvine. Hall invited Doctorow to take up a residency there. Ed claims that he and his wife, Helen, consulted the *I Ching*. It said, "You will cross a great water." Helen said, "That's the Mississippi. Let's go." So they piled their three children in the car, packed up, and left. And, out in California, Doctorow finished the much-admired *Book of Daniel*.

GEORGE DELACORTE and Helen Meyer had built a great publishing house for the time, and its paperback operation was a success, though not quite able to meet the standards set by Bantam and New American Library. They ended up doing what their competitors did: In 1976 they sold the company to Doubleday for $35 million. That gave the giant publisher the one thing it had lacked—a mass market paperback business.

Jim Wade was around at that time. "I vividly remember the day," he told me, "because I was going down the elevator and George Delacorte was standing next to me. I had a date with an agent, and George said to me, 'Walk with me a while.' Well, it's George Delacorte, for God's sake! So we walked together quite a way, talking about the sale, and why it had been done. And before he left me he turned to me and said, 'Do you want to know why I've never retired?' As I remember it, he had already celebrated his eightieth birthday. I said, 'Sure George.'

" 'Because I would have died!' "

George T. Delacorte, Jr., stayed with us into his ninety-seventh year. He died in 1991.

Helen Meyer stayed on as president until 1979. She died in 2003 at age ninety-five. The company, of course, then became something else.

14

NEW AMERICAN LIBRARY, BANTAM, FAWCETT

New American Library

> Victor was kind of overwhelming, really. I was very
> impressed because he just had a certain special quality about
> him, a kind of inventiveness. No one else was reaching out
> in the directions he was going.
>
> —MARC JAFFE

Victor Weybright was born and raised on a working farm in Maryland, the seventh generation of Weybrights, wanting nothing out of life, because he had it all. A do-or-die Anglophile, he spoke with a perfect British accent. The three young acolytes who worked for him at New American Library—Truman Talley, Marc Jaffe, and E. L. Doctorow—bowed to his editorial gifts, his absolute touch for finding the right book at the right time.

For instance, the right book at the outset of Weybright's career with New American Library was *I, the Jury* by Mickey Spillane. When NAL had had its fill of Spillane through five huge bestsellers and seemingly billions of copies, Weybright sought relief, and variety, by turning to such literary works as *Doctor Zhivago,*

The Naked and the Dead, Ralph Ellison's *Invisible Man,* and any-thing written by William Faulkner. The first son, you might say, was his stepson-in-waiting: Truman Macdonald Talley. (I should disclose here once more that "Mac" Talley is the editor for this book.) Mac Talley was also a child of privilege. He was born and raised in New York City, went to its best schools, and when asked which boarding school he would like to attend, he said Deerfield Academy, because he liked the name. He was accepted without undergoing an interview.

I got to know Mac in the years when he and I were working at the Viking/Penguin empire run by Peter Mayer. I discovered that Truman Talley had never lost the innocence of his youth. When he was thrown into the Battle of the Bulge—Germany breaking through American lines in its last-ditch effort to turn the war around—Mac was in the midst of the fighting. He wasn't wounded, but when a medic came by and asked how he was do-ing, Mac replied as would a character out of Trollope: "Well, my feet are numb now, but I used to fish a lot in the Deerfield River in the early spring, and I let my feet get numb. It was no problem."

"Christ," said the medic, "let me see one of your feet. Where is it numb?"

Mac pointed to several toes. The medic took one look, recog-nized frostbite, and said, "You're headed back." He had saved Talley from the loss of his toes, and possibly even a foot.

Talley's father died in 1942; he was fifty-one years old and had enjoyed a supreme career running Fox's *Movietone News.* His biggest coup came in 1937 at a time when German dirigibles were flying back and forth from Germany to the U.S. Each diri-gible was filled with hydrogen, a flammable fuel. "My father was worried about that," Mac told me, "and proceeded to have a cam-eraman stationed at every landing place in northern New Jersey." There was only one cameraman present that day in 1937 at the Lakehurst, New Jersey, Naval Air Station when the *Hindenburg* burst into flames. *Movietone* got the exclusive, which meant that every newspaper and every magazine that wanted to run pictures of the disaster had to buy the rights from Mac's father.

In 1947, Mac Talley was back at Princeton and the editor of the humor magazine, *The Princeton Tiger.* He invited Victor Weybright, who was seeing Mac's mother, to speak at a spring semester dinner. "He gave a very amusing talk," Mac said, "at the end of which he said the magic words, music to any undergraduate's ears—'If any of you are interested in the publishing business, come see me.' " Mac was the first Princeton grad to see Victor.

In August 1949, Mac was invited by Weybright to work side by side with him. In January 1950, Mac's regal boss married his mother, Helen, and so now the good-hearted Truman Talley was serving his stepfather.

WHEN LAST WE saw Ian Ballantine, he had left Penguin Books, and Victor Weybright and Kurt Enoch (see chapter 13) were now in charge of Penguin in America, handling the books that Allen Lane sent them. Enoch was a German refugee from Hitler and a former head of Tauchnitz, a German paperback company. So he had a very good idea of how paperbacks worked. Weybright and Lane had met during the war; Victor was stationed at the American embassy in London, in charge of American lend-lease arrangements with England. "In London I had been a friend and admirer of Allen Lane," Weybright wrote in his somewhat pompous but fascinating memoir, *The Making of a Publisher.* "We were the same age with a genuine interest in publishing, art, public affairs, gardening and farming." But Weybright and Enoch were frustrated trying to sell such titles from Lane as *Edible Fungi* and *Wildflowers on the Chalk.* In 1947, Weybright and Enoch parted with Penguin and immediately formed a new paperbound company that would be called New American Library. Weybright and Enoch each got 42½ percent from Penguin. In addition,

THE TIME OF THEIR LIVES

the printer W. F. Hall kicked in $700,000. "It was the best invest-
ment in support of a publisher that any printer had ever, to my
knowledge, made," Victor said. "Within three years, despite the
constant need for working capital, we were on a fully current basis." NAL soon began publishing its Signet imprint for fiction and
Mentor Books for nonfiction, especially the classics.

MARC JAFFE'S EARLY LIFE was not as privileged as Truman Talley's, but it was similar in some ways. He was born and raised in
Philadelphia. His father was a doctor, "one of those good old
general practitioners who got two dollars a house call," according
to his son. Like Talley, Jaffe went to a very good private school,
and then went on to Harvard. He graduated in June 1942 and
hoped he could become a combat correspondent. The major he
talked with said, "Mr. Jaffe, we have a lot of combat correspondents, but we do need infantry officers." So Marc joined the
Marines and was assigned to the First Marine Division, Second
Battalion. Not long after he landed on Peleliu.
    The battle of Peleliu, one of the fiercest in the Pacific for the
United States, found Second Lieutenant Jaffe as a forward observer, so he went in with the first wave of marines—"riflemen
and machine gunners," he said, "and all the rest for about five or
six days. Our unit suffered more casualties in that campaign than
any other single unit in the Pacific North." He then fought at Oki-
nawa. Marc told me, "I always said to myself when I got back—
'I got through this. I can get through anything.'"
    After the war, still looking for a life in journalism, Marc came to
New York and found a job with *Argosy* magazine. But he wanted
more. Someone sent him to see literary agent Armitage Watkins of
the Watkins agency. While he was there, Armitage called Victor
Weybright: "There's a young man here I think you might want to
see, because he's had this experience working on a men's magazine, and he went to Harvard." Weybright agreed to see Jaffe.

"He gave me a test. He asked me to give him a report on a book they were considering, *Tales of the South Pacific,* by an unknown author, James Michener. I wrote the report—this was the spring of 1948—and I went off to Cape Cod for a little rest and recreation. I got a letter there saying, 'You're hired. Come in and go to work at $55 a week.' " (Hah, when I got my first job at *Sport* magazine three years later, I was also hired on for $55 a week.)

Jaffe learned a lot about what would be his life's work from his decade at NAL, especially having worked for Victor Weybright, this one-in-a-million unquenchable individual.

E. L. DOCTOROW attended Kenyon College and graduated in 1952. He was drafted into the army in 1953. When he came back, he married Helen Setzer, and he became a reader for Columbia Pictures' New York office. "I was reading a screenplay or book a day," he told me, "and writing synopses and making judgments as to whether there was possible movie potential. As a matter of fact, that's how I came to write my first novel, *Welcome to Hard Times.* Westerns were popular then, and I was reading so many terrible westerns that I decided I could lie about the West better than the people I was reading."

One day, Doctorow's boss at Columbia, Albert Johnston, came to him. "There's a book we've got to get our hands on," he told Doctorow. "I can't get it from the publisher, but my friend, Victor Weybright at New American Library, has a set of galleys. He said we could look at it but not take it out of the house. So I want you to go over and sit at NAL and read those galleys." It was a novel by Glendon Swarthout called *They Came to Cordura.* Columbia ended up producing the film, starring Gary Cooper and Rita Hayworth.

"I finished in a couple of hours," Edgar said, "and I went in and talked to Victor Weybright, told him what I thought of the book (not much), but that it could probably be a film. Six months later he called up and offered me a job at NAL." Doctorow went to work for Victor in 1959.

"Victor liked a certain kind of diversity in his editorial staff," Edgar said with a low-key chuckle. "I was lucky. Marc Jaffe had left NAL to go to Bantam, so what Weybright called 'the Jewish seat' was available. And I qualified in that regard. I started out as an associate editor, writing flap and promo copy and seeing reprints through production. Months later I became a senior editor, and I was there for five years." It was an excellent five years for his later he executive duties with Dell.

WHEN MARC JAFFE started at NAL, he was one of three editors. The others were Donald Demarest and Arabel Porter. Weybright took to Demarest, as he wrote in his memoir, because "he was a scholar with incredibly fine taste reinforced by a British education." As for Arabel Porter, a graduate of Swarthmore, she remained closely attached to Quaker ideals, and it showed in her literary attainments.

"She was a very warm person," Marc Jaffe told me, "very sensitive to the words on the page. That's really what she was all about."

When Weybright in 1952 agreed to start a literary journal, *New World Writing,* it was Porter he turned to as his "presiding genius" for the magazine. And genius she was—she turned *New World Writing* into a splendid, widely quoted literary journal. Arabel Porter's work with *New World Writing* over the seven years of its life at NAL was much like that of Barbara Epstein, who cofounded *The New York Review of Books* in the following decade. Weybright wrote about Porter in his memoir: "Her exemplary spirit reflected our inner grace more perfectly than any of my own conduct or rhetoric." (Note the perfection of this sentence: a solicitous bow to his editor, a slight demeaning of his own "conduct," topped by an ode to joy for *his* company's standard of grace.)

In his term with NAL, Marc couldn't get over how this one-man gang worked. "Victor was ruddy, very large, and just had a special quality about him. I remember him coming into the office back from weekends. You'd see twenty books that he'd gone through. And we would sit around gaga.

"Victor had a gut feeling as an editor that was unparalleled. Others were probably as sensitive to what the audience liked, but I can't think of anybody who was more sensitive. He also had this sense of discovery, often in categories," Marc mused. "I bet he said to himself, 'Alberto Moravia, *The Woman of Rome.* The time is ripe.' And we published all the rest of the Moravias, and about a half dozen other Italian writers." Marc may be correct about Weybright's courtship of the Italians, but I find it hard to think of this as a Weybright revelation. The original idea belonged to Roger Straus and his wife, Dorothea, who discovered and began publishing Italian writers in hardcover for Farrar, Straus.

"One of Weybright's keenest and most original intuitions," Marc went on, "was the decision to publish African-American writers. He felt that they had a place in mass-market publishing, and we published a lot of them—Richard Wright, William Gardner Smith, Chester Himes, Willard Motley (*Knock on Any Door* was a big hit), and, of course, Ralph Ellison."

Weybright also had a sixth sense, as he'd had with African-American writers, about trying to corner the market on the great new writers of war. He bought Norman Mailer's *The Naked and the Dead* and Irwin Shaw's *The Young Lions.* And one day in 1951 he received galleys from Scribners of a long first novel by one James Jones called *From Here to Eternity.* Since he slept only four hours most nights, Victor stayed up and read it all. The next morning he told his editors—"This is a must-have book." He paid Scribners an advance of $101,000 for *From Here to Eternity,* becoming the first mass-market publisher to cross the six-figure line. He justified the payment by making the book a seventy-five-cent "Signet Triple," that is, the equivalent of a three-volume novel.

He'd done that originally with Ayn Rand's *The Fountainhead,* and it had worked.

These acquisitions were basically made during the working day, but one weekend in 1952, Victor Weybright did something he had never done before—he interrupted a publisher's weekend to gain the rights to a book he desperately wanted.

He had received an advance copy of J. D. Salinger's *Catcher in the Rye,* which was about to be published by Little, Brown. "I read it that evening," he reported in his memoir, "and went into a cold sweat lest the reprint rights should be seized by a competitor if I waited until Monday morning. I tracked down Arthur Thornhill on the telephone, made a deal, and discovered later that we had beaten the field, most of whom did not receive the advance copies until the Monday or Tuesday following. Although *The Catcher in the Rye* was not enormously successful in hardcover, we managed to sell millions of copies." Later developments in the Salinger story, however, were not happy for NAL.

MARC JAFFE HAD begun his NAL duties as the mystery and western editor, which he enjoyed. "I had had some preparation," he said. "As a kid I was a great pulp magazine reader. Oh, I loved that western pulp and the mystery pulp. My uncle was the super reader, and he brought them all into the house." But soon he was handling J. D. Salinger, who was desperately unhappy about the NAL cover for his book.

"I met Salinger," Marc said, "because at the time I was sort of the editorial liaison for the covers. I didn't design them, of course, but I sat in on every art meeting." Kurt Enoch was then responsible for covers. He assigned James Avati, a first-rate illustrator, to do the *Catcher in the Rye* cover. It showed Holden Caulfield, wearing his red hunting hat turned backward, walking on a busy Manhattan street with dubious women on the side. The blurb read: "This unusual book may shock you, will make you

laugh and may break your heart—but you will never forget it."
The cover, Marc Jaffe said, broke Salinger's heart. "He told me,
'This is not my book, and if it were up to me, I would have my
books mimeographed and distributed in that form.' We had a
conversation. I told him about the need to attract the general
marketplace—that you had to have a picture on the cover, you
had to have copy. He would have none of it."

The cover went out as NAL wanted it. Five years later, when
NAL's license ran out, Salinger took the rights back.

Marc Jaffe soon had other things to do. He became intimately involved with Mentor, NAL's highbrow imprint. The idea originated
with Weybright, Marc said. "He wanted to create a series of philosophy writers." There were those who felt that while Jason Epstein
was claiming his Anchor Books to be the first imprint of its kind, it
was Mentor Books that had come first. With a little smile on his
face, Marc said, "Jason Epstein spent quite a long time with Arabel
and me talking about his ideas. Well, the kinds of books he was
planning to publish—anthropology, physics for the general reader,
philosophy, sociology, new translations of literature—were pre-
cisely the kinds of books that Mentor had already been publishing."
Marc spoke about a number of original projects he had originated
and licensed for Mentor. One, *Great Dialogues of Plato,* is still in
print. Mentor became a proud imprint in the paperbound world.

IT WAS ALL different for Truman "Mac" Talley when he came to
work at NAL: It was his first job, after all, and he felt that he
didn't know anything about book publishing. He had the further
burden of working for his stepfather. I asked Mac to describe
Weybright: "He was not a big man. He was portly." Mac grinned.
"He loved port, and that, I think, makes you portly. And he was
always very demanding of himself."

About his own beginning at NAL in August 1949, Mac told
me, "For the first five years I'm sure I was of no possible value,

monetary or otherwise, to New American Library." But Victor Weybright was patient with him. "After several years of apprenticeship and tutelage," Weybright wrote in his memoir, "Truman Talley developed into a rapid and perceptive reader and a superb negotiator for publication rights." In 1958, Mac was promoted to editorial vice president and made what may have been his most significant contribution to his stepfather's house.

That year, NAL published a fifth novel by an author whose works, published elsewhere, had not even earned out their small advances. "We bought this fifth Ian Fleming book from Macmillan for not much more than $8,000 in desultory bidding," Mac told me. The book was titled *From Russia with Love*. Mac read it and liked it so much that he began to read the author's early books.

"The first four James Bond books in hardcover and paperbound were flops," Mac said. "Two of them were done originally for Pocket Books, and two were done by Popular Library. Victor wasn't caught up by Fleming, even though he let me buy the novel. But I was. I was walking down the corridor one day and a little bulb went off in my head. And right away I went to talk with my boss. I said to him, 'Victor, I want to buy the paperbound rights from Macmillan to the first four books. I think I can get them for $1,000, which would be found money for Macmillan.' He said okay, and we got the first four for a total of $5,000."

"No more than two months go by and Tom Guinzburg calls me from Viking. 'Mac,' he said to me, 'I understand you have been buying the paperback rights to the early books of James Bond. How would you like to buy the next three?'

"I said, 'Tell me more.'

"He said, 'They're not written yet, but one of them is to be named *Thunderball* and one of them is to be named *Goldfinger,* and the third one I don't think Ian Fleming knows yet what it will be. Viking paid $25,000 pooled for the three. If you would pay us $25,000 pooled for reprint rights, we have a deal.'

"So I go to Victor, and Victor likes the idea right away. But Kurt Enoch was a stumbling block. He thought $25,000 was too much to pay a failed writer. So Kurt demurred. Then I think he subsequently talked with Jack Adams, his sales vice president, and found that he was enthusiastic. So I was able to go back to Tom Guinzburg, and say, 'You've got a deal.'"

Between 1957 and 1964, NAL's popular fiction imprint, Signet, sold millions of Bond books. Mac Talley was quoted in *Two-Bit Culture* as saying that over a four-year stretch Fleming's ultimately twelve books accounted for one-third of the house's revenues. Here's what Victor had to say in his book about Talley's triumph. "I had taken the plunge on Ian Fleming." The truth: Victor was plunged into the Fleming sea by his stepson.

ONE OF E. L. DOCTOROW'S first assignments at NAL was to serve as the house editor for Ian Fleming. "I didn't have much respect for his books," Edgar said. "I thought they were slyly racist and sexist. I expected not to like Fleming, but I liked him immensely. A modest man, actually, with a fine sense of humor. I had by then published my first novel, and he was very gracious. 'You must continue to write,' he said to me."

Edgar also handled Ayn Rand's books. "These were books that had gone through printing after printing, so it was just a matter of figuring out how to refresh the package. But I didn't like the books. I thought they were execrable, and I didn't like her. She asked me what I thought about the books. So I told her selfishness and self-interest hardly needed proselytizing. She suggested that of course I was naïve. She was a hideous woman."

But he enjoyed the work he was doing at NAL even when Victor Weybright gave him what he thought was an odd assignment. "I want to start a science line," Victor told him, "and I'm going to make you the science editor." Doctorow asked him why. And he said, "Well, you went to the Bronx High School of Science, didn't you? Everyone knows you get a better education there than you do at MIT." So Doctorow became the science editor. But he also became the house editor for the Signet Shakespeare Classics, and worked with old and new NAL novelists. "We were doing a lot of first-rate stuff then," he said, "like Faulkner and Pasternak and Ellison. It was a great thing to send out these titles by the tens of thousands and sell them for pocket change." We certainly lived up to our motto of 'Good Reading for the Masses.'"

Doctorow outdid himself in 1960 when he pulled off a coup for NAL. As soon as Adolf Eichmann was captured, he got hold of Henry A. Zeiger to write an instant book about how it happened. The book came out one month after Eichmann's arrest. It sold 500,000 copies.

ONE OF THE THINGS I wanted to ask Doctorow was what I had asked Toni Morrison: Had being an editor helped him in his writing? "I think it did," he said. "At NAL we went through the trade lists; we got everything from the major houses. And," he said with a smile, "it was very encouraging to see how many bad books were being published. The fact that something was printed did not mean it was coming down from heaven. At Dial I did some heavy editing, and I think knowing how books were put together and applying that knowledge taught me to be as objective an editor of my own books as I was of others."

So the editors had their good times at New American Library, but now it was the 1960s and different currents were stirring in the country. The publishing world felt the impact of those currents, particularly sweeping over the mass-market lines.

SIMPLY PUT, IT all began in 1960 with the first corporate takeover of a mass-market publisher: The Times-Mirror Company bought New American Library.

In 1959, NAL had sold thirty-three million books with record-breaking sales. But NAL was no longer a powerhouse of its own. Victor Weybright still had the knack for finding books, but he and Kurt didn't have enough capital to buy them all. Also bothering both Weybright and Enoch was the concern over their estates. Enoch would soon be in his seventies, and Weybright wasn't much younger. It was Victor who suggested to Enoch that they make a token overture to the Times-Mirror Company, a company both men liked. Victor especially felt at home with the Chandlers, who owned the company. He called Norman Chandler, the head of the family, a "duke." So the token overture became a full-scale merger. In 1960, Times-Mirror took over all of NAL's stock, and, in return, Enoch and Weybright received generous shares of Times-Mirror stock. But the next few years were tough on the partners.

Marc Jaffe was the first to leave the company. He might have stayed, but he kept saying to himself, " 'I want more responsibility. I want to have something I can call my own.' And Victor," Marc said, "wasn't quite ready to give up that body of responsibility, neither fiction nor nonfiction." Jaffe went to Dell for a year and a half, then moved to Bantam, where he came into his own.

E. L. Doctorow was a bracing replacement for Jaffe and enjoyed the job until the Times-Mirror consultants began coming around. "They were bringing in the McKinsey people to look us over," Edgar said, referring to the management consultants, "and I said, 'I gotta get out of here,' even though it had been a great place to work." Arabel Porter was upset, too, by the intrusion of "foreign" elements in their life. Victor offered a rather feeble excuse to her: "We can't stay in the horse-and-buggy days forever, Arabel." In 1964, Doctorow moved to Dial Press. Shortly thereafter, Arabel joined Houghton Mifflin. Of course, Weybright and Enoch had board membership in the Times-Mirror Company, but in the early sixties, both were replaced as heads of the house.

I think Mac Talley must have felt the change the most. Before Times-Mirror took over, Mac had been on what seemed like a fast track to succeed his stepfather. He was doing what he had been so good at doing—finding, like his stepfather, books in paperbound that would have otherwise been neglected. Back in 1958, Mac was sent by Viking the manuscript of Jack Kerouac's *On the Road.* "I read it overnight, and I felt that the novel really caught the feeling and the mood of these restless, young types of a certain time who are rushing hither and yon to what they did not know."

Viking's rights director, Keith Jennison, was in a hurry for Mac to buy the book. "He told me, quite frankly," Mac said, " 'We have a sales meeting coming up, and to give it some talking points I want to be able to tell the salesmen that we have sold this book to New American Library for paperback.' Jennison said further, 'All I really would like to have for an advance is $4,000.' " Mac immediately got Victor's approval. "Viking's hardcover sale," Mac said, "was 22,000. We sold a million copies within the first paperbound year."

Mac Talley batted .500 in his last two years at NAL, chasing after two novels he thought would be perfect for his stepfather's house—quality fiction attached to a great story. The first one was a manuscript by a nearly unknown writer who called himself John le Carré. Mac was taken not only by the plot, but by the clarity of le Carré's prose. He thought of a way he might be able to buy *The Spy Who Came In from the Cold,* which would be published in 1963. Jack Geoghegan, the president of Coward-McCann, had bought the novel from le Carré's British publisher. Le Carré had written two previous mystery stories—*Call for the Dead* (1961) and *A Murder of Quality* (1962)—which no one had bought. Talley told his colleague Ed Burlingame (who had joined NAL in 1968 and later went on to have a brilliant career at Lippincott and Harper's), "You read these right away, and if you like them, we'll buy them for little or no money from whoever else did them. Then I can go to Geoghegan and say, 'Hey, we're about to do these two mysteries by le Carré, and shouldn't we have first crack at *The Spy Who Came In from the Cold*?'

"So we did sign up the two earlier ones and got them in the works, and Jack Geoghegan called me and said, 'I hear you. If you will offer $30,000 for the paperback rights, the *Spy* is yours.' And I thought, *Wow, I've got it*. And I went to Victor and to Kurt for their okays. And both of them said, 'Oh, spy novels. There haven't been any good spy novels since the time of World War I.'"

Talley lost the book (it was bought by Dell), and it became the No. 1 hardcover fiction bestseller in 1964. "At that point," Mac said, "Kurt Enoch asked to see me. He was sitting in his office looking at the *Times* bestseller list. 'This book of yours,' he said, 'seems to be right at the top of the bestseller list. A very smart idea of yours.'" He had completely forgotten that he'd declined *Spy*. Talley had to tell him, "We don't have the book. You and Victor both said no."

His last shot for NAL came just before he left the company in late 1964, with Mary McCarthy's *The Group*. Let Mac tell the story.

"From Harcourt Brace, I was sent the galleys of *The Group*. The sub rights director said to me, 'If you will pay $150,000, NAL will have this book.'

"I loved it. I went around, wrote memos and all the rest of it, and said, 'Kurt, Victor, this is McCarthy's breakthrough. It's the book that everybody's going to read, because it's about six Vassar girls and their problems with men, etc.' Victor was all for it, but Kurt said, 'Well, $150,000—that's a lot of money.' And I said, 'This is as close to becoming a sure bestseller as I'm aware of.'

"Kurt was unimpressed, but he talked to Jack Adams, NAL's sales vice president. I don't think Jack knew Mary McCarthy's name from beans, but he liked its possibilities for being a leader.

And there was this hole in our schedule a year and one or two months down the line. So Kurt came back and said, 'See if you can get it for $150,000.'

"So I called up the rights person, who said, 'I'm sorry but you didn't respond in the last couple of days. It's now up to $200,000.' I went back and told them, 'You've delayed me. They've raised the ante. Happily they said yes. *The Group,* of course, became a top bestseller and later a top movie."

Eventually Mac couldn't stay with the company anymore. Monday morning he went into Victor's office and said, "Victor, I'm sorry, but I'm going to start looking elsewhere."

Later on, Victor and Mac connected again, starting a small hardcover house called Weybright & Talley. But it didn't last, and Mac—the happy memories of the fifteen years he had spent with a great paperbound house still with him—went his own way; he became a successful finder of important books for various houses under his own imprint. And here he is, still editing those books, always doing the best he can to make a writer's work and a writer's world as good as it can be.

VICTOR WEYBRIGHT'S custom was to wake at 4:00 every morning, find the pot of hot coffee beside his chair, and read for the next four hours. He would then go to the office, which was still empty, and prepare for the day.

At the end of the day he and his wife in the evening would, as a *Newsweek* magazine article described, "collect at his apartment best-selling novelists, visiting English editors, Greek translators, advance-guard poets, reviewers, publishers, and agents." It seemed like an around-the-clock ordeal for this odd and brilliant and difficult and audacious human being, but it wasn't an ordeal for him at all. Not ever.

The only thing that troubled him at the end was what he called "the everyday dehumanization of life." Victor Weybright had the misfortune of living long enough to face the computer. "At this point when the computer goes haywire," he writes solemnly, "the publisher must step in to atone for the failure of the machine. In a way," he adds, "this is my outlook on life."

What else would you expect from one who, from the beginning, took his pleasure by continuously performing as the plowboy, the person who drove the harrow.

INTERLUDE:

THE GOTHIC ROMANCE

In 1962 a young Jerry Gross edited *Editors on Editing: What Writers Need to Know About What Editors Do,* an anthology of essays on the art and craft of editing. Revised three times, the book is still in print. His first job in publishing was in 1953 as a first reader for Henry Simon at Simon & Schuster. Soon afterward he entered mass market paperback publishing, first at Ace Books, then at Paperback Library, Warner Books, and New American Library. Years at hardcover houses followed. Since 1987 he has been a fiction and nonfiction freelance editor and book doctor, working with agented and unagented writers and speaking at writers' conferences around the country. Jerry has always enjoyed editing popular fiction and nonfiction, but let him tell you how he created a category for the paperback public that still entertains readers wherever books are sold.

JERRY GROSS

One weekend in 1959 my wife and I went to my parents' home for Sunday dinner. Hanging up my jacket in their bedroom, I noticed a battered, dog-eared hardcover edition of Daphne du Maurier's *Rebecca*, published in 1938. "Mom," I said, "I can't believe you're still reading *Rebecca*. You must know every line by heart by now."

"Honey," she answered, "they don't write like that anymore."

Those words gave me an idea for a new category of popular fiction: the gothic romance. I went to work every morning at Ace for the next three months as usual but got permission from Ace's publisher, A. A. Wyn, to develop my idea in the third-floor reading room of the Forty-second Street public library. There was a reference book there entitled *Book Review Digest* that contained excerpts of book reviews organized by year and by genre, and in it they had the good old three-line abstracts of book reviews organized by genre: historical novels, westerns, mysteries, etc. One of the genres was gothic romances, but they were all in hardcover. Not one of them was a paperback. I put a thick pile of 3×5 index cards and a dozen #2 pencils on the desk and decided to write down the titles of the more interesting, best-reviewed titles.

During the next few weeks I read many of these gothic romances, beginning with the year 1938—the year *Rebecca* was published—and bought the paperback rights to many of them. I soon realized that they all followed a formula as consistent and as clear as a recipe for Betty Crocker chocolate cake. I isolated the elements and wrote a report describing them to our art director at Ace and said to him: "We're going to create a new category of books, and I need you to translate the components of the category into visual terms. I want a category format that my mother and aunts will be proud to be seen reading." (They wouldn't read most popular paperback fiction because the covers were so lurid, they were embarrassed to buy them.)

"Make the heroine look like a very refined upper-class blond young woman, with good cheekbones. Give her no more than the barest hint of cleavage. She's running toward you, a terrified look on her face. Behind her is a dark castle with one light in the window, usually in a tower. Make the tower tall and thick. Believe me, they'll get the phallic imagery." (And they did!) "Behind her is a dark night, lit only by a moon half in shadow or by a jagged burst of lightning. The woman is obviously in danger and trying to save her life." The art director brilliantly captured all the editorial elements I suggested, and that's how the familiar look of the gothic romance was born.

Editorially, the gothic romance was a variation of *Jane Eyre*. The heroine was always an innocent young woman, usually a governess, and the hero was the dark-haired, handsome, laconic master of the house who falls in love with the heroine but suffers in frustration as he watches her be charmed by his blond, wastrel younger brother. But it is only when she is alone with the master of the house that she feels deep, strong emotions she had never experienced before. In chapter after chapter the heroine becomes the victim of many dangerous accidents (or were they accidents?), but she is rescued by the dark-haired hero. Finally, after 160 pages, she discovers the evil that lurks in the tower, is saved from certain death by the quiet master, discovers the sordid past and lying nature of the blond younger brother (who is shipped off to Australia!).

Finally, on the last page, she falls into the hero's arms, they kiss passionately, and she discovers the source of those delicious, powerful emotions.

The novels were romantic fantasies with no overt sex, but with a great deal of seething sexuality. Nevertheless, they were chaste enough so that my mother and my aunts and millions of other women could read them in public without being embarrassed. The gothic romances became much sexier as the years passed by, but they are still on bookshelves, still fueling the romantic and erotic dreams of millions of readers.

Bantam

Other CEOs might emphasize production, marketing,
or finance. I wanted Bantam to be editorially oriented
from top to bottom.

—OSCAR DYSTEL

The real Bantam came to life only when Oscar Dystel took it over
in 1954. You have read in the Simon & Schuster chapter how, in
1944, Marshall Field of Chicago scooped up S & S, along with
its new paperback imprint, Pocket Books. Next, Field wanted to
buy a healthy book publishing house: Grosset & Dunlap. But
a band of brothers—from Harper's, Little, Brown, Random
House, Scribner's, and Book-of-the-Month Club—repulsed the in-
vader, took over Grosset, and decided they would form their own
paperback imprint. The Curtis Circulation Company, which was
one of the thriving magazine distributors, had also invested in the
new house, and extended its distribution tentacles to paperbound
books. And Ian Ballantine would see to the new baby. Bantam
took out a six-page insert in *Publishers Weekly* to introduce its
first twenty paperbacks. It was a shrewd list, offering such books
as *The Grapes of Wrath, Life on the Mississippi,* Zane Grey's
Nevada, Rafael Sabatini's *Scaramouche,* Elliot Paul's *The Last
Time I Saw Paris,* and *What Makes Sammy Run?* But nothing
seemed to go well internally. Ian Ballantine liked to do what he
liked to do, and the publishers who owned Grosset began picking
at him. By 1952 he had moved on, and Bantam went looking for
its General Patton.

Oscar Dystel's name came up; he was a Patton of sorts, a tough
leader, wherever he went. Both before World War II and right after, Oscar had edited such magazines as *Parents, Coronet, Col-
lier's,* and *Look.* The problem was that he had no book publishing
experience. It was Simon Michael Bessie who came to his aid.

By 1944, Bessie was directing the Office of War Information's desk in Algiers, and Oscar was working for him. And they both worked for Cass Canfield, who ran the OWI in Algiers and France. After the war, Bessie left magazine publishing to become an editor for Canfield at Harper's (see chapter 8). When Bessie found out that the Grosset group was looking for somebody to take over Bantam, he gave a strong recommendation to Cass (one of the publishing group's owners) on Oscar's behalf.

A meeting was set up between John O'Connor, who was then president of Grosset, and Oscar Dystel. At the end of an intensive three-hour interview, O'Connor said to Dystel, "I think you might be qualified to take on Bantam." But Oscar said he wasn't sure he was quite ready for the task. He told O'Connor he wanted to study the company's records before he gave him his decision.

"Fine," O'Connor said, "I'll send you everything—secretly."

Oscar took his time; he wanted to do more than read Bantam's profit-and-loss statements. "I knew nothing about book publishing," Oscar told me. "So what I did, I took off, visited wholesalers around the country. I found the major problem was returns. I said to everyone I met, 'Send them back!' That was the magic word. They came in truckloads, cleaned out our inventory, and I got involved—deeply." Now he was ready to rehabilitate Bantam.

In early December 2003, I went to visit Oscar in Rye, New York. It was just three weeks after the loss of his wife, Marian, after a sixty-five-year marriage, and he was still stunned by her death, as he would always be. Oscar lives in a large, splendidly appointed apartment in a senior citizen center, obviously for well-to-do seniors. Two aides take care of him around the clock, and his secretary of thirty-four years, Barbara Essick, who has a family of her own nearby, sees to everything else in his life. Oscar met me at the door. He was wearing tan slacks, a brown golf sweater, and he was leaning on a cane. He was heavier than he once was, his face round and just as sweet as ever. He smiled wanly at me. We talked about his wife, and his grief over Marian's death. As the talk turned to Oscar's life at Bantam, he seemed to pick up energy. His face lost some of its sadness, his voice was stronger and surer, and his memory kicked in about those most fulfilling years of his life.

One of the first things he told me was that in less than two years at Bantam, he had three titles that each sold over one million copies—Leon Uris's *Battle Cry,* Pierre Boulle's *The Bridge on the River Kwai,* and John Steinbeck's *East of Eden.* These titles are a fair indication of Dystel's philosophy about books, particularly the battle between popular fiction and literature, which was always a bigger battle in the mass-market business. It came down to this, said Oscar: "Can we afford the book because it's a great book. Or can we take the book that can't miss?" All three of those titles were commercial successes in hardcover, and, in the case of John Steinbeck, a literary/commercial bestseller (that book had been bought by a previous editor in chief, Walter Pitkin.)

For Oscar, the best of those books was his first one, *Battle Cry* (1953). "I'd fallen in love with it," Oscar said. "Saul David, our editor in chief, loved it, too. There was a tremendous amount of enthusiasm throughout our house."

Walter Minton, who came to talk with me about his career as CEO at Putnam's, told me with some pride that *Battle Cry* was one of the first books he'd worked on, claiming that he did the original work on the jacket "and everything else." Here's how it came to Putnam's:

"Howard Cady, who was then Doubleday's San Francisco editor," said Walter, "knew Leon Uris. At the time he was a newspaper driver on the San Francisco *Call-Bulletin.* He was also trying to be a writer. He came around one day with a large envelope and said to Cady, 'Howard, I've got these stories and I'm writing a bunch of them down. But I don't know how to put them together.'

"And Howard told Leon, 'There's something that's been invented just for you.'

"And Leon Uris said, 'What is it?'

" 'Leon, it's called chapters.' "

Walter Minton bought the book for Putnam's. It was a No. 4 bestseller in 1954. Oscar Dystel loved it and engaged in his first auction for the paperback rights to *Battle Cry*. "Came the auction day," Oscar said, "I was sitting across from the subsidiary rights woman at Putnam's. Saul and I had agreed on a figure from $22,000 to $25,000. But I was naïve. I said to her, 'What do you want?' She shrugged. I said, 'Would you take $18,000?'

"She bristled. 'This is not the way we do things. You've got to make a bid.' I look over at Saul David. He's holding a hand up by his head, all five fingers showing. I offered $25,000.

"It was a tie, the same number offered by Pocket Books, the biggest paperback house in the country. The rights person said she'd have to discuss this with her people. Then I whipped out my two-page pocket memorandum, indicating the marketing Bantam would do on the book. I had prepared by calling the advertising director for the movie of *Battle Cry* that they were working on. I reached him on his boat in Catalina. Told him we were going to recruit marines, they would go to wholesalers and explain their love of the book. That afternoon a message came: We got the book. It was a battle cry for the country," Oscar said, "that Bantam was in business."

In 1959, Saul David left to work in Hollywood. In 1961, Oscar lured Marc Jaffe away from Dell to become a vice president and editorial director of the house and its twenty-two editorial hands. The immediate trouble was that he came on board just as Oscar Dystel found himself pinned in a corner by his own doings.

IT HAD ALL BEGUN for Oscar when he was out in Hollywood, looking for possible movie tie-ins. He also wanted to see his dear friend, David Brown, a Hollywood producer. One night Oscar found himself at dinner in the Lanai Room at the Beverly Hills Hotel with David and his wife.

He thought that David's wife seemed a bit off, maybe because she was coolly plainspoken. When, for instance, Oscar asked her, "How come an attractive woman like you waited so long to get married?" this woman, whose name was Helen Gurley Brown, elaborated, in front of her husband, on various affairs she had had with various men. "I'm looking at David," Oscar told me, "and he's not having any problem with it, so I said to her, 'Well, have you thought about writing about it?'

" 'She said, 'Sure, I'm thinking about it.'

" 'If you're serious,' " said Oscar, " 'don't forget to send it on to me.' " And, right off, he suggested a title: *Sex and the Single Girl.*

Three weeks later, back in New York, Oscar opened a package from Helen Gurley Brown that contained her manuscript. "It was at that time," Oscar told me, "that I was still searching for a new editor. I read through the manuscript and thought, *This is not for us.* Very suggestive stuff, full of four-letter words." He passed it on to Grace Bechtold, one of his finest editors, especially adept at women's fiction. She came back and said to Oscar, "You can't publish a book like this."

"Mistake No. 1," Oscar said, "came when I told my managing editor, Bob Walter, who was at that L.A. dinner with me, to write a reject note to Helen. He gave me a copy. He had written two sentences. Sure enough, four days later I got a call from Helen, in tears: 'How can you do this? You encouraged me about the story of my life, and you reject me summarily.'

"I felt terrible. I said, 'Please send it back.' " She did, and Oscar decided to give it to Bernard Geis, the young man who had come up with the name Bantam for the new imprint and was now running his own small publishing house, leaning toward erotica.

Oscar's last words to Geis were, "Don't forget where this came from!"

About a month later Oscar received a copy of the Brown manuscript from Geis, much revised and much, much better. He felt it might be publishable. *Sex and the Single Girl* was published by Bernard Geis in 1962.

"Mistake No. 2," Oscar said with bitterness. "There are things about me that I couldn't contain—being a cheapie, cheapo. I asked Bernie, 'So, are you ready to sell it?' He said yes, and that he wanted $25,000 from me for the paperback rights. How could he do that to me? I asked him if the hardcover sales had reached fifty thousand yet. He said no. I said I'd wait to see how he did with it." This is where Oscar Dystel's newly arrived editor began shaking his head. Marc Jaffe, a tall stand-up guy with a bristling mustache and the posture of a marine (which he was), said to his boss, "What are you doing here, playing games with this guy and this book? Get it now before the price goes out of sight."

"Next thing I knew it was No. 8 on the *Publishers Weekly* nonfiction bestseller list." Oscar went back to Geis, hat in hand, only to learn that someone had offered Geis $90,000. Could Oscar top that? Bernie asked Oscar. He could.

That same day Oscar flew back to California and had dinner in the same dining room at the same hotel with the same dinner companions, David Brown and Helen Gurley Brown. "We were sitting around talking about everything but this book," he told me. "Finally, as I left the dining room, she came over to say good night. She kissed me on both cheeks, and she said, 'If you were the last man alive, you'd never get the rights to this book.'"

The paperback edition of Oscar's title, *Sex and the Single Girl,* wound up at Dell, and Oscar received a thank-you from Helen Meyer. Bernie Geis sent Oscar a box filled with bottles of Scotch. Oscar sent it back, and they didn't talk to each other for months.

One day, out of the blue, Oscar got a call from Geis. "Listen," he said, "I owe you something. I have a manuscript I want you to read." So he sent it on to Oscar, who read it and exploded in excitement. He told his colleagues it would sell about a million copies. With incredible promotion from the author, Jacqueline Susann, and her husband, Irving Mansfield, *Valley of the Dolls* was the No. 1 fiction bestseller in 1966. By July 1967 the Bantam paperback had sold four million copies; another four million were gobbled up by the end of the year. According to Barbara Seaman's biography of Jacqueline Susann, called *Lovely Me,* Susann found that *The New Grolier Multimedia Encyclopedia* listed *Valley of the Dolls* as the bestselling novel of all time, with 19.3 million copies sold. Jacqueline's next two books were also No. 1 bestsellers—*The Love Machine* and *Once Is Not Enough* in 1973. Jacqueline Susann died from breast cancer in 1974, but her novels live on.

IT WAS SAUL DAVID who recommended Marc Jaffe to Oscar. Marc had had a successful ten-year run at NAL, then went to Dell for just a year and a half. Oscar met with Marc several times, finally offering him the job as vice president and editorial director. "He was an enigmatic personality," Oscar wrote in his memoir about Jaffe, "but he brought a refined sense of taste to our operation. Over the years, I thought we worked supremely as a team."

One of the reasons why Dystel and Jaffe lived that way was because they each held one side of the coin. Jaffe, in his love of fiction, leaned toward its literary value. Oscar wasn't equally interested in literary values. He always claimed a parallel between success in magazine publishing and in book publishing: "a theory absolutely transferable to my new world of books. No matter how good the publishing team may be," Oscar asserted, "the heart of our business was a good book that people enjoyed reading."

Sometimes a strain appeared because of their different sensibilities. I remember when the Book-of-the-Month Club's judges made John le Carré's *Smiley's People* a Main Selection (they had previously done the same thing for the first two books in the le Carré trilogy *Tinker, Tailor, Soldier, Spy* and *The Honourable Schoolboy*), I received a call from Jaffe. He asked me what I thought of the novel. I told him I loved it, as had our judges. There was a pause, and then he asked me if I thought it would sell. It was obvious to me that Oscar was by his side, nervous about the novel's possibilities. I told Marc we thought *Smiley's People* would sell fine since the author's first two had worked so well for us. And it did.

"Actually," Marc said later, "le Carré was not the kind of an author that Oscar got turned on by. But really, we got to work together in an interesting way because he understood what I was after when I was trying to acquire a book that was not necessarily his sort of gut book."

When I was doing the research for my chapters on the paperback revolution, I had a long conversation with Marc. He lives in Williamstown, Massachusetts, but when he comes to New York, the Harvard Club is his home. It was there, in the first week of December 2005, that I sat in an overstuffed chair and listened to him exclaim: "I have never been bored in my fifty-five years in publishing. I can say that. *Never.* Not one day did I go into the office feeling I was going to be bored. I sometimes may have felt frustrated for various bureaucratic reasons, but never bored."

Beyond Marc Jaffe's plainspoken advice to Oscar Dystel about buying Helen Gurley Brown's book, the odd thing about Marc's first year at Bantam was that he felt a little lost. "We didn't have a single bestseller," he told me, "and I was wondering, 'Am I really going to be able to do this?'"

He received some good advice from Arthur Thornhill, Sr., at Little, Brown. "I remember going to Boston," Marc said, "because that was sort of the routine along with going out to lunch at Locke-Ober with Arthur. He'd have a couple of Canadian Clubs, and then maybe a third. And I would be sipping away on my first. And I started complaining, I guess, about the fact that I couldn't find anything. 'Look,' I said, 'it's not working out. What am I doing wrong?' And he was very understanding. He said, 'Marc, relax. There are plenty of good books around. Don't worry. But you have to be smart enough to pick 'em.' "

That conversation was just what Marc needed, and he began to pick 'em in his own way. He brought in *The Guinness Book of World Records,* which, he says, "was sort of a whole business by itself," and a big moneymaker for the house. Then he told me how he had rescued a character from his pulp magazine days, a figure called Doc Savage that even I remembered. "It occurred to me," Marc said, "why not bring Doc Savage back? Oscar said 'Sure.' We must have published fifty of those Doc Savage books."

With the help of Allan Barnard and Grace Bechtold, a Bantam Modern Classics imprint was launched in the mid-sixties. Then the team commissioned a series of foreign language dictionaries, which had never been done by a paperback publisher. Marc also played a pivotal role in bringing Holden Caulfield to Bantam.

One day in 1963, Oscar got a call from Arthur Thornhill, Sr., J. D. Salinger's hardcover publisher. Thornhill told Oscar that the NAL reprint license for *The Catcher in the Rye* was about to expire, and Salinger wanted another house to create a cover that worked for him. That would also free up two other Salingers—*Franny and Zooey* and *Raise High the Roof Beam, Carpenters.* Oscar caught his breath and took the next flight to Boston, where he met with Arthur in his Beacon Hill office.

"The first thing I asked Arthur," Oscar told me, "was if I could talk to Salinger."

"Absolutely not," Arthur said. "You have to talk with his agent, Dorothy Olding."

"Well, then," Oscar asked, "what does he want?"

"He wants to design the cover himself."

"No problem!" I said. "We'll publish it in a brown wrapping paper cover if he wants that, just as long as the title is legible."

The deal was made. Salinger's design had the title and author's name printed in yellow capitals on an orange-red background. He also chose the typeface and the ink color, even specifying the cover varnish and the paper stock. No one saw Salinger. His instructions came through Dorothy Olding. "The Bantam edition of *The Catcher in the Rye,*" Oscar said, "regularly sold half a million copies a year, beginning with our first printing in 1964. By 1978 the book had gone through forty-six Bantam printings." Salinger also created the covers for *Franny and Zooey* and *Raise High the Roof Beam, Carpenters.* In 1964, *Franny and Zooey* sold 938,000 copies, Bantam's No. 2 fiction title for the year.

OSCAR'S ART DIRECTOR, Len Leone, was not overjoyed about losing the right to design the Salinger covers, because covers were his babies, but he understood that it was for the greater good. I was lucky to work side-by-side with Len when I was a kid at *True* magazine, and he was the young and promising assistant art director. He had a marvelous touch then, assigning artists to illustrate stories and then putting together clean, open layouts for the story, letting the pages breathe. I knew he would be going places.

"Leone was a major factor in changing the visual impact of the mass-market paperback book," Oscar told me. "The Len Leone look was a white background for the back of the cover. And every square inch wasn't taken. Many imitators came later." Len Leone himself put it this way: "When I first came to work everybody was buying emotional, highly realistic, low-key cover art. We decided to bring an airy, light thing to the covers. From there evolved the white cover, using highly realistic painters. And Bantam went to better cover stock for maximum fidelity."

Marc Jaffe told me how Leone and others helped make Bantam

"more of a force in the publishing business and out in the reading world in the late sixties and through the seventies. There were five, six, maybe seven people who really created an energy that I don't think existed in any other publishing company at the time. I mean, you had great individuals—Alfred Knopf, Bennett Cerf, and others. But ours was very much a group effort: Oscar, a great, great manager; Len Leone, a great art director; Esther Margolis, a wizard who found new ways to market and sell books; Grace Bechtold, who became a specialist in the health and fitness area; and Allan Barnard, who I hired and who was probably the sharpest mass-market editor of them all.

"Allan was very crucial in terms of selection, certainly," Marc went on. "I mean he came in with David Reuben's book, which he had in proof, *Everything You Always Wanted to Know About Sex* (*But Were Afraid to Ask)*. To be honest, I don't think I ever read the book to this day. But he put it on my desk and said, 'Marc, believe me, we've just got to buy this book.' What could I do? So I said, 'OK, Allan, go to it.' That was not a big-money acquisition, but, boy, that book sold three or four or five million copies.

"So, you see, we sort of fed off each other's energy in a way that certainly was not true at New American Library. There you had two brilliant guys, Kurt Enoch and Victor Weybright, but they liked to drive their own cars."

ESTHER MARGOLIS, whom I visited in early 2007 at her office, which houses her twenty-five-year-old Newmarket Press, was pleased to drive Bantam's family car when asked to, which was often. She appreciated the Bantam atmosphere. "I grew up amidst twenty-seven first cousins," she said, "within a five-block radius in Detroit. That was quite a community of family." She joined Bantam in 1962, and became one of the most innovative and effective publicists in the paperback field. Taking a cue from the promotional exploits of Jacqueline Susann and her husband, Esther initiated the book tour as a solid part of the sales promotion for leading Bantam titles every month. She bought into Oscar's insistence on what he called "a corporate culture in which everyone had to *listen.* So we had a lot of meetings to discuss covers, advance publicity, promotion, advertising—and especially to consider what titles we would seek for purchase." Esther became Oscar's shadow, in a way, filling the meetings with novel ideas to make the books work. In 1971 she became a vice president of the company.

One of the things she was most proud of was the teamwork involving what they called "Bantam's Extras." The first one came in 1964, when, eighty hours after the Warren Commission's report on the assassination of President Kennedy was released, the complete text—with illustrations, an introduction by Harrison Salisbury of *The New York Times,* and other articles by *Times* writers—went on sale all over the country. Bantam charged one dollar for the 786-page book, and the first printing was 700,000. They ended up with 1.6 million books sold. McGraw-Hill later published it in hardcover, and we offered it to our members at the Book-of-the-Month Club. Between that first Extra, and the last one in 1975—*"They've Killed the President": The Search for the Murderers of John F. Kennedy* by Robert Sam Anson—there were fifty-six instant books all told. Some worked better than others, but none carried the impact of that first Extra.

OSCAR DYSTEL ALWAYS had the reputation of being an excellent listener, especially when his editors were discussing titles they would like to own. One day in 1973 Allan Barnard went to Oscar's office. He had obtained a hardcover manuscript for a book that would be published by Doubleday. He read it immediately, and he asked Oscar to please read it as soon as possible. Oscar took the manuscript home with him and stayed up all night reading the book.

The next morning when he came into the kitchen with the manuscript, his son, John, asked, "Whatcha got, Pop?"

Father said, "It's a book about a shark."

"Wow!"

"That was what I needed to hear," Oscar said. "I knew Allan was on to something. I allowed him to buy reprint rights if we could make a preemptive bid of $20,000. I told him, 'Go to $25,000 only if you have to. I don't believe Doubleday knows the real value of what you have.'

"A little later, Allan came to me and said he'd made a preemptive bid of $50,000. I was upset, pissed off. But the $50,000 was the floor, giving Bantam the right to top the highest bid by 10 percent. This is said to have been a Dystel innovation from many years back.

"The bidding," Oscar said, "went to $500,000. We took it for $550,000."

That was just the beginning for Peter Benchley's rousing novel, *Jaws*. Tom Congdon, who was Benchley's Doubleday editor, came to Bantam seeking advice about the design for the hardcover dust jacket. Oscar wrote in his family memoir, "I was flattered by Congdon's request for advice at all. Here was one hardcover publishing representative who didn't look at us with disdain as an insignificant reprinter."

Len Leone outdid himself for the Bantam jacket. The painting showed the silhouette of a woman swimming on the surface of the ocean, while a monstrous, open-jawed great white shark surged toward her from below. The tremendous cover art was appropriated by Universal Studios, and it became the symbol of the movie used in promotional advertising everywhere. Allan Barnard had struck again. And Len Leone, too.

IN AUGUST 1975, Bantam struck once more, raising the temperature of the mass-market paperback industry to a new boiling point in the auction for *Ragtime*. As Oscar Dystel put it in his memoir, "It became a landmark in the race for paperback blockbusters."

Oscar's limit for Bantam's participation in the auction, in which there would be twelve suitors, was $1.5 million. The problem for Oscar was that while he liked E. L. Doctorow's novel, it wasn't completely in his gut. "One of my motives in *Ragtime*," Doctorow revealed in a Book-of-the-Month Club *News* piece, "was to write a novel that was totally accessible, that could be read by people who don't usually read books, as well as by readers who like the art." Oscar Dystel, I'm sure, would have agreed with that statement, but to him it was still a literary work. It was Marc Jaffe who loved *Ragtime* the most at the house and hoped that Bantam's betting limit of $1.5 million would work.

"Before I left for the day," Oscar said, "I reminded Marc Jaffe that I didn't want Bantam to spend a nickel more than $1.5 million. Later that night Victor Temkin, Bantam's lawyer and Oscar's dear friend (who still calls him every day), called me to report: 'We won the book with a bid of $1.85 million.'

"So much for the power of the CEO. I lost my composure and screamed back at him. Our break-even point was selling two million copies at a cover price of $2.25. We calculated the gross break-even figure rather than the net. But the competition had toughened so much that we felt forced to step out on a limb time after time."

In hardcover, *Ragtime* was the No. 1 novel of the year. It took a lot more time for the paperback to earn out.

TWO YEARS LATER, in 1977, an Italian conglomerate that held a half ownership in Bantam sold it to Bertelsmann. And Bantam turned sorrowful. They kept Oscar on as a "consultant" and gave him a corner. "But nobody would listen to me," he said. "I sat there week after week."

In late January 1980, Esther Margolis, after seventeen years with Bantam, was getting ready to leave and start her own publishing house, which she would call Newmarket Press. "I get this call from Oscar on a Saturday," she recalled. "He had been in Palm Springs with Marian, and I was surprised that he was back in New York. He said he wanted me to come to a meeting the next day at the Olympic Towers in New York. So I go there, and Marc is with him, and he told us that he had been called back to New York by Bertelsmann. They told him they were removing him from all his jobs. They took everything away from him. It was just awful. It was a total betrayal. In my period with the company, it went from five million dollars in sales, and three salespeople, to 120 million dollars in sales, and becoming the number-one paperback publisher in the world."

At that time, Bantam also controlled an estimated twenty-two percent of the paperback industry. It didn't matter; their golden age was over. In 1979 someone at Bantam okayed the all-time highest offer for paperback rights, $3,208,875, for Judith Krantz's *Princess Daisy*.

There were reverberations.

This old family scattered in different directions, many of them still able to find reasonable employment in the business they loved, but no longer living together.

Fawcett

If a major paperback player read something early and said, "I love this," and took a big floor, it made things happen for a book. It generated that kind of enthusiasm very early. Paperbacks were very powerful.

—LEONA NEVLER

Until I came to New York in 1950 from Lynn, Massachusetts, the biggest city I had ever been in was Boston. My hope was to live in New York forever. One of my earliest jobs in publishing was as sports editor of Fawcett's *True* magazine. At that time *True* was by far the largest men's adventure magazine in the country, with a monthly circulation of about 1.8 million. After two years, Fawcett announced that business had faltered and everybody in the company would have to take a 10 percent pay cut. This didn't sit well with the editor of *True*, Ken Purdy, since his magazine was a robust moneymaker for the company. So he quit *True* to become editor of *Argosy*. I went with him, as did several other renegades. It was a short gig. We all quit within a year because *Argosy*'s owner had reneged on various promises he had given Purdy. For the next six years, while my wife, Rosa, was having babies and I was needed at home, I worked as a freelance editor and writer.

One of the people I worked for was Ralph Daigh, who had originally hired me for *True*. When I became a freelancer, he asked me to put together a bunch of one-shot magazines on individual sports. I did a couple on pro football and boxing. I would come to Fawcett several days a week and use their production people to help me put out the magazines properly.

The feeling I got coming back to Fawcett, even as a part-timer, was—*Wow!* How incredibly had the energy level risen at the company, with men and women, most of whom seemed to be young, dashing back and forth not just to see to their magazines, but also to get a new business going. The new name of the game was paperback publishing.

Five years back, in 1949, Ralph Daigh had joined the game in a revolutionary way. First, he signed up New American Library to distribute its Signet and Mentor lines. Then, a year later, he founded an imprint he named Gold Medal Books. The gimmick was that Gold Medal would only publish original works in paper-back. Some thought this might be illegal because the contract with NAL forbade Fawcett, one of the largest independent news-stand distributors, from publishing its own paperback imprints. But the clause in the contract didn't say anything about doing *original* paperbacks. Fawcett tested the air by publishing two an-thologies from their most successful magazines: one for men, *The Best of True Magazine,* and the other for women, *What To-day's Woman* [a bestselling magazine of the day] *Should Know About Marriage and Sex.* No one complained.

Because of their generous contract to writers—they offered a minimum advance of $2,000 and a one-cent-per-copy royalty on the first run, and also let the authors keep all other rights—Gold Medal was able to find some first-rate books and authors. In 1950, Tereska Torres's lesbian novel *Women's Barracks* became the first paperback "original" bestseller. Other early Gold Medal authors were John D. MacDonald, the creator of Travis McGee, and Mickey Spillane (who was quickly picked off by NAL). Gold Medal also published two early novels by Kurt Vonnegut, Jr., *Canary in a Cat House* and *Mother Night.*

Gold Medal Books' first editor in chief was Jim Bishop, who went on to write *The Day They Died* books—Lincoln, John Kennedy, and Jesus Christ, among others. The Gold Medal books were startlingly successful. "In its first six months," Ralph Daigh reported, "we had printed 9,020,645 books, and people seemed to like them very well."

And so they did. Gold Medal kept making a lot of money for the company. Henry Morrison, who started his career working for the Scott Meredith Literary Agency, remembered that "when Scott was on vacation, and his brother, Syd, was out for the day, I'd open the mail. Scott was very concerned that all checks be de-posited the same day. And you'd slice open those envelopes from

Fawcett Publications, and all these checks would fall out. Sometimes it was a couple hundred thousand dollars."

I was pleased to meet some of the people who were intimately involved with Gold Medal. One was Rona Jaffe, an attractive, saucy woman, who was very smart and took to fooling around with the higher-ranked Fawcett players. Rona became an associate editor on two new imprints, Crest Books and Premier Books. She soon quit Fawcett to write a novel about her experiences. *The Best of Everything* (1958) is still around, to be read and watched on the silver screen.

Succeeding Jaffe as associate editor was another young woman, Leona Nevler. I was happy for Leona because she was born and spent her early years in my hometown of Lynn, Massachusetts. I'd known her there. We spent at least one early school year in the same class. When I bumped into her at Fawcett, we shook hands, asked about each other, and then she was on her way. After that, I hardly saw her again until my Book-of-the-Month Club days. By then she had become an admired woman throughout the industry, an editor and discoverer who always performed with a fierce sense of duty.

LEONA NEVLER HAD begun her book publishing career in Boston in 1948 as a secretary to Angus Cameron at Little, Brown. She later became the first secretary at Little, Brown to be promoted to editor. "It was a big deal," she said. "It was James Sherman, who was the treasurer, who suggested that they give me the author contracts to do, which made it possible to give me the promotion." Alas, her career came to an end there after Cameron was sent into exile (see chapter 12 on Little, Brown). "They fired me," she said simply, "along with other people who were Angus's supporters."

She began reading for the New York office of J. B. Lippincott on a freelance basis. It was there that she came upon a novel that would change her life and the lives of a lot of other women, too. The novel was titled "The Tree and Its Blossom." She told one of Lippincott's editors, Alan Williams—*the* Alan Williams—she had a manuscript that was "very good."

"They had five readings," Leona told me, "and it went to Philadelphia [Lippincott's headquarters]. And it came back. They decided not to do it."

At that point, Leona was seeking a job with the Julian Messner publishing house. She talked with Julian Messner's widow, Kitty Messner. (Mr. Messner had died in 1948, the same year, by the way, that his company published Frances Parkinson Keyes's *Dinner at Antoine's* in hardcover.) The job was a marketing job, not editorial. Kitty Messner told her, "I don't want to hire you now, but I want you to work for me on some basis." Leona said okay, and she gave Kitty "The Tree and Its Blossom" to read. Kitty agreed to publish it if Leona would do the editing. Leona readily agreed.

"Just as I was working on the book," she told me, "I got hired at Fawcett." But she continued to edit the manuscript, which was written by a twenty-nine-year-old woman who lived in New Hampshire. Her name was Grace Metalious. The title of the book had been changed to *Peyton Place*.

As she dissected page after page, Leona confessed, "I did what I have never done again as a result. I put some suggestions to Grace *on* the manuscript. She was so upset with me because I wrote on her manuscript that she went ape-shit." (Other authors mentioned in this book with a similar aversion to marked-up manuscripts include Gore Vidal, Norman Mailer, and Bruce Catton.)

"Grace came to New York," Leona said, "and I took her to lunch at the Absinthe House, where she toyed with shrimp salad and drank three martinis. This was on October 12, and we had the next day off. So I invited her to my apartment. We went over the manuscript and I cooked something for her—she didn't really eat, she drank some beer. My roommate was due to come back at 5 P.M. She was an odd person, too, and I didn't want to bring them together. I also felt, since my boyfriend [Jim Silberman] was a rival publisher, I couldn't take her to Jim's for dinner. In addition, she was wearing jeans, and in those days you couldn't use a credit card in places where you wore jeans. So I let her go. "She went off into the night, and apparently she drank all night. She was kind of crazy anyway, and an alcoholic. She was supposed to get back to me the next day or two. When I didn't hear from her, I called Kitty. She had been sleeping on Kitty's doorstep." Leona and Metalious did get together again, and Leona finished the editing job.

At Christmas, Leona got a present from Kitty: $1,000. "It was more than she had to do," Leona said. "But on the other hand, I mean, it really saved her company." (There was a piece in *The New York Times* a couple of years ago about Hollywood director John Waters's penchant for giving and receiving "perfect" Christmas gifts. His favorite present ever, he said, was a swatch of flowered wallpaper from the studio of Grace Metalious.)

Louis Menand, in a recent issue of *The New Yorker,* called *Peyton Place* "the biggest small-town novel of all." The story of a town with sordid secrets was a *New York Times* bestseller for fifty-nine weeks, and it lifted Leona's reputation throughout the industry. I can hear Ralph Daigh saying, with intensity in his voice, "Weren't we lucky to get her?" He meant Nevler, of course.

IF IT HADN'T been for Ralph Daigh, I don't believe Fawcett would have ever come close to breaking through, as it did, in the paperback revolution. There was no one else at Fawcett with his collection of skills accumulated over the years. Daigh was a plain-talking, rugged-looking tough guy. He wore a mustache, which made him look just like one of those riverboat gambler heroes in a *True* magazine illustration. In *Between Covers,* John Tebbel tells how Daigh came to Fawcett: "At his summer resort, in 1926, Wilford Fawcett encountered a solidly built young busboy named Ralph Daigh, who turned out to have a talent for writing. . . . When the growing firm moved into new offices, Daigh went along and helped develop the pulp magazines that Fawcett was beginning to publish."

The founder, Wilford Hamilton Fawcett, was a Minnesotan. He was also called "Captain Billy" because he had been a captain in the First World War. Right after the war he started a bawdy cartoon and joke magazine called *Captain Billy's Whiz Bang.* From there, he and his four sons plunged headfirst into the magazine business. Competing with houses like Dell and Macfadden, the Fawcetts built a comparable magazine empire: *True Confessions, Mechanix Illustrated, Motion Picture, True, Woman's Day,* and a host of other titles. In 1940, Fawcett launched Fawcett Comics, with a new superman, Captain Marvel. Wilford Hamilton Fawcett had died that year, but sons Roscoe, Gordon, Roger, and Wilford Jr., with major help from Ralph Daigh, became book publishers.

AT THE BEGINNING, Nevler worked for William Lengle, who had been with Fawcett for years and had a reputation in the company for groping young women. "He was a doddering old man at this point," Leona said. "He claimed to be fifty; he was seventy and was sort of mired in the past. His claim to fame was that he'd been Dreiser's secretary.

"In those days," Leona recalled, "we weren't allowed to acquire anything of consequence. Mostly, we would buy junky old things that NAL had already reverted." The big change came when Ralph Daigh went after *A Walk on the Wild Side* by Nelson Algren, which was owned by Farrar, Straus. "It wasn't easy for Ralph," Leona remembered. "Pocket Books had offered $50,000 for it. It had to go to Marshall Field, who at that point owned Pocket Books. Someone came into Field's office and said to him, 'You're not going to buy that dirty book, are you?' And Field said, 'I am not.' So there was the book, up for grabs, and Ralph had the courage to buy it for $50,000. It had some consequence for the company." Well, yes. It opened up the purse strings.

In 1957, Leona bought her first big book, *By Love Possessed* by James Gould Cozzens. Soon after, for $100,000, Ralph Daigh bought the book that no hardcover publisher would touch, save Walter Minton at Putnam's: *Lolita*.

One of Leona's most complicated triumphs was William L. Shirer's *The Rise and Fall of the Third Reich*. Fawcett was ready to put up $400,000, but Leona first had to find a way to convert a huge book into a paperback. "The prevailing wisdom was that you couldn't bind the mass market paperback that was going to be more than one inch thick. At the last minute, before I was getting ready to make our offer, I asked our production guy, 'Are you sure we can't do bigger than an inch?' It turned out that Fawcett's printer, W. F. Hall, had a brand-new binding machine capable of handling a two-inch-thick book. Someone at Fawcett persuaded Hall not to share this information immediately with other paperback companies. This enabled Fawcett to buy the book without major competition. The 1,600-page epic sold for $1.65 a copy, the first paperback to be priced at more than $1.00. "And it worked," Leona said. "It made people really pay attention to Fawcett."

Thinking about those days, Leona told me that paperback publishing was much easier than hardcover publishing is now: "Because if a major paperback player read something early and said, 'I love this,' and took a big floor, it made things happen for a book. It generated that kind of enthusiasm very early. Paperbacks were very powerful."

Indeed. In 1965, Fawcett paid $700,000 for James Michener's *The Source.* Fawcett bought the next Michener, *The Drifters,* by becoming the first house to pay an advance of one million dollars. That money also included the paperback rights to all of Michener's previous books. Ralph Daigh, who was then the president of Fawcett, claimed that all of his company's advances of $500,000 or more had earned out.

LEONA ALSO BUILT a notable backlist for Fawcett. She bought John Updike's earlier books at the time she purchased his latest novel, *Rabbit, Run.* She also acquired *Couples,* which sold three million copies in mass market paperbacks. It was Leona Nevler who started the successes of such authors as Mary Stewart, Phyllis A. Whitney, Victoria Holt, and Norah Lofts—popular women novelists who, for a long time, were bigger in paperback than they were in hardcover.

But Leona's great success, as she admitted to me, was achieved in the oddest way. It happened in 1968, when the paperback industry was more rational than it would ever be in the 1970s.

Clyde Taylor, the subsidiary rights director of Putnam's, was getting ready to sell the rights to Mario Puzo's *The Godfather.* "Clyde and I were very friendly," Leona said. "And on a Friday we were having lunch, and he said, 'This manuscript of Puzo's is really terrific. And Bill Targ [the editor in chief of Putnam's] has slipped it to Bantam. And Targ's going to settle for $60,000. Can you read it this weekend, so I can stave off the sale?'

"I said, 'Well, yeah, I can read it, but you know I can't make a move without Ralph Daigh, and he is in Nantucket.' I did read it and loved it, and I told Clyde that. But I had to reach Ralph. When he was in Nantucket, he was kind of hard to get by phone—he was either fishing or golfing; and as this progressed, NAL and Dell were in it. When I finally got to Ralph, he said, 'OK, OK, beat it, whatever.'

"By that time the price had gotten up into the $300,000 area, and Clyde was getting tired of the slow pace. He said he would sell it to the first person who called back with more than $400K. And Dell did."

At almost the same time, Leona explained, Dell had bought a novel by Leslie Waller. "A deal for the Waller was made between Dell and Putnam's for around $60,000. Helen Meyer had apparently not been consulted about this book, and she was upset. She insisted to Putnam's that they rescind the buying price and sell it to her for $30,000." That didn't sit well with Walter Minton, and Leona soon got a call from Clyde. She remembered him saying, "Walter and I are getting very fed up with Dell. If you, Fawcett, will cover Dell's bid, we will sell it to you."

"Ralph Daigh was very courageous," Leona said, "because Roger Fawcett and George Delacorte lived in the same apartment building, and they were always one-upping each other. But he allowed us to go ahead and take the book for $410,000." Leona added, "*The Godfather,* before the movie, sold something like ten million copies."

Mario Puzo knew nothing about what had happened until his editor, Bill Targ, took him to lunch at the Algonquin to tell him the news about the sale that had closed that morning. Mario, who was heavily in debt at that time—"piss-poor," Targ said—looked at his editor and said, "I don't believe a fucking word you've told me." Those were the crazy days in the paperbound world, but such days were beginning to wear down.

IN THE 1970s, Fawcett, like many other houses, hardcover and soft, came under the money crunch. The economy was taking a bad downturn, interest rates were moving sky-high, and paperbacks weren't selling the way they had before. To top it off, Fawcett was a company totally owned by the surviving three male brothers (one brother had died) and one sister. And none of

Captain Billy's brood was interested in the business. In 1977, three years after Ralph Daigh's retirement, CBS bought Fawcett.

Leona Nevler became vice president and publisher of Fawcett Books, but the company had grown fragile. In March 1981, Leona became head of CBS's Fawcett Books Group, which was still the fourth-largest paperback publisher in the United States but was in financial trouble. That didn't last long. In October 1981, Leona resigned from the company she had been a part of for twenty-six years. She eventually moved on to other houses, for she was always in demand.

ONE LATE AFTERNOON in July 2004, I went downtown to the offices of Penguin Group USA—Viking, Penguin, Putnam's, Dutton, etc.—where I had worked for nine years in the 1990s. This time I was coming to see Leona Nevler. She had a small room and was editing a manuscript for Berkley, Putnam's paperback imprint. She greeted me with a cautious smile, told me that the book she was working on was "so good." What she didn't say to me, but it was in that smile of hers, was *"Please don't stay long; I want to get back to this."* She looked the same as she always had, ageless, slim as a model, well dressed, her eyes as clear and sharp as ever, and no time for small talk.

The city we were born in never came up. I told her what I was doing—writing a book about "the good old days" of publishing, her days as well as mine—and that I had interviewed about a hundred and twenty of her colleagues. "I want to talk with you," I said, "about your life in those years." She was wary at first, then warmed up and told me all that you have been reading about here. Then she said politely that she had to finish what she was doing, so I couldn't stay as long as I had hoped. I understood. How could I not understand? She was working on something she wanted to make better. I told her, "I'll call you again to set up another interview." It never happened. On December 10, 2006, she fell on the street and died in the hospital soon after.

I went to her memorial service a couple of days later. It was difficult to be there. Although the speakers said so many of the things they should have said about this singular figure of the golden age, I kept wishing Leona herself were there to talk to. I thought of what Emerson said: "This time, like all times, is a very good one, if we but know what to do with it." Leona knew. I also recalled something that Sam Vaughan had written that connects with Leona and perhaps with many others of us, too. In this instance Sam was writing with honest sentiment about the allure of his trade:

"That box called Book may sit silently for centuries until you lift the lid. Then you have to work at it. You have to care, and if you give yourself to it, it will give itself to you. No wonder for many of us, it is love."

SOURCES

1: YOU ARE WHAT YOU PUBLISH: FARRAR, STRAUS AND GIROUX

Interviews

Paul Elie, New York City, May 4, 2004.
Jonathan Galassi, New York City, July 20, 2004.
Robert Giroux, Tinton Falls, New Jersey, May 14, 2004.
Elisabeth Sifton, New York City, April 13, 2004.
Roger Straus, New York City, December 9, 2003.
Hugh Van Dusen, New York City, October 20, 2004.

Books and Periodicals

Elie, Paul. *The Life You Save May Be Your Own: An American Pilgrimage.* New York: Farrar, Straus and Giroux, 2004.
Farrar, Straus and Giroux. *Roger W. Straus: A Celebration.* Farrar, Straus and Giroux, 2005.
Giroux, Robert. Introduction to Bernard Malamud, *The Complete Stories.* Farrar, Straus and Giroux, 1997.
———. Introduction to Flannery O'Connor, *The Complete Stories.* Farrar, Straus and Giroux, 1971.
———. Interview. *The Paris Review.* Summer 2000.
Hollander, John. Presentation from the American Academy of Arts and Letters of the Award for Distinguished Service to the Arts. Response by Robert Giroux, December 17, 2003.
Malamud, Bernard. *Long Work, Short Life.* Chapbooks in Literature Series. Bennington College, 1985.
Parker, Ian. "Showboat" (on Roger W. Straus). *The New Yorker.* April 8, 2002.
Roger W. Straus, obituaries. *The New York Times,* Christopher Lehmann-Haupt; *Publishers Weekly,* John Baker; *The New York Observer,* Philip Weiss.

SOURCES

Singer, Isaac B. *The Jewish Daily Forward* (special section on Singer), June 25, 2004.
———. *Collected Stories.* Author's Note. Farrar, Straus and Giroux, 1982.
Straus, Dorothea. *Under the Canopy.* George Braziller, 1982.
Williams, Alan D., ed. *Fifty Years: A Farrar, Straus and Giroux Reader 1996.* Farrar, Straus and Giroux, 1996.
"Xavier Rynne," R.I.P. *Denver Catholic Register,* May 20, 2002.

2: WISHING FOR A FAIR WIND: GROVE PRESS

Interviews

Richard Gallen, New York City, January 15, 2004.
Herman Graf, New York City, March 2, 2004.
Fred Jordan, Croton-on-Hudson, New York, March 10, 2004.
Barney Rosset, New York City, January 30, 2004.
Richard Seaver, New York City, July 7, 2004.
Nat Sobel, New York City, July 11, 2005.

Books and Periodicals

Coser, Lewis A., Charles Kadushin, and Walter W. Powell. *Books: The Culture and Commerce of Publishing.* Basic Books, 1982.
Gontarski, S. E., ed. *The Grove Press Reader, 1951–2001.* Grove Press, 2001.
Lovett, Robert Morss. *All Our Years: The Autobiography of Robert Morss Lovett.* Viking Press, 1948.
Rembar, Charles. *The End of Obscenity: The Trials of "Lady Chatterley," "Tropic of Cancer," and "Fanny Hill."* The Notable Trials Library, published by arrangement with Random House, 1968.
Rosset, Barney. *Photographs of Joan Mitchell.* Danziger Gallery, New York.
Rosset, Barney. *War Photographs: China in Conflict, 1944–45.* Janos Gat Gallery, February–March 2002.
Rosset, Barney, ed. *Evergreen Review Reader.* Two vols., 1957–1966, North Star Line, 1993; 1967–1973, Four Walls/Eight Windows, 1998.
Rosset, Barney. "The Art of Publishing." *The Paris Review,* Winter 1997–1998.

3: A QUEST TO KNOW MORE ABOUT THE WORLD: GEORGE BRAZILLER

Interviews

George Braziller, New York City, November 2004.
Herbert Mitgang, New York City, August 23, 2004.
Arthur Rosenthal, New York City, January 23, 2004.
Richard Seaver, New York City, July 7, 2004.
Thomas Wallace, New York City, November 5, 2004.

SOURCES

Books and Periodicals

George Braziller. Interview by Phong Bui. *The Brooklyn Rail*. February 2005.
Lewis, Jeremy. *The Life and Times of Allen Lane*. London: Penguin, 2006.
Madison, Charles A. *Book Publishing in America*. McGraw-Hill, 1966.
Matisse, Henri. *Jazz*. George Braziller, 1983.
Seaver, Edwin. *So Far, So Good: Recollections of a Life in Publishing*. Lawrence Hill Books, 1986.

4: AN UNCERTAIN PARTNERSHIP OF EQUALS: ATHENEUM

Interviews

Simon Michael Bessie, New York City, February 5, 2004.
Herman Gollob, New York City, December 13, 2004.
Thomas Stewart, New York City, September 23, 2005.
Katherine McNamara, New York City, September 29, 2006.
Betty Prashker, New York City, March 16, 2004.
Stanley Kauffmann, New York City, August 25, 2004.

Books and Periodicals

Bessie, Simon Michael. Interview. *Archipelago*, 2004.
Cerf, Bennett. *At Random: The Reminiscences of Bennett Cerf*. Random House, 1977.
Dictionary of Literary Biography, Vol. 46. Gale Research, 1986.
Haydn, Hiram. *Words and Faces*. Harcourt Brace Jovanovich, 1974.
Scribner, Charles, Jr. *In the Company of Writers*. Charles Scribner's Sons, 1990.

5: A MOST UNUSUAL COG IN THE PROFESSION: ST. MARTIN'S PRESS

Interviews

Thomas Dunne, New York City, November 21, 2005.
Richard Marek, New York City, August 16, 2005.
Thomas McCormack, New York City, October 8, 2004; November 21, 2005.
Anne McCormick, New York City, March 2, 2005.
Sally Richardson, New York City, April 20, 2005.
Eleanor Shatzkin, New York City, November 30, 2005.
Michael Shatzkin, New York City, November 17, 2005.
Thomas Stewart, New York City, September 23, 2005.
Robert Wyatt, New York City, January 7, 2006.

SOURCES

Books and Periodicals

Dictionary of Literary Biography. Vol. 46. Gale Research, 1986.
Edwards, Anne. *Road to Tara: The Life of Margaret Mitchell.* Ticknor & Fields, 1983.
Tebbel, John. *Between Covers: The Rise and Transformation of Book Publishing in America.* Oxford University Press, 1987.

6: INDEPENDENT PUBLISHING AT ITS HEIGHT: THE VIKING PRESS

Interviews

Aaron Asher, New York City, November 18, 2005.
Richard Barber, New York City, December 3, 2004.
Kathryn Court, New York City, February 13, 2006.
Thomas Guinzburg, New York City, January 28, 2004; March 27, 2006.
Gerald Howard, New York City, June 28, 2006.
Elisabeth Sifton, New York City, April 13, 2004.
Corlies Smith, New York City, February 6, 2004.

Books and Periodicals

Ellmann, Richard. *James Joyce.* Oxford University Press, 1959.
Jennison, Keith. *The Best of Times.* Marshall Jones, 1995.
Steinbeck, John. *Journal of a Novel: The East of Eden Paper.* Penguin Books, 1964.
Williams, Marjorie. *The Woman at the Washington Zoo.* Edited by Timothy Noah. Public Affairs, 2005.

7: THE CURIOUS FAMILY ESTABLISHMENT: DOUBLEDAY

Interviews

John Appleton, New York City, June 9, 2005.
Vilma Bergane, Tarrytown, N.Y., November 2007.
Nelson Doubleday, Garden City, N.Y., May 15, 2006.
Lisa Drew, New York City, May 25, 2004.
Charles Harris, New York City, September 27, 2004.
Judith Jones, New York City, February 25, 2004.
Anne McCormick, New York City.
Betty Prashker, New York City, March 16, 2004.
John Sargent, Jr., New York City, November 29, 2005.
Eleanor Shatzkin, New York City, November 30, 2005.
Michael Shatzkin, New York City, November 17, 2005.
Sally Richardson, New York City, January 22, 2005.
Samuel Vaughan, New York City, February 24, 2004.

SOURCES

Books and Periodicals

Bessie, Cornelia and Michael. "On Publishing" (interview by Katherine McNamara, part 1). *Archipelago*, Vol. 1, No. 4. www.archipelago.org.
———. "On Publishing" (interview by Katherine McNamara, part 2). *Archipelago*, Vol. 2, No. 1. www.archipelago.org.
Cerf, Bennett. *Dear Donald, Dear Bennett: The Wartime Correspondence of Bennett Cerf and Donald Klopfer*. Random House, 2002.
Doubleday, Frank Nelson. *The Memoirs of a Publisher*. Doubleday, 1972.
Fitzgerald, Ed. *A Nickel an Inch: A Memoir*. Atheneum, 1985.
Gross, Gerald. *Publishers on Publishing*. Grosset and Dunlap, 1961.
Madison, Charles A. *Book Publishing in America*. McGraw-Hill, 1966.
McCormick, Ken. Oral History, 1972.
Reynolds, Paul R. *The Middle Man: The Adventures of a Literary Agent*. William Morrow, 1972.
Scribner, Charles, Jr. *In the Company of Writers*. Charles Scribner's Sons, 1990.
Tebbel, John. *Between Covers: The Rise and Transformation of Book Publishing in America*. Oxford University Press, 1987.

8: THE COMPANY THAT WAS ALWAYS ABOUT CASS: THE HOUSE OF HARPER

Interviews

John Appleton, New York City, June 9, 2005.
Simon Michael Bessie, New York City, February 5, 2004.
Cass Canfield, Jr., New York City, December 11, 2003.
James Fox, New York City, June 10, 2005.
Harvey Ginzberg, New York City, March 10, 2004.
Ashbel Green, New York City, March 30, 2005.
Ann Harris, New York City, November 10, 2004.
Marc Jaffe, New York City, December 8, 2004.
Jack Macrae, New York City, May 26, 2004.
Richard McAdoo, Marlborough, New Hampshire, November 13, 2004.
Fran McCullough, New York City, April 18, 2005.
Walter Minton, New York City, December 17, 2004.
Arthur Thornhill, Jr., New York City, November 2003.
Hugh Van Dusen, New York City, October 20, 2004.
Marion "Buz" Wyeth, Westchester County, N.Y., April 15, 2005.
Genevieve Young, New York City, September 20, 2004.

Books and Periodicals

American Society of Journalists and Authors, Newsletter of September 2003.
Bessie, Simon Michael. Interview. *Archipelago*, 2004.

SOURCES

Canfield, Cass. *Up & Down & Around: A Publisher Recollects the Time of His Life.* Harper's Magazine Press, 1971.

Cass Canfield. Columbia Oral History (courtesy of Genevieve Young).

Exman, Eugene. *The House of Harper: One Hundred and Fifty Years of Publishing.* Harper & Row, 1967.

Marcus, Leonard S., ed. *Dear Genius: The Letters of Ursula Nordstrom.* HarperCollins Publishers, 1998.

Silverman, Al, ed. *The Book of the Month: Sixty Years of Books in American Life.* Little, Brown, 1986.

Targ, William. *Indecent Pleasures: The Life and Colorful Times of William Targ.* Macmillan, 1975.

9: GIVE THE READER A BREAK: SIMON & SCHUSTER

Interviews

Robert Bernstein, New York City, September 15, 2005; November 2005.

Nina Bourne, New York City, September 27, 2005.

Jane Friedman, New York City, October 26, 2006.

Robert Gottlieb, New York City, April 12, 2005.

Mildred Marmur, Larchmont, New York, June 20, 2004.

Norman Monath (telephone interview), California, 2004.

Connie Sayre, New York City, September 12, 2005.

Anthony Schulte, New York City, April 2, 2004.

Seymour Turk, New York City, January 2006.

Books and Periodicals

Bernays, Anne, and Justin Kaplan. *Back Then: Two Lives in 1950s New York.* William Morrow, 2002

Eller, Jonathan R. "Catching a Market: The Publishing History of *Catch-22*" in *Prospects* 17. Cambridge University Press, 1992.

Gottlieb, Robert. "The Art of Editing" (interview by Larissa McFarquhar). *The Paris Review*, Issue 132, Fall 1994.

Korda, Michael. *Making the List: A Cultural History of the American Bestseller, 1900–1999.* Barnes and Noble Books, 2001.

———. *Another Life: A Memoir of Other People.* Random House, 1999.

Lee, Charles. *The Hidden Public: The Story of the Book-of-the-Month Club.* Doubleday, 1958.

Madison, Charles A. *Book Publishing in America.* McGraw-Hill, 1966.

Monath, Norman. *Know What You Want and Get It!* Forge Books, 2002.

Schwed, Peter. *Turning the Pages: An Insider's Story of Simon and Schuster, 1924–1984.* Macmillan, 1984.

Tanenhaus, Sam. *Whittaker Chambers: A Biography.* Random House, 1997.

Tebbel, John. *Between Covers: The Rise and Transformation of Book Publishing in America.* Oxford University Press, 1987.

SOURCES

10: THE PLACE THAT RAN BY ITSELF: RANDOM HOUSE

Interviews

Betty Ballantine, Bearsville, N.Y., May 29, 2004.
Robert Bernstein, New York City, September 15, 2005; November 2005.
Nina Bourne. New York City, September 27, 2005.
Jason Epstein, New York City, September 14, 2006.
Charles Harris, New York City, September 27, 2004.
Robert Lescher, New York City, December 3, 2003; January 7, 2004.
Gloria Loomis, New York City, February 16, 2006.
Robert Loomis, New York City, March 28, 2006.
Mildred Marmur, New York City, June 24, 2004.
Charlotte Mayerson, New York City, March 2, 2001.
Toni Morrison, Princeton, N.J., October 28, 2005.
Alan Rinzler (telephone interview), Los Angeles, California.
Anthony Schulte, New York City, April 2, 2004.
James Silberman, New York City, February 23, 2005.
Nan Talese, New York City, August 2006.
Samuel Vaughan, New York City, February 24, 2004.

Books and Periodicals

Cerf, Bennett. *At Random: The Reminiscences of Bennett Cerf.* Random House, 1977.
————. *Dear Donald, Dear Bennett: The Wartime Correspondence of Bennett Cerf and Donald Klopfer.* Random House, 2002.
Commins, Dorothy. *What Is an Editor?: Saxe Commins at Work.* University of Chicago Press, 1978.
Haydn, Hiram. *Words and Faces.* Harcourt Brace Jovanovich, 1974.

11: LIVING IN A DREAM WORLD: ALFRED A. KNOPF, INC.

Interviews

Aaron Asher, New York City, November 18, 2005.
Robert Bernstein, New York City, September 15, 2005.
Nina Bourne, New York City, September 27, 2005.
Jane Friedman, New York City, October 21, 2006.
Robert Gottlieb, New York City, April 12, 2005.
Ashbel Green, New York City, March 30, 2005.
Judith Jones, New York City, February 28, 2004.
Stanley Kauffmann, New York City, August 25, 2004.
Alfred A. Knopf, Jr., New York City, March 23, 2004.
Anne McCormick, New York City, March 2, 2005.
Toni Morrison, Princeton, N.J., October 28, 2005.
Daniel Okrent, New York City, May 29, 2006.
Anthony Schulte, New York City, April 2, 2004.

SOURCES

Books and Periodicals

Alfred A. Knopf obituaries. *Chicago Tribune*, August 12, 1984; *Los Angeles Times*, August 12, 1984; *The New York Times*, August 12, 1984.

Alfred A. Knopf, Inc. Records 1873–1996. Harry Ransom Center at the University of Texas at Austin.

American National Biography. Vol. 12. Oxford University Press, 1999.

Blanche Knopf obituary, 1966, by Seymour "Sy" Brody. Jewish Virtual Library.

Cerf, Bennett. *At Random: The Reminiscences of Bennett Cerf.* Random House, 1977.

Current Biography Yearbook. Marjorie Dent Candee, ed. H. W. Wilson, 1957.

Dictionary of American Biography. Supplement Eight. Charles Scribner's Sons.

Dictionary of Literary Biography. Vol. 46. Gale Research, 1986.

Fadiman, Clifton. *Fifty Years: Being a Retrospective Collection of Novels, Novellas, Tales, Drama, Poetry, and Reportage and Essays.* Alfred A. Knopf, 1965.

Gottlieb, Robert. "The Art of Editing" (interview by Larissa McFarquhar). *The Paris Review*, Issue 132, Fall 1994.

Knopf, Alfred A. *Publishing Then and Now, 1912–1964.* New York Public Library, 1964.

Lemay, Harding. *Inside, Looking Out: A Personal Memoir.* Harper's Magazine Press, 1971.

Madison, Charles A. *Book Publishing in America.* McGraw-Hill, 1966.

McNamara, Katherine. "Reminiscence. Lee Goerner." *Archipelago*, Vol. 3. No. 3. www .archipelago.org.

Tebbel, John. *Between Covers: The Rise and Transformation of Book Publishing in America.* Oxford University Press, 1987.

12: A FATHER AND SON STORY: LITTLE, BROWN

Interviews

Roger Donald, New York City, February 23, 2005.

Harry Houghton, Katonah, N.Y., June 18, 2003.

Joseph Kanon and Robin Straus, New York City, January 29, 2007.

Richard McAdoo and Marcia Legru, Temple, New Hampshire, November 13, 2004.

William Phillips, Belmont, Mass., January 19, 2007.

James Silberman, New York City, February 23, 2005.

Arthur Thornhill, Jr., New York City, November 2003.

Books and Periodicals

Bell, Millicent. *Marquand: An American Life.* Atlantic/Little, Brown, 1979.

Brooks, Paul. *Two Park Street.* Houghton Mifflin, 1986.

Hart, Stan. *Fumblefinger.* Abeel Publishers, 1999.

Madison, Charles A. *Book Publishing in America.* McGraw-Hill, 1966.

One Hundred and Fifty Years of Publishing, 1837–1987. Little, Brown, 1987.

Tebbel, John. *Between Covers.* Oxford University Press, 1987.

SOURCES

13: BALLANTINE, AVON, POCKET BOOKS, DELL

Interviews

Betty Ballantine, Bearville, N.Y., May 29, 2004.
Carole Baron, New York City, September 14, 2005.
Robert Bernstein, New York City, September 15, 2005; November 2005.
E. L. Doctorow, New York City, April 4, 2007.
Lawrence Hughes, New York City, January 13, 2004; March 7, 2007.
Stanley Kauffmann, New York City, August 25, 2004.
Richard Marek, New York City, August 16, 2005.
Esther Margolis, New York City, March 22, 2007.
Peter Mayer, New York City, January 23, 2006.
Henry Morrison, New York City, August 3, 2005.
Robin Straus, New York City, January 29, 2007.
Seymour Turk, New York City, January 2006.
James Wade, New York City, November 2005.
Robert Wyatt, New York City, January 7, 2006.

Books and Periodicals

Davis, Kenneth C. *Two-Bit Culture: The Paperbacking of America*. Houghton Mifflin, 1984.
Hare, Steve, ed. *Penguin Portrait: Allen Lane and the Penguin Editors, 1935–1970*. Penguin Books, 1995.
Korda, Michael. *Another Life: A Memoir of Other People*. Random House, 1999.
Peterson, Clarence. *The Bantam Story: Thirty Years of Paperback Publishing*. Bantam, 1975.
Seaman, Barbara. *Lovely Me: The Life of Jacqueline Susann*. William Morrow, 1987.
Tebbel, John. *Between Covers: The Rise and Transformation of Book Publishing in America*. Oxford University Press, 1987.

14: NEW AMERICAN LIBRARY, BANTAM, FAWCETT

Interviews

E. L. Doctorow, New York City, April 4, 2007.
Oscar Dystel, Rye, N.Y., December 5, 2003.
Marc Jaffe, New York City, December 8, 2004.
Esther Margolis, New York City, March 22, 2007.
Walter Minton, New York City, December 17, 2004.
Leona Nevler, New York City, July 8, 2004.
Truman Talley, New York City, January 15, 2005.

SOURCES

Books and Periodicals

Bonn, Thomas L. *Heavy Traffic and High Culture: New American Library as Literary Gatekeeper in the Paperback Revolution.* Southern Illinois University Press, 1989.

Davis, Kenneth C. *Two-Bit Culture: The Paperbacking of America.* Houghton Mifflin, 1984.

Targ, William. *Indecent Pleasures: The Life and Colorful Times of William Targ.* Macmillan, 1975.

Weybright, Victor. *The Making of a Publisher: A Life in the 20th-Century Book Revolution.* Reynal & Company, 1967.

Index

INDEX

INDEX

INDEX

INDEX

INDEX

INDEX

Macmillan USA, 114–16
Macrae, Elliot, 267
Mad magazine collections, 390
Madeline books (Bemelmans), 173
Madonna Red (Carroll), 370
Magic Barrel, The (Malamud), 32
short story, 31
Magus, The (Fowles), 375
Mailer, Norman, 5, 12, 65, 76, 303, 334, 365, 373, 417, 418, 422, 427, 460
Make Way for Ducklings (McCloskey), 173
Making of a Publisher, The (Weybright), 423
Making of the President, 1960, The (White), 93
Malamud, Anne, 32
Malamud, Bernard, 27, 31–33, 227
Malcolm X, 62, 207
Male Chauvinism: How It Works (Korda), 286
Malone (Beckett), 48
Malone, Dumas, 358
Malouf, David, 79
Malraux, André, 283
Man in the Gray Flannel Suit, The (Wilson), 258
Man with a Load of Mischief, The (Grimes), 370
Man with the Golden Arm, The (Algren), 185
Manchester, William, 238–39, 365, 375
Manchild in the Promised Land (Brown), 293
Mann, Thomas, 318
Mansfield, Irving, 448, 452
Mansfield, Katherine, 318
Mao Tse-tung, 46
Marek, Richard, 135–37, 407, 411, 415
Margolis, Esther, 409, 452–53, 456
Marmur, Mildred "Milly," 298, 303–4
Marquand, John P., 76, 355–57
Márquez, Gabriel García, 231, 297, 335
Martin, Judith ("Miss Manners"), 108–9
Martin, Pete, 156
Martin, Steve, 371
Martyred, The (Kim), 79
Mason, Bobbie Ann, 4

Massee, Mae, 172–73
Mastering the Art of French Cooking (Child/Bertholle/Beck), 324–25
Masters, William Howard, 372
Matisse, Henri, 84–85
Matisse, Pierre, 84
Matson, Harold, 187, 374
Matthiessen, Peter, 154, 165, 284
Maugham, W. Somerset, 186, 190–91
Maule, Harry, 276, 283
Mauriac, Claude, 79
Maxwell, William, 328, 360
Mayer, Peter, 174, 393–94, 395–96, 396–97, 397–98, 400, 406–408, 416, 422
Mayerson, Charlotte, 8, 283, 303
McAdoo, Richard, 224, 239
McCarthy, Cormac, 285
McCarthy, Eugene, 199
McCarthy, Joe, 358–59
McCarthy, Mary, 435–36
McClelland, Jack, 360
McCloskey, Robert, 173
McCormack, Lida, 117
McCormack, Thomas, 117
McCormack, Thomas, Jr., 112–14
adoption and childhood, 116–17
at Doubleday, 117–20
at Harper & Row, 120–21
as playwright, 122, 141
at St. Martin's Press, 114, 122–23, 123–26, 126–29, 129–34, 135–38, 140–41
McCormack, Sandra, 127, 133
McCormick, Ann, 123–24, 186, 196
McCormick, Ken, 117, 118–20, 124, 182–83, 185–87, 196, 201, 205, 207
McCullough, Colleen, 242
McCullough, David Willis, 368
McCullough, Fran, 8, 216, 231–32, 239, 240–41, 243
McElderry, Margaret, 94
McEwan, Ian, 286
McGrath, Charles, 373
McGraw-Hill, 116, 364, 453
McIntosh, Miss (Steinbeck's agent), 151

McIntyre, Alfred, 348–49, 353–54, 354–55, 357
McIntyre, James, 346–48, 354–55
McKenzie, Ian, 121–22
McKinley, William, 223
McNamara, Katherine, 110, 199, 203, 310–11
McPhee, John, 21
Mehta, Sonny, 309–10, 339–40
Melville Goodwin, U.S.A. (Marquand), 357
Memoirs of a Publisher, The (Doubleday), 187
Memoirs of Hecate County (Wilson), 228
Menand, Louis, 5, 80, 461
Mencken, H. L., 313, 318
Mentor Books. *See under* New American Library
mergers. *See* acquisitions and mergers
Merlin magazine, 47, 48–50
Merrill, James, 94
Merton, Thomas, 24, 27, 35
Merwin, W. S., 94
Messner, Kitty, 460
Metalious, Grace, 459–61
Meyer, Helen Honig, 9, 60–61, 217, 408, 409–10, 410–12, 414–16, 418, 419–20, 465
Meyer, Victoria, 176
Michener, James, 99, 102–3, 210, 255, 425, 464
Milford, Ken, 234
Milford, Nancy, 234, 236
Miller, Arthur, 21, 75, 150, 151, 164, 387–88
Miller, Henry, 41, 42, 46, 58–60
Miller, Lew, 91
Millett, Kate, 183
Milosz, Czeslaw, *xi,* 37
minorities. *See* African-Americans; anti-Semitism; gays and lesbians; women
Minton, Walter, 198, 229, 230, 444–45, 463
Misfits, The (A. Miller), 394
Mishima, Yukio, 322
Miss Manners' Guide to Excruciatingly Correct Behavior (Martin), 109
Miss Piggy's Guide to Life, 7, 336
Mitchell, Joan, 42–43

INDEX

INDEX

493

INDEX

494

INDEX

INDEX

Spock, Dr. Benjamin, 36, 403
*Spy Who Came In from the
    Cold, The* (le Carré), 182,
    434–35
Stafford, Jean, 327
Stainback, Berry, 263
Stalin, Svetlana, 225
Stanford, David, 148, 155
Stein, Gertrude, 280, 306
Stein, Irving, 253
Steinbeck, John, 147, 150,
    151, 442, 444
Stevens, Wallace, 318
Stevens, George, 156, 157
Stevenson, Adlai, 215
Stewart, Mary, 464
Stewart, Tom, 106–11
Stillness at Appomattox, A
    (Catton), 201–202
Stone, Irving, 206
Stone, Robert, 3–4
Story of Civilization, The
    (Durant/Durant), 249–50
Stories of John Cheever, The,
    339
Story of O (Réage), 62
Story of Philosophy, The
    (Durant), 249
Strange Fruit (Smith), 394
Strange Victory (documen-
    tary), 42
Straub, Peter, 12, 135
Straus, Robin, 409–10
Straus, Dorothea, 20, 427
Straus, Harold, 36, 321–22
Straus, Roger W., Jr., 5, 7,
    17–24, 25, 27–28, 33–35,
    38–39, 39–40, 427
    See also Farrar, Straus and
    Giroux
Straus, Roger (son), 21–22
Strauss, Helen, 99–101
Studs Lonigan trilogy
    (Farrell), 45
Styron, William, 8, 90, 92,
    154, 289, 290
Success (Korda), 303
Sula (Morrison), 298
Summit Books. *See under*
    Simon & Schuster
Susann, Jacqueline, 386, 448,
    452
Swarthout, Glendon, 425
Swinburne, Algernon Charles,
    347

Tai-Pan (Clavell), 102–4
Tales of the South Pacific
    (Michener), 99, 425

Talese, Nan, 8, 285–86,
    287–88, 291–92, 296
Talese, Gay, 287, 291–92
Talley, Truman "Mac," 156,
    421, 422–23, 429–31,
    431, 434, 436
Tallulah (Bankhead), 226
Tanizaki, Junichiro, 322
Targ, William, 215, 235, 464,
    465
Taylor, Clyde, 464, 464–65
Taylor, Frank, 394–95
Taylor, Helen, 152, 159
Taylor, Peter, 27
*Teach Us to Outgrow Our
    Madness* (Oe), 47
Tebbel, John, 211, 316, 317,
    462
Temkin, Victor, 455
Tenth Muse, The (Jones), 180
Teriade, Efstratios, 83–85
Theroux, Paul, 4–5
They Came to Cordura
    (Swarthout), 425
*"They've Killed the
    President": The Search
    for the Murderers of
    John F. Kennedy*
    (Anson), 453
Thief of Time, A (Hillerman),
    4
Thief's Journal, The (Genet),
    62
This Side of Paradise
    (Fitzgerald), 102
Thomas, Evan, 224–25, 231,
    233–34, 237, 238, 240
Thomas, Hugh, 231
Thomas, Lewis, 168
Thomas, Norman, 224
Thomas Dunne Books. *See
    under* St. Martin's Press
Thompson, Hunter S., 273–75
Thompson, Jim, 11
Thompson, Lovell, 352
Thorn Birds, The
    (McCullough), 242
Thornhill, Arthur, Jr., 238,
    341–43, 343–46, 349,
    367, 369, 370, 372–73,
    376, 428
Thornhill, Arthur, Sr., 100,
    341–43, 343–46, 348,
    350–51, 361, 362, 366,
    367, 371–72, 375–76,
    449–50
Thornhill, Joseph, 348
365 Days (Glasser), 80
Thunderball (Fleming), 430

Thurber, James, 223, 246–47
Ticknor & Fields, 177
Tim (McCullough), 242
Time Inc., 343, 375–76
Time-Life, 76–77
Time-Life Books, 81
Time magazine, 183, 248
Times Literary Supplement,
    161, 368
Times-Mirror Company, 417,
    432–33
Tin House literary quarterly,
    54
Tinker, Tailor, Soldier, Spy
    (le Carré), 449
Tipping Point, The
    (Gladwell), 371
Tobey, Carl "Bud," 413–14
Toffler, Alvin, 298
Toland, John, 8, 290–91
Tolkien, J.R.R., 392
Tom Sawyer (Twain), 117
Tomkins, Calvin, 236
Tommyknockers (King), 167
Topper (Smith), 417
Torchbooks. *See under*
    Harper & Row
Torres, Tereska, 458
Tough Guys Don't Dance
    (Mailer), 373
Townsend, Robert, 337
Train, John, 154
*Transactional Analysis in
    Psychotherapy* (Berne),
    61
Transit of Venus, The
    (Hazzard), 11
transition literary magazine,
    78
Traver, Robert (John D.
    Voelker), 121–22
Tree Grows in Brooklyn, A
    (Smith), 218
Tregaskis, Richard, 280
Trevor, William, 173
Trillin, Calvin, 377
Trilling, Lionel, 249
Trocchi, Alex, 48, 50
Tropic of Cancer (H. Miller),
    41, 42, 46, 58–60, 63
    United States Supreme
    Court and, 59
Trout Madness (Traver),
    121–22
True Grit (Portis), 262–63
Truman, Harry, 186, 192, 199
Tuchman, Barbara, 339
Tunnel of Love, The (De
    Vries), 368

496

INDEX

Williams, Alan, 28, 100, 101,
152, 166–67, 177, 369,
460
Williams, J. Randall, 350
Williams, Joan, 94
Williams, Marjorie, 167
Williams, T. Harry, 334
Williams, William Carlos, 280
Wilson, Edmund, 5, 20–21,
102, 228, 301
Wilson, Sloan, 258
Wilson, Woodrow, 272
Winds of War, The (Wouk),
374
Winesburg, Ohio (Anderson),
149
Wolf, Wendy, 148
Wolfe, Thomas, 3, 368
Wolfe, Tom, 4, 21, 37, 273
Wolff, Helen, 80, 292
Wolff, Kurt, 80, 292
Womack, John, Jr., 334
*Woman at the Washington
Zoo: Poems and
Translations, The*
(Williams/Noah),
93–94
Woman of Rome, The
(Moravia), 427
*Woman's Room,
The* (French), 3

women (in publishing),
183–85, 217–18,
240–41, 286, 296–97,
408, 409–10, 410–12
as editors, 8–9, 18–19, 148,
180–81, 204–7, 217–18,
231–33, 402, 406–8
Women's Barracks (Torres),
458
Woodburn, John, 360
Woodiwiss, Kathleen E.,
399–400
Woolf, Virginia, 293
Woolsey, John M., 282–83
Words & Faces (Haydn), 91,
94, 96
World According to Garp, The
(Irving), 407
World Without End, Amen
(Breslin), 170
"Worst Baseball Team in
History, The" (Breslin),
159
Wouk, Herman, 24, 118,
186–87, 365, 373–74
Wretched of the Earth, The
(Fanon), 62
Wright, Lee, 402
Wright, Richard, 295, 427
Wuthering Heights (Brontë),
402, 417

Wyatt, Robert, 396, 399, 400,
408, 414–15
Wyeth, Marion "Buz," 228
Wylie, Elinor, 318
Wyn, A. A., 439

Yale University
Residential College Seminar
programs, 3
*Year the Yankees Lost the
Pennant, The* (Wallop),
142
Yearling, The (Rawlings), 271
Yevtushenko, Yevgeny, 199
Young, Genevieve "Gene," 8,
214, 217, 218, 225,
233–34, 234–35, 236–38,
240–41, 243
Young Lions, The (Shaw), 427
Youngblood Hawke (Wouk),
118
Your Income Tax (Lasser),
253

*Zapata and the Mexican
Revolution* (Womack,
Jr.), 334
Zeiger, Henry A., 432
Zelda (Milford), 236–37
Zenith Books. *See under*
Doubleday & Company

498